Praise for
Mind in the Making

"We need to get these important messages out, and parents are clamoring for it."
>   —T. Berry Brazelton, M.D., emeritus professor of pediatrics, Harvard Medical School, and founder, Brazelton Touchpoints Center

"[Ellen Galinsky's] latest book...just put her in the 'Child Development Expert Hall of Fame.'...My recommendation: get a copy of this book, give a copy to another parent, and recommend that every library and early childhood educator has one on their shelf. *Mind in the Making* is one of those rare and glorious books that will make a difference in our children's lives and futures."
>   —Dr. Michele Borba, *Today Show* contributor and author of *The Big Book of Parenting Solutions*

"[This book is] literally a mind-expanding contribution to the field and will have a huge impact on how teachers and parents think about and understand children's learning and development, and hopefully their interactions with them."
>   —Sue Bredekamp, early childhood education consultant

"It may well be the next iconic parenting manual, up there with Spock and Leach and Brazelton, one that parents turn to for reassurance that all is more or less okay, reminders of how to make it better, and glimpses of what's to come."
>   —Lisa Belkin, *The New York Times*

"Education goes far beyond the subjects we typically teach in school. Life skills like focus and perspective taking are essential to building human potential. *Mind in the Making* will be a powerful new resource for teachers and families."
>   —Gaston Caperton, president of the College Board

"A valuable resource! Ellen Galinsky's extensive research reveals important insights into the science of early learning."
>   —Adele Faber, coauthor of *How to Talk So Kids Will Listen & Listen So Kids Will Talk*

"*Mind in the Making* is the central component of a creative, multi-faceted initiative that clarifies paths to lifelong learning—related to discoveries about brain development and how learning builds on the structure and function of the brain. It is a valuable contribution based on solid research that yields practical benefits."

—David A. Hamburg, M.D., Weill Cornell Medical College, and president emeritus of the Carnegie Corporation of New York

"*Mind in the Making* is a tour de force. In Galinsky's hands, the latest scientific discoveries about how children learn are carefully molded into seven seemingly simple but profound skills that predict success in the 21st Century."

—Kathy Hirsh-Pasek, professor of psychology, Temple University, and coauthor of *A Mandate for Playful Learning in Preschool*

"A book of incomparable quality about what is best for children and why in today's world. *Mind in the Making* helps you assemble the ingredients in your own kitchen for rearing children who are intelligent, emotionally secure, and equipped to succeed."

—Roberta Michnick Golinkoff, professor of education, psychology, and linguistics and cognitive science, University of Delaware, and coauthor of *A Mandate for Playful Learning in Preschool*

"The future of our society depends on how we treat our children, and this remarkable book, richly illustrated with examples from the latest scientific research, provides an engaging and well-informed characterization of the developmental challenges children face. It will be of enormous value to parents, educators and policy makers, and serious students of child development."

—Philip David Zelazo, professor, Institute of Child Development, University of Minnesota

"*Mind in the Making* shows why early learning and development matter more than ever. A highly cogent, remarkably accessible, and important book."

—Michael Levine, executive director, Joan Ganz Cooney Center

"Ellen Galinsky has been one of our most thoughtful as well as passionate advocates for children. In this book she assembles the latest fascinating research from the very best scientists in the field and presents it clearly and accurately, in a way that parents and others will find most valuable."

—Alison Gopnik, professor of psychology, University of California at Berkeley, and author of *The Philosophical Baby*

National Association for the Education of Young Children

1313 L Street NW, Suite 500

Washington, DC 20005-4101

www.naeyc.org

Founded in 1926, NAEYC is the world's largest organization working on behalf of young children, with nearly 90,000 members, a national network of more than 300 local, state, and regional Affiliates, and a growing global alliance of like-minded organizations.

MIND IN THE MAKING

THE SEVEN ESSENTIAL LIFE SKILLS
EVERY CHILD NEEDS

ELLEN GALINSKY

HARPER
An Imprint of HarperCollinsPublishers

HarperCollins books may be purchased for educational, business, or sales promotional use. For information please write: Special Markets Department, HarperCollins Publishers, 10 East 53rd Street, New York, NY 10022.

For more information about this book or other books from HarperCollins,
visit www.harpercollins.com

This special edition created for the
National Association for the Education of Young Children
ISBN 978-0-06-204129-6

Designed by Gretchen Achilles

Library of Congress Cataloging-in-Publication Data

Galinsky, Ellen.
    Mind in the making : the seven essential life skills every child needs / by Ellen Galinsky.—1st ed.
        p.   cm.

    1. Children—Life skills guides. 2. Child development. I. Title.
HQ781.G35   2010
305.231—dc22

                                                                2009051549

10 11 12 13 14   ID/RRD   10 9 8 7 6 5 4 3 2 1

*For my mother, Leora Osgood May, for my father, M. H. May,
for my daughter, Lara Galinsky, my son, Philip Galinsky, and my
husband, Norman Galinsky. You are my greatest teachers.*

*For parents and teachers everywhere
and for a time when caring for and teaching children truly have
the importance and respect they so deserve.*

CONTENTS

ACKNOWLEDGMENTS

In the journey to write *Mind in the Making* there have been so many people who not only made this journey with me, but made it possible.

First I want to thank my publisher Bob Miller. From the moment I met him years ago at an event honoring Fred Rogers, I knew I wanted to work with him. When he made an offer for this book, it was a dream come true, but the reality of what he has brought to this book far exceeds what I could *ever* have imagined. As an expert communicator himself, he knows when to push, when to praise, what's important, and what's not. Bob represents the ideal editor from the past, but one who is reinventing the future of publishing today. It is an honor and a privilege to work with him.

When I joined HarperStudio, I gained another pivotal relationship—with Debbie Stier. Like Bob, Debbie is one of the most insightful, creative, energetic, forward-thinking, and supportive people I have ever met. The future of publishing will be entirely different and so much better because of her.

I also want to thank Katie Salisbury of HarperStudio. Katie has managed every step of the production of *Mind in the Making* and all of its complexities with grace and perfect professionalism.

And Toni Sciarra Poynter. Toni, my editor for *Ask the Children,* has been my brilliant editorial consultant for *Mind in the Making.* She has been my first, middle, and last reader. Every conversation with Toni—via e-mail, over the phone, or in person—brings me joy, deeper insight, and new understandings. I look forward to having these conversations with Toni forever and I am deeply grateful to her for so enriching my life and work.

Jim Levine, my agent and my friend, for decades has been after me to write a book that synthesizes and extends my work in child development and the workforce. It is no exaggeration to say that without Jim—

without his probing questions or his superb ability to know how to create the right books—*Mind in the Making* would not have happened.

Two people have taken this entire journey with me—Hank O'Karma and Amy McCampbell of New Screen Concepts, the award-winning production company. We selected the researchers we wanted to profile together, we interviewed and filmed them together, and we have discussed what we have found together. We have weathered the storms of travel (including a very late-night drive home when there were tornados and flying was made impossible) as well as the joys of travel. Hank has the most incredible ability to understand what's significant amid the mountains of research we pursued, to see the world as children see it, and to capture this magic and communicate it on film and in words. Amy brings the artistry of a great filmmaker and the savvy of a new parent to *Mind in the Making* and has been a touchstone throughout. The publication of the book is only a way station in my journey with Hank and Amy, and I look forward to the years of continuing to work on joint projects that enrich our understanding of what early learning is and thereby change the national and international conversations about its importance.

I am deeply grateful to the staff of the Families and Work Institute (FWI) for their insight and support during the writing of *Mind in the Making*. It is hard to be fully immersed in running an organization and write a book at the same time, and it is a tribute to the strength of this organization that it worked so well. A colleague who spent a few weeks at Families and Work Institute recently told me that being at FWI was a transformative experience—she had never experienced a place where people so enjoyed working and had such pride in the difference they are making.

Very special thanks go to Lois Backon, FWI's senior vice president. I turn to her sage wisdom for issues large and small, and she always has that critical insight or idea that propels our work forward in the right— and often in a new—direction. She helps us to be ahead of the curve. I am also grateful to her for ensuring that I had (hopefully) inviolate times that I could pull away from the institute's daily work to write.

And Sharon Huang, FWI's director of our larger initiative, also called Mind in the Making. Sharon has been my closest partner at the institute on all things Mind in the Making. Her joy in this work is unparalleled, her brilliance in guiding this initiative for the Families and Work Institute is also without measure, and her positive can-do attitude is a gift that I value every day. Special thanks to Sharon for assembling a group of interns to work with us on fact checking the references for *Mind in the Making*. Among these interns, Courtney Dern took a leadership role in managing the process with skills that show she is headed for an extraordinary career.

I also want to thank the board of directors of Families and Work Institute. When I said that I wanted to write *Mind in the Making*, they said "Of course." When we have talked about the strategic details of this work, I have always left the meetings with energy for new possibilities. Our board has said that FWI is a "treasure," but they have been the engine behind our success. My deepest thanks to our board chair, Mike Carey. I know how uniquely lucky I am to have a mentor with such profound talents—someone who has been responsible for helping to create the field of work and family life. Special thanks also to our former board chair, Dee Topol, who has been a pioneer in creating a future we all want in the work-life and child-care fields; and to Ted Childs, who gives speeches about game-changing events, but is himself one of the most significant game changers in workforce diversity around. Ted has always made it possible for FWI to do the work it should be doing.

Thanks to Morra Aarons-Mele of Women & Work for being our exceptional social media strategist and to Camille McDuffie of Goldberg McDuffie Communications, Inc., for being our extraordinary public relations strategist. What a team! Very special thanks to Andy Boose, my lawyer and friend over the years.

Mind in the Making has had many funders over the years. It would have been impossible to have taken this journey to capture the classic and cutting-edge research on how children learn best without their support and wisdom. I list them below, but want to thank a few very special people by name: Tony Berkley from the W. K. Kellogg Foundation for being such a visionary and remarkable guide; Marge Petruska from the Heinz Endowments for being the person I always go to with a problem when I don't see an answer and emerge from the conversation with fantastic solutions; Alan Dworsky from the Popplestone Foundation for his inspiring leadership; Kate Liebman from the Marks Family Foundation for encouraging us to create learning modules for parents and for helping us shape them in the best way; Luba Lynch from the A. L. Mailman Family Foundation for being the wise "venture funder" in the early childhood field; and Owen Rankin of Johnson & Johnson who so believes in this work.

Also very special, special thanks to Kathy Bonk of the Communications Consortium Media Center and to Andrea Camp, a consultant to the Kellogg Foundation and, through the Civil Society Institute, a funder of the Ask the Children study on learning that led to the Mind in the Making initiative. I am grateful beyond words for their guidance. I am also very grateful to Susan Magsamen of the Johns Hopkins Neuro-Education initiative for being such a trusted advisor. Thanks, too, to the wonderful Sue Lehmann. And I am forever grateful for the deep and inspiring relationships I have with Marilyn Smith and J. D. Andrews, former executive directors of the National Association of the Education of Young Children, and with Mark Ginsberg, its current executive director. Thanks as well to Robert and Marisol DeLeon for their counsel.

And in the beginning, there were four funders who inspired me to tackle what has now become *Mind in the Making*—the incomparable and iconic David Hamburg and the gifted Michael Levine, both then of the Carnegie Corporation of New York, and the trail-blazing Margaret Mahoney, then of the Commonwealth Fund. There was also the late Irving Harris of the Harris Foundation who said yes to our convening one of the first conferences on the brain development of young children at the University of Chicago in 1996 and then helped us turn it into a seminal event. Finally, there have been some very special friends and colleagues, especially the visionary late Fred Rogers and his gifted wife, Joanne, Bill Isler of Family Communications, and Maxwell King of the Fred Rogers Center for Early Learning and Children's Media at Saint Vincent College. All have helped in more ways than they know. In fact, long conversations with Bill helped me find the "voice" to best communicate this complex research.

The Families and Work Institute and I are thankful for:

The Lead Mind in the Making Funders: The W. K. Kellogg Foundation, the Heinz Endowments, AT&T Family Care Development Fund, the

Popplestone Foundation, MetLife Foundation, Johnson & Johnson, and the John D. and Catherine T. MacArthur Foundation.

Additional Mind in the Making Funders: The Procter & Gamble Company, the Robert Wood Johnson Foundation, Citigroup Foundation, Arizona Community Foundation, Freddie Mac Foundation, and Carnegie Corporation of New York.

Funders of Learning Modules for Early Childhood Teachers: The Heinz Endowments, AT&T Family Care Development Fund, Lucent Technologies Foundation, Geraldine R. Dodge Foundation, A. L. Mailman Family Foundation, Pritzker Early Childhood Foundation, Vivendi Universal, the Prudential Foundation, and American Business Collaboration.

Funders of Learning Modules for Families: The Marks Family Foundation.

Dissemination and Outreach Funders: The Heinz Endowment, the James and Judith K. Dimon Foundation, the David and Lucile Packard Foundation, and the A. L. Mailman Family Foundation.

I also want to thank the more than seventy-five researchers who welcomed us into their labs with our questions and cameras. We feel as if we are the guardians of a treasure—their work—and we thank them for sharing it with us, and thereby with so many others. I am also deeply grateful to them for fact checking my descriptions of their work as well. I am also grateful for the Society for Research in Child Development's online research library.

I am especially thankful for the generous help of Kathy Hirsh-Pasek of Temple University and Roberta Golinkoff of the University of Delaware. Not only are they renowned researchers themselves, they have been caring friends who have been willing to review the lists of researchers we were considering, suggest others, and review my (many) outlines for the book. In so many ways, *Mind in the Making* has been our journey together. And special thanks as well to Phil Zelazo of the University of Minnesota, Alison Gopnik of the University of California at Berkeley, Clancy Blair of New York University, and Edward Zigler who have been there with wisdom throughout. I am grateful to Maggie Jackson, author of *Distracted*, for introducing me to some of the best researchers on attention and for many insightful conversations on this subject. And there is Jack P. Shonkoff of Harvard University, who has been a leader among leaders in bringing research on the early years to policy makers and the public. We count it among our most profound blessings that Jack has worked with us on Mind in the Making from its earliest days.

I want to thank the exceptional colleagues who helped create the Learning Modules for Teachers with us and have continued to work with us on making them better and better. Each of them is truly amazing: Peg Sprague of United Way of Massachusetts Bay and Merrimack Valley, Nina Sazer O'Donnell of the United Way of America, author Amy Dombro, Marilou Hyson of the National Association for the Education of Young Children, and FWI's consultant, Mary Beth Harvey.

I also want to thank the many education leaders who have experimented with implementing these modules in their communities and on perfecting them. I'd like to recognize the following people in particular, who helped lead the implementation of the modules in their states: in New Mexico, Lois Vermilya, Ellen Biderman, and Diana Montoya of the University of Mexico's Family Development Program; in Pennsylvania, Harriet Dichter, deputy undersecretary of the office of Child Development and Early Learning, Michele Walsh (and previously Kelli Thompson) and all of the regional Mind in the Making liaisons at the Pennsylvania Key; in Florida, Mimi Graham of Florida State University and Craig Jones of the University of West Florida; in Massachusetts, Joan Matsalia and Emily Barr of the Harvard Achievement Support Initiative, Peg Sprague and Geetha Pai of the United Way of Massachusetts Bay and Merrimack Valley, and Betsy Leutz and the late Libby Zimmerman of Connected Beginnings Training Institute; in Arizona, Diana Abel of Rio Salado Community College; in New Jersey, Theresa Caputo of Professional Impact New Jersey; in Oklahoma, Debbie Ihrig and Jan Figart (and previously Tori Rafferty) of the Community Service Council of Greater Tulsa; and in Rhode Island, Leslie Gell of Ready to Learn Providence.

Thanks also go to the many parents and grandparents who contributed by sharing their insightful stories with us. They so enrich this book: Morra Aarons-Mele, Penelope W. Armstrong, Jessica Bacal, Lois Backon, Amy McCampbell Baluzy, Shelley W. Boots, Erin Brownfield, Jillian D. Cosgrove, Judy David, Karen S. Diamond, Lisa D'Annolfo Levey, Kate

Liebman, Joan M. Matsalia, Jacqueline Miller, Robert S. Miller, Shanny Peer, Richard Rolka, Elizabeth Rubin, Stacey Rubinstein, Johanna Seppäläinen, Mackenzie Anderson Sholtz, Michelle St. Pierre, Melissa A. Wardy, Tyler Wigton, Carolyn Yost, and Susan Zoll, among others. And then there is Eric Pansewicz of the Transportation Security Administration who rescued my computer, lost in travel, and got it back to me in less than twenty-four hours.

Finally, thanks to my family—to my gifted and loving sister, Sally Ruth May, and her daughter, my beloved niece, Sasha Rau. Enduring thanks to Norman who has helped me every day in thousands of ways make *Mind in the Making* the book I want it to be. Very special thanks with love to Valerie, Antonio, and Richie. And most of all, I thank my children, Philip and Lara. I don't think I have ever been so nervous as when I sent them the sections of the book where I mentioned them by name and so overjoyed when they gave me an exuberant green light to include their stories in the book. Of everything in my life, I am the most proud of them—for the caring, contributing, and exceptional adults they have become.

INTRODUCTION

AN EXERCISE: WHAT IS LIFE LIKE TODAY?

Think about some words that describe what life is like today. What words come to mind?

Did your words reflect the challenges of living in a complicated, distracting world? Did you think of words that describe feelings of being rushed, time starved, of having too much to do and not enough time to do it? Did you focus on the uncertainties, the changes that ricochet in our economic systems, or the volatility of relationships in a diverse and unpredictable world? Did you focus on the moments that give you pleasure, large and small?

Life today can be all of these things—complex, distracting, fast moving, 24-7, and stressful. It is also joyful and full of exciting possibilities. We know that if it is this way for us, it is only going to be more so for our children. We all want the best for our children, but how do we help them not only survive but thrive, today and in the future?

It is clear that there is information children need to learn—facts, figures, concepts, insights, and understandings. But we have neglected something that is equally essential—children need life skills.

What do I mean by skills? Take the words often used to describe the world: *complicated, distracting.* Or the words about time: *24-7, rushed, time starved, too much to do and not enough time to do it.* To navigate this world, children need to focus, to determine what is important and to pay attention to this, amid many distractions. Focus is one of the essential skills we need to promote in our children.

Or take the words used to describe the complexity of life in an uncertain, even volatile world. Another essential skill is the ability to understand others' perspectives—perspective taking—despite whether we end up agreeing or disagreeing with them.

There are three *essential* points about these life skills:

These skills are not only important for children; we as adults need them just as much as children do. And, in fact, we have to practice them ourselves to promote them in our children. That's why I call them life skills.

We don't need expensive programs, materials, or equipment to promote these skills. We can promote them in everyday ways through the everyday fun things we do with children.

It is *never* too late to help children learn these life skills, no matter what their ages.

So many books for parents make us feel guilty or that we have made mistakes. This is a different kind of book—not a guilt trip but a book that helps us understand children's development in new ways, with hundreds of to-do suggestions.

These are the conclusions I have drawn from my own research, from spending more than eight years interviewing more than seventy researchers on children, and from reading more than a thousand studies to write *Mind in the Making.*

AMAZING BABIES

One theme from the research on children and learning is that babies' brains appear to be wired to help them understand and know about the world in specific ways, and that this learning begins long before babies can be *taught* this kind of knowledge.

Babies four months short of their first birthdays already have what I call a *language sense:* they can detect statistical patterns in which sounds go together in their native language (or languages) to determine the beginnings and endings of words in a "sea of sounds," as the studies of Jenny Saffran of the University of Wisconsin show.

Since babies that young can't talk, how can researchers possibly know this? Babies—like all of us—are drawn to anything new. So the researcher gives babies something to listen to or look at that is new to them and they look or listen until they get bored. At that point, the researcher presents them with other things to listen to or look at and can tell from the babies' reactions which things the babies view as new (measured by longer listening or looking times) and which they see as familiar (measured by shorter listening or looking times).

So when Jenny Saffran and her colleagues presented babies with a made-up language and, in subsequent studies, with a language they didn't know, they found that babies seem to use an almost statistical-like process to learn that certain sounds are likely to follow other sounds in that language. As a result, the babies became bored with and stopped listening to the made-up or the unfamiliar language after a while, but showed renewed interest when they were presented with *new* combinations of sounds.

Similar studies have shown that infants six months old and even younger have a *number sense:* they can detect the difference between large and small numbers of things—such as the difference between eight and sixteen dots, or the difference between a large and a small number of times that a puppet jumps or a car honks its horn, as seen in the studies of Elizabeth Spelke and her colleagues of Harvard University.

And they have what I call a *people sense:* they focus on people's intentions rather than seeing what people do as random movements in space, as shown by the studies of Amanda Woodward of the University of Maryland. By six months, they can tell the difference between who's helpful and who's not, which Kiley Hamlin, Karen Wynn, and Paul Bloom of Yale demonstrate by showing the children a puppetlike show where a round circle with big eyes tries to reach the top of a hill and is helped up to the top by a square but pushed down the hill by a triangle.

After the children view the show, an experimenter who doesn't know what has happened in the experiment (so as not to influence the babies) enters and places the triangle and the square on a tray in front of the baby to see which one he or she reaches for. Will the six-month-old reach for the character that helped the circle achieve its goal (the helper) or the character that prevented the circle from achieving its goal (the hinderer), or is there no pattern to the babies' choices? Of course, the researchers sometimes used the triangle as the helper and the square as the hinderer. Hamlin says:

We found impressively that almost one hundred percent of the babies in a number of different studies preferred the more positive character.

Yes, babies' capacities are truly amazing, but even more amazing is that we now know how to take advantage of these capacities to help babies and their older sisters and brothers develop the essential life skills that will serve them throughout their lives.

EXECUTIVE FUNCTIONS OF THE BRAIN

Another theme in the research is that the skills I see as crucial—based on reviewing the research on children and on my own research on the adult skills needed for the twenty-first century—all involve, in one way or another, the *prefrontal cortex* of the brain. Child development researchers call these *executive functions* of the brain.

Some people don't like the word *executive* because it conjures up an image of a boss in your brain ordering you around. Instead, think of executive brain functions as managing, not ordering. We use them to manage our attention, our emotions, and our behavior in order to reach our goals. Nor are they just intellectual skills—they involve weaving together our social, emotional, and intellectual capacities. They begin to emerge during the preschool years and don't mature until young adulthood. Here are some key aspects of executive functions:

They are always driven by goals.

They involve using our working memory to keep a number of different things in mind at the same time while paying attention, thinking flexibly, and inhibiting our tendency to go on automatic pilot. If you think that's easy, ask someone to say the word *joke* quickly fifteen times. Then ask, "Tell me quickly, what's the white of an egg called?" Chances are the person will be on automatic and say "yolk"—not "white."

Executive functions pull together our feelings and thinking so that we can reflect, analyze, plan, and evaluate.

Stanislas Dehaene of the Collège de France in Paris calls the prefrontal cortex and its functions a "neuronal workspace" whose main purpose is to "assemble, confront, recombine, and synthesize knowledge," allowing "our behavior to be guided by any combination of information from past or present experience."

Adele Diamond of the University of British Columbia believes that executive functions predict children's achievements as well as IQ tests do or even better, because they go beyond what we know and tap our abilities to *use* what we know.

THE SEVEN ESSENTIAL LIFE SKILLS

SKILL ONE: FOCUS AND SELF CONTROL

I've already pointed out how important focus and self control are in today's 24-7 world where we are flooded with information, tempted by multiple distractions, and need to multitask more than many of us would like. In many workforce studies I've conducted, it has become clear how important focus is to being all that we can be, both at work and at home.

Likewise, studies of children's development have begun to uncover the importance of self control. For example, in the Marshmallow Test, a classic study conducted by Walter Mischel of Columbia University, when children were given a choice between one marshmallow now or two marshmallows later, some could wait for the larger treat and some just couldn't. Those who could wait were more likely to do better in many ways as they grew up, including pursuing their academic and personal goals with less frustration and distraction. These correlations, he notes, "are clearly statistically significant" but in no way doom children.

Focus and self control involve many executive functions of the brain, such as *paying attention, remembering the rules,* and *inhibiting one's initial response to achieve a larger goal.* And they can be taught, as shown by the studies of Michael Posner and his colleagues of the University of Oregon.

SKILL TWO: PERSPECTIVE TAKING

Think about something you bought that you didn't know you wanted until you saw it. The people who created that product could anticipate the needs and wants of customers like you. And the people who marketed that product could present it in a way that stood out, despite the clutter of everything else on the store shelves. The late Peter Drucker, known as the father of modern management, calls this an "outside-in perspective"—seeing things as a customer would see them—and deems it responsible for launching the most successful new businesses.

Or think about the latest conflict you've had with somebody—the person who shot off an e-mail in haste, who said something insensitive when you were going through a hard time, or simply couldn't understand what it's like to walk in your shoes. That person lacks the skill of what I call perspective taking.

Perspective taking calls on many of the executive functions of the brain. It requires *inhibitory control,* or inhibiting our own thoughts and feelings to consider the perspectives of others; *cognitive flexibility* to see a situation in different ways; and *reflection,* or the ability to consider someone else's thinking alongside our own.

Although perspective taking is rarely on lists of essential skills for children to acquire, research makes it clear that it should be. According to Ross Thompson of the University of California at Davis, this skill helps children by making the social world they live in more predictable and memorable. And Alison Gopnik of the University of California at Berkeley reports that studies show children who can understand others' perspectives do better in kindergarten because they're better able to understand what their teachers want and expect.

Perspective taking affects how we deal with conflict. Larry Aber of New York University found that decades of efforts to reduce aggression by teaching children problem-solving skills were only moderately successful because the children most likely to be aggressive interpreted ambiguous situations as hostile when there wasn't enough information to be certain—they jumped to false conclusions about others' intentions. But a curriculum aimed at teaching children to understand other people's intentions and behaviors by using children's books, discussions, writing exercises, and role-play situations has had promising results: the children are less likely to jump to conclusions about the behavior of others, they get into fewer conflicts—and the reading scores of those who initially had the most substantial behavior problems have gone up, too!

SKILL THREE: COMMUNICATING

Kathy Hirsh-Pasek of Temple University says that observing children learning to communicate is observing the mind at work. Communicating well involves executive functions of the brain—for example, *reflecting* upon the goal of what we want to communicate and *inhibiting* our point of view so that we can understand the viewpoints of others. These are not simple tasks, as my workplace research reveals. When we surveyed a nationally representative group of employers, asking them to name the gaps in skills they found among new entrants to the workforce, by far the largest proportion cited spoken and written communication skills.

What we do as parents and teachers matters a great deal in developing children's communication skills. The studies of Anne Fernald of Stanford University show that the singsong way we talk with babies—slowing down our speech, stretching out and enunciating sounds melodically over two octaves, or what I call *parent-speak*—engages their attention and communicates emotion. She has also found that infants who hear more child-directed speech from their caregivers are able to learn new words more quickly and efficiently. Other research shows that even the sequence of our words and coupling our words with pointing and looking (what I call *parent-gesture* and *parent-look*) facilitate language development.

By taping parents interacting with their children at the dinner table and during story times and playtimes, as well as by interviewing parents, Catherine Snow, David Dickinson, and Patton Tabors of Harvard University found that families talk in many different ways with their children, but some ways promote future literacy more than others. Three attributes particularly stand out:

When reading books or talking at the dinner table, parents talked about issues that went beyond the "here and now."

Parents used a sophisticated vocabulary.

There was support for children's literacy.

SKILL FOUR: MAKING CONNECTIONS

Think about your most recent "aha" moment—when you suddenly understood something that you didn't understand before. Chances are this "aha" moment involved seeing a new connection.

Making connections begins with sorting and categorizing—for example, young children can see that spoons and forks go together because both are used to eat. It also begins with an understanding that one thing can stand for or represent another—that a photograph of the family dog represents the real dog. This skill underlies an understanding of all the subjects we study in school, including math.

Robert Siegler of Carnegie Mellon University and Geetha Ramani of the University of Maryland noted that children entering kindergarten differed in their ability to understand mathematical ideas and wondered if it had anything to do with playing board games. They created a simple game based on Chutes and Ladders in which they asked children to spin a spinner and say the corresponding number names in order to advance on the game board. For example, if a child is on space number five and is going to advance two spaces, she has to say "six and seven." This game proved effective in increasing children's ability to count, to understand which numbers are bigger or smaller than others, and to read numbers. Children playing the same game—but with colors, not numbers—didn't make the same advances in their ability to understand these mathematical ideas.

By playing this and similar board games, children are not only gaining information but also getting better at the skill of making connections. They're learning, for example, that the number on the spinner stands for a rule—how many squares they can advance—and that there is a linear relationship between the numbers from one to ten, where each number in the sequence is one larger than the previous number.

Making multiple connections is a skill that becomes possible during the later preschool and early school-age years and beyond as the prefrontal cortex of children's brains matures. It calls on executive functions of the brain, including *working memory, inhibitory control*, and *cognitive flexibility*.

You can help children see connections in their everyday lives by playing matching games and asking how two things are the same or different. Researcher Philip David Zelazo of the University of Minnesota uses just such a task to assess executive functions, asking children to look at cards with three pictures of objects and to figure out how the objects go together in one way (for example, by color) and then in another way (for example, by shape or size).

Making unusual connections is the basis of creativity. Adele Diamond says:

> *The essence of creativity is to be able to disassemble and recombine elements in new ways.*

In the information-overloaded world of today and tomorrow, creative thinkers have an edge, as Kathy Hirsh-Pasek points out:

> *In a Google generation, where there are facts at your fingertips, the person who will later be called boss will be the person who can put those facts together in new and innovative and creative ways.*

SKILL FIVE: CRITICAL THINKING

At its core, critical thinking is the ongoing search for valid and reliable knowledge to guide beliefs, decisions, and actions. Like the other essential life skills, critical thinking develops on a set course throughout childhood and into adulthood, but its use must be promoted. And like the other skills, critical thinking draws on executive functions of the brain. It parallels the reasoning used in the scientific method because it involves developing, testing, and refining theories about "what causes what" to happen.

Even when you're watching television with your kids, opportunities abound for helping them learn to think critically. When they see an ad, ask them what they think the advertiser is trying to sell, whether the ad is effective (do they want to buy the product?), and how they can find out whether the advertiser's claims are true or false.

SKILL SIX: TAKING ON CHALLENGES

As we know far too well, life is filled with challenges. And challenges—even positive ones—can be stressful. The National Scientific Council on the Developing Child, directed by Jack P. Shonkoff of Harvard University, has reviewed the research on children and stress and has concluded that, while there are different types of stress, the key factors in whether these experiences ultimately have a positive or tolerable or toxic impact on children's development are how long the stress lasts and whether or not children have safe and dependable relationships with people to whom they can turn for support.

I think we should do more than help children cope with or tolerate challenges. We need to help them learn to *take on* challenges. Carol Dweck of Stanford University has found that children who avoid challenges have a *fixed mindset:* they see their intelligence as a fixed trait and therefore are reluctant to undertake challenges that "stretch" them. Children who are willing to take on challenges have a *growth mindset,* seeing their abilities as something they can develop. Children with a growth mindset do better in school. Dweck has also found that if adults praise children's efforts—"You are working hard!"—rather than their intelligence—"You are so smart!"—we can help our children learn to "love challenge."

SKILL SEVEN: SELF-DIRECTED, ENGAGED LEARNING

Several years ago, I was invited to write a paper on three gold-standard early childhood programs that have been studied for decades as the models for profound and positive development, learning, and adulthood success in children from very challenging backgrounds. I did something unusual. I reached out directly to the people who had created and evaluated the impact of these programs—Larry Schweinhart of the HighScope Perry Pre-school Project, Craig and Sharon Ramey of the Abecedarian Project (they are now at Georgetown University), and Arthur Reynolds of the Chicago Child-Parent Centers (he is now at the University of Minnesota). I asked each of them what they thought they had done that mattered most.

Of course, these researchers talked about many things that made a difference, among them the importance of viewing social-emotional and intellectual learning as being linked and helping children find something they care about learning and then pursuing that. But I also heard another message that has not been communicated loudly or frequently enough. Each of these programs became a "community of learners," a place where administrators were learning, teachers were learning, parents were learning, and children were learning. As Nobel Prize winner James Heckman of the University of Chicago puts it, "motivation begets motivation." My interviews revealed that the adults fostered children's motivation by being motivated themselves.

There is much in this research on children and learning that is inspiring and insightful. And there is much that is very practical. It shows us just how capable our children are, and it helps teach us how to build on these capacities. There are everyday simple things that you can do—whether you are getting your kids ready for school, dealing with a battle between them, taking them to the market, or just having a conversation. My purpose in writing *Mind in the Making* is to provide you with tools that are everyday, easy, and fun that you can use to promote these essential life skills. And my larger purpose is to enlist you in what has become a mission for me—to help children learn for life, and live to learn!

CHAPTER ONE

SKILL ONE: FOCUS AND SELF CONTROL

AN EXERCISE: ATTENTION, PLEASE

Think about the last time you wanted to pay attention but the situation around you was noisy and confusing—lots of stuff was going on. How did you respond?

Could you pay attention or were you easily distracted?

Could you remember what you wanted to say? Could you remember what the other person said to you?

FOCUS AND SELF CONTROL IN A 24-7 WORLD

Being in a situation with noise, confusion, and lots of stuff going on is not atypical in this era of 24-7 information, of being tethered to our computers, BlackBerries, or iPhones with expectations of constant availability and instant responses. Many of us feel overscheduled and rushed; we worry about distractions, about multitasking too much, and about the barrage of information that floods us daily.

The analogy of flooding is an apt one. When I asked a group of parents to describe how they felt about "life these days," many used images of floods—of sinking, feeling overwhelmed, finding it hard to come up for air or to think clearly when there's such an onrush of everything to do. Conversely, when I asked parents to describe when they felt most successful as parents, they used the word *focus*—again and again: "I feel good when I can really focus on my children without the other things I have to do crowding out my time with them."

Many kids, too, feel rushed, overscheduled, and stressed. In one of my studies, more than one in three young people (35 percent) in the fifth through the twelfth grades said that they felt stressed very often or often.

Kids also sense when their parents feel overwhelmed—39 percent rated their parents as frequently stressed. Some even have techniques for finding out if their parents are really paying attention. One teenager told me that he'd routinely say something ridiculous when telling his parents about his day at school. In the middle of a sentence about math class, he might say, "a goldfish was on the grass," to see if they were really listening. Other younger children said they put their hands on their parents' faces when they were distracted, saying things like "Earth to Mom" or "Earth to Dad."

Just as our kids worry about us being overwhelmed, we also worry about them: we see them doing their homework while texting their friends and listening to their iPods and wonder if they can really learn this way. In fact, at a community meeting where I spoke recently, someone advocated bringing back "good old-fashioned boredom."

The more time I've spent interviewing and filming the best researchers on early learning, the more I've come to the conclusion that focus and self control are central to the other essential life skills I write about in this book. Put simply, if we want to achieve our goals amid everything else that's going on, we have to learn to be focused and we have to learn to have self control.

FOCUS AND SELF CONTROL . . . MAYBE AS IMPORTANT AS IQ

Jeanne Brooks-Gunn of Columbia University and a group of other academics recently reviewed six studies that followed children over time, offering a rare opportunity to evaluate what kinds of skills or knowledge acquired early in life matter most to children's later success. They compared children's school achievement in math and reading between the ages of eight and thirteen to assessments of these same children when they were between ages four and six.

What did they conclude? Out of literally hundreds of analyses, only three skills that children had when they entered school were strongly related to their later success in reading and math. Two are obvious: the children who had good math and reading skills when they entered school had good math and reading skills years later. But the third skill is less obvious. It was *attention skills*—the more penetrating our attention, the richer and deeper our learning. As Brooks-Gunn says:

> *Attention [skills] allow children to focus on something in a way that maximizes the information they get out of it.*

Adele Diamond of the University of British Columbia has been a pioneer in studying what scientists call the *executive functions* of the brain—because these are the brain functions we use to manage our attention, our emotions, and our behavior in pursuit of our goals. She believes that executive functions predict children's success as well as—if not better than—IQ tests:

> *Executive functions [are] different than what people usually think of when they think of IQ. Typical traditional IQ tests measure what's called* crystallized intelligence, *which is mostly your recall of what you've already learned—like what's the meaning of this word, or what's the capital of that country? What executive functions tap is your ability to use what you already know—to be creative with it, to problem-solve with it—so it's very related to* fluid intelligence, *because that requires reasoning and using information. There's a big overlap between fluid intelligence and executive functions.*

Executive functions, which emerge during the preschool years and don't fully mature until early adulthood, appear to have a bearing on school success, too:

> *If you look at what predicts how well children will do later in school, more and more evidence is showing that executive functions—working memory and inhibition—actually predict success better than IQ tests.*

Philip David Zelazo of the University of Minnesota, also a leading researcher studying executive functions of the brain, sees more of an overlap between IQ and executive functions. For example, we might not do well on an IQ test because we're distracted and can't pay attention. Also, having a good working memory matters in both IQ and executive functions. Like Diamond, Zelazo notes that executive functions enable us to *use* our knowledge:

> *If you ask what is the difference between these two constructs, I think it would be that it is possible to have knowledge of what one's supposed to do—but for various reasons to have difficulty acting in light of that knowledge.*

Executive functions take place in the *prefrontal cortex* of the brain. I love the term that Stanislas Dehaene uses to describe this part of the brain—a *global neuronal workspace:*

> *It's a theoretical construct, but the human brain contains a set of areas that are much more tightly interconnected to each other—like hubs in airports.*

The prefrontal cortex is responsible for the ability to exchange information across the high-level areas of the brain, Dehaene says, so that our behavior can be guided by our accumulated knowledge. That's the beauty and the purpose of executive functions: they enable us to control ourselves, to reflect deeply, and to consider things from multiple points of view, as we'll see below.

JUST WHAT ARE FOCUS AND SELF CONTROL?

We all think we know what we mean when we talk about focus and self control, but just how are they defined? Based on my knowledge of the research and my conversations with parents "in the trenches," I see them as having four components: focus, cognitive flexibility, working memory, and inhibitory control.

1. FOCUS

Researchers talk about "attention," but I use the word *focus* because it's the word parents use, and it has an inclusive meaning. For young children, researchers talk about being "alert" and about "orienting" (being able to position their attention in the right direction to achieve what they want to achieve—think of a fourteen-month-old trying to get Cheerios onto a spoon in order to feed herself or himself). For older children and adults, focus includes those two aspects, plus being able to concentrate—that is, to remain alert and oriented for a period of time, bringing our other skills to bear on a project or task despite internal and external distractions.

On the following page is a quiz where you can score yourself on focus. Note, however, that I developed these questions simply to help you think about yourself; they're not from a standardized diagnostic test. Circle the number that describes how well the statement describes you.

Add up your scores in the far right-hand column:

If your overall score is between 20 and 15, then you rate highly on focus.

If your score is between 14 and 9, then you are in the middle category and could use some work on this skill.

If your score is 8 or below, then this is a skill you could improve.

Here are some ideas from parents on how they improve their focus:

I try to set a goal with specific milestones—such as getting a certain number of items checked off the to-do list. Then I build in some rewards—such as taking a mental break and surfing the Web after completing five tasks.

Listening to music helps me focus.

I'm someone who starts a million projects at once and rather than finish one, I move on to the next. If I feel this happening, I just stop and remind myself how great it will feel to finish something. This encourages me to not move on to the next thing, but rather to stop and finish what I'm doing.

FOCUS

	EXACTLY LIKE YOU	VERY MUCH LIKE YOU	SOMEWHAT LIKE YOU	NOT TOO MUCH LIKE YOU	NOT AT ALL LIKE YOU	YOUR TOTAL SCORE
1. I typically get so absorbed in what I'm doing that I stay with it for a long time	5	4	3	2	1	
2. I'm easily distracted	1	2	3	4	5	
3. I have a hard time keeping my mind on things	1	2	3	4	5	
4. I can keep my energy at just the right level so that I can concentrate when I need to	5	4	3	2	1	
						OVERALL SCORE

I do what I call "setting myself up for success" by breaking down a big project into tiny, almost ridiculously easy steps, particularly at the beginning—it might be as simple as getting some information I need. I take one tiny step each day and then tell myself, "You've done it! That's it for today on that project." Often, removing the pressure to continue makes me want to do more, so sometimes I take a couple of steps in one day—Zowie! The incremental, achievable steps give me a constant sense of progress and success. By the time I get to some of the more difficult steps, I've built a large body of knowledge and information, and a lot more confidence than when I started.

At the end of the chapter are numerous other suggestions that you can try with your children.

2. COGNITIVE FLEXIBILITY

With a young child, researchers talk about the skill of shifting one's attention (for example, a baby looking at you when you speak and then looking at your friend when your friend speaks); with older children and adults, researchers talk about cognitive flexibility. You can see cognitive flexibility in action when your child pretends. She might pretend to be a dancer, and then another child comes along and changes the script— now they're playing superheroes, and your child goes with the flow. As an adult, cognitive flexibility is at work when you understand a problem from your own and your boss's differing points of view. Adele Diamond defines cognitive flexibility as being able to:

flexibly switch perspectives or the focus of attention; and

flexibly adjust to changed demands or priorities.

On the following page are questions from my quiz about cognitive flexibility, so that you can calculate your score:

If your overall score is between 20 and 15, then you rate highly on cognitive flexibility.

COGNITIVE FLEXIBILITY

	EXACTLY LIKE YOU	VERY MUCH LIKE YOU	SOMEWHAT LIKE YOU	NOT TOO MUCH LIKE YOU	NOT AT ALL LIKE YOU	YOUR TOTAL SCORE
1. When I try something that doesn't work, it's hard for me to give it up and try another solution	1	2	3	4	5	
2. I adapt to change pretty easily	5	4	3	2	1	
3. When I can't convince someone of my point of view, I can usually understand why not	5	4	3	2	1	
4. I am not very quick to take on new ideas	1	2	3	4	5	
					OVERALL SCORE	

If your score is between 14 and 9, then you are in the middle category. If your score is 8 or below, then this is a skill you could improve.

3. WORKING MEMORY

When I first began studying the research on focus and self control, I didn't understand how working memory fit into the equation. But the more I've delved into this subject, the clearer the connections. For example, just as I'm falling asleep, a mental to-do list for tomorrow floats into my mind. When I wake up, unless I can remember what was on the list, I can't decide what I should focus on first.

Adele Diamond defines *working memory* as holding information in your mind while mentally working with it or updating it. The examples she gives are:

relating one idea to another;

relating what you're reading now to what you just read; and

relating what you are learning now to what you learned earlier.

Thus, working memory is critical for making sense of anything that unfolds over time; for example, understanding something we read or something we are listening to (such as a lecture we hear in school or the dialogue in a television show). It is also important for tasks like:

doing mental arithmetic; and

prioritizing the order in which things need to be done.

On the following page are some questions about working memory, so that you think about your own working memory:

If your overall score is between 20 and 15, then you rate highly on working memory.

If your score is between 14 and 9, then you are in the middle category.

If your score is 8 or below, you could work on this skill.

WORKING MEMORY

	EXACTLY LIKE YOU	VERY MUCH LIKE YOU	SOMEWHAT LIKE YOU	NOT TOO MUCH LIKE YOU	NOT AT ALL LIKE YOU	YOUR TOTAL SCORE
1. I can hold a couple of ideas in my mind at the same time	5	4	3	2	1	
2. If I'm reading, it's hard for me to remember what I have just read	1	2	3	4	5	
3. I can add large numbers in my head	5	4	3	2	1	
4. I don't always remember what I plan to do first and then second	1	2	3	4	5	
					OVERALL SCORE	

Here are some suggestions from parents on how they improve their memories:

I learned an exercise that involves strengthening my memory. It has several rules: I make a circle by lifting both my arms and crossing them in front of me. I then lower them, and when I lift them again I switch between the right and left arms crossing in front. Finally, I add a new level of complexity, like breathing in when I lift my arms up and breathing out when I bring them down.

When I meet new people, I repeat their names and then I try to relate the name to the people in some way—maybe to something they are wearing or something about their face. I try to take a mental picture in my mind with their name on the photograph. Or I say to myself, "This is Eric with blond hair, not my friend Eric with black hair."

I play the game my doctor uses in my annual physical exam (is he testing my memory, my balance, or both?): Pick a line to walk on, one foot in front of the other. Then subtract 7 from 100, then 7 from that, and keep going.

I think of crossword puzzles as my insurance policy for keeping my memory sharp as I age.

If all else fails, write things down. Every Sunday night, I make a to-do list in categories. During the week, things get added and crossed off. And on the next Sunday, I transfer what hasn't been accomplished or I drop it because it now, thankfully, seems unimportant.

I have a to-do list for work, but for less critical things I refuse to make lists, as a way to tune up my memory. At the grocery, for example, I make it my business to remember what we need. I must say that there's no memory enhancer like remembering how cranky I get when I don't have milk for my morning coffee!

4. INHIBITORY CONTROL

Think about your day so far and tally up the times you were on automatic pilot—when you didn't really have to think or make tough decisions about what you were doing, such as getting up, getting dressed, brushing your teeth, or getting your favorite food for breakfast. These tasks didn't require much conscious focus or self control; you just did them.

Now think about the times that were just the opposite—where you had to make a real effort to stick with the task and be intentional about what you wanted to achieve. These times demanded what is called *inhibitory control*—or what some researchers, such as Mary Rothbart of the University of Oregon, refer to as *effortful control.*

Adele Diamond defines inhibitory control as "the ability to resist a strong inclination to do one thing and instead do what is most appropriate." Here are some examples:

being able to pay attention even when there are lots of distractions, such as paying attention to your child when you've just had an unpleasant conversation with someone else and this conversation is preoccupying you;

sticking with something you are doing after you've had an initial failure—inhibiting the strong inclination to give up;

being able to stop and think before you act, such as not blurting out something but thinking through what you really want to say or not hurting someone who has hurt you (tit for tat); and

acting appropriately when tempted to do otherwise, such as continuing to work on something even when you're bored.

You'll notice that inhibitory control involves controlling your *attention,* your *emotions,* and your *behavior* to achieve a goal. Diamond elaborates:

[There's] inhibition at the level of attention—you want to inhibit distraction. You can be in a noisy room and you want to focus on the one person you're trying to listen to, so you're trying to inhibit

what you're hearing from others. Or you can be looking for a sign on the road and you want to inhibit all the other distractions and try to hone in on that sign you're looking for.

Diamond goes on to say that distractions can be internal or external, but inhibition is needed *both* for focused or selective attention *and* for staying focused on what you want to hold in your mind (aiding working memory). She continues:

There's also inhibition at the level of behavior, where you want to resist doing what might be your first impulse but would not be the most appropriate or the best thing to do in that moment. [Perhaps] you're working on an assignment and it's getting boring and there's something much more fun to do and you would really like to stop working and do the more fun thing, but you say, "No, I have to exercise the discipline to finish this work," and you make yourself do it. You inhibit the strong pull to go do something more fun.

We also need inhibition if we have an initial failure on something we are doing—inhibition helps us resist the strong urge to simply give up. And inhibition is critical in social relationships. Diamond explains:

Let's say there's a friend you haven't seen in many years, and maybe your first impression when you see your friend is "My God, how much weight you've gained!" But you don't want to say that; you don't want to hurt your friend's feelings. You inhibit that statement, and instead you say something to make your friend feel good.

Finally, inhibition can help you break the cycle of hurting one another (tit for tat to get back at someone who has hurt you).

On the following page are questions about inhibitory control, so that you can get a sense of how you stand on this capacity.

If your overall score is between 30 and 22, then you rate highly on inhibitory control.

If your score is between 21 and 13, then you are in the middle category.

INHIBITORY CONTROL

	EXACTLY LIKE YOU	VERY MUCH LIKE YOU	SOMEWHAT LIKE YOU	NOT TOO MUCH LIKE YOU	NOT AT ALL LIKE YOU	YOUR TOTAL SCORE
1. If I'm in a noisy room, I can still pay attention to the person I'm talking to	5	4	3	2	1	
2. I have trouble screening out things that are going on around me	1	2	3	4	5	
3. When I'm interrupted by someone who needs me—at work or at home—I can switch gears and pay attention	5	4	3	2	1	
4. I tend to blurt out what I'm thinking, even if it might hurt someone else	1	2	3	4	5	
5. If others are having dessert, I usually have one, too, even when I want to lose weight	1	2	3	4	5	
6. I stick to what I need to do, even when I'm not successful right away and I want to give up	5	4	3	2	1	
OVERALL SCORE						

If your score is 12 or below, that means you could work on this skill.

If you are like me, depending on what's going on in your life and how well you feel you're coping, you could score your "best self" or your "worst self" in any given category of this quiz. That variability is actually in keeping with what the research tells us: these skills shift and change. Diamond explains:

> *Executive functions are very fragile—so no matter how good your executive functions are, your executive functions will look terrible if you're sleep deprived [or] if you're stressed.*

A DAUGHTER'S PERSPECTIVE: EXECUTIVE FUNCTIONS *ARE* FRAGILE!

When my father died, I had very little patience for problems beyond the usual. It was as if all my mental bandwidth was devoted to dealing with this big thing that was preoccupying my attention and focus, with very little left over for anything else. I remember a knotty problem that had circulated for a week among about a dozen people at work while I was away at my dad's funeral, and when I got back, the memo came back to me without a single solution; the problems were still there! And I looked around the conference table and said, "Do you realize that in the week it took this piece of paper to circulate to all these people and come back to me unchanged, *a person died* and left this world forever?" And they all sat back and looked at me, like, "*Whoa.*" And I thought, "Oh. Now I understand why the company offers bereavement days. Guess I should have taken some."

If we find it difficult sometimes to maintain our focus and self control, imagine what it's like for our children, who don't have our decades of practice and experience. These are difficult skills, which may be why they're so fundamentally important. On the other hand, these skills are like muscles—the more we work on them, the stronger they become. So there's always hope for our kids—and for us, too!

IMPROVING OUR OWN FOCUS AND SELF CONTROL IN AN ERA OF *TIME FAMINE*

In business-speak, we say, "We have to walk the talk"; in parent-speak, we say, "Actions speak louder than words." These are easy to say, but not so easy to do, as I know too well from working on these skills myself. And as fate would have it, just as I began to write this section of the book, my daughter, Lara, called, testing the strength of my skill. I had carved out time to write (and uninterrupted time is hard for me to come by), but she wanted my help in thinking through a paper she was writing for a graduate course. Competing goals!

When my son was a teenager and wanted to talk about something, he would suddenly appear nearby and silently hang around. I thought of it as "hovercrafting": he was like a helicopter in a quiet holding pattern, circling around me. I soon realized that if I kept on doing what I was doing, he'd move away, but if I literally swiveled around and started to talk about something—anything—usually he'd tell me what was on his mind. You can probably guess that as a busy parent I sometimes swiveled—shifted my attention—and sometimes I didn't.

As we all know, turning away from something we really want to do can be wrenching. Time feels so limited these days. According to our research, more than six in ten of us are experiencing what we call a *time famine.* I've learned that I have to remove myself physically from what I'm doing if I want to pay full attention to someone else. I often walk to another room (certainly away from the computer, where the "you have mail" sound pings, frantically calling to me).

A WRITER'S PERSPECTIVE: DON'T TURN ON THE BELL!

The best thing that ever happened to my work life was to get a new computer and not know how to turn on the little bell that pings to tell me I have e-mail. I intend to never learn how. It has calmed me down so much to have this silence. I check my e-mail plenty obsessively and I don't miss an urgent message. But I no longer get an adrenaline shot a hundred times a day on someone else's schedule.

I choose when I visit e-mail and don't just react to "the bell." This simple change has been instrumental in helping me begin to hear myself think again.

That morning when my daughter, Lara, called, I thought of those little kids putting their hands on their parents' faces to capture their attention. I didn't want to be like that for my daughter when she needed my help. I used my "change of scene" technique for focusing and went into another room while she talked to me.

Was it a good experience? Not entirely. She was struggling with the topic of an assignment. I didn't know much about the subject, so my one suggestion "was not really helpful." But Lara and I both gave me points for trying. And I know that the more I exercise this skill, the more I can help her—even as an adult—with this skill itself, if not with the paper.

THE ORIGINS OF FOCUS AND SELF CONTROL:
A VOYAGE INTO THE WOMB

When we talk about improving our focus and self control, we're talking about improving a process that calls on multiple parts of our brain and is rooted in a developmental chain that began before birth. Put simply, we *increase our energy* to respond to something that has happened, and then, if we're successful, we *bring ourselves under control* and ultimately are able to be goal directed. It can be depicted like this:

SOMETHING HAPPENS ➡ WE RESPOND ➡ WE BRING OURSELVES UNDER CONTROL

T. Berry Brazelton of Harvard Medical School, the man who is often called "America's pediatrician," recalls when and how he became aware of this process. It was the early 1970s, and many pediatricians—as well as many other people—didn't fully understand the capacities of newborns. He remembers:

We still didn't think babies could see or hear. Where did we get such a stupid idea?

But he observed something different. He saw that newborns had many unique ways of being connected to what was happening around them. It seemed to him that if we as adults could find better ways to tune in to what infants were doing, we could better understand their experiences. To help doctors and families interpret the "language" of the newborn, Brazelton created the Neonatal Behavioral Assessment Scale as a translation and assessment tool:

The thing that came to me as I worked with babies was that valuing [a baby's] state of consciousness—deep sleep, light sleep, in-between, wide-awake alertness, fussing, crying—was the most critical way of seeing what a baby was like.

Brazelton had observed that the typical newborn pediatric examination at that time overstimulated most newborns, and they managed this stress by shutting down—such as by turning away or falling asleep. From this observation, he realized that the way a baby responds to stimulation tells us a lot about the baby's inborn temperament (which we'll explore in chapter 6, on taking on challenges). He also realized that shutting down is a *positive* response—it's the beginning of self control.

I have accompanied Brazelton into the hospital rooms of newborns and their parents immediately after childbirth and watched him use the Brazelton Neonatal Behavioral Assessment Scale with these tiny infants in their first few moments in the world. He holds the baby gently and exclaims over him or her to the parents and then conducts his assessment, which includes stimulating the newborn with a flashlight and a rattle. These babies, born just minutes or hours before, typically startle at the noise or light and then find a way to recover—by sucking a finger, shutting their eyes, or turning away from the commotion (in the language of the Brazelton assessment, they are *regulating* their state of consciousness).

The way the baby calms down tells the parents and pediatrician something about how this particular baby responds to a new and somewhat challenging experience. Brazelton then talks to the parents about their child's style of controlling emotions and about how important this skill is to the child's later development.

Amazingly, the origins of focus and self control begin even before birth. I have watched very pregnant mothers undergo fetal examinations during which they can actually watch their unborn babies on sonogram machines as they start to a buzzing sound, grimace in response, and then find ways to calm down. Some even suck their thumbs! The kind of technology that lets us travel into the womb wasn't available more than thirty years ago when my children were born, but I can clearly remember how different each of my children was before birth: if there was a loud sound, Philip kicked and Lara glided!

AN EVEN MORE FANTASTIC VOYAGE: INTO THE BRAIN

In a tribute to Michael Posner when he retired as a professor of neuroscience at the University of Oregon, two of his colleagues wrote: "Michael Posner is one of the most creative and influential psychologists of the past century." Why do they and others feel this way? Because Posner has pioneered the study of attention systems in the brain from far-ranging perspectives—from actual images of the brain in action to studies of the genetics of attention, from studies of temperament to training studies to determine if our attention systems can be improved.

In our several-hour conversation, Posner narrated a voyage into the interconnected networks of the brain that control attention:

> We all know what it is to be in an alert state. We often change our level of alertness when we get a warning signal—for example, that something important is going to occur—and this alerting function is carried out by networks of neurons in different parts of the brain.

Posner described how signals are sent and received across different parts of the brain:

The cells [in the brain] don't actually come together. Instead, there's a narrow gap between the cells, which is called the synapse. *At one part of the synapse, a transmitter or chemical is released that swims across the synapse and changes the electrical characteristics of the next neuron. That's how information is transmitted in the nervous system.*

An important part of the brain for alertness is called the *locus coeruleus,* a name from Latin that means "blue spot." It is deep within the brain, but it sends signals to the *parietal lobe,* in the back of the brain. Its job is to integrate information from our senses. As Posner explains, signals are sent to two parts of the parietal lobe, a higher part of the network that is involved in voluntary switches of attention and a lower part that is involved when our attention is captured by something. So we might be paying voluntary attention to one thing, but a sudden movement or a noise somewhere else captures our attention and moves us to focus on something else.

Signals are also sent to the *anterior cingulate gyrus.* Think of the anterior cingulate gyrus as involved in the control of the emotional parts of the brain and the more cognitive parts. Mike Posner says:

The anterior cingulate gyrus is involved in the resolution of conflict between different responses that you might make.

Signals also go to the *prefrontal cortex* in the front of the brain. The functions the prefrontal cortex helps carry out are called executive functions, as I've said, and include working memory and self control.

Here's an example of how these systems work. You're at home, and a scream distracts you and shifts your focus. In an instant, you weigh the source of the noise and your responses. You run through some of the possibilities. Was the noise from inside or outside? Was there an accident outside? Is it an animal or a person? Is there an intruder? Did something happen in my house? Is someone hurt? Are the kids in danger? Am I in danger?

If the answer seems to be no, you can go check out the situation more calmly. If the answer to any of your questions seems to be yes, then both emotional and rational messages about where to place your focus start to cascade with all the options, like a multiple-choice test with dozens of possible answers: find out what happened, call 911, grab the kids, run to the person who's screaming in pain, run away from the intruder. Then the executive function sorts through the possibilities and you decide what you're going to do and in what order. And all of this happens in seconds.

This is an example of an emergency, but these systems are working on innumerable tasks, large and small, in times of calm as well as in times of duress. Posner says:

> These three networks of attention we think are all important. In adults, they cooperate in many tasks, but they [also] have a certain amount of independence.

I find it astounding that we can now follow how the networks inside our brains connect, because until fairly recently, scientists didn't have the technology to observe brains in action at all. As we follow these networks, we can see that focus and self control involve multiple areas of the brain that operate our senses, our emotions, and our intellect.

HOW BABIES TELL US THEY'RE PAYING ATTENTION

Focus and self control begin with paying attention. As you can see from Brazelton's work, this is an ability that children are born with. Infants—who can't yet talk, who can't even point to what they want—reach out to others through crying and making other noises, through moving, but especially through focused attention in the form of looking: the deep and solemn stare of the newborn, the inquisitive gaze of the three-month-old, or the wide-eyed, wriggling joy of the six-month-old when you walk in the door.

Imagine you have never noticed how a baby reaches out to the world through paying attention. It's a pretty miraculous sight.

A PARENT'S PERSPECTIVE:
JASON GETS THE "KICKIES"

At six weeks, Jason didn't smile much, but by three months, he gave us lots of smiles. We knew he was waking up to the world by his body language, especially his habit of kicking his legs in rapid, intense forward motion when he saw something he liked or when he seemed to want to communicate something. We called it "kickies."

We had a balloon tied to the side of his changing table. This was the first object to be the recipient of kickies. He loves the changing table and the parade of ever-changing balloons.

Now, at fourteen weeks, he kicks violently, waves his hands, furrows his brow, and makes intense eye contact with me. It's almost as if he wants to show me his progress. He's saying, "Mommy, listen to me! Watch me!" And I'll watch him and talk to him, and his cadences match mine. We have a call and response, he and I. He'll follow conversations—his little head volleying back and forth, trying to figure out the pattern and rhythm of adult conversation. And he'll burble to interrupt, so we smile, and he smiles back. It makes me feel like a million dollars. And even when I notice that his mobile gets a similar reaction, it's okay.

A PARENT'S PERSPECTIVE:
MOHAWKS ARE THE MESSAGE

Even as a young baby, long before he could talk, my son had a sparkle in his eyes that let me know he was alert and wanted to participate. It's all about the eyes and hands for a young baby. Once, I found a toy stuffed bird that had a "Mohawk" of plumage on the top of its head, similar to my son's hair at that time. I made a big show of asking the bird, "How did you get the same hairstyle as my son? That's *his* hairstyle, you rascally bird," etc. My son thought it was hilarious. He chortled wildly and punched the air repeatedly to make me understand that he was excited and wanted me to do it again. I rarely felt that we didn't understand each other.

Much of the research on what goes on in the minds of the youngest children—as you'll see throughout this book—is based on the fact that infants have times of being alert, when they learn about the world by looking, listening, and responding. *When, how,* and *what* they pay attention to will be our ticket to still another fantastic voyage—into their "minds in the making."

A PARENT'S PERSPECTIVE: STARING IS NOT RUDE

Since we live in a metropolitan area, we take the train and the subway frequently. We're a "baby-wearing" family: since birth, Adam has been in slings and other baby carriers. Typically, babies sleep a lot while being carried, but not our Adam! He was usually busy studying the faces of the people sitting next to us. In the adult world, it's not polite to stare at strangers for long periods of time. To break the ice, I explained that Adam is very curious and wants to learn about different people. I'd often end up chatting with the person for the whole trip. I realized that Adam and I could make someone's day a happy one simply by giving them smiles and attention—a small gift that can make a big difference!

THE CONNECTION BETWEEN STRESS AND SELF CONTROL

Clancy Blair's research into children's development was fueled by an observation years ago:

When I found out that [a child's ability to pay] attention is probably the best predictor we have of understanding a child's level of cognitive functioning [at] age six, age ten, age twelve, and so on, I thought, "Well, that's really interesting. I wonder what it is about the ability to quickly shift the focus of attention or to focus attention or to [get used] to novel stimuli?" It just led to a whole host of different questions.

It also led to a study that he and his colleagues began in 2002 in which they have been following a group of children from infancy into their school-age years. Now a professor at New York University, Blair is unusual in that he studies both the emotional and the intellectual development of children and how these interact to affect children's readiness for school. Typically, researchers study one or the other—in fact, the field of psychology separates cognitive psychology from the other branches of psychology—but when we want to look at how the brain pays attention, these divisions don't serve us well. Blair says:

> When children are having behavior problems—when they're having a temper tantrum or are acting in a way that is really exuberant or very negative—[that] really inhibits the child's ability to listen and focus.

At best, Blair says, children should "have their emotions work with them, not against them."

To assess how children's emotional control relates to their cognitive abilities and school readiness, Blair measures children's cortisol levels. *Cortisol* is known as the stress hormone. Its production in the adrenal glands (above the kidneys) is stimulated and regulated by the pituitary gland at the base of the brain. Cortisol (as you'll learn in more detail in chapter 6, on taking on challenges) provides a barometer of how much stress we're experiencing over time and can be easily measured in saliva. Blair and his team do this with four- and five-year-olds by giving them pieces of cotton rope to chew on:

> We ask children to think of [their] favorite food and what [they're] going to have for lunch and [to] put this piece of cotton rope in their mouth and chew on it like a puppy dog.

Since it takes about twenty minutes for cortisol to appear in saliva, the experimenters give this exercise to children three times during their forty-five-minute assessment. The first sample, taken when children begin the assessment, actually measures children's stress level twenty minutes beforehand; the second, taken twenty minutes later, measures their cortisol levels at the beginning of the assessment; and the third, taken at the end of the assessment, measures their responses midway through the assessment.

Between "rope-chewings," Blair and his team give the children a number of tasks aimed at evaluating various aspects of their school readiness skills. He fondly calls one of the tasks, which evaluates children's inhibitory control, the "glorious peg-tapping task":

> In the peg-tapping task, you sit down with the child and you hand them the peg [a wooden stick] and say, "Can you tap this?" And children usually don't have any trouble with that—[they] tap away. And we say, "Okay, we're going to play a tapping game, now that we know you can tap. The tapping game is when I tap one time, you tap two times, and when I tap two times, you tap one time." We establish [that] children understand the rule with a few practice trials.

They go through this task sixteen times, mixing up the times that the child is asked to tap once when the experimenter taps twice, and tap twice when the experimenter taps once. In other words, the rules of the game keep changing, and the children need to apply their focus and attention to follow what's going on. Blair says:

> What happens with four-year-olds is, in general, they'll hang in there with you for a few taps—then they'll just start mimicking your tapping. There's a strong tendency to mimic what the experimenter is doing, and the inference is that the rule has just sort of evaporated out of the child's mind.

This exercise measures children's ability to remember the rule (*working memory*) and to overcome their automatic response of copying what they see the experimenter doing (*inhibitory control*). That's why the peg-tapping task is a good measure of the executive functions of the brain.

Blair has found a connection between children's cortisol levels and their ability to do the peg-tapping task. The children who do the best on this task show a moderate increase in stress and then, importantly, a decrease. In other words, children's ability to control their emotional response to a slightly challenging situation (going into a room near their preschool classroom with an experimenter and being asked to play a number of new games) is linked to their ability to remember the rule, follow it, and inhibit their natural tendency to copy what the experimenter is doing.

Thus one aspect of maintaining focus and self control involves the ability to manage stress. Measuring cortisol in studies of this skill makes this connection very evident.

ATTENTION DEFICIT DISORDERS AND EXECUTIVE FUNCTIONS OF THE BRAIN

There is general agreement among researchers that ADHD is an impairment of executive functions of the prefrontal cortex. Adele Diamond explains:

> There are three kinds of ADHD—attention deficit hyperactivity disorder—according to the diagnostic manual. There's ADHD of the hyperactive type; there's ADHD of the inattentive type; and there's a combined type of ADHD.

Diamond notes that the truly inattentive types appear to be quite different from the other types of ADHD that include hyperactivity. They differ in the brain systems and genes involved, in how they respond to medication, and in the way they are manifested in behavior and in mental functioning. She is launching a study to determine if an early childhood program that fosters development of executive functions can reduce the incidence or severity of ADHD. She predicts that it can.

F. Xavier Castellanos, a professor of child and adolescent psychiatry, a director of research, and a director of an institute for pediatric neuroscience at the NYU Child Study Center, has been studying ADHD for many years, including at the National Institute of Mental Health, where he was chief of the ADHD Research Unit. In an article on the NYU Child Study Center Web site, he writes that ADHD is caused by a mix of genetic and experiential factors and that it is affected by the level of dopamine—

a neurotransmitter, or chemical, responsible for sending nerve signals across a synapse between two neurons in the brain. He feels that future studies must focus on the underlying mechanisms of ADHD, which include difficulty with:

Inhibition: There's a difference between children with and without ADHD in the ability to avoid distractions and stop themselves. This can be tested by a "stop task," where children are asked to respond as fast as they can when told to "go," and then to stop when they are told to "stop." Children with ADHD are more likely to need the stop signal to occur earlier in the process for them to be able to stop themselves.

Ability to defer gratification: Children with ADHD may be more likely to choose an immediate reward over a reward that will happen later, even when the delayed reward is a bigger or better reward.

Estimating time: People of all ages with ADHD are likely to be less accurate in estimating how long things will take.

Working memory: Children who have the inattentive form of ADHD have a harder time holding different things in their memory at the same time.

Castellanos writes:

We believe that by measuring patients' working memory, and/or their ability to reproduce or estimate temporal durations, and/or their ability to delay gratification, we will learn about some of the physiological components which can result in the symptoms we call ADHD.

By testing these "scientific guesses," he hopes that we can become better at understanding the different types of ADHD and thus better at preventing and treating it.

From what we know now, promoting the skill of self control and focus provides a promising new direction in efforts to reduce attention deficit disorders.

WHEN SHOULD WE BEGIN PROMOTING FOCUS AND SELF CONTROL?

The skill of focus and self control begins to develop in the early childhood years, but it doesn't fully become established until the later teen and early adult years. The prefrontal cortex is among the last parts of the brain to mature. Adele Diamond says she is repeatedly asked:

> "How can you say that a three-year-old or a four-year-old is capable of any kind of executive function? [The] prefrontal cortex is too immature." The analogy I like to use is: Think about a two-year-old's legs. Your legs at age two are not at their full adult length; it may take ten or fifteen years to reach their full adult length— they're very immature. But even with those immature legs, a two-year-old can walk; a two-year-old can even run. So the legs, even in their immature two-year-old state, are capable of serving a lot of the functions that legs are supposed to serve.

She concludes:

> An immature prefrontal cortex is capable of supporting a lot of the functions it's supposed to support. So even babies, toddlers, and kindergarten children are capable of exercising executive functions to some extent.

HOW CAN FOCUS AND SELF CONTROL BE IMPROVED?

I find Adele Diamond's analogy to walking and running very logical. How well would we walk and run if we weren't allowed to do so until our legs were fully grown? When we see children crawling, pulling themselves to stand, and demonstrating other cues of readiness, don't we naturally encourage them to strengthen and train their muscles, nerves, and bones to perform these complex skills by helping them to (literally) take "baby steps"? It should be no different with the skills of focus and self control—and the good news is, it's possible.

Researchers are increasingly convinced that families and teachers should be much more intentional about promoting these life skills, especially in the preschool and school-age years, and they've begun to experiment with ways to do so.

Michael Posner and his colleagues gave four-year-olds and six-year-olds five days of training in attention skills on the computer and compared them to comparable groups of children with no training. The results? Even with such a brief training, the children had less trouble with "effortful" or inhibitory control. Not surprisingly, the six-year-olds learned more than the four-year-olds. The researchers also found that when children's ability to pay attention improved, their reasoning and thinking skills also improved.

Adele Diamond and her colleagues have evaluated an initiative that promotes children's executive function skills called Tools of the Mind, a curriculum developed by Elena Bodrova and Deborah Leong based on the theories of Russian psychologists Lev Vygotsky and Alexander Luria. Four- and five-year-olds in a state-funded preschool program for lower-income children were randomly assigned either to regular classes that met state standards or to classes that met state standards but also used this curriculum. Teachers in the Tools of the Mind classes spent 80 percent of their classroom time promoting executive function skills in fun and playful ways (some of which I'll describe later).

Even though this curriculum required no special equipment or even highly trained teachers, the researchers found that the children using Tools of the Mind became much better at working memory, inhibitory control, and cognitive flexibility skills.

Although I'm *not* advocating for this or any of the other curricula or materials I mention in this book, my point is that executive function skills can be improved, if it is done in the right way.

HOW CAN YOU PROMOTE FOCUS AND SELF CONTROL IN CHILDREN?

SUGGESTION 1: HELP INFANTS AND TODDLERS LEARN TO BRING THEMSELVES UNDER CONTROL.

My suggestions below for improving focus and self control largely involve children in the preschool years and older, when executive functions of the brain begin to come on line. But even our youngest children can start to learn important basic skills of self control. Here are some ways you can help very young children bring themselves under control:

Observe in order to understand what helps your child maintain self control and focus. Maybe you'll notice that your child calms down when you carry her to a quiet place. Maybe you'll notice that your child becomes calmer when you use words to describe his feelings. When you follow your child's cues, you're not *imposing* control on your child; you are helping your child, even in infancy, *learn to take the lead* in managing himself or herself, because you're providing the calm place or the words that you observe are helpful to your child. This is a very, very important point and why you need to be a detective in figuring out what your child does that is most helpful in calming her down.

Use the technique that you know works best for your child. Heidelise Als of the Harvard Medical School suggests holding your baby to help him or her simmer down:

As you let go, the baby may lose control again. You have to stay long enough so your support takes hold in the baby. You will feel the baby taking over. The baby has come back to balance.

You will need to experiment to find what calms your baby down. When my son, Philip, was very young, I found that turning the lights off and on usually captured his attention and he calmed down.

Acknowledge your baby's successes. T. Berry Brazelton says:

Every time babies put themselves together in the face of stress or stimulation, they're getting internal feedback that says, "You learned. You just did it!" And if they do it over and over, it becomes part of their equipment. When the adult reinforces these internal feedback systems, but doesn't take them over, we are giving that baby not only the chance to learn, but also a chance to experience the excitement of learning.

SUGGESTION 2: WEAVE THESE SKILLS INTO EVERYDAY ACTIVITIES IN FUN AND PLAYFUL WAYS—NO DRILLS, "TEACHING," OR EXPENSIVE GAMES OR TOYS NEEDED.

If sharing the research on encouraging focus and self control in older preschooler and school-age children results in more "drill and practice" exercises or in more expensive games that parents are supposed to buy, then we're not heeding the lessons of the research itself. Adele Diamond cautions:

I think that we should be focusing on helping children get better at these skills early. I'm hesitant to use the word teach, *because when you say* teach, *people have this image of children sitting like little college students in their seats with somebody lecturing at them.*

Promoting these skills should involve weaving them naturally into everyday activities in school and at home in playful and fun ways. Read on for many examples and ideas.

SUGGESTION 3: PROMOTE FOCUS—ENCOURAGE YOUR CHILDREN TO HAVE "LEMONADE STANDS."

When Lara was about six or seven, she and her older friend Katie had a lemonade stand. During warm-weather weekends, they positioned themselves in front of Katie's house on the edge of a country road, shouting out to everyone who walked or drove by: "Try our lemonade—it's delicious!"

The work that went into their lemonade stand was phenomenal. It involved counting the number of customers from their last day of sales and then using that number to figure out the amount of lemonade to make; going to the store and buying the ingredients with their profits; reading and following the recipe; keeping track of money; making change for customers; and making signs as well as practicing marketing and sales techniques. In addition, there was the focus and self control needed just to be at the stand for long stretches of time! I have a favorite photograph of their lemonade stand. Katie and Lara sit side by side on a log in front of a child-sized table. Their huge smiles reveal missing teeth, and their lemonade sign has some backward and upside-down letters. Just from looking at this old photograph, I can still feel their passion for what they were doing.

Lemonade stands have become my metaphor for something that children care a lot about. Every child needs lemonade stands throughout childhood. Caring strongly about interests beyond oneself engenders true focus.

Antonio, my now sixteen-year-old grandson, is a good example of what lemonade stands can mean in a child's life. Valerie, a single mother at the time, would come home from work to find Antonio at ten or eleven lost in the world of video games, his homework thrown on the kitchen table untouched. At Valerie's insistence, Antonio would make halfhearted promises to do his homework, rush through it at the highest speed possible, and tune back in to his world of gaming and texting.

One day Antonio and some friends were harassed by a ganglike group of older kids on their way home from school. No one was hurt, nothing was stolen, but their confidence in being able to walk home from school safely was rattled.

Down the street from Antonio's apartment was a tae kwon do school. Antonio prevailed upon Valerie, his other grandparents, and Norman and me to enroll him. He became hooked, pouring the kind of energy into learning martial arts that he had poured into video games. His initial goal was to be able to defend himself if anyone ever tried to mess with him again, but soon he had other goals—to learn tae kwon do and to earn a yellow belt, then a green belt and a blue belt.

Valerie told me that Antonio's schoolwork began to improve, so I asked him why. He said simply, "Learning tae kwon do taught me to *focus*."

Children obviously don't need to be bullied by bigger kids to find their own lemonade stands. Their true interests are evident—if we only look. And their interests will change as they grow up. Antonio has moved from tae kwon do to a passion for the Yankees and for playing baseball.

A PARENT'S PERSPECTIVE: TRUCKS AND MORE TRUCKS

This game began in the grocery store. I always name items and point them out. I label everything! I also say things like "Do you see something yellow? Do you see something shaped like a square?" My son turned this into the truck game. He loves trucks, so whenever we see a truck we talk about it . . . big truck, big digger, big bulldozer! He sees them before my husband and I do. He watches so intently that we won't miss a truck in the entire state!

SUGGESTION 4: PROMOTE FOCUS—PLAY GAMES THAT REQUIRE CHILDREN TO PAY ATTENTION.

Here are some examples:

Guessing games. For example, "I am thinking of an animal with a name that sounds like a rat."

"I Spy." In this game, you tell the child what you spy ("I spy something in this room that is green") and the child has to guess what it is. This is also a good car game.

Puzzles. You can buy puzzles or make your own by cutting or tearing magazine photos into odd-shaped pieces and having your child "find the picture" by putting the pieces back together.

Red Light/ Green Light. In this game, one person plays the stoplight and the other children try to touch him or her. The child playing the stoplight stands about fifteen feet away from the other children, who are positioned at a starting line. The stoplight child turns his or her back to the other children and says, "Green light!" The other children move as fast as they can toward the stoplight child, who at any time can say, "Red light!" and turn to face the other children. Any child who is spotted moving by the stoplight child after a red light is called is out of the game. The game continues in this way. The stoplight child wins if all the children are out before anyone is able to touch him or her. If someone succeeds in touching the stoplight child, then that child becomes the stoplight for the next game.

Musical Chairs. Make a circle of chairs and have each child line up behind a chair. Then put on some music and remove one chair. The children circle around the chairs while the music is playing, but when you stop the music, each child must sit down on a chair. The child without a chair is out. Keep playing, removing one more chair each time. Continue until you have only two children and one chair left. The child who sits down on that last chair when the music stops is the winner. You can also play this game using pieces of construction paper instead of chairs. The object of the game is to stand on the paper.

Bell Game. Diamond suggests a game used in Montessori programs. You give a bell to each member of the family:

The game is that you're all to walk. It doesn't matter what the formation is—you can walk in a circle or in a line—but the goal is that nobody should make a sound with the bell.

As the children get better at the game, you can up the ante: have the children walk faster or move in more complicated patterns. Diamond notes that this game is a good one to calm children down before bed.

SUGGESTION 5: PROMOTE FOCUS—READ STORIES TO CHILDREN IN WAYS THAT ENCOURAGE THEM TO LISTEN.

As adults, we know that listening—really listening—feels almost like a lost art. The world speeds by, and often we speed by at the same pace. Listening requires focus and powerful inhibitory control. Think of a time when you've been listening to someone else and how much you've wanted to stop listening and break in with your ideas, your thoughts, and your opinions—it's not so easy to inhibit that urge.

Listening games encourage children to focus, remember, and practice inhibitory control. When you read to preschoolers, ask them to listen to a line or two of a nursery rhyme or a favorite book and repeat it with you. Think of the lyrical words from *Goodnight Moon* by Margaret Wise Brown, saying goodnight to the stars, goodnight to the air, and goodnight to "noises everywhere."

Ask your children to singsong the words of favorite refrains in books with you, or stop and ask them to finish the sentences. These everyday games involve children focusing and remembering.

A PARENT'S PERSPECTIVE: MUSIC BABY

Sam is pretty verbal now, but before he could even talk, he loved music. At about six months, he could amazingly mimic the tunes and even word sounds. He also could do the hand motions to things like "Open and Shut Them" and "The Itsy Bitsy Spider." It really hits home how much they remember—even at such a young age. Now, twenty-one months old, Sam sings at the top of his lungs and loves to dance. He even has concerts with his sister.

The Tools of the Mind curriculum uses a simple line drawing to help children listen. Adele Diamond reminds us what four-year-olds are like when they each have a story to tell:

The typical scenario is that nobody wants to listen—everybody wants to tell his or her story. If you ask a four-year-old to wait, you might as well save your breath.

Diamond explains how one classroom tool promotes listening:

What they do is they give one child a picture of a mouth and the other child a picture of an ear, and they explain that "ears don't talk, ears listen." With that concrete reminder in front of them, the child [holding the ear picture] listens. It's amazing. I wouldn't have believed it if I hadn't seen it. The child doesn't talk, the child listens—[even] the child who would never have listened otherwise. After a few months, the pictures aren't needed anymore. The children have internalized them—and the behaviors they represent.

Adele Diamond jokes that when she has told her friends about this device, they all want it for their adult meetings!

SUGGESTION 6: PROMOTE FOCUS—SELECT COMPUTER GAMES THAT PROMOTE PAYING ATTENTION.

If you buy computer games for your children, get ones that promote the development of focus. Michael Posner describes three of the games they created for the training of four- and six-year-olds. These games are not available commercially, but there is further information about them on the Web site http://www.teach-the-brain.org/learn/attention/index .htm. My point in describing them is to point out what might be good features to look for in games for your children.

The first game involves a cartoon cat and mud. The children are given a joystick to move this cartoon cat around on a computer screen. At first the cat is surrounded by grass, but patches of mud begin to appear on the screen. The task is to keep the cat away from the mud. Posner says:

[The children] have to really control the cat very carefully to get it on the grass and not the mud. Of course, no one likes getting [into] the mud. The kids really get into this.

When the children move the joystick to the left, the cat moves left; when they move the joystick to the right, the cat moves right. The children then have to learn to move the cat forward and backward—tasks designed to be more difficult. This game involves *learning how to focus on the task, remembering the rules for moving the cartoon character,* and *continuing to respond to the changing situation.*

In another computer game called Chase, the task is to control a cartoon umbrella to keep the cat dry. This game involves the same principles as the "mud" game.

To develop the skills of *anticipating and orienting,* Posner and his team use a third computer game. In the easier version, the children are given the task of moving the cartoon cat to find a duck in a pond. The game is then made more difficult by having the duck swim underwater and having the child anticipate where the duck might emerge. Also very important are exercises that teach the child to resolve conflicts between possible moves they might make in this game.

I heard Bing Gordon, when he was chief creative officer of Electronic Arts, an interactive game company, speak at a symposium on learning in the digital age. He talked with great passion about the learning potential in games. It is clear that video games can promote destruction and violence or they can promote amazing thinking skills. So when you select games for your children, review them carefully. Are they helping children improve their thinking skills in constructive ways?

SUGGESTION 7: PROMOTE FOCUS—SELECT TELEVISION SHOWS THAT HELP CHILDREN PAY ATTENTION.

Daniel Anderson of the University of Massachusetts at Amherst was one of the earliest researchers on children's television and is among the most prominent and well respected. He became involved in this research in the 1970s through his interest in studying attention. He says:

I had given a lecture to a large class on child development about the development of attention. After the class, a student came up to me and asked, "Professor Anderson, if young kids are so distractible and have trouble sustaining attention, how come my four-year-old brother can just sit and stare at Sesame Street?" Being a young professor, I thought I had to know the answer to everything, and I said, "It only seems like your brother is paying attention. In fact, the TV is producing [constant movements] and those are constantly distracting him. Every time he's getting ready to look away, something changes and he looks back again."

Although this answer satisfied the student, it didn't satisfy Anderson, who set out with a graduate student to review the literature on children's attention to television. There was no literature—the field was too new. So Anderson decided to do his own study. Little did he suspect then that this would become his life's work!

In an early study of children from one through four years old, Anderson and his colleagues found that he had been partially correct—children did not pay continuous attention to TV: they looked and they looked away. However, the researchers did find that paying attention to television increased with age, and that led them to question *what* children pay attention to when they watch television. At that time, many people thought the children were captured by the television production itself, especially productions that were fast paced, highly edited, and jazzy (like commercials).

To investigate this question, Anderson and his colleagues created four different shows. All had the same programming elements, such as cuts, pans, zooms, sound effects, and voice quality. The first version was the original *Sesame Street* show—just as it had been created; the second was reedited so that the shots were cut together in random order; the third version had the words played backward; and the fourth was in Greek (literally, it was dubbed in Greek). They showed these segments to children ages two, three and a half, and five. They found that children paid much less attention to the distorted segments than to the normal segments. Anderson comments:

In fact, some of the five-year-olds would vociferously complain about the show: "Hey, mister, your TV's broken." Or they'd ask their mom to change the channel.

So children weren't captured by the television production—they were captured by its content, especially when the content told a meaningful story.

Another debate focused on whether television distracted children, taught them to have less focus. In fact, Anderson has found that when the content is *age-appropriate, meaningful, and educational* not only do children learn from it, they learn to pay attention. He says:

If you design programming with a curriculum and if that curriculum is designed with a particular audience [and] age group in mind, television can be a powerful teacher.

But his many studies and those of others have revealed a number of issues that we should be concerned about. In Anderson's words:

Watching aggression begets aggression. It's very clear that children, at young ages, will imitate aggressive acts that they see on television. It's also clear from a lot of research that children will learn the ways of thinking that lead to violence—retaliation, categorizing people as good guys and bad guys.

There is also little evidence that children under two learn much from television:

In a whole series of studies, we find if children under two experience something on TV, they show much less indication of having learned the information than if they have an equivalent live experience.

So it is important for you to take a strong role in selecting the television programs that teach the values you want your child to learn. It is equally important that these programs help (not hinder) children's growing capacity to focus. Even more important is that you use television to trigger conversations. Anderson says:

> *If a parent is wise, they can use a television program as a launching point for an important discussion about the world, about the child, or about how the child is interpreting the world.*

SUGGESTION 8: PROMOTE FOCUS—REALIZE THAT BACKGROUND TELEVISION CAN BE DISRUPTIVE.

While age-appropriate and meaningful television can promote children's capacity to focus, television can also be a distracter, as another of Anderson's studies reveals:

> *The study came about because I spent a day at home with my daughter when she was a twelve-month-old. It just happened to be a big news event day—the Waco incident [a siege that began on February 28, 1993, when the Federal Bureau of Alcohol, Tobacco, and Firearms attempted to search the Branch Davidian Ranch in Waco, Texas].*
>
> *I had the TV on all day, and I began to wonder if her behavior was in some way being disrupted by that show. It took us about ten years to finally get around to doing the study. Rather than using an event like the Waco incident that had violence [for our study], I thought, "What about a TV show that any parents might watch and would think would be perfectly good if their child was present?" We used the program Jeopardy!*
>
> *We asked parents to come to the Child Study Center with their one-, two-, or three-year-old child and to spend an hour in our playroom with their child and to minimize their interactions with the child. We had a lot of toys for the children to play with, and we videotaped the parent and child during this hour.*

For half of the children, the television was turned on, playing *Jeopardy!* for their first thirty minutes in the Child Study Center and then turned off for the last thirty minutes. The other half had the opposite schedule—the TV was off, then on:

> What we were interested in was the child's behavior: did the child act any differently when the TV was on [or] off? We knew that the children would not pay much attention to the TV, because it's an adult TV program that they don't understand—and that was true. The children only looked at the TV about five percent of the time.

Among the measures the researchers used to assess the impact of the TV on the children was the length of time they focused on play episodes. They selected this measure because Anderson knows that it is a good predictor of children's ability to pay attention when they are older. And they did find that having the TV on in the background made a difference:

> We found that children's play episodes were about half as long when the TV was on.

In addition, the researchers looked at how long children spent in intensely focused play, the maturity of their play, and how long they spent playing with one toy before moving on to a new toy:

> We [also] found that episodes of focused attention were only about three-quarters as long when the TV was on, [but] surprisingly we didn't find that much difference in play maturity. Also, when the TV was on, children would tend to move from toy to toy.

Obviously, television is not just "background noise" to children. It affects the quality of their play and their focus, giving Anderson concern about TV's effect on children's later development. So limit the amount of background television that your children come into contact with.

SUGGESTION 9: PROMOTE COGNITIVE FLEXIBILITY— HAVE CHILDREN PLAY SORTING GAMES WITH CHANGING RULES.

One such sorting game is called the Dimensional Change Card Sort Task. Developed by Philip David Zelazo of the University of Minnesota and his colleagues, it involves *working memory* (because there are different rules that children have to follow), *cognitive flexibility,* and *reflection* (see chapter 4, on making connections, for a fuller description of this game). The task involves sorting different types of objects. In this example from Zelazo, there are flowers and cars in three different colors: red, green, and blue. Here's how it works:

Two-year-old children are just asked to "put all the flowers in one pile." With three-year-olds, you can ask children to put all the flowers in one pile and all the cars in another pile. With four-year-olds, you can first ask the children to sort the pictures by *color,* putting the blue, green, and red objects in three different piles, and then change the rules and ask them to sort by *shape,* putting the flowers and cars in two different piles.

Adele Diamond, who uses a similar game in her research, notes:

Three-year-olds have no trouble sorting by either shape or color. The problem comes in when [they] have to switch. Typically, three-year-olds cannot switch; they keep sorting by the first dimension. Even though they tell you on each trial what dimension is currently being used and how to sort by it—so they know what they're supposed to do—they can't get themselves to do it.

The majority of four-year-olds, however, can sort by changing rules.

You can create your own sorting games for children by pasting computer clip art or drawings onto cards, but the pictures and colors have to match *exactly* so that the task is very clear and not confusing to children.

SUGGESTION 10: PROMOTE COGNITIVE FLEXIBILITY— ENCOURAGE CHILDREN TO PRETEND AND TO MAKE UP PRETEND STORIES.

Imagine two preschool children playing in the kitchen. One child pretends to be the grown-up, picks up a magazine that's lying around, says it's a sandwich, and pretends to eat. The other pretends to be the baby, picks up the cardboard tube from an empty roll of paper towels, says it's a bottle, and drinks from the bottle. The "baby" then pretends that the bottle spills, and the "adult" pretends to wipe it up.

Just in this simple act, the children are using themselves to represent other people—a grown-up and a baby. They are using objects (a magazine and a paper towel tube) to represent something else (a sandwich and a drink). And they are adapting to changed circumstances. Each of those actions involves cognitive flexibility. Look at how often that kind of thinking happens when children pretend.

A PARENT'S PERSPECTIVE: THE STORY GAME

In the car, we play the Story Game, where we take turns elaborating on a story line, a little at a time. This is a good game for my three girls of different ages (four, seven, and ten). The first person starts a story, tells a little of it, and then "passes" it to the next person, who continues the story however she likes. Everyone likes going first (to set the time, place, and character), but it's also fun and challenging thinking up the next part of the story and listening to the ways the stories can suddenly change.

SUGGESTION 11: PROMOTE COGNITIVE FLEXIBILITY— GIVE CHILDREN PUZZLES.

Doing puzzles also involves the skill of cognitive flexibility. The children must look at each puzzle piece from many different perspectives as they turn it in their hands, trying to figure out how and where it will fit into the puzzle.

SUGGESTION 12: PROMOTE WORKING MEMORY— PLAY GAMES THAT HAVE RULES.

When children play games with rules, they must remember the rules as a guide to their action. Do you remember playing "Simon Says" during your own childhood? It's a great example of a simple game with rules. The rule is, the child is not supposed to follow your directions unless you say "Simon says." For example, if you say, "Simon says, 'Touch your toes,'" your child should touch her toes, but if you just say, "Touch your toes," without saying "Simon says," your child must remember the rule: not to make a move unless you say "Simon says."

You can make the game more complicated by giving two directions at the same time: "Simon says, 'Touch your toes and touch your nose.'" Giving children two actions involves even more memory.

A PARENT'S PERSPECTIVE: NAME THAT TUNE

Daryl (now a teenager) is a smart kid but with learning disabilities that made learning sounds and letters difficult, plus he has a fair dosage of attention deficit disorder. I was inspired to play a game that met his needs (he loves music) and my own. We spend a lot of time in the car, and I'm a fan of the "oldies but goodies" radio stations (not exactly his faves), so we made a deal: if he could identify the singer—vintage Beatles, Rolling Stones, Elton John, Eagles, Aretha Franklin, and others—I would add money to his allowance. Not only would this train his ear to distinguish a guitar from a piano, a soloist from a group, and a characteristic twang from a mellow harmony, but he could also learn to read their names on the digital printout, and he could earn money—something that interested him greatly! And I was happy listening to my kind of music and sharing these great tunes with him. He's older now, but we still play this game, to our mutual delight. Now, if only I could get him to reciprocate: if I identify one of his favorite singers vintage 2008, he pays me! So far that hasn't happened.

SUGGESTION 13: PROMOTE WORKING MEMORY— ENCOURAGE CHILDREN TO PRETEND.

Let's go back to the scenario that I described above, with one child pretending to be an adult and another pretending to be a baby. Now let's imagine that the child playing the adult says, "I have to go to work." The baby says, "You can't leave. I don't have a babysitter." This simple action involves recalling that babies shouldn't be left without someone to take care of them. Children are supposed to stay true to their character and to remember what they should or shouldn't do in the plots that they themselves create.

SUGGESTION 14: PROMOTE WORKING MEMORY— HAVE CHILDREN MAKE PLANS, FOLLOW THE PLANS, AND THEN DISCUSS WHAT THEY ACCOMPLISHED.

In the school my children attended, there was a traditional activity that took place every morning. The children—from preschool through grade school—would have circle time in their classrooms. Each child would be asked to plan his or her first activity, making choices about the morning's work. Preschool children would be asked if they were going to work in the block corner, the dress-up corner, the story corner, and so on. The older children would be asked if they were going to work on writing in their journals, at the math table, and so on. The children would go off to their chosen first assignment and then come back at midmorning to another circle time to report on their work. There would be discussions about what they had learned.

What a good idea, I thought. There's nothing worse than a child treating parents as if we're "Entertainment Central," whining, "There's nothing to do! I'm bored!" So when Philip, six years old, told me one Saturday morning that he was bored, I sat down with him and we made a list of all of the things he liked to do and posted it on his bulletin board. Any time he complained that he was bored, we went to the list and he would choose an activity. As at his school, I'd ask him to make plans about how he was going to carry out this activity and then report on how it went. Little did I know at the time that he was exercising his "working memory." I did know that this strategy was a great way to deal with "good old-fashioned boredom," which doesn't feel so good when it comes in the form of a child whining, "There's nothing to do!"

SUGGESTION 15: PROMOTE INHIBITORY CONTROL— PLAY GAMES WHERE CHILDREN CAN'T GO ON AUTOMATIC PILOT.

Here I'll share some of the tasks that researchers use to test or teach inhibitory control—in other words, *to help children remember the rule and to inhibit what they would do automatically.*

Peg-Tapping Game. In the peg-tapping game, children are supposed to do the opposite of what you do. If you tap once, they're supposed to tap twice. If you tap twice, they're supposed to tap once. You can play this game with three-year-olds, but it's best for children four and older. You can also make the game more complicated by increasing the number of rhythms (I tap four times, you tap twice, etc.).

Day-Night Task. When shown a picture of a black background with a yellow moon and stars, children are supposed to say "day." When shown a picture of a white background with a yellow sun, they're supposed to say "night."

Adele Diamond has found that children begin to master this task after the age of four. When, however, she shows them abstract pictures that are not the opposite of what they're supposed to say (such as a purple background with red marks for "day" and red with purple checks for "night"), preschoolers can easily learn to make the correct response. They can even learn to say "cat" for the day picture and "dog" for the night picture without making mistakes. It's seeing a day picture for night and a night picture for day that makes this task difficult.

Stroop-like exercises. For children who know how to read, you can give them the word *red* written in green print, and the word *green* written in red print. Children are supposed to say the color they see, not the word that's written. This task is difficult because our automatic response is to read the word, not to look at the color. This effect was first reported by psychologist John Ridley Stroop in his PhD thesis in the 1930s.

Here are some more games from parents and educators:

"Simon Says, Do the Opposite." In this game, the task is to do the opposite of what the leader says. If you say, "Simon says, 'Sit,'" children are supposed to stand. If you say, "Simon says, 'Wave your right hand,'" children are supposed to wave their left hand. If you say, "Simon says, 'Be noisy,'" children are supposed to be quiet. You can play this game alone with your child or with a group of children. If a child doesn't do the opposite, he or she is out. The child left at the end becomes the winner and can become Simon for the next round.

Say "ten" fifteen times. Then you ask, "What's an aluminum can made out of?" Richard Weissbourd of Harvard University, who shared this game with me, says, "This one seems to work almost always. People say 'tin,' not 'aluminum.'"

Say "joke" fifteen times. Then you ask, "What's the white of an egg called?" Weissbourd says that this game is "another consistent success. People say 'yolk,' not 'the white of an egg.'"

Say "pots" ten times. Before beginning, explain the rules. If you say, "Red light," the child is supposed to say, "Stop," and if you say "Green light," the child is supposed to say, "Go." Then ask the child to begin by saying "pots" ten times. Andrea Cameron of the University of New Mexico says that her family would play this game in the car. When the adults said, "Green light," her kids inevitably would say, "Stop."

Now that you know the rules for games like these, I bet you can invent lots of other games that give your children practice in self control.

SUGGESTION 16: PROMOTE INHIBITORY CONTROL— SELECT COMPUTER GAMES CAREFULLY.

Earlier I discussed how computer games with certain characteristics might be used to encourage focusing skills. Researchers also use computer games with older preschool and elementary-aged children to assess and promote inhibitory control. These games ask children *to inhibit what they would do automatically and instead follow changing rules.* These games are not available commercially, but my point in describing them is to give you an idea of what to look for in the games you select. For example:

Hearts and Flowers. This is a computer game that Adele Diamond uses in her research. Every time children see a heart on the computer screen, they press a button on the screen that is on the same side as the heart. For example, if they see the heart on the left side of the screen, they press the left button. If they see the heart on the right side, they press the right button.

Then Diamond adds a complication: the children are told that when they see a flower, they're supposed to press the button on the *opposite* side of the screen—"Press the button on the left side when the flower is on the right, and on the right side when the flower is on the left."

Once children can do this, Diamond alternates hearts and flowers. She has found that children can call out the rules—"Hearts same side, flowers opposite side"—but they often impulsively press the same side when they see flowers. She reasons that the "problem seems to be translating the rule into the correct response when switching back and forth." This is true for school-age children as well.

Flanker tasks, such as Feed the Fish. This computer game used by Adele Diamond incorporates a technique called the *Eriksen flanker task.* There's a big fish in the middle of the computer screen. The task is to feed this fish. If the fish is pointing right, children need to press the right-hand button to feed the fish. If the fish is pointing left on the screen, they press the left-hand button. So far, so good.

As I'm sure you've guessed by now, once children master this task, it's then made more complex. In fact, the point of a flanker task is to add competing and distracting symbols. In this particular game, Diamond adds other smaller fish on the screen. Sometimes they swim in the same direction as the big fish, but sometimes they swim in the opposite direction. It's much harder to keep track of the direction of the big fish when there are lots of small fish, but it's a great task for promoting inhibitory control.

For older children, Diamond and her colleagues make the game even harder by including a reverse flanker task. Here sometimes the children have to pay attention to the fish on the sides (the flanking fish) and ignore the fish in the center or they switch between the flanker and reverse flanker games. The clues are the color of the fish—they tell the children what to do.

Diamond notes that if you use only the standard flanker task, children can master this task by about age seven. However, if you include the reverse flanker task, you continue to see developmental improvements throughout adolescence.

SUGGESTION 17: PROMOTE FOCUS AND SELF CONTROL—MAKE SURE YOUR CHILD IS WELL RESTED AND HAS BREAKS.

As the researchers I've interviewed point out, these skills are fragile. Children who are well rested are better at paying attention and inhibiting automatic responses.

However, it's not just a matter of being well rested. None of us can work flat-out, without breaks. Recess, though it appears to be going the way of other old-fashioned practices, was created for sound reasons. We need time off in order to do our best work. Anthony Pellegrini, an educational psychology professor at the University of Minnesota, has spent twenty-five years on school playgrounds studying how recess affects children's adjustment to school and has found that having a time-out at recess maximizes students' ability to pay attention in class.

SUGGESTION 18: TAKE CARE OF OURSELVES— WE NEED REST AND BREAKS, TOO!

Being well rested and taking breaks are just as important for adults as they are for children. I know this from my research on adults in the workplace. We have an image of work as running a marathon without stopping, but we work better in sprints.

Remember the paper my daughter was writing for her graduate class—the one where I was not so helpful? Because it was a new subject for her, too, she felt she had to cram and was working on this paper, in addition to her job, until the middle of the night. Finally the day came when the paper was due, and Lara was upset. She didn't think she was doing a good job; she was exhausted and confused; her voice was shaky. I then spoke to her a few hours later and her voice was strong, back to the voice I know so well. What had happened? She had gone to a yoga class and returned better able to concentrate and think through her final points for this paper.

The bottom line: if we're stressed out, it is a lot harder for us to help our children learn focus and self control.

SUGGESTION 19: PRACTICE FOCUS AND SELF CONTROL.

In addition to taking time for rest and recovery, what would it take for you to exercise your own skills of focus and self control? We teach by doing as much as by saying.

A PARENT'S PERSPECTIVE: HAVE SELF CONTROL TO TEACH SELF CONTROL

Patience is very hard for both of my children (ages seven and ten), especially when it comes to asking questions. They find it hard not to interrupt if they want to know something, especially when I am on the phone. So I ask them to take a second and ask themselves, "Is this so important that it can't wait?" This helps them think twice.

I've also been better in the last year about finishing what I'm doing before doing something for them, saying, "Just a minute, let me finish what I am doing." Too often I would just drop what I was doing and respond to them. Not a good precedent!

A PARENT'S PERSPECTIVE:
SLOW DOWN; DON'T GO SO FAST

When Jeremiah was around two and a half, he started stuttering. Even though we read that stuttering is typical at this age, we were concerned because my husband stuttered as a child. After consulting books and specialists, we realized that we had to slow our speech way down and try to stop interrupting him and each other. This has been harder than it sounds. We both talk a lot and tend to interrupt. We continually have to make a conscious effort to talk slowly.

Recently, Jeremiah was going through a particularly intense week or two of stuttering, so we'd do things like saying—at the beginning of dinner—"We are all going to try to talk slowly tonight." Jeremiah also spoke more slowly, which reduced the amount that he stuttered. It seems like the more aware we are of slowing down our speech, the easier it is for him to speak smoothly.

Gil Gordon, an expert on telecommuting, wrote a book called *Turn It Off.* He calls for having times when we are unplugged—turning off the TV, not answering the phone, turning off the computer. One parent I know has a "no-multitasking zone." She suggests spending time with yourself or your child *as if* your child has grabbed your face ("Earth to Mom, Earth to Dad") asking for your attention. Maggie Jackson writes in her book *Distracted* that paying full attention is a gift we give ourselves and others.

DO YOU WANT ONE MARSHMALLOW NOW OR TWO MARSHMALLOWS LATER?

In the late 1960s, Walter Mischel, then at Stanford University and now a professor at Columbia University, conducted an experiment that has become a classic for very good reasons. Mischel calls this experiment the Marshmallow Test (though they sometimes used cookies or pretzels). In this experiment, four-year-olds are taken into a lab room with a one-way mirror so that the adults can see into the room but the children can't see out. The researcher puts a plate in front of the children. On one side of the plate is one marshmallow and on the other side of the plate are two marshmallows. Beside the children is a bell that they can push down and ring. The experimenter tells each child:

This is a bell—the "bring-me-back" bell.

Mischel explains the goal of this appetizing exercise:

We were trying to set up situations in which young children make a choice between two of something that [they] prefer later or one of something that [they] prefer a little less now. The whole point of the experiment is to set up an intense conflict between the two.

The experimenter tells the child:

If you have to choose, would you like to have one marshmallow now or would you like two?

And most children say, "Two!" The experimenter then says:

Here's how we play the game. I am going to leave the room. While I'm gone, if you can stay here and wait for me to come back, then you get two marshmallows. If you don't want to wait, you can make me come back right away, but then you get one marshmallow, not two.

In the experiment, the children were left for as long as fifteen minutes, but they could always bring the experimenter back by ringing the bell. Mischel remarks:

The kids who know how to [delay gratification] are superb at it and it's quite wonderful to watch them.

And he is right. Some children turn their backs on the marshmallows or sit on their hands. Others stick out their tongues but don't lick the marshmallow. Others sing little songs to keep themselves distracted or shake their heads as if to say no, no, no. One child even put his hand out to take the marshmallows, but used his other hand to steer the offending hand away from temptation.

Mischel observed that the children who were the best at delaying gratification didn't focus on the "hot" stimulus, the marshmallows, but instead distracted themselves by shifting their attention to looking at or doing something else. If children think about the marshmallows and "how yummy and chewy and sweet they are," they're likely to ring the bell earlier than the children who distract themselves by "thinking about how marshmallows are a lot like cotton balls or they are a lot like puffy clouds."

This experiment began in 1968 in his children's nursery school, the Bing School at Stanford University. Years later, as he heard his children talk about their friends in high school, he began to see a pattern—that the children who had waited longer for the marshmallows seemed to be doing better. That prompted Mischel to recontact these children and follow them into midlife. Here are some of the correlations he found:

The longer the young children were able to wait at age four, the better the SAT scores, the better the ratings of their ability to control themselves and to pursue their academic and other goals successfully—[as reported] by parents and by teachers—and the better their own reports about how they were doing as people in their early thirties.

He explains why delaying gratification can be so important:

*The advantage for the young child who knows how to delay grati-
fication is that they're likely [to] be able to pursue academic and
personal goals with less frustration, with less distraction.*

Mischel notes that this can have other repercussions later in life as
well. He says that the skill of delayed gratification

*shows up in many ways. For example, in middle life, there's less
drug use—not that there isn't any, but there's less. Similarly, there's
a higher educational level obtained. [These individuals are] much
less likely to have lowered self-esteem, to engage in bullying behavior with other people, to develop a sense of worthlessness, to feel
that they are failing in their interpersonal relationships.*

Given these correlations, Mischel and his colleagues have begun to
see if they can teach children to control their attention and thoughts and
thus delay gratification, by making suggestions to the children like the
following:

*You can think about fun things while you are waiting, like Mommy
swinging you on the swing or singing happy songs to yourself.*

They've found that the same child will behave differently if given this
kind of help:

*We can get very dramatic differences in the same child simply from
cuing the representation of the goodies [as] not so hot, not so appealing, but [as] more cool, more abstract, more informative.*

Mischel believes that these executive function skills should be promoted and reinforced by families and schools because they enable children to become able to manage frustrations and distress in ways that
don't derail them from pursuing the goals that are important to them.
*Remember: focus and self control are always exercised in the service of pur-
suing an important personal goal.*

The Marshmallow Test is a simple test, but a valuable one. However, Mischel makes it clear that if you try this with your own child, it doesn't predict his or her destiny:

> *The correlations are clearly statistically significant, but that in no way means that a youngster who at age four didn't wait a long time is in any way doomed. Far, far from it!*

SOME FINAL THOUGHTS

Alison Gopnik in her 2009 book, *The Philosophical Baby,* notes that a focus on inhibition *must* not come at the expense of taking away children's inborn imagination and passion to explore and learn. She writes that

> *inhibition has a downside if you are primarily interested in imagination and learning. To be imaginative, you want to consider as many possibilities as you can, even wild and unprecedented ones. . . . In learning, you want to remain open to anything that may turn out to be the truth.*

Keeping the fire in children's eyes burning brightly and keeping their engagement in learning strong are what is most essential to me.

CHAPTER TWO

SKILL TWO: PERSPECTIVE TAKING

AN EXERCISE: YOU CHOOSE

Imagine you've come home after a bad day, totally exhausted. You talk to three people. One says, "You think you had a bad day. That's nothing compared to mine!" Another says, "Why did you let that happen? You should never have let that other person talk to you that way. You should have put your foot down . . . walked away . . . [fill in the blank]." The third person says, "I am so sorry. What happened?"

How do you react to each of these people? Which statements make you feel better or worse? Which ones make you want to talk? Or walk away?

I've used this exercise in perspective taking in many workshops and find that people's reactions are very similar. Whether we're parents, teachers, or business leaders, we usually prefer to talk with someone who is attuned to our point of view and avoid someone who is critical or competitive.

Perspective taking has many aliases. In relationships, we use phrases like "We see eye to eye" . . . "We clicked" . . . "Here's where I'm coming from" . . . "Walk a mile in my shoes" . . . "He just doesn't get it." In business, we do research on what customers want—R & D, focus groups, and brainstorming. We spend millions making products more "user-friendly," software more "intuitive," and Web sites more "sticky."

I doubt we'd have so many terms to describe something that isn't crucial to human success. As ubiquitous as it is, perspective taking isn't easy, as anyone knows who has ever shouted obscenities at a computer, tried unsuccessfully to get a cap off a bottle or a snack from its wrapper, attempted to resolve a major (or, for that matter, minor) conflict with someone, or looked at the news headlines about conflict in the world.

In fact, it is far easier to want others to take our perspectives than it is to understand the perspectives of others. Sometimes we think we know how others see things, but when we actually ask, we may be surprised.

AN EXERCISE: GUESS SOMEONE'S WISH

Select a person who is close to you—your partner, an older child, a parent, a coworker, or a friend. Now guess how this person would answer this question: "If you had one wish to most improve things at home . . . at work . . . in our community, what would that wish be?" Then ask this person the question. Were you correct in what he or she would wish? Why or why not?

A PARENT'S PERSPECTIVE: WHY CAN'T MY BEST FRIEND SEE THE LIGHT?

My best friend and I were recently discussing the current political scene. We go way back, having attended the same college. We share similar backgrounds and have comparable goals. With so much in common, I assumed we'd have the same perspective on politics. But it became very apparent that our views were totally different. I was shocked and even held it against her for seeing things so, well, "wrong."

How could we look at the same set of circumstances and come up with entirely different ways to address them? And how could I have so misjudged this person I thought I knew so well?

I suppose I hadn't been really looking at her life and how it might shape her views: that her experience living in the suburbs might differ from mine living in the city; that she has two preadolescent stepdaughters while I have one preschooler; that her husband works in the financial world while my husband and I work in entertainment. If I really paid attention to who she is, as opposed to making assumptions, we might have a reasonable dialogue—which, of course, would lead to my changing *her* mind!

Although this parent comes to see why her best friend would see politics differently than she does, she still wants to change her friend's mind. If understanding different viewpoints is hard, treating others as we would want to be treated—following the Golden Rule—is harder still.

An exercise that I have used in workshops is to ask people to recall a terrific and a terrible experience where they were in some way dependent on another person—their doctor, their boss, their child's teacher. The good experiences are retold with a lot less emotion than the bad ones:

I went to see a doctor about an "allergic reaction"—where I got violently sick from something I had eaten. Looking down his half-rimmed glasses at me, he told me that it wasn't an allergic reaction. If my throat had closed, that would have been an allergy, but not having an upset stomach. He then implied that I had emotional problems, and that's why I "felt" sick.

I had a regular parent-teacher conference with my child's teacher. She started by telling me what my child had done wrong in school—with not a single good word about my child—and then asked, "Is something going on at home that might be causing these problems?" I felt as if I'd flunked as a parent.

One day I got to work very early because I had to leave early. It was the last day of baseball camp for my son and there was a baseball game and a picnic for the parents. I had cleared it with my boss, but when I walked out the door, he gave me a poisonous look that seemed to say, "I know that you aren't really serious about your job and I will remember this when it is time to decide on raises."

AN EXERCISE: DEPENDING ON OTHERS

Think about a terrific and a terrible experience that you've had in which you were dependent on someone else. What made it a terrible experience? What made it a terrific experience? What does this tell you about how you would like to be treated by others?

Most of my workshop participants respond to these questions by saying that they want to be listened to, understood, and treated with respect. If there are problems, they want the other person to know what it's like to be in their shoes and to deal with them in a positive, compassionate way.

Then I put the participants in a role-play situation where one person pretends to be the professional and the other pretends to be the client in one of the difficult situations they've just described: for example, a parent-teacher conference to discuss some problems the teacher sees with a child. In front of the rest of the group, they play out these roles, usually pretty well. But then I throw in a wild card. A person (played by one of my colleagues) bursts into the parent-teacher conference, pretending to be another parent. In front of the other parent and the teacher, he furiously accuses the teacher of losing his child's favorite sweater.

Typically, the person playing the teacher strikes back: "I did *not* lose your child's sweater. Your child lost it, and you know why, too—he's so flaky, that's why he's always losing everything."

Whether you identify with the parent or the teacher in this situation, it's obvious that it is not easy to take someone else's perspective, especially if you feel wrongly accused or attacked in front of others. You may feel the teacher was right to defend herself, but turn the situation around and look at it from the first parent's perspective. The teacher probably lost the goodwill she was trying to establish with the first parent ("If she bad-mouths someone else's child so easily, who knows what she's saying about my child?"), and she certainly has dug a trench between herself and the parent whose child is missing a sweater. What would you do in this situation?

If I think about the disagreements that my husband and I have, they usually result from the fact that one of us has not taken the other's perspective. And if I think about the conflicts in my office, they often have the same root cause; for instance, someone has shot off an e-mail in haste without considering how it will be read by others.

It's not surprising, then, that being able to take the perspectives of others is a platform to success. Think about the most persuasive ads you see or the products that you choose to buy. The person who created them understood how customers feel and what they might need and want.

THE BRAIN BASIS FOR PERSPECTIVE TAKING

I've often wondered why perspective taking, despite being so important to human relationships and to life success, is not considered an essential skill for thriving. We rarely teach it explicitly at home or at school. Perhaps that's because it's equated with empathy, which may be considered intuitive and therefore difficult to teach, or perhaps it's discounted as a "soft" emotional skill.

While empathy is certainly a component of perspective taking, brain research shows that perspective taking is more complex. MIT researcher Rebecca Saxe has used *functional magnetic resonance imaging* (fMRI) to map which parts of the brain are recruited when people think about the perspectives of others. She has found that a special part of the cortex—the part of the brain where complex thinking takes place—lights up when people think about the thoughts of others. A number of other parts light up, too.

When you consider the tasks involved in perspective taking, it's not so surprising that the brain lights up in multiple places. Perspective taking involves the intellectual skill of discerning how someone else thinks and feels; it requires assembling our accumulated knowledge of that person, analyzing the situation at hand, remembering similar situations, recalling what others have told us about such situations, putting aside our own thoughts and feelings, and trying to feel and think as another person must feel and think.

Saxe and others are credited with an important scientific breakthrough in finding that this skill calls upon the executive functions of the brain. It requires *inhibitory control*—we must inhibit our own thoughts and feelings to take on the perspectives of others. It also requires *cognitive flexibility*—that is, the ability to view a situation in different ways. Finally, it requires *reflection,* as we ponder someone else's thinking as well as our own. Perspective taking is truly a social-emotional-intellectual (SEI) skill.

TO PROMOTE PERSPECTIVE TAKING IN CHILDREN, WE HAVE TO LEARN IT OURSELVES

A PARENT'S PERSPECTIVE: WOULD I LIKE A TO-DO LIST WITH MY CEREAL IN THE MORNING?

It's the end of the summer and there's a lot my son needs to do to get ready for school, but like most fifteen-year-olds, he's procrastinating. My wife and I talked about it last night and decided to give him a to-do list with boxes he could check off when he finished each task. We would leave it for him on the breakfast table in the morning. I was so caught up in thinking about myself—that I didn't want a last-minute, just-before-school-starts crisis—that I never thought about how he might feel about getting a to-do list with his cereal in the morning. But as the evening wore on, I had second thoughts. How would I feel if I got to work in the morning and found that the boss had left a to-do list with check boxes on my desk the night before? Even the thought of it made me furious. So why did I think this would work with my son? If I didn't think I would respond positively to something, chances are my son wouldn't, either. There have to be other ways of dealing with his procrastination.

This father makes a critical point. Before we can teach perspective taking to our children, *we* have to learn it. For me, the "aha" moment that there might be such a thing as perspective taking came in 1982, when my children were school-aged. I read a book by Judy Dunn and Carol Kendrick entitled *Siblings*. Although it was an academic book, I was drawn to it for far more than professional reasons: what mother of an eight-year-old and a thirteen-year-old wouldn't want to help her kids get along better? I still have my copy. It is well worn, underlined in pencil, with key points circled in red ink. Clearly, I read it more than once.

This was the first book on siblings that was based on an observational study; it followed forty families in England over time. It challenged the common wisdom of the 1980s that young children were egocentric, only able to understand experiences from their own vantage point. Dunn and Kendrick observed something very different:

> *well before age 3, children are unequivocally skillful at reading, antici-pating, and responding to the feelings and plans of their baby siblings.*

They called this phenomenon "understanding the other."

It was a few sentences at the end of the book that I recalled, surprisingly almost word for word, more than twenty years later. The authors concluded that, although many factors (such as temperament) influence how siblings get along, parents *do* things that make a real difference:

> *In families where the mothers discussed caring for the baby as a matter of joint responsibility and talked about the baby as a person from the early days, the siblings were particularly friendly over the next year.*

What does that mean? It means that those mothers (mothers were more likely to be the focus of studies than fathers in that era) who helped the older child understand the baby by saying things like "The baby is crying. Why do you think he's crying? Do you think he's hungry or needs his diaper changed? Let's try to feed him and see if he stops crying" had children who were more likely to fight less and get along better as they grew up.

I realized that if I was going to help my children learn to take each other's perspectives and be more friendly with each other, I was going to have to see the world as each of them saw it. To teach this skill, I needed to learn and use it myself.

For example, my son used to get furious at his little sister. To my husband and me, his outbursts seemed like unexpected bolts of lightning— and he would get into trouble. Applying the notion of perspective taking, I decided to step back and watch my children, paying special attention to the scenes that led to an outburst. When I did, I discovered that my daughter wasn't the innocent victim I had assumed. She was doing subtle things to annoy her brother, like chewing with her mouth open. I also could see that from her perspective, her behavior was a way of getting her big brother's attention. These clues had been invisible to me until I looked at the situation from each of their perspectives.

Later, during what we called "special time" (a family tradition of spending time alone with each child, usually at night), I explained to Philip what it must be like for Lara to have such a big and competent brother (though she was no slouch herself). I told him to think of her teasing as quicksand. He had to look for it, avoid it—and never fall into it. He got it right away, and her subtle provocations had a lot less power.

I told Lara that I had warned Philip about the "traps" she was setting for him and that if she wanted her brother's attention, she didn't have to annoy him to get it. We began to plan times for them to do things together, and that helped too.

Once I understood the power of perspective taking, I could use it in many other parenting situations. For example, my daughter seriously pursued gymnastics as a child. Because of her smaller size, she was usually close to the front of the line in summer camp competitions. She began to feel that one counselor "wasn't fair." She always gave Lara and the other kids at the beginning of the line lower scores than the kids who came later in the lineup. When Lara complained bitterly about this counselor, I tried to help her see things as the counselor might. The counselor didn't have a standard in her mind for what constituted a good score until she saw several kids do the routine. So naturally, the kids doing the routine first suffered. Once Lara understood why this counselor might be tougher on the kids in the front of the line, she stopped being angry at the counselor. In fact, she asked to talk with her.

To her credit, the counselor listened to Lara and decided to vary the lineup for each routine. Lara was clearly taking a risk here. Some adults might not like a young person telling them anything, much less that they were scoring unfairly. But Lara talked to the counselor in a calm way, saying how she was feeling, using I messages, not you messages: "I feel bad that I and the other kids in the front of the line seem to get worse scores than the kids at the end of the line." She didn't accuse or criticize. It was a skill that has stood Lara in good stead, and she has continued to use it with teachers in high school and college and, most recently, at work with someone who was engaging in nonproductive behavior.

WHY PERSPECTIVE TAKING IS IMPORTANT FOR CHILDREN

Although perspective taking is rarely considered an essential skill for children, research tells a different story. Ross Thompson of the University of California at Davis emphasizes how perspective taking helps children make sense of their own and others' experiences. Studies have found that young children who learn perspective taking have a better adjustment to kindergarten. It helps them understand what their teachers want and expect. And there are connections between this skill and learning to read.

FROM ALONENESS TO TOGETHERNESS: HOW PERSPECTIVE TAKING EMERGES IN INFANTS

In the years since *Siblings* was published, there has been a virtual explosion of fascinating new studies revealing the significance of perspective taking, how it develops, and how parents and teachers can promote it. Paradoxically, one of the most important findings about understanding others came from examining our essential aloneness in the world.

Daniel Stern, now of the Université de Genève, contested the 1970s orthodoxy that infants are born without a sense of self—that their experiences at birth are fused with their mothers'—and that children's mission in growing up is to separate, become individuals, and become independent. Stern turned this model upside down, arguing that we're born alone, and that the process of growing up is "learning to be with others."

How did he reach his radical conclusion? As happens with many interests that captivate us as adults, the roots went back to his own childhood:

The real reason I got interested in children who can't [yet] talk comes from when I was little. We had a Czech nursemaid and she spoke only Czech. I spent most of my time with her and I learned to understand Czech and much less English. When I was about two, I got very sick and was in the hospital for five months or so. When I

*got to the hospital, people realized that I didn't speak English. And
in those days, the idea of having a nursemaid come to the hospital
was out of the question.*

Because he didn't understand what was happening to him at the hospital, Stern became a watcher of behavior:

*I became totally attuned to what people were doing, what happened
to their faces. I would listen to them, but I would listen to the music
and not the lyrics, because I didn't understand the lyrics.*

His interest in being a "watcher" affected his career path—from MD
to neuroscience to child psychiatry—but ultimately, he found his way
back to watching behavior by using a lightweight television camera (a
microscope for looking at behavior, as he describes it) to record the interaction between mothers and infants.

As you can imagine, it's extremely difficult to fathom what is going
on in infants, but Stern developed some ingenious methods. Using freeze
frames and slow motion, he saw that these interactions were like natural
choreography—a dance. The babies moved in striking synchrony with
their mothers: the mother would move her arm, and the baby would
move his or her arm to mirror the mother's.

These split-second analyses seemed to contradict the "fusion model."
Stern began to suspect that *if* an infant "knows" that his arm is moving
one way and his mother's arm is not, then the infant's experiences are not
totally fused with those of the mother.

Stern also noticed infants reaching for things. The baby clearly wanted
something, planned to get it, and then completed the action. If the baby
missed the object, the baby would "correct" the action and reach for the
object again. But if the mother went through the same process—reaching
for something the baby wanted and missing it—the baby didn't do anything to correct the situation. This was also a clue that infants "knew" in
some fundamental way that they were different from their mothers.

The moment, years ago, when I viewed Stern's films of that lyrical
back-and-forth *dance* between mother and child, the way I literally saw

adults and children connecting—in both my professional and my personal life—was transformed from black-and-white into brilliant color. To say that I was transformed is putting it mildly. These everyday moments between parent and child happen all around us all the time—from the playground to the park to the supermarket checkout line—but if you tune in to them and realize how magical they are, I am sure that you will be transformed, too: the child does something, the adult seemingly unconsciously mirrors the child's action, and vice versa. As the child grows, the dance becomes more and more elaborate. At first the adult more or less mimics the child, but over time, the interplay becomes complex: movements and sounds become actions and words, then interactions and conversation. A relationship is born and nurtured.

AN EXERCISE: WATCH FOR THE DANCE

As you go about your daily activities, observe adults and children together. Watch for the dance between adult and child. What does the child do? What does the adult do? What happens when the child has had enough stimulation? If the dance pauses, how do they get back into the dance again? Isn't this normal process amazing?

What more appropriate way for Stern to test his fusion-nonfusion theory than with Siamese twins? They were five months old when Stern found out about them, and he had one week to observe them before surgery to separate them:

I went there every day with my cameras. They didn't look at each other, because their heads were too close.

They did, however, suck each other's thumbs:

So I wondered, could they—being almost one organism—could they tell the difference as to whose thumb they were sucking?

Stern found that if he pulled the child's own thumb out of that child's mouth, the child would try to bring it back. But *if the baby was sucking the other kid's thumb and I took the other kid's hand away, the baby wouldn't do anything with his arm, but he'd bring his head forward. So he already knew whose finger he was sucking in the sense that his response was an entirely different way to reestablish the sucking contact. And that impressed me. I figured these guys are living together all the time, and already there's a distinction between these two.*

Based on his experiments and his evolving theory of human development, Stern placed perspective taking as part of one of the foundational tasks of human development:

I began to see—you're born alone, essentially separate. You can tell the difference, and what you need to do with your developmental gains is to learn new and richer ways to be with somebody else.

A PEOPLE SENSE

Stanislas Dehaene of the Collège de France in Paris refers to a *number sense* in describing how infants' brains appear to be wired for math. Similarly, infants' brains appear to be wired for understanding other aspects of their world, so I adopt this terminology to describe how infants have a capacity to grab onto information about people, language, objects, space, and numbers before they could have been taught this.

Let me explain what I mean by a *people sense* by sharing the findings of research by Amanda Woodward of the University of Maryland. Remember, Stern observed that infants respond differently when they or their mothers reach for something. Think for a moment about the act of a mother reaching. How would an infant understand this? Would the infant see this action as a series of physical movements through space, or would the infant understand, in some way, that his or her mother was trying to get something; that is, the mother has a goal? And how could a researcher figure out what the baby understands about this very simple act?

That was the challenge that Woodward gave to herself. Whereas Stern used film to explore the mind of the infant, Woodward used the *familiarization* procedure developed by Robert Fantz in the 1960s. This procedure is based on the finding that when babies—like all of us—see or hear something repeatedly, they tire of it and pay less attention each time it is repeated. Researchers measure how long young children watch (or listen) before they get bored. The next step in a familiarization procedure is to present babies with other experiences to determine which they see as *new* (measured by longer looking or listening times) and which they see as *familiar* (measured by shorter looking or listening times).

In this experiment, Woodward places six- to nine-month-old babies on their parent's lap, facing what looks like a puppet stage. On the stage are a ball and a teddy bear. They see a person (one of Woodward's research assistants, or an experimenter, as I usually call them) reach onto the stage and grab the teddy bear again and again.

When babies become bored, the stage curtain is lowered and raised to reveal some changes. Woodward explains:

> In one new event, the research assistant's reaching to the same place, but there's a new toy there. Instead of reaching for the bear, she's reaching for the ball.

The other event is just the reverse. The experimenter reaches for the bear, which is now on the opposite side of the stage. Woodward's question was: do infants focus on the adult's *goal*—reaching for a teddy bear? If so, they'd pay more attention if the adult has a new goal—reaching for the ball. Or do they focus on the adult's *physical action*—an arm moving through space? If so, they'd pay more attention to the adult reaching on the opposite side of the stage for the teddy bear. Woodward finds:

> Beginning at about five or six months, babies look longer at events where the person is acting toward a new goal.

Woodward went further with another experiment, replacing the person's arm with a robot arm. There, she found that the infants looked longer at the new action—reaching to a different place than before. Woodward concludes:

> *This suggests that by five or six months, babies, like adults, are tuning in to the relation between person and goal as being really critical to making sense of human behavior. They're interpreting the actions of people as being goal directed.*

These five- and six-month-old babies have a rudimentary sense of others' perspectives (i.e., their goals and intentions) before they could possibly have been taught it. It is one aspect of having a people sense, and it underlies children's later awareness that people can *differ* in their intentions, likes, dislikes, thoughts, and feelings.

CRACKERS VERSUS BROCCOLI: HOW PERSPECTIVE TAKING DEVELOPS IN THE TODDLER AND PRESCHOOL YEARS

Alison Gopnik of the University of California at Berkeley has been a leader in understanding how we develop *theory of mind,* becoming aware that others have different beliefs, desires, and intentions from our own. This awareness is essential to what I call perspective taking. One of Gopnik's first questions was: when do children understand that one person might want one thing and another person might want something else?

When she began to pursue her studies, as I've mentioned, young children were typically seen as egocentric and self-absorbed:

> *For literally thousands of years, most people thought that very young children just didn't have very much going on—they were impulsive, passive, just soaking up the sensations around them.*

One reason this view held sway for so long is that very young children aren't facile with language. So Gopnik needed to find a nonverbal way to delve into what children understand:

We know that even very, very young babies pay a lot of attention to facial expressions, so we felt we could use facial expressions to tell the children what the other person wanted.

To test this, Gopnik and her colleague Betty Repacholi (who was the experimenter in the original research) devised a study: Gopnik gives children two bowls of food—one containing raw broccoli and one containing crackers shaped like goldfish. She lets the children taste the food and finds—no surprise—that most children would rather eat the crackers than the raw broccoli. Then Gopnik tastes the food from each bowl. Sometimes she acts as if she likes the same thing they do—the crackers— and sometimes she acts as if she prefers the raw broccoli:

I would have some of the crackers and go "Oh, yuck, crackers." And I'd have some of the broccoli and go "Umm, broccoli," as if I really like the broccoli.

Gopnik accompanies the tasting with exaggerated expressions, making a face of total disgust when she tastes the crackers and a face of pure pleasure when she tastes the broccoli. The children, often busily chewing crackers, observe her "I love broccoli" expression with thoughtful perplexity. She says:

So what's happened? We've given the children information in a form that they can understand that tells them that what I like is different from what they like. They like crackers and I like broccoli.

Then she puts her hand out and asks the children to "give me what I like":

We discovered that eighteen-month-olds would give me the crackers if I acted as if I liked the crackers. But they would give me the broccoli if I acted as if I liked the broccoli. So even these very little children already seemed to have realized, "Okay, this is a strange person—she likes broccoli. But if that's what she likes, then that's what I'm going to give her."

On the other hand, fourteen-month-old children give her the crackers, no matter which food she demonstrates that she prefers. They can't seem to understand that someone else would like to eat something different than they do.

This finding helped Gopnik and her colleagues map out when children learn about differences in people's likes and dislikes—leading to her next question: when do children understand that others could *think different thoughts* than they do?

Again she devised an ingenious experiment. She fills a crayon box with paper clips. Then she shows the closed box to children and asks them what's inside. All the children guess that there are crayons inside. Gopnik opens the box and shows them the paper clips. Then she closes the box and asks the children:

What did you think was inside this box when you first saw it?
And what will someone else think is inside this box?
What will your friend in child care think is inside this box when he sees it all closed up like this?

She found that three-year-olds answer "paper clips," seemingly unable to fathom that they or other children might not know what they *now* know—that there are paper clips in the box. But by the age of four, children seem to have figured out the difference. They'll say that they originally thought there were crayons in the box, and that other kids would think the same:

The four-year-olds—still preschoolers just beginning to understand what's going on in the world—seem to have figured out that someone else could believe something different from them.

Other researchers have found that, in fact, infants do respond to *false beliefs* (as such conundrums are called) before the age of four. In one experiment, Renée Baillargeon of the University of Illinois at Urbana-Champaign shows fifteen-month-olds a yellow box, a green box, and a toy slice of watermelon. The baby repeatedly sees the experimenter hide the watermelon in the green box and reach for it there. When the experimenter leaves the scene and the watermelon is then moved from the green box to the yellow box, the babies detect a violation (i.e., look reliably longer) if the experimenter returns and looks for the watermelon in the yellow rather than the green box. In other words, babies seem to "expect" the experimenter to look in the green box where the slice of watermelon was originally left. This result seems to indicate that children understand false beliefs earlier than previously supposed. What is going on?

Rebecca Saxe of MIT has begun to shed light on these contradictory findings. Using fMRI technology, Saxe finds that the brain region used when children think about others' thoughts and feelings (what she calls *social cognition*, an intellectual understanding of the social world) is still developing in the early years. While very young children have a rudimentary understanding of false beliefs, they can't express the complexity of this knowledge until they're older. Saxe says:

> *In order to predict what somebody else is going to do if they know different things than you do, if they believe different things than you do, or if they see different things than you do, you have to be able to step out of your own perspective and step into their perspective. Another way to say that is, you have to be able to inhibit your own knowledge. If you look at [children's] ability to be able to inhibit one answer in order to respond based on somebody else's perspective, that's an incredibly important accomplishment, and it's developing a lot, changing a lot, between ages two and six.*

This is a fascinating example of how knowing where something happens in the brain allows us to better understand how it happens. In this instance, it also reveals complexity of these functions: the part of the brain that enables us to take another's perspective develops earlier than the part that enables us to inhibit our own knowledge in order to express it (inhibitory control takes place in the prefrontal cortex of the brain).

Interestingly, although children seem able to sense false beliefs earlier than researchers may have thought, under certain circumstances, adults have trouble with this. Promoting perspective taking is a lifelong endeavor.

A PARENT'S PERSPECTIVE:
WHAT WOULD CAPTAIN HOOK DO?

Peter Pan, Wendy, Tinker Bell, and Captain Hook—my daughter loves them all. I spend many evenings pretending to "walk the plank" with a cardboard tube held at my back or sprinkling pixie dust so we can fly (well, really run around with our arms in the air).

But it's also been interesting to see the limits in what my daughter understands about the characters. For Christmas, a friend got her a Peter Pan play set, complete with dolls of the main characters. Sara seems to understand their basic personality types: Peter Pan = nice boy; Wendy = sweet girl; Captain Hook = mean man who says "Arrrgh!" Sometimes I'll suggest we pretend that Captain Hook has kidnapped Wendy, and Peter Pan must save her. But Sara won't hear of it. It's almost as if, because *she* would never be mean to Peter Pan or Wendy, she can't make Captain Hook be mean, either.

Like Gopnik, Baillargeon, and Saxe, for many years Ross Thompson of the University of California at Davis has been studying children's false beliefs (or *mistaken beliefs,* as they are also called). In one experiment, using a puppet stage that looks like a kitchen, children watch a puppet show that involves mistaken beliefs:

A puppet has a snack that's a favorite snack and puts it in the refrigerator, expecting to eat it later on. The puppet leaves the room, and then somebody else comes in and moves the snack from the refrigerator into the cabinet.

The first puppet returns and wants his snack. Thompson asks the children where the puppet would look for the snack: in the refrigerator (where the puppet left it) or in the cabinet, where the child knows it really is?

Thompson has found that some children learn perspective taking better than others and wanted to know why. He suspected from his own and others' research that how children gain insight into "what goes on in people's hearts and minds" depends on how parents interpret "the every-day events of their lives."

To test this idea, Thompson created an experiment where he asked a group of mothers to recall a recent time when their child misbehaved. He found that some described the situation in detail, including why the child misbehaved, while others told a story that was, as he puts it, "just the facts."

Thompson elaborated on his finding that parents have different styles of expressing feelings by developing another experiment where he asked parents to read a book about feelings to their three-year-old children. There weren't many words in the story, so parents could interpret this book in any way they wished—they could read the book straight through or they could fill in the story, providing rich detail about the emotions portrayed in the pictures.

Thompson and his colleagues hypothesized that parents who elaborated on the feelings in the story would have children with a more developed understanding of others' minds and better perspective-taking skills. To his surprise, he found that this hypothesis was not true. The way parents talked about feelings was not related to how well children understood the thoughts and feelings of others. But Thompson did not give up on his hunch:

> We began to wonder whether we were getting [at] it too early. So we followed up with the same children at age five. And we found that how the parent had read at age three did predict the child's understanding at age five. We had just caught it too early.

PROBLEM SOLVING ISN'T THE PROBLEM: HOW PERSPECTIVE TAKING DEVELOPS IN THE SCHOOL-AGE YEARS

One of the things I love about conducting research is that it's an adventure. Like scaling a mountain peak or kayaking in rough waters, the researcher sets out on a journey, armed with experience and knowledge, but never fully knowing what he or she might find. Sometimes the path is clear, but usually it's fraught with uncertainty and unexpected challenges. That was certainly Ross Thompson's experience in trying to understand how parents' sense of comfort with their own emotions affects children's ability to understand others' thoughts and feelings. He had a hunch; it didn't prove true, but he didn't give up. He repeated the experiment when the children were older and then found what he had suspected.

The experiences of Larry Aber of New York University have been similar. In a completely different field, the study of aggression, Larry Aber had findings from his and others' research, but they weren't very strong findings. So he, too, kept looking.

You may wonder: what does perspective taking in preschoolers have to do with aggression in school-age children? But there is a connection, and it is only one of the many benefits of perspective taking: children who can understand others have less of a need to strike or hurt others.

Aber has been especially interested in aggression in younger children because it can escalate into greater aggression during the teen and adult years—and interfere with children's learning. He wanted to know: What are the roots of aggression in children? When in a child's life is aggression likely to flare up? Does it continue to escalate or can it be prevented, and if so, how? In other words, can more constructive ways of dealing with conflict be taught? Aber says:

> Children who get in fights with other children, children who disobey—who are constantly in conflict with other children and teachers—are on a path where they're not learning now and they're going to learn less in the future.

The saying goes: "If children are sad or mad, they can't add." As I've said, Aber's research has been fascinating because it has had its twists and turns. He says:

> When one child pushes another, the early thinking was that children who responded aggressively to that push had an impoverished reper- toire of options—they only knew how to push back or to push harder.

As a result, there were twenty years of attempts to improve children's "repertoire" of problem-solving skills. Did these efforts yield results? Yes, but "only a little bit," Aber said. So the question became why.

Building on the prior laboratory work of Kenneth Dodge, Aber and his colleagues began to study through their field-based research what goes on in children's minds when they are provoked. They asked children in their classrooms how they would respond to an ambiguous hypothetical situation—such as one child bumping into another in a school cafeteria and spilling a drink on the second child. Which children would decide to push back harder? And which children would decide to use other problem-solving skills, and why?

They discovered a missing link, a link they call an *appraisal process*. In the spilled-drink scenario above, for example, the child who has been bumped makes an immediate assessment of the situation: Was this an accident? Maybe this kid doesn't like me? Maybe this kid is trying to hurt me?

For the children who assume that others are out to get them, having skills to handle conflict is relatively worthless. They have what researchers call a *hostile attribution bias*. These words are a mouthful, but what they mean is that some children immediately interpret ambiguous situations as hostile when there isn't enough information to be certain—they jump to conclusions.

Given this insight, efforts to curb aggression in children of all ages have moved to include what Larry Aber calls *attributional retraining;* that is, helping children step back when something happens to them and make sense of the situation. Teachers using this approach help children gain perspective on the situation, realize that they don't have enough information to know why they were bumped, and look for clues to understand whether this was an accident or a hostile act. Once you teach children this skill, Aber says, "you've opened the gate to their using problem-solving skills."

Larry Aber and his colleagues have evaluated this approach with children in the New York City public schools and have found that it works—children become less aggressive.

HOW CAN YOU PROMOTE PERSPECTIVE TAKING IN CHILDREN?

SUGGESTION 1: PRACTICE WHAT WE PREACH.

Children who feel listened to, who feel understood, become better able to listen to and understand others. Of course that's easier said than done. It has helped me, though, to recognize that perspective taking is an essential skill in parenting and that to practice it, I have to put aside my own reactions. So I give myself assignments. When I listen to someone I disagree with, I ask myself: "What could this person be thinking?" The more I exercise this skill, the better I become at using it, especially in stressful moments.

SUGGESTION 2: VIEW TEACHING CHILDREN TO BE WITH OTHERS AS EQUALLY IMPORTANT TO TEACHING THEM INDEPENDENCE.

Go back to the parenting books you've read and I'm pretty sure you will find that most focus on helping children learn to become independent, with less emphasis on connecting with others. They may reflect the fusion theory that children are born with no sense of self and that their main task is to become independent. As we now know, independence is by no means the whole story. In fact, we spend most of our lives, in one way or another, in communities with others.

A PARENT'S PERSPECTIVE: I AM TRULY AT A LOSS

Mikey is three and only now expressing the Terrible Twos—meaning he's especially fussy, cranky, and stubborn. Nothing like the sweet angel I've known. He's just started preschool—and the teacher tells me he's bossing around the other kids.

I'm somewhat savvy, and I like to think I know how to manage this challenging period. But for additional reinforcements I turn to my handy parenting guides. "Talk to him on his level" . . . "give him some choices" . . . "be patient, it's only a phase" . . . advice that certainly embraces my child's growing independence.

But what I'm also worried about—and what's not so comprehensively covered—is: How much is this demanding attitude affecting his relationships with the other kids in his class? How long before his classmate Julian can no longer stomach being told what to do and doesn't want to be his friend anymore? This compounds my concern about how to raise Mikey as an only child without his becoming completely self-centered. I'm truly at a loss!

Most of us don't really think about exactly how to teach children to be with others. Of course we want our children to learn to get along with other people. But as we now understand it, the task is much more exciting than that. One of our main jobs is to teach children to understand others' perspectives as an essential aspect of learning to live with others. That "dance" we engage in with our children from the moment they're born is the beginning of their lifelong engagement with others. And through that caring dance, we can help children learn how to build bridges of understanding among people.

There are innumerable opportunities to do this right in our own backyard, so to speak. Take what I call the *Authority Stage,* from my research on the stages of parental growth. This is the period when parents are dealing with children between eighteen months and four or five years old. Children at this age begin to exercise their newfound prowess and say, "No!" "I won't!" and "You can't make me!" The parent who has been taking care of and protecting the child now has to shift into a greater authority role and confront the issue of power. Parents have to decide what kind of authority to be, how to set rules, how to enforce rules, and what happens when children break rules. Throughout these years, we're helping children develop their competencies (i.e., become independent), but we're also teaching them to relate to us as authorities, and that's all about perspective taking.

I used to drive my children back and forth from school when they were little, and they often fought in the backseat of the car, making the drive anything but pleasant. When I saw that part of my responsibility was to teach my children to be with others, my view of my role as a parent was transformed. First, I began to accept that sibling rivalry was a fact of life. I used to want it to disappear, so I reacted to it that way. "Stop fighting!" I would say again and again, to little avail.

Instead, I shifted my own perspective and began to see their fights as opportunities to help them learn to deal with conflict, rather than as a burden to me. I began to realize how few of us ever learn to deal with conflict directly. So I called a family meeting. My daughter was about four and my son was nine. I said, "The fighting in the car when I am taking you to school makes it hard for me to drive safely. I'm not interested in who starts the fights and I'm not interested in whose fault it is. I am only interested in who has a good idea for stopping the fights. I am going to write down all of your ideas so that we can try out some of them."

It took a while for my kids to get over trying to blame each other, but the piece of paper for writing down good ideas did wonders. I also used what I now think of as a problem- or dilemma-resolving technique:

1. **Identify the dilemma, problem, or issue.**

2. **Determine the goal.**

3. **Come up with alternative solutions.** They can suggest as many alternative ideas as they can think of to resolve the dilemma, but they can't pre-judge any idea. In other words, they can't immediately say, "This would never work."

4. **Consider how these alternative solutions might work.** After writing down each idea, go back and ask them what would work *and* what wouldn't work about each idea. This helps them learn to evaluate the pros and cons of solutions.

5. **Select a solution to try.** After trying the solution out for a while, have another family meeting to discuss what's working and what isn't working about this solution.

6. **Evaluate the outcome, and if the solution isn't working, try something else.** When things start to fall apart, as they inevitably do, try to figure out why, repeat the process, and come up with another solution to try.

As you can see, I was teaching my children perspective taking along with problem solving. When evaluating each solution on the list, they had to think about it from their own and from the other's perspectives. So the idea my daughter suggested—that her brother should just leave her alone—wouldn't work and wouldn't happen, as they both realized.

One of the first workable solutions they came up with was that each should get a "car-kit." This was simply a small empty bag that they would fill with a few favorite toys before each trip in the car. They thought that if they were busy and weren't bored, they might not argue with each other as much. I liked that idea for several reasons. First, it was their solution, not mine. As I know from working with adults, if people come up with solutions on their own, they're more likely to try to make them succeed. Second, having them playing actively in the car was much better than passively distracting them with music (now it would be a car video), because using distractions with older children doesn't teach them much about resolving problems.

The car-kit idea worked for quite a while. When it stopped working, their next agreed-upon solution was to put a pillow between them so that they wouldn't accidentally bump into each other in the car. Finally, they decided that they wanted to do things together. They took one of my tape recorders and invented their own radio show, interviewing each other. It gave my son an opportunity to perfect his imitations of cartoon characters (a skill he uses today with kids).

SUGGESTION 3: UNDERSTAND THAT A WARM AND TRUSTING RELATIONSHIP IS THE STRONGEST FOUNDATION FOR LEARNING PERSPECTIVE TAKING.

As I've mentioned, although perspective taking emerges as children grow up, not all children are equally good at it. What makes the difference? In addition to finding that parental comfort with emotion makes a difference, Ross Thompson found that the children who had trusting relationships with their parents—relationships that made them feel safe and secure—were later more adept at understanding others' perspectives.

Thompson sees that this is true in early childhood programs as well. If a child was having a temper tantrum and the teacher responded, "What a terrible time to have a temper tantrum!" children were less adept at reading and understanding others' feelings and thoughts. When teachers expressed empathy and understanding about the tantrum ("You must be really upset about something"), children "came to realize that there are human needs underlying these emotions."

I want to emphasize that empathizing and understanding the feelings that lead to tantrums does not mean allowing them. These teachers help children learn different ways of expressing negative feelings without being hurtful.

SUGGESTION 4: HELP CHILDREN FEEL KNOWN AND UNDERSTOOD.

AN EXERCISE: THINK BACK TO YOUR CHILDHOOD

Can you remember a time when you felt known and understood? What did the adult do to make you feel that way? How did you react? Can you think of a time when you felt misunderstood? What did the adult do to make you feel that way? How did you react?

I remember a particular moment in my childhood when I was trying to get away with something and my father made it clear to me that he knew exactly what trick I was up to. He stopped me, but not in an angry or mean way. I don't remember his words, but I do remember a comforting feeling, even though I was being disciplined.

In an *Ask the Children* study I conducted on how kids feel about their working parents, I asked children: "What would you like to tell the working parents of America?" The response of many, in essence, was "Understand me":

[Parents should] try to communicate with their children more because in today's society a lot of parents don't even know what is going on with their children.

Don't be afraid to talk with your kids. They may act like they don't want you talking to them, but it is actually very important that you do.

Remember, as one child put it:

You are not your children—respect and understand our viewpoints and needs.

Children who don't have any adults who they feel "know" them or who are "there for them" have a harder time connecting with others as adults.

To help infants feel known and understood:

You can be attuned to your infants by imitating what they are doing, such as repeating a sound they make. Remember that dance that takes place, almost automatically, between parents and infants—the infant does something and we respond in a way that parallels the speed, sound, and tempo of the infant's action. We can be conscious that as we do this, we're laying the groundwork for our infants to feel understood and thus ultimately able to take the perspectives of others.

What about older children? As children learn language, the communication moves to another level. I remember the pioneering researcher Urie Bronfenbrenner once telling me that good communication is like a Ping-Pong game that becomes more and more elaborate as children grow up.

There are many ways to help older children feel understood. They all begin with putting yourself in your child's place and trying to understand what the world feels and looks like to your child. Sometimes it even helps to get down to your child's eye level so that you're literally looking at things as your child would.

A PARENT'S PERSPECTIVE:
FEELING KNOWN AND UNDERSTOOD

Last night my son learned to play a new game. His mom would write out part of a word (example: _un) and then ask him to find the letter in the alphabet needed to make the word *fun*. With great excitement, he'd point to the letter. According to his mother, Ty couldn't wait to show off his new "trick."

When I walked in the door, I was still on a phone call that I had taken a few minutes earlier. Eager to show me what he could do, Ty and his mom played the game for me. I obviously couldn't cheer and clap for him while I was on the call, so I tried to give him the biggest, if silent, "Hooray!" I could.

To help younger and older children feel known and understood:

Repeat back your child's words or what you think your child is trying to communicate: "You are hungry."

Describe what you see going on, as if you're a sportscaster: "You threw that ball all the way across the yard!"

Ask a question: "Did you like that book we just read? Why did you like/not like it?"

Let them know you've been there: "I know how that feels."

Many parents fear that *tuning in to* their children means *giving in to* them. I think of a child who didn't want to go to school and would get sick in the mornings. Her mother thought she was being manipulative, so she would say, "You are *not* sick. Get dressed and go to school."

But this little girl was feeling sick—that's how badly she didn't want to go to school. It would have been much better to say, "I know you feel sick and you don't want to go to school. You have to go to school today, but I am going to talk with your teacher to see if we can make school a better place for you."

In other words, helping your child to feel known doesn't mean you go along with what he or she is doing.

A PARENT'S PERSPECTIVE: FEWER BEDTIME BATTLES

Bedtime is always a battle these days. Analia usually finds any excuse to stay awake for "just a little bit" longer. After we've read a few books, I announce it's time for "nighty-night." She says, "We can read three more books and then I can go to bed—is that a great idea?" It's late, I'm sleepy, and I grow increasingly frustrated with this game. I'm in no way angry at her—how can I be angry at a daughter who wants to read more? But neither of us is getting to bed any earlier.

So last night, when I announced we were on the final book for the night, the pouty lip made its usual appearance and she said, "But I want you to stay with me." Using her own words, I said, "I know you want me to stay, but it's bedtime. Tomorrow morning I'll come into your room and we can read another book then. Is that a great idea?" This seems to work. Rather than getting into a drawn-out discussion, she turns her head on her pillow, I head off to my room, and, as promised, in the morning we read a little *Green Eggs and Ham*. I guess we both "won."

SUGGESTION 5: TALK ABOUT FEELINGS— YOURS AND THEIRS.

That's clearly a lesson from the research of Ross Thompson and others, and it applies to children of all ages. My saying to my children that their fights in the car upset me is one example. It's important, however, not to burden your children with your feelings. Let's go back to the "bad day" scenario at the beginning of this chapter. If you've had a terrible day, it's better to acknowledge it briefly, even with toddlers and preschoolers: "I've had a hard day, like you sometimes have hard days." Since kids are quick to assume that it's their fault, make sure that you tell them it isn't.

Then share how you're going to recover: "You know how you sometimes have a time-out when you're upset? I need some time to myself and then I will be better."

A PARENT'S PERSPECTIVE: A NIGHT WHEN I FELT BLUE

One night I was feeling a bit blue—tired and a little off-kilter. I explained to my daughter that I wasn't going to be able to play as much because I was sort of sad. She came over to me and asked, "Why are you sad? Is it because you miss your babies?" I didn't really understand what she was talking about and asked her what she meant. Sara said, "Are you sad like Mrs. Darling because you miss your babies?" There's a scene in *Peter Pan* where Mrs. Darling is sitting in the nursery, sadly waiting for her children to come back from Neverland. Sara had remembered that and was trying to understand my mood. Suddenly, I was more cheered up.

SUGGESTION 6: USE EVERYDAY MOMENTS TO TALK ABOUT OTHER PEOPLE'S PERSPECTIVES.

Alison Gopnik found that children can learn this skill in their everyday lives—but *how* it's taught matters. Using the paper clips and crayons example, Gopnik and her colleagues worked with children who "were failing the false belief test" despite being old enough for this skill to have developed. She says:

We actually gave [the] children information about the way [other] people see the world.

When, for example, a child guessed that her friend Nicky would think there were paper clips in the closed crayon box (because she knew that's what was there), Gopnik and her team would call Nicky over to guess what was in the closed box as the first child watched. That way, the child could see with her own eyes and hear with her own ears that her friend Nicky would think there were crayons in the crayon box.

Gopnik makes the point that this information was given in the natural way that children might get this information in their everyday lives—from direct experience:

> And sure enough, we discovered that at the end of that training, the children were understanding these things in a way that they hadn't before.

Gopnik also found that children learn this skill better when they can talk about it. If, for example, you have eight blocks grouped closely together and six blocks spread widely apart, young children will typically think that there are more blocks when they are spread out over a larger space, even though the smaller grouping contains the larger number of blocks. Gopnik reports:

> We told [children] that one set of numbers is bigger than another. We gave them the same amount of encouragement and the same amount of experience [counting the blocks], but we didn't talk about people's minds [that if blocks are spread out, it looks like there are more blocks]. [When] we tested those children at the end of the two weeks, they weren't any better at understanding than they had been in the beginning. And that suggested that there was something very specific about telling children about what the mind was like that actively made a difference in their understanding.

While we tend to think about learning as "instruction," Gopnik points out that children learn the most through having everyday experiences where adults talk about perspective taking:

> It isn't enough to say, "All right, now we're going to have a twenty-minute theory of mind teaching session." What seems to really make the difference is the children's experience in an everyday setting—being with lots of different kinds of people and with people who are attentive to what's going on inside the children.

SUGGESTION 7: GIVE CHILDREN OPPORTUNITIES TO PRETEND.

Watch any group of children who are pretending and you will see them experiment with how others think and feel. They are "trying on" the perspectives of others. As Gopnik says, they are figuring out:

> What's it like if you're the mommy? What are mommies like? What are daddies like? What are babies like? What happens when [the] mommy says this; then what's the daddy supposed to say? Those are ways that children are actually actively experimenting, actively trying to figure out what's going on with other children, [what's] going on in other people's minds.

When we as adults are going to meet new people or visit a new place, we often rehearse the new experience in our minds beforehand. This is pretending "grown-up style." From the toddler years on, give children props and permission to pretend about their experiences; for example, toy airplanes if they've been on an airplane trip; a phone to play office; dress-up clothes to pretend to be different people.

SUGGESTION 8: USE OTHER-ORIENTED DISCIPLINE.

When I wrote the book *The Preschool Years*, I discovered the research of Martin Hoffman of New York University and his concept of *other-oriented discipline,* in which parents make the child aware of the effect of his or her behavior on another person. This may involve pointing out the direct consequences of the child's behavior on someone else: "When you leave food out, our dog eats it and gets sick." Or it can mean pointing out feelings: "I feel terrible for our dog when she gets sick, and I am not too happy about cleaning up after her, either."

Hoffman found that children were more likely to listen to others and be more considerate if parents used other-oriented discipline—except when parents accompanied this message with harsh discipline: severe threats or physical force. The power of the harsh discipline apparently blocks the lessons of the other-oriented discipline.

SUGGESTION 9: TEACH APPRAISAL SKILLS.

Larry Aber and his colleagues have experimented with how teachers can teach appraisal skills in order to reduce aggression. Their research holds many lessons for us as parents.

In their first studies, they followed children from the first through the sixth grades in the New York City public schools. They picked this period in childhood because they've found that aggression can escalate during this time. Initially, they evaluated a curriculum called the Resolving Conflict Creatively Program (RCCP), developed by Educators for Social Responsibility. This curriculum teaches children appraisal skills— how to figure out someone else's intention. It also shows children that they have choices about how they handle conflict and gives them skills for making those choices in their everyday lives. Not surprisingly, Aber found that the more RCCP lessons children were taught, the more competently they handled conflict.

But Aber suspected that the results could be even stronger, so they began work on a second series of studies in the New York public schools with a successor program to RCCP called the 4 Rs Program—Reading, Writing, Respect, and Resolution. This program doesn't separate teaching children to handle conflict from other kinds of academic teaching; it combines what I see as social, emotional, and intellectual (SEI) skills. Each unit is based on a children's book selected for its literary quality and its relevance to the theme. Through discussions, writing exercises, and role-play, children explore the meaning of the book, learn how to appraise complex situations, and then are taught how to resolve conflicts in these situations.

The early results of this research are even more promising. Children are less likely to jump to conclusions about others' behavior. Their mental health is better. And the reading scores for those who initially showed the most substantial behaviorial problems have improved.

Aber's research further confirms that children need to learn how to figure out the intent of others when they're in tough situations with parents and with other children. You can help them by teaching appraisal skills, and there are many ways to do this from the preschool years on:

> Encourage your children to think about people's responses to everyday situations. "Why do you think Aunt Beth got upset when her friend said she looked tired?"

> Ask children to think about characters' intent in books. Take the example of Maurice Sendak's *Where the Wild Things Are*. Ask your child why he or she thinks that Max was causing trouble.

> Ask children to think about intent in the television shows and movies you watch together.

THE FAR-REACHING BENEFITS OF LEARNING PERSPECTIVE TAKING

In the early years, perspective taking helps children begin to demystify their world. In doing so, it fosters security and sets the stage for complex learning. As Ross Thompson says:

> *It's learning that helps children not only understand what goes on in other people's thoughts and minds, but it also shapes their memories for events, [and] it helps them to predict what will happen in the future.*

Studies have found that young children who learn to understand what is going on in the minds of others have a better adjustment to kindergarten. And there are connections between this skill and learning to read. Alison Gopnik says:

One of the things that you need to do to be able to learn how to read is to have what sometimes [is] called metalinguistic skills. That means understanding how reading works and understanding how language works. Understanding how language works requires understanding something about what other people are thinking.

Ultimately, perspective taking is fundamental to children's future, as Gopnik notes:

If we want to be successful and deal with other people, [we need] to understand the people around us—particularly what's going on in their minds.

Without this ability, in Dan Stern's words, the world would be a very lonely place.

CHAPTER THREE

SKILL THREE: COMMUNICATING

Think of a newborn, unable to understand or use a single word. In just a few short years, that same child could know thousands of words and use them to retell an experience, express an opinion, negotiate with you, or crack a joke. That very same child could grow up to use words to plumb the mysteries of the world, discover something new, write epics, and inspire others to hope and dream. Our words have enormous power: to wage war or bring about peace; to change an individual—or an era—for better or for worse. Yet we enter life knowing none, understanding none.

The quest to understand the remarkable process of human growth has inspired many of the researchers in this book. MIT neuroscientist Rebecca Saxe says that even as a child she was awestruck by the question: how do you start with a molecule and end up with a person?

Roberta Golinkoff, a developmental psychologist at the University of Delaware, describes the same wonder in her quest to know how we learn language:

I wanted to understand how kids become the adults that they do. When a child is born, they're saying nothing. By the end of the first year of life, you're lucky if they say "da da." Then by the end of the second year of life, many of them are speaking in sentences. How did that happen?

Tracing the course of how that happens—how children learn to communicate—is a journey into the mind at work, says Kathy Hirsh-Pasek of Temple University.

AN EXERCISE: CRACKING THE CODE

Can you read and understand the following?

Obitsobeemsmobagobicobiknobow

What technique did you use to figure this out? Did you try to sound it out? Did you look for patterns in the letters? Were you able to figure out what I'm saying? If not, I'll tell you later in the chapter.

AN EXERCISE: SAILING IN A SEA OF SOUND

Remember the last time you were surrounded by a language you didn't understand. How did you begin to make sense of what was being said?

A PARENT'S PERSPECTIVE:
THE WHITE AND BLACK CHANGED PLACES

I started studying Spanish when I was forty-three. I was motivated to communicate in order to visit our exchange student's family in Venezuela. I enrolled in classes at our local university, began reading in Spanish, sought out Spanish people to talk to, and listened to tapes from Radio Nacional de España over and over. One moment stands out as evidence of my progress.

It was in the summer after I had begun taking classes. I was sitting on our porch listening to a Radio Nacional tape. Suddenly I realized that instead of listening hard for words that I *could* understand, the words that leaped out at me were those that I *couldn't* understand. It was like going from looking at a photographic negative to looking at a positive. The white and black had suddenly changed places.

When Philip and Lara were young, we spent several summers on the Greek island of Kos. We stayed with German friends, living high in the rugged mountains in Asfendiou, a community of five villages. The history of this island is a checkerboard of foreign occupations—Turkey occupied Kos for almost four hundred years, followed by Italy, then Germany. During the occupations, the Greek people sought refuge in the mountains. When the occupations ended in 1948 and Kos was reunited with Greece, many abandoned their mountain homes, some even leaving plates in their cupboards and baskets in their windows, and returned to the seaside. The families now living in these semiabandoned villages are a collection of nationalities, with no Americans and just a few English speakers. I was surrounded by multiple languages, so my mind turned into a running tape recorder, practicing the simplest of phrases again and again—"good morning" in Greek (*Kalimera*), "good morning" in German (*Guten Morgen*)—trying to remember new sounds and translate them into words I could understand.

Animals can communicate. My fish used to thrash around their aquarium if it was feeding time and one of us came nearby. And my dog Lola is a great communicator. If she wants a dog biscuit, she goes over to the cabinet where the box is kept and stares at me until she captures my gaze. She then turns and looks upward, directing my attention to the cabinet door. If I don't look at the cabinet, she stares back at me and then at the cabinet again, literally pointing with her nose. Finally, bingo—she gets her biscuit! She understands a number of words, like *ball, bone, biscuit,* and *bye-bye.* She even seems to understand sentences. If I say, "Norman is coming" (versus just "Norman"), she runs to the window, barking, puts her paws on the sill, and looks out at the driveway. If Norman is already at home, she goes to look for him elsewhere rather than running to the window. I have even experimented with her comprehension of words. If I am holding an adult conversation near her, her ears are typically motionless, but if I quietly and without emphasis insert her name into a sentence, her ears begin to wiggle up and down, back and forth, even though she remains resting on the floor.

As truly fantastic as I know she is (and she is!), Lola obviously can't use words to express herself. Communicating using complex language is uniquely human. And while language is among our greatest capacities, it's also a weakness for many. In a survey my organization conducted with employers, here is one of the questions we asked:

There is a debate about whether there is a gap between the competencies that employees should learn in school to succeed at work and the competencies they actually do have. Please tell me the most important general skills and competencies you look for in new hires that often fall below your expectations.

We found remarkable uniformity in employers' top two concerns— "spoken communication skills" (29 percent) and "written communication skills" (28 percent). Every other skill was mentioned by only a handful of employers.

So what happens between the time that children are born and the time when many enter the workforce apparently lacking these skills? First, children need to acquire the tools of language—the ability to comprehend, speak, and read words—but then they need to learn to use those tools with power and precision—i.e., to communicate. That is the story of this chapter.

CHILDREN ARE BORN PRIMED TO COMMUNICATE

Charles Nelson, now of Harvard Medical School, has used a brain-imaging technique to find that infants as young as one or two days old already "recognize" their mothers' voices. Small sensors are placed on the babies' heads to record and measure the electrical activity in the brain, which is recorded on a computer. Then a little earphone is placed in the baby's ear and the baby hears a continuous tape recording of the mother's voice alternating with a stranger's voice saying "Hi baby, hi baby, hi baby." The computer screen displays separate readings of the baby's brain activity in response to each voice. Nelson describes the experiment:

The only way [this baby] would recognize its mother's voice—because this particular baby was born just in the last day or so—would be having learned about its mother's voice when it was a fetus.

Deep within the brain, in an area called the *hippocampus*, memories of the mother's voice have been stored before birth. Since the hippocampus is connected to the emotional part of the brain, the *limbic system*, these earliest memories clearly have emotional connections.

Patricia Kuhl, a scientist at the University of Washington and the first recipient of the Bezos Family Foundation Endowed Chair for Early Childhood Learning, notes that in the last ten weeks or so of pregnancy, the child's auditory system becomes ready to receive and remember sounds:

> *What can they hear in the womb? It has the sounds of the [mother's] heartbeat, of bodily workings—a very noisy environment. And the baby is getting bone-conducted sound. So the mother's voice resonates in the bone structure of her body. Infants prefer their mother's voice at birth due to their experience in the womb.*

Kuhl likens this sound to listening to someone talk through the cheap walls of a motel room:

> *It's kind of muffled; you can hear that someone's talking, but you cannot tell what words or sounds are being produced—a kind of "waa-waa-waa-waa" sound pattern. Dad's voice doesn't make it through [this sound barrier], because it's not loud enough. Eighty decibels is beyond a shout, and that's what it appears to take to get through the [surrounding] tissue and overcome the noise in the womb. It takes about two weeks after birth for babies to prefer Dad's voice.*

Not only is the mother's voice preferred, but so is her native language:

> *If she spoke French while she was pregnant, babies will prefer French over Russian or English or other languages.*

What if the home is bilingual? One pioneer in early language research, Janet Werker of the University of British Columbia, lives and works in the multilingual community of Vancouver, Canada. She has found that while monolingual babies prefer their native language at birth, infants exposed to two languages in utero prefer both of those languages at birth.

Newborns' auditory systems are better developed than their sight systems, so the importance of language and voices to children's development is evident from the start. But are infants especially attuned to voices? Janet Werker and Athena Vouloumanos of New York University conducted an ingenious experiment to find out. Werker explains:

> We give [newborns] the opportunity to suck on a pacifier connected to a computer. Every time [they] deliver a strong suck, they get to hear either a speech sound or a nonspeech sound. So we have alternating minutes where they hear speech or nonspeech.

The nonspeech sounds are sound-wave analogues to speech—that is, the important information in the speech signal has been replaced by a simple tone, which Werker describes as sounding somewhat like a hypothetical chorus of Martians. They found that babies prefer to hear speech:

> Athena and I found that babies sucked a lot more during those moments when they heard speech than they did [during] the moments when they had the opportunity to hear nonspeech.

PARENT-SPEAK?

Some breakthroughs occur because the right person is in the right place at the right time. That was certainly true for Anne Fernald and her groundbreaking insights on infant-adult communication. In college she had been interested not in the study of language per se, but in language as literature, as poetry. After completing college in the late 1960s, she moved to Germany with her husband for his work:

> We went for one year and ended up staying eight years. When I went, I was an outsider to that language. By the end of that time— a quarter of my life—I was pretty good at German.

I watched myself move into fluency. I paid attention to all the cues that I used in talking to people that told me what the meaning was before I knew the grammar, before I knew the vocabulary.

Our children were born there. Becoming a parent in another language is a wonderful experience because it gave me distance [on the process].

What drew me to the study of language was a moment of epiphany. One of my dear friends had a baby a few months before our second daughter was about to be born, and I was asked to be the godmother of this child. [I] went to the hospital on the second day and my friend put her newborn child into my hands to introduce us.

To her own surprise, Fernald introduced herself to her godchild in singsong German:

I immediately thought: now where did THAT come from? I didn't hear people talking to me that way when I was a child, and I don't talk to my daughter in German. And this child doesn't know any language at all. Was this a performance for her German-speaking mother? Or was I just intuitively trying to engage with this newborn baby?

Not only was Fernald acutely aware of her words, but she was also struck by the fact that she was *singing* them. When her own baby was born a few weeks later, she found herself singing the same kind of melody to her newborn—this time in English.

A PARENT'S PERSPECTIVE: BABA-WAWA TALK

When my children were babies, I called bottles "babas" and water "wawa." If I said "bottle" or "water," the names didn't register as quickly as if I said "baba" and "wawa."

Fernald's experiences in a new country led her into what has become a lifelong study of communication, beginning as a volunteer in a scientific center studying infant development in Germany and continuing to graduate school and then to Stanford University, where she is now a professor.

In her first days as a volunteer, Fernald accompanied a pediatrician to a hospital for a study he was conducting of how physically close mothers get to their newborns when they speak to them. There she saw families from Germany, Turkey, Yugoslavia, Sicily, and Greece:

What caught my ear was that they were all, in some sense, singing the same melodies in one language [or] another to a little two-day-old child who didn't know any language. [They were] using those melodies that I heard myself making to my little goddaughter.

In her own first study, Fernald recorded German mothers talking to their newborns, analyzing the tones of their voices as one would analyze music. She found that the range of their voices stretched across two octaves.

Patricia Kuhl has conducted similar studies of the way adults talk with babies:

When we brought men and women into the laboratory with their children, we would engage them in a conversation in which they would be talking to us, and then they would naturally turn and talk to the baby. So we get this wonderful contrast between adult-directed speech and infant-directed speech.

Although the scientific term is *infant-directed speech*, and I am calling it *parent-speak*, Kuhl calls this way of speaking *motherese, parentese,* or *caregiverese:*

[The voice] increased by an octave, it's much slower, and the sounds are like golden nuggets. They're very clearly articulated and stretched out in time, and their frequency differences are much bigger.

Fernald wondered if infants actually prefer infant-directed speech to adult-directed speech, and she developed one of the first auditory preference methods to address this question. The technique entails her recording mothers' adult-directed and infant-directed speech:

I had the moms speak to me and speak to their four-month-old. So the mom might say to me, "Well, I don't take [my children] out so much, because it's been raining a lot," but to her baby, she says, "Hey, sugar bear! Hey, sugar bear!" I selected little sections of that speech and put them on tape.

Then she "trained" other four-month-olds so that if they turned their heads one way, they heard infant-directed speech, but if they turned them the other way, they heard adult-directed speech. She alternated the sides, so the findings wouldn't reflect a preexisting preference for the right or left side:

We found babies would turn more in the direction [that would] turn on the infant-directed speech.

This finding led Fernald to the next logical question in cracking the communication code: was it the music of the voices that the babies preferred, or was it the actual words?

[In] the next experiment, [babies] heard the very same speech but filtered so the adult-directed sounded like "hmmmm, mmmmm," and the infant-directed sounded like "hmmmmm, mmmmm."

You'll have to use your imagination to translate these *hmmmmm*'s into singsong infant-directed and regular adult-directed sounds, removing the words and just using pitch. If you can, try it with a baby. Fernald found:

Sure enough, [the] four-month-olds showed an even stronger preference for the pitch contours of the infant-directed speech.

PARENT-LOOK: OOCHIE, WOW, AND JOY

In studying how adults talk with babies, Janet Werker noticed that adults don't exaggerate just their speech; they also exaggerate their facial expressions. She and her colleagues investigated how adults from two very different cultures—English-speaking and Chinese-speaking mothers—connect with their four- to seven-month-olds. They gave the mothers several topics to talk about with their babies (for example, bringing them home from the hospital, taking them to get their first shot)—topics purposely chosen to evoke a range of emotions—and filmed the mothers as they did so. They then had observers code the mothers' facial expressions according to standard facial-expression coding schemes. They found three typical faces that they called:

Oochie: an expression adults use to express concern, caring, comfort, and love. It involves pursed lips and is playful.

Wow: Werker says that this looks somewhat like an adult expression of surprise. The eyebrows are raised, the mouth is wide open, and there is an upturning in the lips that softens the edge of excitement, turning it into something that their coders consistently labeled as amazement, pride, and love.

Joy: Werker says that a content analysis of adult ratings of this expression indicates that it reflects an unmistakable look of joy and love.

Werker summarizes the meaning of this and other studies she has conducted:

Babies are prepared at birth to listen to language. Moreover, they've already learned something about the characteristics of their native language or languages and are prepared to listen accordingly.

While originally researchers thought that babies were born able to discriminate differences among the sounds in all the languages around the world (for example, the difference between the *d* sound in English and in Hindi), recent evidence indicates that "babies are probably not universal listeners at birth." Werker says:

> They can discriminate many, perhaps most, of the sounds from the world's languages, but they can't discriminate all possible sounds. Experience seems to be required to allow that discrimination to emerge.

That's where immersion in language combined with facial expression, or what I call *parent-look*—precisely what Werker saw parents do— is crucial:

> Over the next several months of life, [babies] listen to the sounds of language, they pay attention to the facial expressions that accompany those sounds, [and] they pay attention to the entire communicative context in which language is so richly expressed.

From birth on, babies are ready to listen and watch, and we as adults typically talk and look in ways that, in Werker's words, enable the infants to

> pull out the properties—the consonants, vowels, and other properties of their native language[s]—that will eventually give them the categories they need to go on to learning words, syntax, [and] to learn to become both comprehenders and speakers.

WHY PARENT-SPEAK, PARENT-LOOK, AND PARENT-GESTURE MATTER IN THE FIRST TWO YEARS OF LIFE

Some people think babies aren't learning about talking until they start to babble or say actual words, but that couldn't be further from the truth, as many parents realize.

A PARENT'S PERSPECTIVE: A POLITE BABY

I definitely believe that my children were learning the meaning of words before they could babble or say actual words. The fourth word that my son said was *thank you*, and he said it at the correct times. How else could that be explained?

Think of interactions during those first months and year as forming the foundation of children's skill in communicating. The way we talk, the expressions on our faces and in our eyes, what we look at, even our gestures are the basis upon which learning to communicate is built.

Of course, we can teach only what we ourselves have learned. So as we promote communication skills in our children, we have to develop them in ourselves. *We have to learn what we want to teach* . . . and it all begins with how we talk, how we look, and what gestures we use with our young children.

PARENT-SPEAK AND PARENT-LOOK CONVEY FEELINGS IN A MORE PRONOUNCED WAY

We communicate our feelings through our parent-speak, word-songs, and our parent-look *oochie, wow,* and *joy* faces to babies. Fernald says that, long before they can understand the verbal language of feelings, babies begin to put these cues and clues together to begin to differentiate among a range of emotions:

> *Babies begin to learn about emotional cues not yet carried by language, because at six to seven months they don't yet have the ability to learn those words and those meanings.*

I remember startling Philip when he was a few months old. Something surprised me, I yelled, and he got upset. I had no idea that my emotions were being transferred so easily.

Why does this matter? Because it indicates that children typically learn things we view as more cognitive or intellectual, like language, through the filter of feelings.

PARENT-SPEAK HELPS BABIES LEARN TO REGULATE THEMSELVES

We all know how soothing it can feel to be touched, and how parents provide soothing touches to children by rocking, cradling, and stroking them. But most of us don't think about the caressing power of our voice. Think of the tone of voice we use with babies as similar to touch—it regulates the baby as one of the first steps in the baby's learning self control, which is fundamental to learning to communicate.

Anne Fernald observed that parents also use their tone of voice to manage their infants' behavior, typically to praise or to prohibit. Curious to know if tone by itself was sufficient to regulate the child, she tape-recorded parents saying things that conveyed approval or prohibition in several different languages—French, German, Italian, Japanese, British English, and American English. She and her colleagues then tested five-month-old American babies with these "messages" in unfamiliar languages:

> These little American babies would hear the praise and they would smile and relax; they would hear the prohibition and they would stiffen a little and their eyes would widen. These sounds—in a different language, from a total stranger—had predictable effects on babies' behavior.

AN EXERCISE: THE MEDIUM IS THE MESSAGE

If you have a baby in your life, try this exercise: use just your tone of voice to convey meaning. For example, try speaking nonsense words in a stern voice, and then saying the same nonsense words in a pleasant, happy voice. How does your baby react?

PARENT-SPEAK HELPS CHILDREN LEARN TO DETECT WORDS IN A SEA OF SOUNDS

Remember the made-up word I used at the beginning of this chapter: *Obitsobeemsmobagobicobiknobow?*

If you broke the code by sounding it out or by looking for patterns in the letters, you discovered that it was not one word but a sentence. It comes from a language I learned as a child called "ob language." The rule for this language is to put an *ob* sound before every vowel sound. I am fluent in ob—I can sing, rattle off long sentences, and talk with my sister, who is also fluent. We used to speak ob at the dinner table to say things we didn't want our mother to understand. Little did we know that she soon broke the code and infiltrated our secret talk, but she waited until we were adults to tell us!

If you translate my ob sentence into English, it is: "It seems magic, I know." I wrote this sentence because the more I know about how children learn to communicate, the more magical it seems to me.

Part of breaking the code of a language is figuring out word boundaries: the sounds that mark the beginnings and endings of words. Jenny Saffran of the University of Wisconsin likes to use the example of "pretty baby" to explain how complex this is. When we speak, we don't typically pause before and after words to indicate where they begin or end, so "pretty baby" could be "pre ty ba by" or "pre tyba be," etc.

In fact, however, every language contains statistical regularities. There are not many words in English that begin with *pre*. So the statistical likelihood that *pre* will be followed by *ba*, as in *baby*, is low, whereas the likelihood that it will be followed by *ty*, as in *pretty*, is relatively high. Saffran wondered whether babies have an ability to learn language by detecting these statistical patterns. Answering this question would illuminate a debate about learning language—how much of this capacity in infants is innate versus learned. If children can detect patterns, then they can use this capacity to *learn* where words begin and end.

Saffran and her colleagues used the *familiarization procedure* I've described previously: when babies, like all of us, hear (or see) something again and again, they become tired of it and pay less attention each time it is repeated. They have *habituated,* to use the scientific term. If you present babies with new sounds—or something *babies hear as new*—they will listen longer. If they listen for a shorter time to the old sounds than the new ones, it suggests that they have become familiar with the old sounds.

In order to avoid presenting the babies with words they might have heard before, Saffran made up new words. These words are unintelligible: *pabiku golatu daropi tibudo.*

Saffran and her colleagues conducted a series of studies with eight-month-olds. In one study, the babies heard the made-up words *pabiku golatu daropi tibudo* repeatedly for two minutes (a flashing light also helped them pay attention).

Then the eight-month-olds were exposed to the same "words" they had heard before (*pabiku golatu daropi tibudo*) or new part-words, made by combining the final syllable of one word with the first two syllables of another word, such as *tudaro pigola.*

AN EXERCISE: FINDING THE PART-WORDS

Can you go back to the four words of Saffran's made-up language and find the new part-words? For some of us, it's not so easy, is it?

Presumably it isn't so easy for infants, either—perhaps many of the new words they hear seem as strange to them as these made-up words do to us. Yet the study showed that eight-month-olds listened longer to the part-words than to the whole words, indicating that they had become familiar with the sound patterns in the whole words. Jenny Saffran and her colleagues say that the infants' performance is all the more impressive because the made-up words contained no pauses, no cues other than the "sequential statistics inherent in the structure of words."

Saffran and her colleagues used a similar technique to present Italian words to English-learning eight-month-olds and came to the same conclusions. It's amazing to think that children just four months short of their first birthdays can detect statistical patterns to determine the sounds that go together and eventually the beginnings and endings of words in what Saffran has called a "sea of sounds."

She and a colleague also found that children were even more facile in detecting word boundaries in infant-directed speech. The way we typically talk to infants—speaking more slowly, enunciating words, pausing between sounds, and varying the pitch of our voice—makes learning language much easier.

PARENT-LOOK AND PARENT-GESTURE HELP CHILDREN DIRECT THEIR ATTENTION TO WHAT WE THINK IS IMPORTANT

Voice tone is only one of the tools we use to help infants shift their focus. Amanda Woodward has been a leader in uncovering how children learn to associate, or map, words with the things they represent (such as the word *dog* with the actual dog). It starts with the ability to direct attention and focus. She gives a grown-up-world example of how this works:

> *Imagine you're standing on a street corner and somebody is looking up high. You tend to shift your own eyes to see what that person is looking at. It's an automatic response. It's hard to stop yourself from doing it. In fact, people sometimes use that automatic response to play jokes on other people. If you're playing touch football, a good way to fake out your opponent is to look in one direction and throw the ball in the other direction. It works every time, even though everybody knows it's the oldest trick in the book.*

AN EXERCISE: FAKING IT

Try this trick with your child. Pretend to throw a ball in one direction and then shift and throw it in another direction. What happens? How many times do you have to do this before your child "gets it"?

Woodward explains:

It turns out that babies, like adults, have the propensity to follow
another person's eyes from pretty early in life.

Some studies have found this tendency emerging as early as three months.
It's well developed by nine to twelve months.

Just as singsong parent-speak helps children begin to pick out what
Patricia Kuhl calls the "golden nuggets of sound" that will someday have
meaning, parent-look—shifting our focus to what we want children to
look at—helps them learn words as well.

When babies follow our gaze, we are actually *telling* them with our
eyes what we think is important. And as we saw in chapter 2, on perspective taking, from Woodward's finding that babies prefer to follow our
intentional actions rather than the actions of a robot, babies appear to
have what I call a *people sense,* meaning that they appear wired to focus
on people's intentions far before anyone teaches them to pay attention to
what others seem to intend. Babies use this focus on people's intentions
as a guide to learning language. By nine months or so, babies begin to
learn actual words, lots of them.

Woodward has explored how babies' focus on intention guides language learning. In one study, she used two different methods to introduce
thirteen-month-olds to a word they'd never heard (a made-up word) and
an object they'd never seen.

In one method, the baby (sitting on his or her parent's lap) is across
a table from two experimenters. The first experimenter looks at the baby
and then looks over at the new object, pointing to it. (This reminds me of
the way my dog Lola looks at me and then at the cabinet, pointing with
her nose when she wants a dog biscuit.) The second experimenter does
the same, but just when the baby looks at the object, the second experimenter names it: "Look, Alice, it's the *gombie.*"

In the second method, the procedure is the same except that the
second experimenter doesn't connect with the baby—she or he watches
what is happening on a video monitor—but as before, just when the
baby looks at the object, the second experimenter names the gombie.
Both groups of children see the gombie being named nine times. They
also see another object that isn't named.

Do babies learn the name of a new object simply by *association* (hearing a new object being named when they're looking at it)? Or are babies more likely to learn a new word if adults seem to have the intentional goal of teaching them the new word by naming the object while pointing and looking at it? To find out, a third experimenter comes into the room and puts the gombie and the other unnamed object on a tray and asks the baby to "get the gombie."

Infants who saw the experimenter name the gombie while looking and pointing to it are much more likely to get the gombie. But if the experimenter was looking at the video monitor while naming the toy, some of the babies actually go over to the video monitor to try to find the gombie!

These experiments reveal that we're helping children learn language not only with *parent-speak* and *parent-look,* but also with our hands, by gesturing or pointing to what we want children to focus on. I call this *parent-gesture.*

PARENT-GESTURE HELPS CHILDREN LEARN TO COMMUNICATE

Before I learned about this research, I never considered gesturing as a tool we use to help our children learn to communicate. Susan Goldin-Meadow of the University of Chicago has studied gesturing (including with deaf children in hearing families) and finds that the gestures are signals to children, telling them what parents think is important.

One of the most familiar gestures is pointing. Children themselves begin to point around eight months or later. Kathy Hirsh-Pasek of Temple University fondly calls this "the royal point," because it is such an important milestone in the development of communication skills. Goldin-Meadow has found that pointing and other gestures are the first steps that all children take into language:

I like to say that children enter language hands first!

A PARENT'S PERSPECTIVE: A LANGUAGE ALL HER OWN

My toddler had a lot to say before she could say it. When she was eighteen months old, she created some gestures to let us know what she wanted. She tilted her hand a certain way near her mouth to tell us she wanted her bottle. She rested her head on her two hands as though they were her pillow in order to tell us she was tired. And she loved to play in water. She showed us she wanted water-play by tapping the index finger of one hand into the palm of the other—mimicking the motion of water from the tap spilling into her hands.

Goldin-Meadow finds that children use gestures *before* their first words. They will point to their bottle before they say "ba-ba." My son, Philip, used to thump his hand back and forth against his mouth to tell us he was hungry, before he said the word "hun-gree."

Parents tend to translate children's gestures into sentences, giving children words to begin to express themselves. In studying fifty-three children over time, Goldin-Meadow and her colleagues have found that children who used more gestures to express themselves at fourteen months were more likely to have larger vocabularies at forty-two months. In a subsequent study of fifty children from fourteen months to fifty-four months, they found that children with larger vocabularies when they were older were more likely to have used gestures when they were younger. More important, the children more likely to gesture have parents who are more likely to gesture. Because of the design of these studies, one can't conclude that parent-gesture *causes* better language skills (because these parents might be doing other things that affect their children's language development in addition to gesturing). Goldin-Meadow and her colleagues are now conducting an experimental study, but given the evidence thus far, she concludes:

Mothers, [fathers, and other caregivers] who are attentive to their children's gestures have children who pick up words a little faster.

PARENT-SPEAK HELPS CHILDREN LEARN TO RECOGNIZE AND SAY WORDS

Roberta Golinkoff calls the first words that babies recognize "anchors," as they allow babies to recognize new words that come after them. In fact, her research shows that even as early as six months of age, babies can recognize a new word that comes after their own name but not when it comes after someone else's name. It's not that they know the *meaning* of the word, but familiar, frequently heard words like their own name and "Mommy" serve as a wedge or anchor into the speech stream. This happens perhaps earlier than one might think. Kathy Hirsh-Pasek says:

> We [have] learned that babies pay attention to their own names by four and a half months of age. Babies know "Mommy" and "Daddy" by six months.

At around seven months or so, they begin to babble. And when they begin to look and point as well as babble and point, Hirsh-Pasek says, they can communicate what they want.

She and Golinkoff tell a story in their book, *How Babies Talk*, about Golinkoff's son, Jordan, clearly wanting something when he was fourteen months old. He was pointing at the counter, and Golinkoff tried to decipher what he wanted by naming everything in sight—the jelly, a spoon, the cheese. Jordan shook his head vigorously at each suggestion. Finally she said "sponge." He leaned back in his high chair, finally relaxing because his mom had figured out what he wanted.

Often the first words, when babies are somewhere around a year old, are "Mama" or "Dada." It is a magical milestone.

A PARENT'S PERSPECTIVE:
NOT THE FIRST WORD I HOPED TO HEAR

My son lives in a bilingual home. His father is Spanish and I am Finnish. I always thought that his first word was Äiti, or more like "Äihtiiih," when he was a tiny, tiny baby. Äiti is "Mom" in Finnish, and I desperately wanted to hear that. After all, it was a word I use tons of times each day! Well, I wasn't so lucky. At close to sixteen months, as I was changing his diaper one day, I think I heard the first clear and deliberate word: "*Papa.*" It took me a split second to realize that this was an actual word! His first word was naming his father, not me.

A PARENT'S PERSPECTIVE: UPS MAN, NOT DADDY

My son was just learning to talk and knew three words—*cat, light,* and *Daddy.* One lovely Saturday afternoon, we were walking in our neighborhood and I was carrying him in his sling, chatting with some neighbors. My son saw our friendly (and cute) UPS man delivering packages and loudly shouted out, "Daaaddddyyyy!" much to my embarrassment and my neighbors' amusement. My husband, who was feeling a little neglected around then, didn't find it so hilarious. But I explained to him that if you know only three words, *Daddy* is closer to *UPS Man* than *cat* or *light*, and to give us a break. We still laugh about it whenever we see the UPS truck.

By eighteen months, most young children have a number of words and can string them together to create the beginnings of sentences. I remember one of Philip's first communications to us. I tend to use nicknames for the people in my family. One of Philip's early nicknames was Flipper, bestowed because of the way he propelled himself around his crib. One day he said to me, "No Flipper." I looked at him, astonished, and he repeated it again with more emphasis: "No Flipper." And then he said, "No Flipper! Ippy." So we called Philip "Ippy." As he grew up, Ippy underwent many transformations (you can imagine all the names I can create out of Ippy). In high school, we called him Mr. Ip. He "permitted" his family to use this special name for him when he became an adult, though Mr. Ip was replaced by Dr. Ip when he got his PhD.

Obviously, their own names are particularly important to young children and they're more likely to learn new words that follow their names.

They're also more likely to learn words at the end rather than in the middle of sentences. Anne Fernald describes her study of this:

> The way [we conduct naming experiments is] to show the child two pictures, [for example, of] a baby and a doggie. You ask, "Where's the baby?" Or "Where's the doggie?" However, if [you] change the sentence a little bit and you say, "There's a ball over there," and put [the word "ball"] in the middle instead of at the end [of the sentence], they fall apart completely. They can't get it.

Fernald has found that by around eighteen months, children are more able to pick out words in the middle of the sentence. In addition, infant-directed speech becomes less important to their learning new words.

At that age, studies show that children's vocabularies seem to take off—young children are learning many new words per day. Fernald elaborates:

> [Babies at] twelve, fifteen months may learn one word a week— very slowly building vocabulary. Then around eighteen months they pick up the pace and parents will notice, "He learned three new words today," or "He learned five new words or ten new words this week." [It's called] a vocabulary explosion because it's a change in rate of language learning.

A PARENT'S PERSPECTIVE:
PICTURES WORTH A THOUSAND WORDS

I wanted to capture the way my daughter was learning language, so I got out my video camera. On the morning of the shoot, I dressed Carrie in a pretty pink outfit that would look good on camera, found a slimming outfit for myself, and yelled, "Action." I don't think I'm being too much of a stage mother when I say that Carrie "performed" beautifully. Right on cue, she threw out lots and lots of nouns, naming all her favorite objects around the house (shoe, ball, apple, juice). And, as evidence that she was starting to expand her words beyond nouns, she threw in a "bye-bye" and "hot."

Soon after the cameras were turned off, a spurt obviously began! Before I knew it, Carrie was trying on new words for size at an amazing pace. And I did my part, talking with her as much and as often as I could. Unfortunately, I got busy and didn't tape her again until she was twenty-four months. And at that point, what came out was far more sophisticated—sentences like "I finished yogurt now." Looking at these two videos, I felt like I had a ringside seat for something that otherwise might have been hidden.

PROCESSING LANGUAGE IN THE TODDLER YEARS AND BEYOND

Computer scientists trying to create voice recognition computers have struggled to create a machine that can recognize all the variations in voices—loud, soft, gruff, silky, southern, midwestern, and so on—something children are able to do by their second year. In her most recent research, Fernald has examined how efficiently children process new words:

> The baby is sitting on Mom's lap in a little booth and there are two pictures on two monitors that the child is looking at, to the left and to the right.

Let's say that on the left monitor is a picture of a dog and on the right monitor is a picture of a baby, though the positions of these pictures are changed throughout the experiment. When the child hears, "Where's the baby?" the researchers look at how the child processes this information and when the child begins to shift attention to look at the picture that has just been named. Does the child begin to shift his or her focus upon hearing the first syllable "bay," or does the child wait until the whole word, "baby," is said? Fernald says:

> At eighteen months, the shift is quicker [than when they were younger]. By twenty-four months, just nine months later, all they need to hear [is] "Where's the bay—" and they're out of there. So at that point they can already place their bets based on hearing half the word.

Fernald calls this *efficiency of processing* or *fluency of processing*. She explains why they are so important—if a child doesn't need to wait until the end of a word to "grab it," he or she is ready for the word that comes along next:

> When you're a very young language learner, what comes next is likely to be new, so the [more efficiently] you can process familiar words, the [better able you are] to attend to the new information that comes along and potentially make use of it.

They have found this to be the case. Children who processed language more quickly when they were younger had greater vocabulary growth in their second year.

How parents talk with children matters as well. In a longitudinal study of Spanish-speaking children, Fernald and her colleagues found that the children of mothers who spoke more, used different words for the same object, used different types of words, and spoke in longer phrases to their children at eighteen months, not only had larger vocabularies but were faster at processing words at twenty-four months. As Fernald puts it, these "little differences can add up to a big effect":

> For the young child, there are always new things to be learned in almost every sentence they hear. So that advantage, small as it is, can add up to a big advantage later on, because the capacity for learning is then increased.

ANNE FERNALD'S PERSPECTIVE:
WHAT ARE THEY SAYING ABOUT EGGPLANTS?

I had an experience in Japan a few years back when I attempted
to learn Japanese that reminded me [of the importance of grabbing
words as they fly by in everyday language]. I was laboriously learning these Japanese words. I learned the [word that] means "eggplant," and somebody spoke it in a sentence. I was so grateful to
them for speaking a word that I actually understood [that] I stopped
and said, "I know that word!" I proudly beamed with the satisfaction
of knowing the word, [but then] the rest of the sentence had gone
on without me. The verb was lost on me. I had no idea what to do
with that eggplant!

LANGUAGE AND LITERACY

Catherine Snow, a professor at Harvard Graduate School of Education
and a renowned expert on language development, began her studies
when very little was known about how children learn language—it was
truly a new frontier. She says:

> I could review the literature on language development in a week-
> end, because there was so little of it in 1967. Now, of course, it's
> become an enormous field, which has produced thousands of books
> and dozens of journals. It's a very exciting and vibrant field—but
> at the time when I started, there were just a couple of studies that
> had been published.

Among the debates in the field, as mentioned, was the question of
how much language is innate versus learned. Snow and her colleagues
David Dickinson and Patton Tabors began what has become a landmark
study: The Home-School Study of Language and Literacy Development.
The idea was to look for a group of families where the children would
be at risk for not developing strong literacy skills and determine over

time which experiences the families and schools provided that made the biggest difference in children's development in language, literacy, and reading:

> *We started with a group of eighty or so low-income families with three-year-old children. We visited the families at home and [at school] every year when the children were three, four, and five. And [we've] tested the children every year starting when they were five on language and literacy skills.*

Among the techniques they used were taping family dinnertime conversations, story times, and playtimes, as well as interviewing parents. I love the idea of taping dinnertime conversations and wonder what ours would have sounded like when our kids were little. Dinnertime was such an important time for all of us to be together.

AN EXERCISE: WHAT DO YOUR DINNERTIME CONVERSATIONS SOUND LIKE?

Listen to your mealtime conversations as if you are a researcher. What did you learn?

One parent tried this and found that she was not having a conversation, but listening to soliloquies from her oldest and youngest child, while her middle child remained quiet. So she began to work on weaving the one-way comments into a conversation and including this middle child.

Over the years, three findings from the Snow, Dickinson, and Tabors study have been most predictive of children's language and literacy skills:

> **While reading books or talking at the dinner table, parents talk about issues that go beyond the here and now.** Snow says that this talk involved telling stories or getting the child to respond to questions like "What do you think is going to happen next?" Or "Why do you think that happened?" They used what Snow calls "extended discourse":

Extended discourse means talk about topics that goes on longer than just a sentence or two. So, for example, when these more successful families read books, they didn't just read the book and then ask questions like "What's that?" or "What color is it?" They asked questions like "Why do you think [the character in the story] did that?" [They asked] questions that involved the children in analysis, in an evaluation of the book, but also questions that gave them a chance to talk through their understanding of the story.

They also often encouraged children to tell stories about their own lives that mirrored the stories in the book: "The little bear was scared. Do you remember when you were scared?"

Parents use a sophisticated vocabulary. Snow says:

In these dinner table conversations, of course, there's always a lot of talk about "Eat your peas" and "Keep your elbows off the table" and "Pass the noodles," but in some of the families, in addition, there's wonderfully interesting conversation about what proposals the governor just suggested for the new budget, or how the construction of the expressway is going to influence the neighborhood. And these conversations are full of wonderful words like budget *and* governor *and* proposal *and* neighborhood—*words that children might not use [and] probably don't understand fully. We found that families that used words like that in their dinner table conversations had children with much larger vocabularies two years later.*

So part of vocabulary acquisition is learning the words that are going to be important in school, the words that second-grade teachers think when a child uses them, "Oh, wow, that was a good word; that's a smart kid." Those words are signals about the sophistication of the child's thinking. And of course they are also tools for thinking.

The difference between knowing three thousand words and knowing fifteen thousand words when you arrive at kindergarten is enormous. The child who knows three thousand words knows words like shoes *and* milk *and* jump. *The child who knows fifteen thousand words knows words like* choice *[and]* possibility—*words that index a more complex array of possibilities for dealing with the world.*

Parent-talk does not mean baby talk, talking down to preschool-aged children, or a constant flood of words. Using meaningful, grown-up words with children as they enter the toddler and preschool years helps them learn and appreciate new words.

There is support for children's literacy. Snow says:

These were [families] that had bought children books; that ensured that children [were] read to regularly by parents and by other adults; that had pencils, paper, and crayons around and encouraged children to write. [These were] homes in which the parents themselves also engaged in regular reading, got a daily newspaper, or read magazines or books regularly.

A PARENT'S PERSPECTIVE: EVERYDAY TRADITIONS

I started reading to Jimmy when he was about six weeks old. When he was around four months old, we established a bedtime routine that included reading two books aloud. I would tell him that it was "time for books, nursing, night-night." When he stopped nursing and the routine evolved, it was, "Time for bath, books, night-night." Eventually we'd make jokes like, "Time for bath, going to the zoo, night-night"—he thought this was hilarious.

Reading was one of our first rituals together. Now we also have a ritual called "family sing." A couple of times a week, we go into the living room after dinner, play songs on the guitar, and sing. Jimmy plays his own little guitar or drums, or he just sings. "Family sing" has been a nice time to just be together for the purpose of having fun, rather than trying to accomplish anything like eating a meal or getting out the door to preschool, etc. It's been a good opportunity to talk about taking turns, too. Initially, we let Jimmy choose all the songs, but then we decided that we wanted choices, too.

A PARENT'S PERSPECTIVE: SPECIAL TRADITIONS

A close family friend gave us a copy of *The Polar Express* at my baby shower. I read it to my daughter on Christmas, and signed my name and the date to the inside cover of the book. I plan to have a different family member read it to her each year and sign their name until she is old enough to read it out loud to us. Then she can sign her own name and the date. I hope that this will become a family tradition she remembers her whole life.

Preschool also makes a difference. The Home-School Study of Language and Literacy Development found that three quite equivalent factors predicted children's literacy skills. Catherine Snow summarizes the findings:

1. Teachers use "cognitively engaging talk":

This is very much like the kind of talk that we saw in homes around books—asking the children to consider hypothetical situations or to make future plans; asking children to talk about their own lives and how these relate to the stories in the books.

2. Teachers use more complex, sophisticated words when talking to children.

3. Teachers have a content-oriented curricular plan:

These were preschools in which the teachers engaged the children in learning about letters and sounds, about the world, and about how to analyze and think.

HEAD-TO-TOES TASK—AND LITERACY?

A group of researchers headed by Megan McClelland of Oregon State University found that kindergartners with poor skills in *focused attention and self control*—among other learning-related skills—also had poorer skills in literacy and math. Even more disturbing, the gap widened by the second grade and stayed wide when the children reached the sixth grade.

Since this study relied on teachers' views of children's skills over time, McClelland wanted to do a study of children's focused attention and self control that didn't depend on the perceptions of teachers. She and her colleagues gave more than three hundred children the Head-to-Toes Task in the fall of their preschool year. In this five-minute assessment, children are asked to do the opposite of what the experimenter tells them to do. If the experimenter says, "Touch your toes," the children are to touch their heads; if told to touch their heads, the children are to touch their toes. This very simple task, repeated ten times, assesses the skills we explored in chapter 1, on focus and self control—*focused attention, working memory,* and *inhibitory control.* The children have to pay attention to the directions, remember the rules, and inhibit the tendency to go on automatic and follow the directions of the experimenter.

The results are striking. For one thing, the researchers found that having good focus and self control skills predicted the children's literacy, vocabulary, and math skills in the spring of their preschool year. They also found that those children who improved their focus and self control skills made the greatest gains. In fact, their improvement in the skills of focus and self control was equivalent to having an extra month of prekindergarten in terms of their gains in literacy and math skills, and an extra 2.8 months in vocabulary skills.

The researchers also followed children's performance on the Head-to-Toes Task in kindergarten and found that children with strong self control and attention skills in the fall of kindergarten had higher reading, vocabulary, and math scores in the spring. For example, children who scored high on this task in the fall had spring math scores that were the equivalent of almost 3.5 additional months of math learning, 1.7 additional months of literacy learning, and 1.9 additional months of vocabulary learning. In addition, children with stronger self regulation in the fall demonstrated greater *gains* in mathematics over the school year. Focus and self control underlies other skills that are so essential to children's learning.

WAYS TO ENCOURAGE LITERACY SKILLS IN THE EARLY SCHOOL YEARS

In addition to focus and self control, reviews of the literature on what children need in order to develop good literacy skills and become successful readers include the following:

It's about expression. Catherine Snow says it's important to remember that a central purpose of literacy is to *communicate*. That means not losing sight of the forest for the trees and putting excessive emphasis on mechanics such as sounding out letters or learning the alphabet at the expense of focusing on children expressing themselves.

It's about understanding, not drills. Snow also says that a central purpose of literary skills is for children to *understand* what is communicated verbally or in writing. Again, the danger is "drill and practice" that neglects children's comprehension or dampens their understanding and enjoyment of what they're reading.

Surround the process with enjoyment. In fact, Hirsh-Pasek, Golinkoff, and others have written a book summarizing the research on learning and have issued a mandate for embedding the teaching of skills and content in *playful* ways: "learning takes place best when young children are engaged and enjoying themselves."

Connect the visual with the verbal. Judy DeLoache of the University of Virginia and her colleagues note the importance of helping children *understand symbolic relationships* of all kinds—that pictures stand for objects and that the squiggles on a page stand for written words.

Give children a concept of printed words. Dorothy Strickland of Rutgers University and a lead member of a panel reviewing the research on how literacy emerges, for the National Institute for Literacy, points to helping children acquire a *concept of print*—that pages are read from left to right, that there is a beginning and an end of books, a top and a bottom of pages, and a space around each written word.

Talk, listen, discuss, and imagine. Snow writes about providing children with *meaningful experiences with books* by reading aloud and then talking about books so that children can think about, relate to, and interpret what they've read. Strickland notes that children also need experiences in *listening attentively*.

Encourage children to talk about their ideas. Snow goes on to say that while having a strong vocabulary is crucial, children also need to share their ideas by *talking to others*.

Make it fun to crack the code. Learning to recognize letters and their sounds is very important, too. Adults can help children with this knowledge (called *phonemic awareness*) in everyday, fun, and meaningful activities, such as having all the children whose names begin with a "ba" or a "ka" stand together.

Promote expression in all its forms. Snow calls for encouraging children to use many *different forms for self expression,* such as drawing and painting.

LEARNING TO READ

The neuroscientist Stanislas Dehaene has been studying how the brain processes reading. He notes that while children are born with intuitive ways of understanding certain kinds of information, such as shapes and numbers, brains are not prewired to read:

Reading is a completely novel cultural invention. It's very recent—maybe five thousand years old at most—and until a few centuries ago, very few people on earth were reading. So there cannot have been any specific evolution in the brain for reading. It has to be tinkered out of existing brain material. Yet what we can show is we've "recycled" an existing brain circuit, so that with minimal learning changes, [an individual] can become a good reader.

That system is in the ventral [lower] side of the brain and allows you to recognize objects regardless of their orientation in space, regardless of their location, regardless of their size, and other variations.

In Dehaene's book *Reading in the Brain,* he writes that the world's written languages are all based on the same patterns of lines and angles. This is fascinating because, on the surface, it seems so implausible—for instance, English and Chinese seem to have letters that are very different. Dehaene says:

[It is a] fascinating recent discovery that we seem not only to be using the same brain area for all of the world's languages, but [there are] also very consistent cross-cultural regularities in the very shapes [of letters] that are being used in different languages. Mark Changizi has counted how many times you find intersections like Ts and Ls and Xs and Ys in different writing systems including Chinese, Hebrew, and so forth, and has found an amazing regularity in the statistics of how many intersections are present in the world's languages.

But even more interesting is that these statistics match those of the outside world. So if you take a natural scene [such as a landscape] and you just count how many Ts and Ls are present, you find the same statistics as in scripts. So what must have been happening is that our visual system developed a sort of alphabet of shapes. In fact, what you can show by recording neurons in the monkey brain [is] that different neurons encode these elementary shapes—Ts and Ys and Ls—which are present at the corners of shapes in the natural world.

Of course, the scribes [who created written language in different parts of the world] did not know that these shapes were encoded in neurons in the brain, but intuitively, in a slow process of cultural evolution, they selected these shapes because they were easy to recognize by the brain and easy to learn. So in the end, we have a system [that] is extraordinarily efficient because it is well adapted to the existing structure of the brain. The extraordinary result is that all of the world's reading systems map onto the same brain area.

This is true even when it comes to languages that are read left to right or right to left. Dehaene calls this part of the brain where spoken and written language come together the *letterbox*. Understanding how the spoken language and written language coalesce in the brain is crucial for understanding how children best learn to read—and thus how to teach them. Dehaene has mapped this process into stages:

The first stage seems to be a stage where children try to "photograph" words—they use all of their visual system's ability and they treat letters as three-dimensional objects. In particular, they cannot see that there is a difference between b *and* d, *for instance, because for them it's the same object viewed in two different axes—so that would explain mirror errors that children make. They have to build to a second stage, which is [learning] that these are two-dimensional letters and that the letters individually map onto sounds. It's the grapheme-to-phoneme conversion.*

A *grapheme* is a single letter or set of letters that maps onto the unique basic element of spoken language, which is the *phoneme*. When children learn to read, they have to learn the packages of letters that make up graphemes. Understandably, this process of mapping sounds to letters is quite different in different languages:

There are languages that are very transparent, such as Italian—if you learn the pronunciations of individual letters, you can read

Italian; there are very few, if any, exceptions. In French or English, it's much worse—even when you know your individual letters, you still have a lot to learn because you have to learn many exceptions. At the brain level, we see that this will lead to more activation in this letterbox area. For children, it will take them one, two, or three years more to learn the information in English compared to Italian. So it's no wonder that it's difficult to read in English. It is one of the world's most difficult written languages.

At the brain level, reading takes place as a series of successive steps:

The first is in the retina [of the eye], where individual neurons only see small parts of the word. The word has exploded into a million different neurons firing together to represent the word. We think the brain does that by first recognizing singular letters, then putting these letters together so that there will be neurons that care about pairs of letters, and then these neurons themselves are put together into higher assemblies that care about small pieces of words such as prefixes, suffixes, and altogether this will allow you to recognize an entire word.

So in the second stage, [as] children learn the mappings from letters to sound (from graphemes to phonemes), they are very slow because they take the information one chunk at a time. You can see that because their reaction times for reading are directly proportionate to the number of letters. If the word is six letters, it would take them twice as long as for a three-letter word. In adults, you no longer see [this]; in expert readers, we take the whole string [of letters] and it is all processed at once—whether it is a long string or a short string, at least between three and eight letters.

The implication of these discoveries is that children don't read by recognizing whole words, so according to Dehaene, teaching children to look at the shape of whole words is counterproductive:

We should not care about teaching the contours of the word. This is meaningless for the brain. It might even distract children from the actual job [of learning to read]. The actual job is to understand that there are letters and that each of them maps onto sounds, or that combinations of letters map onto sounds. Indeed, educational research shows that the earlier you teach these grapheme-to-phoneme correspondences, the better you teach reading.

Dehaene says that the jury is out on the best time for teaching reading—whether it is at five or six or seven years old—noting that there are very good results from countries that teach children to read at the age of seven. But the jury is *not* out about the importance of playing sound games with children as a foundation of their learning to read:

We can prepare children to read by playing games that are purely sound based, [such as] rhyming games.

He thinks that these techniques can also be useful in preventing or addressing dyslexia. He notes that there are different kinds of dyslexia:

When we talk about dyslexia, we are talking about multiple categories—but it seems to be the case that the dominant variety comes from a problem with spoken language. These children seem to have a difficulty in discriminating the sounds of language. It can be quite subtle, and it may not impair [their] ability to communicate orally, but when it comes to learning to read, it creates a significant difficulty.

There may be another category of children where the deficit comes from the visual level, and, in particular, it may be a deficit in attending to the locations of the letters and being able to scan the string [of letters in a word] in a way that you can really select one unit [of sound] at a time.

What is striking is that all children benefit from [learning] the sounds of letters. Research is showing that even severely dyslexic children can benefit from these methods.

LEARNING A SECOND LANGUAGE

One key finding of the Snow, Dickinson, and Tabors research is that children have better communication skills when they grow up surrounded by rich and meaningful language experiences. What about children who are non-English speakers? Catherine Snow worries about the children who are deprived of rich language experiences in their native languages during this time. She says:

> The possibility exists that [non-English speakers] could be better spending their time expanding their first language, getting a really strong language base in the first language, and postponing the learning of English somewhat. And it would be nice to know whether it would be better for these children to be in first-language preschools or in English-language preschools, in terms of what they're going to do in second, third, and fourth grade later on.

She knows that nonnative English speakers will need to speak, read, and write well in English during elementary school, but she questions the timing and approach.

There are some other common wisdom assumptions that Snow now knows are incorrect:

The evidence clearly demonstrates that there is no critical period for second-language learning. Snow reports that there's no drop-off in the ability to learn a second language and that older and younger learners make similar mistakes when learning a second language, suggesting that they're using similar cognitive processes.

Younger children don't necessarily learn a second language more easily than older children. Snow notes that older learners actually have some advantages. They can apply learning strategies and literacy skills from the language they already know. And, of course, learning a second language depends on the context. For example, younger learners typically learn a language by full immersion in the language. That sink-or-swim approach helps them become more fluent (as it would help older children, too). Nevertheless, younger children who have these experiences often lose their first language in the process, and that is an extremely regrettable loss.

As Linda Espinosa, an expert on bilingualism, says, we tend to see bilingualism as a problem, but it is really an asset, particularly in the global world of today and tomorrow.

Janet Werker points to other assumptions that are not true:

Infants growing up in bilingual families don't get confused by hearing two languages. Bilingual babies can even tell the difference between two languages using only visual clues. Using the "preferential looking" procedure that I've mentioned a number of times in this chapter, Whitney Weikum, an alumna of Werker's doctoral program, exposed English-French bilingual babies to a person on a television screen speaking English—with the sound turned off—until the babies became bored. When that screen person switched to French—still with the sound turned off, the babies perked up and looked longer again, indicating that they recognized that the mouth movements were different in French than in English. This was true at four months and at eight months. Werker notes that bilingual children might engage in occasional *code switching*—using a word in one language when speaking the other language—but that doesn't indicate confusion.

Bilingual children do not experience delayed language development. According to Werker, there is no evidence that children from bilingual families have more or fewer delays or language disabilities than other children. She says:

In fact, the incidence of language delay and language disability in the bilingual population is virtually identical to what it is in the monolingual population.

However, she does point out that the process of language acquisition may differ in small but important ways between bilingual and monolingual children:

> *At about one and a half years of age up to three or four, the total vocabulary size of a bilingual child is equivalent to a monolingual child, but in a bilingual child, it's divided across two languages. In the early stages of [language] acquisition, the bilingual child's vocabulary is probably not as large in each of their languages as a monolingual child's. Is this a delay? We don't think so. We think it's a difference.*
>
> *Sometimes it can appear that [bilingual children] are getting confused for a period of time, but [they're engaged in] a more difficult task. A bilingual baby has to keep track of two sets of sounds simultaneously and set up categories in each. So if it does end up taking them a little bit longer, it's okay. Ultimately what they have is two sound systems, two vocabularies, and two sets of syntactic rules.*

HOW CHILDREN MOVE FROM LEARNING THE TOOLS OF LANGUAGE AND LITERACY TO USING THOSE TOOLS TO COMMUNICATE

Language and literacy are the tools we use to communicate, but they're *only tools*. One can be very literate but be a terrible communicator—and it takes two to communicate, as this all too familiar story from a mother reveals.

A PARENT'S PERSPECTIVE:
I THINK MY HUSBAND CAN'T COMMUNICATE,
BUT HE THINKS I CAN'T

I am sorry to say that I think my husband is lacking in the communication department. I find this amazing, because he manages a business with over fifty employees and it is his job to help others communicate and problem-solve. When he comes home, it seems he shuts that switch off.

Just this morning we had an incident. I usually take my son to and from day care, but today my husband was doing the shuttling. I got up first—I let our three dogs out, fed them, fed the cat, made the baby his bottle, ironed a shirt for my husband, changed the baby's diaper, and dressed him.

My husband proceeds to go into the bathroom to get ready, leaving me to feed a crying, hungry baby. Needless to say, I got upset and yelled that I needed to leave for work, too—I was late. He responded that if that was the case, I was not communicating—I was simply assuming he would know this. It was my fault.

I've accepted that we both need to work on talking—since he feels it is my fault and I feel it is his fault.

HOW CAN YOU PROMOTE COMMUNICATING WITH CHILDREN?

First, a few dos and don'ts.

Do: Remember the purpose of language.

Language is a tool by which people express their thoughts. Everything children are going to learn, they are going to learn through their ability to understand language and to produce language.
—JANELLEN HUTTENLOCHER, UNIVERSITY OF CHICAGO

Don't: Think that using flash cards is promoting communication skills.

There are so many ways that parents and caregivers can encourage language in young children, and it's not through flash cards—it's through conversations, it's through questioning, it's [through] being responsive to what a child is interested in.
—KATHY HIRSH-PASEK, TEMPLE UNIVERSITY

Do: Know that you are your children's most important guide into the world of language.

Think of yourself as [your] child's greatest plaything. Your voice, your face, the things you do, your actions are what intrigue them most. They have a natural curiosity for the things that humans do.
—PATRICIA KUHL, UNIVERSITY OF WASHINGTON

Don't: Think you have to buy expensive products to teach your child about communicating.

Rather than buy fancy software or expensive toys, the thing to remember is that you and your time are the most valuable things to a child.
—PATRICIA KUHL, UNIVERSITY OF WASHINGTON

Do: Listen and be responsive to your child.

Children learn language in a situation where they talk to you about what they're interested in and you respond.
—CATHERINE SNOW, HARVARD UNIVERSITY

Don't: Drown your child in words.

When your children have had enough stimulation, they'll pull away. Be respectful of this and engage them again when they are ready to reengage.

SUGGESTION 1: CREATE AN ENVIRONMENT AT HOME WHERE WORDS, READING, AND LISTENING ARE IMPORTANT.

In order to promote literacy and communication skills, we must exercise them ourselves. Children learn what they see and live.

In retrospect, I see that this is something that my mother did very well. She was always interested in new ideas and new information right up until the end of her life, at almost ninety-eight years. In fact, two months before she died, we used a quote of hers on my organization's holiday card: "If you stop learning, you stop living."

My childhood home was filled with books, which Mother treasured and which my sister and I treasure now. Before I could read, I remember poring over a book of Russian fairy tales with pictures embossed in glossy colors—gold, purple, and royal blue. They sparkled and were just as fanciful as the stories themselves when I was old enough to hear them.

Mother was always reading and talking with us about what she was reading. In the days before book reviews were posted on the Internet and everywhere else, she had a mutually beneficial arrangement with the owner of the local bookstore. Because he couldn't read every new book but knew his customers would expect him to "provide reviews," he enlisted my mother as a reader. Every few days she would return a book she had finished, share her opinion with the bookstore owner, and pick up the next one. Reading was so important to her that the book club she belonged to before she died now bears her name.

I remember Mother reading anything and everything: the print on the cereal box if she was waiting for her coffee to brew, the ads in the local paper for dogs for sale—everything. And I remember dinner table discussions often being about books we were reading—a tradition I continued with my children.

A love of language, of literature, and of the world it can bring to our imaginations is contagious. I caught it from my mother and am happy to have passed it on to my children and others.

SUGGESTION 2: NARRATE YOUR CHILDREN'S EXPERIENCES WITH PARENT-TALK, PARENT-LOOK, AND PARENT-GESTURE.

Talk to your child from the moment of birth on. Think of yourself as a sports announcer, giving a play-by-play description of what is happening: "Oh, you just woke up. Are you hungry?" But, as I've said, be sensitive to the times when the kids want to tune out.

Use parent-talk with very young children. The music of the sound, the variation in pitch, and the slowed-down speech help infants begin to detect the words in the "sea of sound" that surrounds them.

Use parent-look and parent-gesture. If you want your child to pay attention to something, look at it and point to it.

Name what you're looking at. "Look, Ana, there is a bird. It is flying high in the sky." Remember, children are more likely to remember words if you put them at the end of the sentence or if the words follow their names. Catherine Snow points out that the best talk with toddlers is "simple, concrete, repetitive, and responsive."

Elaborate your child's communication. Whether it's a grunt, a babble, a point, or a word, say more when you respond to your child. "You said Ma-ma. Where is Ma-ma? She is over there. Let's go see her."

Use familiar words again and again. Children will be more likely to remember words they hear often: "Where's your nose?" "Where're your toes?"

Play games. Peekaboo and pat-a-cake are wonderful word games. Our favorite game with Philip came from his once opening the door to a room and saying, "No buv-de d'ere," meaning "Nobody's there." We made that into a family game and always opened doors to rooms, closets, and cabinets, asking, "Who's there?" He would respond with his refrain: "No buv-de d'ere."

Use familiar words in new ways. Roberta Golinkoff says:

Think about how many meanings we have for the word "run." You could say, "Mommy's running," "the dog is running," "the stocking is running," "my nose is running," "my temperature is running high."

As your children move into the preschool years, give old words new meanings.

Use new words. Remember Catherine Snow's findings that children who were better at communicating had parents and teachers who used more sophisticated words. I remember that Lara as a little girl would often say, "That's interesting." Finally she asked, "What's interesting?" (She would have said "What does interesting mean?" but she didn't know the word "mean" yet.)

Use nouns, verbs, and adjectives. Children learn nouns first, but you can introduce them to verbs and adjectives by elaborating what they're saying. When they point to a neighbor's dog, you can say, "That fluffy white dog is named Marshmallow. He loves to run into mud puddles, and then he isn't so white or fluffy anymore."

SUGGESTION 3: USE "EXTRA TALK" AND TALK THAT GOES BEYOND THE HERE AND NOW.

In their book *Meaningful Differences in the Everyday Experience of Young Children,* Betty Hart and Todd R. Risley found, on the basis of an observational study of forty-two diverse parents and children at nine months of age and continuing through thirty-six months, that parents use two different types of language in talking with their children.

One is *business talk*—such as "Stop that," "Do this," or "Come here"—that expresses the adult's needs. This language is matter-of-fact, direct, and doesn't involve many words.

The other is *extra talk*—where parents talk about "what if," "remember," and "what do you think," or use other words that respond to, elaborate, and extend what their children are doing or saying. This rich talk, employing a large vocabulary, is a part of the connection (or social "dance," as they call it) between parent and child, and it conveys meaning and intellectual ideas. Hart and Risley found that this extra talk has a very high correlation with children's performance on IQ tests at three years of age and with their performance on achievement tests in the third grade. When the researchers compared the relative importance of children's socioeconomic status, their ethnic background, and the extra talk they experienced, they found that only the extra talk made a difference in children's academic success.

A PARENT'S PERSPECTIVE:
FINDING THE NEW IN THE FAMILIAR

Our son, almost two, also loves his reading time, often picking the same favorites to read over and over again. One of his favorites is *Good Night, Gorilla,* and he laughs each time we get to the part about the gorilla in bed with the zookeeper. While I can recite that book now by heart, he still loves it. I thought I would be sick of it, but we can still find new things to look at in the pictures and new ways of talking about what's happening in the story. Sometimes, after reading a book five hundred times, you start going beyond the written words and start talking about other aspects of the characters, the scenery, or the plot. Last night, we talked about why the gorilla wanted to get out of his bed and sleep in the house with the zookeeper, and why the armadillo had a bottle in his cage (which is a good topic to bring up lately, since we're working on him giving up his last bottle soon).

SUGGESTION 4: TIE YOUR TALK IN TO WHAT IS INTERESTING TO CHILDREN.

Roberta Golinkoff's research has shown that babies are most likely to learn the names of things that they find interesting, but as they gain the ability to take others' perspectives, they can learn what others like as well. She says:

> At twelve months of age, babies learn words mostly from their own perspective. If they like an object and they hear the name for it, they will learn it—but if you try to teach them the name for a boring object, it's very unlikely that they will learn its name. By nineteen months, they can overcome their admiration for a particular object and learn the name even for a boring object.

Many children have what Judy DeLoache of the University of Virginia and her colleagues call "extremely intense interests"—which they define as a long-lasting passionate interest in a category of objects or activities. They describe the story of a baby who was drawn to the globe light hanging over his changing table, which evolved into a passion for balls of all kinds. Philip had that kind of interest in music from as early as I can remember. At three, he would ask for his drum as soon as he woke up. I recorded the following conversation in a book I wrote at the time, so this is not revisionist history. He said: "I want to play my drum. I'm going to have a band, Mommy. Where's my drum?" Several decades—and a doctorate in ethnomusicology—later, he plays percussion professionally and is the director of a music and dance performance group. Music was his "lemonade stand," my metaphor for something children care passionately about. Children's interests are the launching pads for building communication skills.

AN ADULT'S PERSPECTIVE: THE GIRL IN THE TUTU

I've been a passionate student of ballet and dance for fitness (and sanity) over the past twenty-six years. I started in college and have continued ever since. A few years ago, when my mother was moving out of my childhood home, she divided the family pictures between my sister and me. I was leafing through photos of grandparents, aunts, and family vacations when suddenly I came upon a large black-and-white photo of five little girls, about six years old, standing proudly on tiptoe, arms aloft, wearing shiny tutus and sparkly tiaras. And guess who was right in the middle, smiling her heart out? I hadn't remembered taking any dance lessons, but this photo was apparently so important to me at the time that I'd used my beginning writing skills to print on the back, in big, straggling block letters, the names of the girls—in numbered order, left to right—and the color of the tutu. It was an amazing lesson in how that passion was always there, even though I'd forgotten it for a while.

SUGGESTION 5: TELL STORIES ABOUT YOUR LIFE AND ASK YOUR CHILDREN TO TELL STORIES ABOUT THEIRS.

Stories are what bind us together; they are what tell us that we are part of a family or community. They convey our traditions and our favorite memories.

We always told stories when I was growing up; West Virginia retained that southern tradition. Someone walking by my grandmother's porch would stop to talk, and that would launch a story stretching back generations. I felt that stories were a key to unlocking the realities of the grown-up world.

In my family, we have traditional stories, but my children's favorites are the ones that set me off on uncontrollable laughing sprees. Among those is the story about how their uncle Bill had installed a computer device in his home to tell him if anything was going wrong. One day—when something did go wrong—Bill was away from his desk and the computer call went into the switchboard of the bank where he worked. It kept redialing and saying, "The water temperature is . . ." By the time Bill returned to his desk, the central authorities of the bank had been called in to deal with what they thought was a hoax, but it was only "Oscar," as we had named his computer device. Or there's the story about how I once tried to order lemon sherbet in French (*citron*), but I actually ordered a car (Citroën).

Dorothy Strickland suggests taking children to interesting places (like the zoo) and then having them retell the story of the visit. She says:

> *I say kids who are taken places—and I'm not talking about exotic places—are lucky kids!*

SUGGESTION 6: READ, READ, AND READ SOME MORE WITH YOUR CHILD.

Study after study finds that reading with children is a powerful force in their lives and a pathway to better communication skills. Catherine Snow explains why:

Books do something that a pile of toys on the floor doesn't do. [If] you have a two-year-old child, you [are likely to] say, "Go play." The toys are for the child. But the book is clearly something that adults have to help children appreciate.

Nobody expects a two-year-old child to read a book on his or her own. Now, of course, many two-year-old children might look through books on their own, or even pretend to read them on their own. But if you have a new book, the adult has to be there to help the child understand the book. The book creates a platform on which the conversation takes place. [The adult is there to] interpret, to name the pictures, to describe the action, to explain what's going on.

This is one of the reasons why research shows that families in which children are read to regularly are families whose children are more likely to arrive at school ready to learn, with bigger vocabularies and a greater capacity to participate effectively in classrooms. [It's] because they've had this kind of focused conversation with adults.

Snow's point is essential—books provide a forum for a focused conversation. Learning is powerfully enhanced when children and parents are paying attention to the same thing. Researchers call this *joint attention*. Remember the gombie experiment where babies learned language better when the adult served as a vector for the child's attention: looking at, pointing at, and naming an object. Books offer the ideal opportunity for parent-look, parent-gesture, and parent-speak.

When a colleague heard about the importance of reading to children, he thought that the right thing to do was to read as many books a night as possible to his preschooler. But it's your attitude and approach, not quantity, that matter. If reading is a chore for you, it will seem like a chore for your children. If it's a joyful activity, it will be joyful to them. Even if you just get through the first page of a book but you've had a great conversation, you've given your child a great reading experience.

Here are some of the things you can do with books.

With infants and toddlers:

Get books that young children can't harm when they put them in their mouths—heavy cardboard books, laminated books, or cloth books. Also get books featuring things children can do. That's why *Pat the Bunny* is a classic. Many of us remember patting the soft bunny or feeling the scratchy face of the man in the book; now we can share these experiences with our children.

Point out the pictures. Judy DeLoache has found that very young children don't comprehend that pictures stand for or represent something else. She and her colleagues found that nine-month-olds would actually try to lift the pictures off the page. They also tested fifteen- and eighteen-month-olds to see whether they could transfer new information from a picture in a book to the actual object or from the actual object to the picture. Children were shown pictures of objects they had never seen before (for example, a wire egg holder) with a made-up name (a *blicket*). They found that fifteen-month-olds could recognize the blicket if the drawing was realistic, but not in cartoon form, while eighteen-month-olds could recognize both the cartoon and the realistic versions. The implication of this study is that if you want very young children to learn about new things (zebras, for example), realistic pictures work better than cartoon pictures.

Get books with a catchy refrain that children can begin to remember, such as *Hop on Pop* by Dr. Seuss. As children get older, they love to shout out the refrains.

Create traditions for family story time. In our family, until Philip and Lara were in the late school-age years, we had "special time" at bedtime, when each could select books to read with us.

With preschoolers:

Use books as conversation starters. Ask children to put themselves in the place of the characters and imagine what the characters might be feeling or thinking. Using Judith Viorst's book *Alexander and the Terrible, Horrible, No Good, Very Bad Day* as an example, you could ask: "Why do you think Alexander had such a horrible day? What would you have done if you were Alexander? Would you want to move to Australia?" And if your child likes this book, have him or her look for other Alexander books.

What and why questions are wonderful prompts for discussion. Ask your child to guess what is going to happen next and then see if it comes true.

Encourage your children to ask you questions about the stories. If you answer, share your process for finding the answer: "I didn't remember whether the boy in this story had a sister, so I went back to the beginning of the story to find out."

Select stories whose emotional themes resonate with your child. If your child doesn't like to go to new places or thinks there are monsters under the bed or is interested in dinosaurs, there are books on these subjects.

Select stories that play with language. Children are beginning to know letters and their sounds, and there are many clever books on the alphabet or with great rhyming refrains that help children play "sound games." If there's a rhyme in the book, ask your child how many other words he or she can think of that sound like that word (e.g., *rat, sat, pat, brat, scat, fat*).

Know that reading with your child is what matters. Kathy Hirsh-Pasek collaborated with two graduate students on a study of traditional reading versus reading using electronic books (or e-books). As opposed to the interactive give-and-take when parents and children read together, they found:

The e-book is asking questions and demanding answers and the parent [is] left out of the picture. The child doesn't look at the parent and the parent doesn't get to ask a lot of questions. The parents are mostly saying, "Oh, push that button." So [parents become] directors instead of engagers.

For school-age children:

Make reading a family tradition. You can read stories aloud as a family; these times will become treasured memories.

Select books that extend your children's interests. When he was six, one child I know was interested in everything dinosaur. We got him dinosaur posters, books on dinosaurs ranging from reference books to stories, and plastic dinosaurs so that he could act out dramas with them. As Kathy Hirsh-Pasek says, "Books can take us to worlds well beyond their covers."

Help your children begin to read the books themselves when you sense they are ready to do so. In the beginning, they may memorize the words. If so, help them sound them out. You can play a game where you read one word and they read the next.

SUGGESTION 7: PLAY WITH WORD SOUNDS.

You can communicate a love for word sounds from your child's earliest years by singing and dancing together. As your child gets older, here are some games to help your child learn the beginnings of phonics.

Play guessing games with the first letters of words. "I am looking for something in the market that begins with an *a* sound." "Right, it's apples!" "Your dog Betty Poochie's name begins with a *b* sound. Who else in our family has a name that begins with that sound?" "Betsy!"

Clap the syllables while you say the sounds. Beginning with your children's names is always good. Phil-up (two claps), La-ra (two claps), and so on. But you can also use this technique for "I Spy" games: "I spy something in this room, and its name sounds like this," and make one clap. If they can't guess, give them another hint. "It rhymes with *hair*." "Yes, it's a chair."

Help children begin to blend word sounds to make words. They can also play with taking away sounds. For example, "If Fred's name didn't have an *F* in it, what would it be?" "Red!"

Play the alphabet game. Children think of words beginning with each letter of the alphabet and others have to guess the words.

Give children reading assignments when you go shopping. One of mine was that my kids could select any cereal they wanted as long as sugar was listed after the fourth ingredient. When they were smaller, I gave them pictures of products to match and find on the shelf, like the label from the flour we use for our Sunday morning biscuits. Dorothy Strickland suggests making a marketing list and when you take something off the shelf, have the child cross it off the list.

Play with tongue twisters. See if your child can say: "Peter Piper picked a peck of pickled peppers." Use the nursery rhymes and stories from your own culture for these games.

SUGGESTION 8: ENCOURAGE YOUR CHILDREN TO WRITE.

You can encourage writing long before your children know how to write, by taking dictation from them. When he was three, Philip became intrigued with clowns after seeing slightly scary clowns in a neighborhood Fourth of July parade. He did a series of clown drawings (which I still have—they are whimsical and wonderful). I always asked him what he wanted to say about the clowns. He would say a few words, which I would write down. My practice of making books for my children led Lara at age four to make her own books from construction paper stapled together (which I've kept, too). As she learned to write, she would write some of the letters herself.

When children are getting interested in writing, they pretend to write by making squiggles on the page. These should be appreciated. You can ask, "What are you writing about?" Your children may want you to write the actual words beside their words, or they can write them, usually with their own invented spelling. Catherine Snow feels that invented spelling is beneficial because children have to listen very carefully to the word and stretch the sounds out to try to spell it.

One of the first words that most children learn to write is their own name. Write it for them at first, and then help them learn to write it themselves. Lara loved to write her name with different-colored Magic Markers.

In addition to having the children keep journals, the elementary school my children attended did something else I think was a very good practice. They let the children use invented spelling in their journals, and then their "assignment" was to edit their stories. The teacher would underline misspelled words and grammar errors so that the children could correct their own work. They then wrote down the correctly spelled words and their definitions, making their own dictionaries. Their spelling quizzes were based on the words in their personal dictionaries. This technique taught my kids the rudiments of grammar and spelling without killing their joy in writing and communicating by endless drill and practice that disconnected writing from its basic purpose—to communicate.

SUGGESTION 9: SELECT EARLY CHILDHOOD PROGRAMS WHERE COMMUNICATION SKILLS ARE EMPHASIZED.

The research of Snow, Dickinson, and Tabors has shown that teachers make a difference, especially when they engage in *cognitively engaging* talk, use more complex words when they talk with children, and plan their curriculum activities. Similarly, Janellen Huttenlocher from the University of Chicago conducted a study of more than three dozen preschools where she and her colleagues taped the language of the teacher and then evaluated the impact on the children. Children whose teachers used more complex language had higher comprehension levels.

SUGGESTION 10: GIVE CHILDREN ACCESS TO MANY FORMS OF MEDIA COMMUNICATION.

Painting, drawing, sculpture, collages, dancing, singing, playing instruments, making videos, taking photographs—all are crucial vehicles for communication. Many of the most groundbreaking contributions to human culture communicate in nonverbal form. We need to ensure that our children have access to many types of media to express themselves.

SUGGESTION 11: CONTINUE TO PROMOTE THE SKILLS OF FOCUS AND SELF CONTROL.

Numerous activities you can do with your children are described in chapter 1, on focus and self control. In addition, you can do a variation on the "Simon Says, Do the Opposite" task discussed there by playing the Head-to-Toes Task described earlier in this chapter: If you say, "Touch your toes," the children are to touch their heads; if you say, "Touch your head," the children are to touch their toes.

SUGGESTION 12: EMPHASIZE EFFECTIVE COMMUNICATION.

With school-age children, help them analyze their own and others' communication.

When they read something written by someone else, help them discuss how effective it is in communicating. What message do they think the author wanted to communicate? Is this message well communicated? Is it written too intellectually, or does it affect their feelings? Does that matter to them?

If you know any writers, ask them to talk about their writing with your children. If your child has a favorite author, write a letter to him or her. I wrote to my favorite author when I was ten and she actually wrote back. That made a big difference in my life—it made me feel that writing a book was a goal I might someday be able to attain.

Have children look at their own writing through the perspectives of others. What do they think their teacher will say about it? Their grandmother? Their friends? Why?

IN SUM

Janellen Huttenlocher makes a point that aptly summarizes much of the research on literacy and communication skills:

> *It's very important that language be embedded in a positive environment where everybody is thrilled—not about learning language per se, but learning something [they care about].*

Patricia Kuhl echoes this sentiment:

> *As I've watched my own child grow, there are various times and various things that light her up. As parents and as caretakers of a whole generation of kids, we have to be tuned in to the engagement process.*

Children are born engaged in learning. With our help, they will remain engaged. Communication skills extend their learning by giving them the tools not only to learn from others, but to share what they've learned with others. What better gift can we give them than the ability to send their messages into the world?

> Language development is not an end point. It's a process that starts with the very first smiles, the very first gaze, the very first back-and-forth [connection]. That turns into an opportunity for us to label words and for children to map those words together with their ideas, to understand the intents and minds of others, and to express what they want to say.
>
> —KATHY HIRSH-PASEK, TEMPLE UNIVERSITY

CHAPTER FOUR

SKILL FOUR: MAKING CONNECTIONS

When I was in college, there was a statement that was repeated so often by Vassar professors that it became the subject of cartoons in the student magazine. The phrase was: "Everything correlates." While I certainly know from life and from my own statistical research that not "everything correlates," the moments when learning came alive for me then and still does now are those moments when I can see connections among different facts, findings, or concepts. That's when learning soars—when time seems to stand still.

Making connections was a skill that was reinforced by the grading standards to which I was held in college (a B paper typically was one that made good connections among different pieces of information, while an A paper made unusual connections) and it is a skill that has served me well in life—for example, enabling me to see that becoming a parent prompts predictable patterns of growth and development for us as adults, while others studying adult growth ignored parenthood; enabling me to see and study the connections between work and family life, while others were seeing these as very separate aspects of life; and enabling me to see that we should "ask the children" about their views of growing up, rather than just study them from an adult perspective. These three connections have shaped me professionally and personally in profound ways and have allowed me to make numerous other meaningful and lasting connections and contributions—as well as forge richly satisfying bonds with countless people.

AN EXERCISE: "AHA" MOMENT

Select someone who is close to you and ask him or her to recall an "aha" moment—an insight or understanding that changed the way that person thinks about something. Chances are, this insight will revolve around seeing a new connection.

A PARENT'S PERSPECTIVE:
APPLES DON'T FALL FAR FROM THE TREE

Recently I consulted the school psychologist at my son's school because I had a concern about him but thought if I talked to his teachers, they would think I was just being overprotective.

Basically, my six-year-old son Evan was feeling anxious—he was convinced he wasn't doing a good job and that his teachers were critical of him. I wanted to find a way to convey to his teachers that he was a very sensitive kid. When I mentioned my concern to the psychologist, I was surprised that she did not address the issue by making suggestions for how the teachers could speak to Evan; instead, she talked about how *we* could help Evan to see criticism in a less negative light. She said that he often sees neutral, sometimes even positive comments as negative—that we should encourage him to reexamine what actually happened and help him to identify other interpretations for what had happened.

That rang true for me. When he would say things like "The teachers said it was bad," I would ask, "What did they say, exactly?" He would then say that they told him he wasn't doing his "best work" and to "give it another try."

More than that, I had an immediate flash of self recognition (it was me she was describing!) as well as embarrassment. Here I was going to the psychologist instead of Evan's teachers because I had taken some prior encounter with one of Evan's teachers personally. The apple really doesn't fall far from the tree!

When Philip was two years old, he specialized in carrying bags of stuff around. Wherever he went, he usually took an old canvas bag from L.L.Bean with him. Sometimes it was filled with stuff he brought from home; sometimes he filled it with stuff he found in new places. A friend of mine who occasionally invited Philip to visit the group of three-year-olds she taught at Bank Street School for Children used to tell me that Philip would graduate from being two years old with a degree in hauling and carrying.

A closer look revealed that Philip liked to sort the stuff he was carrying. Sometimes he made piles of things that were the same or similar—children's books or toy animals. Sorting by sameness meant that he was also sorting by differences—big Lego blocks were different from the toy animals that inhabited his Lego world. And sometimes he was sorting for how things connected with each other—a big toy clown was the daddy clown and the small toy clown was the baby clown. Little did I know at the time that this sorting was an early manifestation of the essential skill of making connections.

Alison Gopnik of the University of California at Berkeley sees making connections as pathways into children's learning about how the physical and biological worlds work:

> One important thing that they're learning is what categories things fit into—what makes something one kind of thing rather than another kind of thing? What makes a cat a cat? Or what makes a dog a dog? And it turns out that that's a very important thing to understand. If you can sort the world out into the right categories—put things in the right boxes—then you've got a big advance on understanding the world.

Gopnik notes that those who studied children's development into the 1950s and 1960s didn't think that young children had this capacity until they were considerably older:

> Conventional wisdom was that children didn't really put things in categories until fairly late. What we've discovered is that, in fact, from very, very early, children are putting things in categories—spontaneously. If you give eighteen-month-olds or two-year-olds a mixed-up bunch of objects, they'll start putting them into different groups. They'll hand you all of the pencils versus the [toy] horses,

or they'll put all the little boxes in one hand and put all the little bananas in another hand. So already—before they're even talking [much]—children are spontaneously sorting the world out into its different categories.

Making connections involves putting information into categories as well as seeing how one thing can represent or stand for something else. Ultimately, it involves:

figuring out what's the same or similar;

figuring out what's different;

figuring out how one thing relates to another; and

finding unusual connections, often by being able to inhibit an automatic response, by reflecting, and by selecting something that is connected in a different way. This is a competency that children begin to develop later in the preschool years and strengthen throughout their growing-up years. It involves drawing on the *executive functions* of the brain. Furthermore, it promotes creativity.

While children's capacity to categorize emerges at a much earlier age than previously thought possible, a series of studies over the past three decades has found that there are *precursors* to human knowledge and skills that emerge even earlier—in babies' first months of life. Elizabeth Spelke of Harvard University describes these as *core cognitive capacities* that "come on line" before they could possibly have been taught.

Stanislas Dehaene of the Collège de France in Paris refers to one such capacity as a *number sense*—describing the way that infants' brains appear to be wired for math. I use this terminology to describe other awarenesses infants seem to have: an *object sense* and a *space sense*. These cognitive capacities—which are the rudimentary origins of math, physics, and geometry—are the foundations upon which children have many opportunities to enhance their skill in making connections.

As we saw in the previous chapter, children are making connections all the time as they learn to communicate: they're learning that sounds *stand for* words; that words *stand for* people, places, or things in their world; and (eventually) that symbols *stand for* the words they hear and say. They're categorizing the world through language, linking that which is seen, heard, spoken, and written. So while I focus on certain aspects of making connections in this chapter, I hope you'll see opportunities for promoting this skill in all aspects of your children's lives.

AN OBJECT SENSE

Throughout her career, Liz Spelke has been interested in the beginnings of human knowledge. In some of her earliest studies, she explored how infants understand the properties of objects before they could have learned about them from experience.

In what is now a classic experiment, she and a colleague, Philip Kellman, now of UCLA, brought babies into an infant lab, where they sat on their parents' laps, facing a curtained puppet stage. The curtain rises and the baby sees a tall, upright rod move back and forth across the stage. The rod's middle section is hidden by a long block stretching across the middle of the stage, so the baby actually sees only the top and the bottom half of the rod in motion. Spelke wanted to know:

> *If you show a baby a rod whose top and bottom are visible but whose center is hidden behind another object that's placed in front of it, can babies perceive the complete shape of the rod?*

Kellman and Spelke used the *familiarization procedure* that I've written about in other chapters: when babies—like all of us—see something again and again, they become tired of it and pay less attention each time it's repeated. Researchers measure how long young children watch before becoming bored. Spelke describes this particular experiment:

The first time you show a baby a rod [moving] back and forth be-hind a block, they'll look at it for a fairly long time, but if you show them that same [action] again and again, they'll look less and less until eventually their looking time has gotten quite low.

When babies became bored with the first scene of this so-called play—the rod moving back and forth with its middle hidden by a block—they were presented with an alternating second scene: (1) a rod moving back and forth across the stage *without* the block hiding its middle—in other words, the whole rod; and (2) two pieces of a rod—the bottom half and the top half, moving together across the stage, but with a gap in between them. Spelke says:

The idea is that if babies had [perceived there was] a complete rod in the initial presentation [even though the middle portion of the rod was hidden]—and they've now become bored with it—they should con-tinue to be bored when you show them the complete rod and be more interested when you show them the [two pieces of the] rod with the gap.

And that's exactly what they found—the babies were more interested in the rod with a gap, indicating that they perceived the whole object, even when its middle was hidden:

What babies showed, in study after study, was continued boredom with the complete object and greater interest with the two object pieces. We found this with four-month-old infants.

Spelke reports that newer studies have shown the same pattern with newborns. It's a simple experiment, but its finding is quite profound: it indicates that babies' brains appear to be wired to go beyond the imme-diately available visual information and to perceive objects.

This and other studies revealing that children appear to have these inborn capacities from their earliest days were controversial when they were released, but comparable studies have been increasingly reproduced by other scientists around the world. Exactly how to interpret the studies has remained a subject of some debate and discussion among scientists, but it's now more commonly accepted that these findings are valid. Subsequent experiments have shown that the rod has to be in motion for young children to picture it as a whole.

If you think about it, having an *object sense* is a precursor to physics—the science of how objects (or matter), energy, space, and time interact. It's also the foundation for helping children learn how things in their everyday world work—making connections is fundamental to learning. The toddler who repeatedly tosses a spoon from his high chair onto the floor is making the connection between throwing an object and seeing it fall to the floor. You probably never thought of this as an elementary experiment in physics, but it could be seen this way. Young children will test the outcome of this experiment again and again. And they'll test whether you will keep picking up the spoon, so they can throw it again!

A GRANDPARENT'S PERSPECTIVE:
KIDS SOLVING PROBLEMS

When my granddaughter Karen was five, I showed her the finch feeders on my deck and explained that, although I had done everything I could think of to prevent it, raccoons would climb up to the feeders at night and eat all the food. So, I said, I was sorry I had to abandon the bird feeders. I loved seeing the birds—but it was costing me a fortune in seeds.

Without a moment's hesitation, Karen said, "Grandma, why don't you just bring the bird feeders in at night? Raccoons *are* nocturnal, you know." Problem solved.

A SPACE SENSE

Young children also are sensitive to the geography of the space they're in; that is, they have an early *space sense* that helps them find their way.

One of the early experiments to explore this was conducted by Barbara Landau, now of Johns Hopkins University, with Henry Gleitman of the University of Pennsylvania and Liz Spelke.

These researchers had the opportunity to work with a child who had been blind from birth, a two-and-a-half-year-old named Kelli, to see how she navigated space. They set up a lab room to contain objects in four locations: in the front of the room, Kelli's mother was seated in a chair; on the right side of the room was a basket filled with toys; on the left side of the room was a stack of pillows; in the back of the room was a table. Think of these as forming a diamond shape in relationship to one another.

Table

Pillows   Toy basket

Mother

A researcher led Kelli back and forth twice between each of three destinations—her mother and the pillows, her mother and the toy basket, and her mother and the table. At each destination, Kelli stopped to touch what she found there. Then the researcher left Kelli by the table and asked her to either "go to the toy basket" or "go to the pillows." Kelli had never walked these routes before, but in eight of the twelve times she was asked to do so (or *trials* in research language), she took a new and more or less direct route to the goal.

The researchers then moved each object 90 degrees while maintaining their angular relationship to one another. Kelli was successful in five of the eight trials. To determine whether blind children might be more attuned than sighted children to finding their way using geographic clues, the researchers repeated the experiment with three-year-old sighted children wearing blindfolds. These children had a very similar rate of success to Kelli's.

The researchers concluded that children, both blind and sighted, have a sense of space. Subsequent studies of young children without blindfolds in rooms that have other clues, such as the color of a wall, reveal that young children initially use the geometry of the environment—the distance and the angles among the objects—to help them find their way. As they turn three and older, children learn to make connections using clues that go beyond the geometry of the space—such as color or other landmarks. Barbara Landau believes that children represent various spaces in their minds by creating cognitive maps of their environments.

Studies among an Amazonian tribe without any formal schooling, without any experience with rulers, compasses, or maps, and with very few words in their language dedicated to mathematic, geometric, or spatial concepts, also found that children and adults turn to basic geometric principles to locate hidden objects. The researchers see these findings as further proof of the fact that we are wired to have an intuitive understanding of geometry.

I find this a fascinating idea. I have always joked that I am geographically dyslexic. I remember when I was about ten years old, I was asked to ride in a car with my aunt and uncle and direct them to a place where we were meeting the rest of our family for lunch. I had been there hundreds of times, and in the countryside of West Virginia, with its hills, hollows, and rivers, there were lots of landmarks and not that many different roads to try, yet I led them in circles until they finally had to stop and ask for directions. Perhaps I wasn't given enough experiences to make connections between my inborn sense of space and finding new places!

Whatever their directional prowess may be once they are grown up, children's early sense of space provides a foundation for further learning. They use it to develop increasingly complex understandings of place, space, and geometry. Key to this process is children's ability to use what Landau calls the "stand for" relationships between symbols and objects—for example, that a map or a model stands for a real place. The ability to make this connection among symbols typically emerges in its earliest forms when children turn about three.

Judy DeLoache of the University of Virginia conducted a now classic experiment that traces the development of children's capacity to decipher symbols as they relate to what they stand for. In her lab, she created a miniature three-dimensional room (a scale model) of a regular, life-sized room. Both had the same furniture, arranged in precisely the same way. She showed young children both the miniature model room and the real room to demonstrate how the two spaces matched. Then she had the children watch her hide a tiny toy Snoopy dog in a basket on a side table in the miniature room, telling them that a bigger Snoopy (a stuffed animal) was hidden in the same place in the real room. When she asked the children to go into the real room to find where the Snoopy was hidden, she was surprised by what happened:

To my astonishment, I found out that two-and-a-half-year-old children couldn't do this. I had expected it to be trivial—easy for them—but, in fact, it was virtually impossible.

While the younger children seemed clueless about finding the Snoopy in the real room, randomly running around, looking everywhere, such as under the sofa or behind the coach, the three-year-olds could find the big Snoopy right away. Both the two- and three-year-olds in this experiment were able to return to the miniature room and point out where the miniature Snoopy was hidden, so the younger children's failure was not an issue of memory. DeLoache believes that the younger children have great difficulty making the connection between a miniature and an actual room—a skill that matures, but can be influenced by experience, too. Interestingly, two-and-a-half-year-old children were more successful when they were shown a photograph of the hiding place in the larger room—perhaps because it is easier for children to mentally represent the relation of a picture and what it stands for than of a model and what the model stands for.

Children's capacity to make connections between symbols and what they represent is a critical bridge to human knowledge. DeLoache says:

There's nothing that sets human beings apart from any other species on the planet more than our symbolic capacity. If you think about what you know about the world, a vast proportion of what you know comes through symbolic representation.

Herbert Ginsburg of Teachers College, Columbia University, studies the development of mathematical and scientific thinking in young children. One method he uses is to videotape preschoolers at play. These tapes are striking for how much of a space sense (as well as an object sense and a number sense) they reveal in young children's pretend play, especially with blocks. Watching the tapes is like putting on a new pair of glasses to see children in a new way. Ginsburg comments that until his graduate students begin to look at these tapes, they have no idea how much of children's play revolves around exploring mathematical and scientific concepts.

In one tape, for example, two preschool boys are building with blocks. They have built walls and want to put a roof across the top. One child grabs a block and says, "How about if it don't reach?" Ginsburg notes that the child is asking the other child for a plan if the block isn't long enough. It does fit, and they begin to add other blocks to make the roof. One of the children then says, "We need two more," looks again, and then revises his estimate to "three more" blocks. Building on their space sense, these children are continuing to learn about space, shapes, and numbers. What an impressive example of making connections!

AN APPROXIMATE NUMBER SENSE

While I've always thought of myself as being a geographic dyslexic, it is much more common for people to describe themselves as not having a "math brain." In one of our "ask the children" studies of how older children feel and think about learning, we heard that kind of statement repeatedly: "I suck at math" or "I just don't get math." Susan Levine of the University of Chicago notes:

> People don't go around saying, "I'm not a verbal person," very often, but you very often hear people say, "I'm not a math person."

These statements strike home for me because I had a similar experience with Lara. Although she didn't say this about herself until she was finishing elementary school, it wasn't inherently true. She could work herself into a panic when it came to math (and when she did, it led to hysterical homework nights), but if she was calm, math came easily for her, and she almost always did well on math achievement tests. She and I had many conversations about why and how she had "learned" to feel she was bad at math, even though she wasn't.

Susan Levine finds that, indeed, this view is acquired:

What we're finding in our studies is that early input plays a role in whether children are good at math. Thus, whether people consider themselves a math person or not a math person may be related to the teaching they receive. There may be people who are better or worse at math, but not someone who just can't do it.

Infants appear to be "wired" to understand approximate numbers. Among the leaders in this research is Liz Spelke. She was particularly interested in "our abilities to represent and reason about number" because she sees that these abilities, along with geometry, are "the foundations of human science":

It just may be that these abilities are founded on basic core systems of representation that emerge very early in human life and that— at their foundations—are what make it possible for us to become mathematicians and scientists.

Among their first studies, she and Fei Xu, now at the University of British Columbia, investigated whether infants could tell the difference between large numbers and smaller numbers. They brought six-month-old-babies into the same kind of puppet stage setting they used for the rod experiment. The babies sat on their parents' laps in a darkened room with the stage illuminated from above. When the curtain opened, one group of children saw a series of white posters (which Spelke describes as *arrays*) with eight black dots on each; the other group saw posters with sixteen dots:

[Half the babies] first see an array involving eight medium-sized dots and they got to look at that for as long as they wanted. When they looked away [and then looked back], they would see a new array of eight small dots. The dots [would be] in different positions from the previous array, but always the same number. Over trials, they would see different size dots, in different locations, but always eight dots. Over the trials, their looking time would gradually [decrease]. Meanwhile, a separate group of infants is also seeing successions of [dots], but they're always seeing sixteen dots, not eight.

The researchers used the familiarization procedure, presenting the larger or smaller array of dots over fourteen trials or until the baby was truly bored. When that occurred, the second part of the experiment began: both groups of babies were shown alternating posters of eight and sixteen dots. (To ensure that the children were mainly focusing on numbers, all the nonnumerical factors on the posters were the same: the shape of the dots, their brightness, their density, etc.)

Spelke summarizes the findings:

What we found is that babies who were bored with the arrays of eight dots would be more interested when we showed them arrays of sixteen [and] vice versa—the babies bored with the arrays of sixteen were more interested in seeing eight dots.

Subsequent studies have further refined their findings. They found that while six-month-old babies could also differentiate between sixteen and thirty-two dots, they were unable to differentiate (based on their looking time) between numbers with smaller differences—for example, between four and six or between eight and twelve dots. Ultimately, they found that for babies younger than six months, there's a three-to-one ratio—they can differentiate between four and twelve; for six-month-olds there's a two-to-one ratio (babies can differentiate between eight and sixteen or between sixteen and thirty-two); and with nine-month-olds, it's a smaller ratio—differences of eight and twelve.

Spelke also found that babies aren't just responding to the visual difference in the quantity of dots:

> *We found that babies who could discriminate eight from sixteen dots could also discriminate a puppet who jumped eight times from [a puppet who] jumped sixteen times, and if they failed eight versus twelve dots they would also fail eight versus twelve jumps.*

By using listening, not looking time, they also found that babies could differentiate the number of sounds, such as the honks of a car or chirps of a bird or gongs or beats of a drum. They've concluded that babies are wired to have a sense of approximate number. Spelke says:

> *It's hard for me to see how a six-month-old infant could have learned this.*

AN EXERCISE: GIVE YOURSELF A QUIZ

Look at the people in a room. Can you guess how many there are? Look at the cars parked on a street and guess the number. Guess how many seconds it takes the traffic light to change. How well have you retained a sense of approximate numbers?

A NUMBER SENSE—ADDING AND SUBTRACTING SMALL NUMBERS

Very young children also can track differences between one, two, and three objects, well before they know what counting means.

Rochel Gelman of Rutgers University demonstrates this with preschoolers who have been taught and remember the names of a few numbers, but who have *not* mastered the conventional count list of numbers. Still, they have some intuition that there's a one-to-one correspondence between each object and a number, and that each object can only be counted once, not several times. It might take a while for an adult to discover that a young child is working on learning the conventional count list while harboring an idiosyncratic list of her or his own. To illustrate, if you ask them to count three toys, they might say, "Two, three, five," and do so repeatedly. Gelman tells us that about a quarter of beginning counters do this.

A PARENT'S PERSPECTIVE: BLAST OFF

My nineteen-month-old listens to the older children counting in his child care program. Recently he began using numbers to let us know he's going to jump. He says, "Four, five, seven . . ." and then he bends down and attempts to launch into the air.

In a now classic experiment, Gelman illustrated that even very young children have the capacity to understand when something is taken away or added to a small group of objects. She described her experiment to the children as a game:

The game involved putting two [pie] plates on the table. One had three [toy] mice on it; the other had two. We point to the [plate with three mice and say], "That's the winner plate. Every time you find the winner plate you get a prize, and it goes into this envelope over here."

Even children as young as two and a half are able to grasp the "more versus less" concept and learn that the winner plate has more toy mice and the loser plate has fewer:

We cover these plates [and] shuffle them around. Before we uncover them, [the children are] asked to guess which one has the winner. [Then the plates are] uncovered one at a time. If they find the winner, they're given the prize. This goes on—the shuffling, the covering and uncovering—because we want to be sure that they've [understood it].

Then, Gelman says, they pull the research equivalent of a bait and switch. In other words, she or one of her experimenters secretly removes one of the mice. And the children are surprised! They know that there are supposed to be more mice in one plate than in the other. Gelman reports that the children say things like "'Where'd dat go?' Quite frequently they'll get up and start looking around. 'Where is it?' Or [they'll] go look in my pile of things and bring something over and just stick it [on the plate] and say, 'There's three—one, two, three.'"

Gelman and her husband, Randy Gallistel of Rutgers University, note that even before children turn three, they can understand some of the basic principles of the mathematics of natural (counting) numbers; for example, that it is the number of objects that determines the winning plate and that you can change a number by taking something away or adding something.

Karen Wynn of Yale University has also been a leader in investigating children's understanding of math. She found, as have other researchers, that very young children—babies—can differentiate between small numbers of objects, or as she puts it, "they could tell two from three." But did this mean that babies truly had an understanding that these were *numerical* differences—that is, that two is one less than three? Or did it mean that they were just responding to *physical* or *perceptual* differences, as, for example, a "cow might be different from a tree"?

To find out, she set up an experiment using a puppet stage setting and then testing five-month-olds' looking time:

> They would see one little Mickey Mouse doll placed on a display. We'd bring a screen up to hide that doll, and then they might see a hand coming in and holding another doll and placing it behind the screen, too. Then we'd bring down the screen to show the baby the result.

Sometimes the result was expected—"there would be two dolls like there're supposed to be"—because they had seen a hand adding a doll to the one doll already on the stage. But sometimes it wasn't: "Through a secret trapdoor in the back, we might have secretly removed one doll so there was only one."

Would babies look longer at an incorrect outcome (indicating that it was surprising), at the correct outcome, or would there be no difference?

In the example where we start with one doll and [they see a hand adding] another doll, the correct outcome is two and the incorrect outcomes would be one or three. We found that even five-month-olds will look longer at the incorrect outcome.

They also did experiments with subtraction and had similar findings. Not surprisingly, these results were debated by academics when the studies were first reported, but now have been replicated a number of times—not only with babies, but with animals like monkeys and dogs. Academics, however, do continue to discuss what the findings reveal about children's numerical abilities.

Stanislas Dehaene has found that three parts of the brain are involved in mathematical thinking. Although distinct, these brain networks are interconnected and often operate together. There is a *magnitude* system, located in the *inferior parietal cortex* of both hemispheres of the brain, that supports our ability to have a sense of quantity, to compare numbers, and to perform *approximate* calculations. The second area, a *verbal number system*, located in the language area (or what is called the *Broca* area) of the left hemisphere of the brain, represents numbers in spoken and written form and is the part of the brain where *exact calculations* take place. The third area, located in the *occipitotemporal* region in both hemispheres, represents numbers in their *visual Arabic written* form (such as a 5 or 555).

While babies have a number sense before they can talk or even walk, coordinating these complex brain functions takes time and practice. Wynn summarizes:

What we're looking at in the baby's mind is this approximate sense of number, this sense of the magnitudes and how they relate to each other. But you would never expect a baby or any animal to be able to discriminate thirty-nine from forty, or to tell you exactly how many five times six is.

That must be learned. And much of that learning has to do with making connections.

THE GREAT RACE

Robert Siegler of Carnegie Mellon University has pursued a better definition of this learning process: Exactly how does a number sense turn into
mathematic knowledge? And why does this process take hold better in
some children than others? He explains:

> Number sense *is a term that's been around for a long time. People
> use it in everyday discussions as well as in scientific literature, but
> it's always been extremely vague as to what it meant. We were in-
> terested in figuring out what it really means for how children devel-
> op and why some children develop it more effectively than others.*

To study the development of an important part of number sense—
children's ability to estimate—Siegler and his colleagues give children a
series of number lines, drawn on pieces of paper. For example, a number
line might go from 0 to 100, represented by 0 on the left side and 100 on the
right side of the line. The researchers ask children to put a mark where the
12 goes on one piece of paper, where the 18 goes on another piece of paper,
and where the 82 goes on still another piece of paper. Siegler reports:

> *Young children, at first, think that the numbers at the low end of
> the range are larger than they really are. For example, if you have
> a zero-to-one-hundred line and [ask] a five-year-old, "Where does
> twelve go?" they might put it at around where fifty would really go.
> And if you ask them, "Where does eighteen go?" they might put it
> where sixty-five would go. They generate a pattern of estimates that
> rises far too quickly in the low-number range and then slows down
> in its rate of increase.*

In other words, preschoolers and kindergartners tend to plot number lines logarithmically rather than evenly: as the numbers get higher,
the spaces between them decrease. Older children tend to be more accurate, but some are more accurate than others, especially those from more
advantaged, higher-income families.

Siegler and his colleagues focused on estimation because this knowledge affects later competence in math:

We've found that giving children help in estimating the magnitudes of numbers helps them subsequently—all the way from the end of kindergarten through at least elementary and middle school mathematics.

Although when my children were growing up, I didn't know that children's approximate number sense needs to be refined and developed, this knowledge helps me see some of Philip's early experiences with math in a new light.

Philip was a very creative child. Rather than learn standard math, he ultimately invented his own math system. His system was accurate enough—and in hindsight I can now see that it was probably based on estimation—so that he got by at first. But he secretly knew that he didn't know the "school rules" for math and began trying to avoid everything math when he was seven years old. Like a lot of other parents, we tried to help him with his homework. If and when we could cut through his persistent desire to disappear when it came to math homework, we asked him to talk about the way he solved problems. It became clear to us that he didn't know the school rules for adding and subtracting, but he had his own ways of doing these problems.

In retrospect, I made a good call—probably because his rules were so fascinating to me. I told him it was like being bilingual. There was one language for math that was spoken in school, but he had another language for math, and his language was very inventive. We took the issue out of the school realm, because I didn't want him criticized for being wrong or for making mistakes, and instead found a college student who could work with him. We told her that her first assignment was to decipher Philip's math system, to figure out his rules and write them down. He liked working with a "cool" college student and telling her about his rules for math, so that removed some of the drama from the situation.

Once she knew Philip's rules, her next task was to show him the school rules, or language, for math. She helped him see the connections between his rules and the school rules. Importantly, none of us—Norman, Philip's tutor, his teacher (who was enthusiastic about trying this experiment), or I—criticized his rules or tried to get him to discard them. Eventually he learned the school rules, and math homework was less of a tinderbox than it had been, though it took several years after the tutoring ended for Philip to feel really comfortable with math. What I now see is that this tutoring experience built on his number sense, on his ability to estimate, but at the same time helped him learn exact numbers and standard math rules. Furthermore, it helped him make connections between his system and the school system.

A FORMER NON-MATH-LOVER'S PERSPECTIVE: IT TOOK A WHILE FOR MATH AND ME TO GET ALONG

I had terrible problems with math, starting in third grade. I always attributed it to changing schools between second and third grades, and my new school class was much further along with basic concepts of multiplication. I just never really *got* it. For example, I thought all I had to do to learn the "5 tables" (the first such ones we learned) was to memorize the answers *in order*—5 × 1, 5 × 2, etc. It never occurred to me that these could be given out of order (i.e., I had no true understanding of how multiplication was to be used or what purpose it served) until we had the test, which of course I failed—my first test failure ever, and the first of many math test failures.

I finally learned the multiplication tables by relentless drilling en route to school, but I drew the line at learning the 12s. I was exhausted by then and decided that knowing the 11s was quite enough; 12s were unreasonable. Even now, I only know as far as 12 × 5.

It took one loving math teacher who stuck with me to get me to the point where I was finally getting As and Bs instead of Cs and Ds in math. It took from the third through twelfth grades plus this *one* special person who would not give up, to help me crack that code. Ultimately, all of that failure and striving taught me how to fail and how to strive, even when I felt little hope of success. That was the real lesson I learned from math, and it is one I count to this day as one of the jewels of my education.

Philip and the non-math-lover were both very lucky. Had they been in different schools or not had that one special teacher, tutor, or parent, math might have remained a battlefield—and it is just those kids without such advantages on whom Bob Siegler focuses as he works to translate estimation into knowledge of exact numbers:

> We started asking ourselves what experiences other than counting might encourage children to form a good sense of numerical magnitudes, and we started thinking about board games such as Chutes and Ladders.

Siegler and Geetha Ramani, now at the University of Maryland, realized that one of the differences between less and more advantaged children is that more advantaged children play lots of board games. They wondered whether giving less advantaged children experience with these games could begin to promote their knowledge of numbers and reduce the gap between these two groups of children.

So they modified the game of Chutes and Ladders (removing the chutes and ladders) to create an experimental game called the Great Race. In this game there are ten horizontal squares in a straight number line, each marked with a number from 1 to 10. The word *Start* is written by the number 1 and the word *End* by the number 10. The child and the researcher compete, spinning the spinner and advancing one or two squares forward. According to the rules of the game, they have to say the number name of the square they are on. For example, if a child is on 5 and the spinner tells her to advance two spaces, she has to say, "Six and seven." The first person to reach 10 wins.

They also created another version of the game, in which the numbers are replaced by four colors. Let's say that when the child spins the spinner, it lands on blue, and he is on purple. He would say the names of the colors as he advances—"Red, blue."

Overall, 124 four- and five-year-old children from Head Start centers participated. Roughly half played the color game and the other half played the number game five times over four different sessions, totaling about an hour's worth of game-playing experience.

Those children who played the number game (in contrast to those who played the color game) improved in their knowledge of 1 to 10 in their ability to count, to estimate numbers (to mark the correct location of numbers on a number line), to compare magnitudes (to say which of two numbers was bigger), and to identify the correct names for numbers written out as Arabic numerals.

Ramani notes that not only did these skills improve immediately, but they remained strong nine weeks later. In addition, those children who had more experience playing board games at home (but not card games or video games) had better numerical skills than those who didn't play board games very often.

By playing this and other board games, children are gaining content information about numbers, but they're also promoting the skill of making connections. They're learning, for example, that:

The number on the spinner (1 or 2) *stands for* a rule—whether to advance one or two squares.

Each square on the board *stands for* one number—that is, there is a one-to-one correspondence between the number name and the square.

Each number is *connected* to the next number in a sequence, from small to large numbers.

There is a linear *relationship* between the numbers from 1 to 10; that is, each number in the sequence is one larger than the previous number.

AN EXERCISE: PLAY A BOARD GAME

Play a board game with your child or with a friend. How many connections are you making?

So yes, children are born with a number sense, but unless they learn content and begin to master life skills, they aren't exercising and developing this inborn ability.

Siegler says:

Traditionally, parents in the U.S. have viewed mathematics learning as a kind of talent or ability that some people had and some people didn't have. It was nice if you had it, but not really necessary. It's very different in places like Japan. In Japan, [it is assumed] that every normal person will be able to have a reasonable degree of proficiency [in math]. It isn't just a matter of how interested you are—it's something that is an essential part of being a good child and a reasonable adult.

EXECUTIVE FUNCTIONS: LITERALLY PULLING IT ALL TOGETHER

When a child is thinking about numbers, objects, or space, various parts of the brain are involved, but so, too, are the executive functions of the *prefrontal cortex*. Philip David Zelazo of the University of Minnesota, one of the most thoughtful and creative researchers studying executive functions today, has undertaken research that illustrates how making connections is a fundamental part of executive functions.

One of his experiments with toddlers and preschoolers reminds me of my son Philip's "hauling and carrying" bags full of stuff. Zelazo and his colleagues give young children a collection of toys and ask them to put them into two buckets:

In the initial phase of the Reverse Categorization Task, children are asked to sort toys—mommy toys into one bucket and baby toys into another bucket.

Zelazo reports that this task can be difficult for toddlers:

Young children, two-and-a-half-year-olds, have difficulty even making that kind of systematic discrimination—keeping two rules in mind and using them to guide their behavior.

Zelazo finds that most slightly older children can do it:

> *By three years of age, children have no difficulty—they're able to switch quite flexibly between "the mommy item goes here and the baby item goes there" and "the baby item goes here and the mommy item goes there."*

But then the researchers add greater complexity to the task. The children are asked to reverse the buckets—to put the mommy toys in the baby bucket and the baby toys in the mommy bucket. That proves hard even for three-year-olds. Interestingly, they can state the rules out loud, but just have a hard time following them until they are older.

This is a task that calls on many aspects of executive functions. Children not only have to remember the two rules (*working memory*), but in switching the buckets they must inhibit an automatic response that they've just learned (*self control*) in order to do the opposite (*cognitive flexibility*). They're making one set of connections, quickly followed by a new set of connections.

Another measure Zelazo uses that taps into these skills to a greater degree is called the Dimensional Change Card Sort. In this task, children are shown a deck of playing cards. Each card has one of four different pictures on it: (1) a blue star, (2) a blue truck, (3) a red star, or (4) a red truck. The experimenter begins by telling the child that they are playing the *color* game. There are two boxes with slots for the cards. The experimenter shows the child that red things go in one slot and blue things go in the other slot. Zelazo explains:

> *Children are told explicitly which rule they should be using on every single trial. So they're told to remember, "If it's red, it goes here. If it's blue, it goes there."*

As with many tasks involving executive functions, the rules change. The experimenter tells the children they are going to switch and play the *shape game*. In that game, all the star cards go together and all the truck cards go together. Three-year-olds have difficulty when the rules switch. If they've been playing the color game, they keep sorting by color:

> *You [say to] a child who's sorting by color but is being told to sort by shape, "So we're playing the shape game now, right?" And they say, "Right." And you say, "Okay, where do the stars go?" And they'll point to the right box. And [you say], "Where do the trucks go?" And they'll point to the right box. And you say, "So, where does this truck go?" And they'll turn around and sort it by color.*

It doesn't matter whether the experimenter begins with colors or shapes—young children seem to stay stuck on the original dimension, even when they can state the rules out loud. When asked why, Zelazo says:

> *Young children seem to have difficulty stepping back and reflecting on the fact that they know the color rules and they know the shape rules and they need to make a deliberate decision about which pair of rules is relevant at a particular moment.*

Another measure Zelazo uses is called the FIST (the Flexible Item Selection Task), developed by Sophie Jacques for preschoolers. Here the experimenter sets out three cards, each showing a picture (for example, of a large red boat, a small blue boat, and a small yellow teapot). The experimenter asks the child to pick out "two pictures that go together in one way," without any explicit directions about which way they might go together—that is, to make connections. The child might match the large boat and the small boat. Then the experimenter asks the child to pick "two pictures that go together in another way." Again, the instructions aren't explicit. The child might select the small blue boat and the small yellow teapot because both are small.

Being able to make connections—unusual connections at that—involves in this instance *remembering two rules at the same time, inhibiting an automatic response, thinking flexibly,* and *reflecting.* Reflection is critical, Zelazo maintains, for children to succeed on these tasks. Reflection involves stepping back, considering alternatives, and then acting, drawing on a higher level of consciousness that begins to become possible at four years of age and above.

Why are these abilities important? In an article for families, Zelazo writes that the development of these capacities provides many new cognitive possibilities for children, enabling them to understand more complex rules, to reason about what is right and wrong, to better understand their environment, to plan, and to make decisions, as well as to consider others' perspectives and predict their behavior. These are the capacities, Zelazo says, that enable children to be ready for and succeed in school.

Learning to make unusual connections also promotes children's creative thinking. Adele Diamond of the University of British Columbia says:

The essence of creativity is to be able to disassemble and recombine elements in new ways.

In so many conversations with employers, I hear them bemoan the absence of creative thinking in employees. As I noted in the introduction, Kathy Hirsh-Pasek rightly observes that facts are "at your fingertips" in today's world, so the person who stands out is the person who can make connections among things that are known, to come up with solutions and innovations not yet known or even imagined.

THE LINKS BETWEEN CREATIVITY AND SOCIETAL SUCCESS

Professor of learning research at MIT Mitch Resnick thinks that the ability to make unusual connections—to think creatively—is fundamental not just to children's success, but to our society's success. He says:

For a number of years, people have realized that our society is going through a transformation from the industrial society of the nine-

teenth century that was sparked by the steam engine and the rise of factories. People have been searching for ways of thinking about the nature of this new society. There's no doubt that information is much more important than it ever was before. We also know that we're drowning in information.

We're now talking about the "Knowledge Society," [but] it's not just about access to information but our ability to build knowledge based on the information we have access to. As I look ahead, I think the key to success in the future (and the key to satisfaction in the future) is not just going to be how much we know, or what we know. I think that the ability to think and act creatively will be the key distinguishing quality that will allow people to succeed and be satisfied in their lives.

THE ARTS AND THE BRAIN

AN EXERCISE: WHAT COMES TO MIND WHEN YOU THINK OF THE ARTS?

Think of a list of words that you associate with art. What's on your list?

Did you have any words that describe how the arts contribute to the richness of our lives?

Did you have any words that emphasize a direct connection between the arts and cognitive achievement?

I wouldn't be surprised if you used words that describe how the arts contribute to the fullness of our lives, but I would be surprised if you also included words that emphasize the connections between the arts and other cognitive endeavors. Many people don't know about these connections. Why else would the arts be among the first on the chopping block when school budgets face a difficult economy or pressures to increase test scores? Why else would people see the arts as helping us be "well rounded," but not emphasize the links between a pursuit of the arts and other more intellectual measures of attainment?

Studies, however, tell a different story. Michael Gazzaniga of the University of California at Santa Barbara notes that for a number of years, studies have shown that there is "a correlation between kids who go into the arts and academic performance." What was not known is why. Gazzaniga continues:

Is this correlation because [these kids] have more "get-up-and-go," or is there actually something about [the arts] that changes, increases, and improves cognitive skills?

In response to this question in the scientific field, the Dana Foundation convened a consortium to investigate learning, arts, and the brain and produced its findings in a 2008 report. Gazzaniga, the chair of this inquiry, describes its findings:

There is growing evidence that learning of the arts—whether it be music, dance, drama, painting—has a positive impact on cognitive life.

There are at least two pathways by which learning of the arts affects cognitive life. The first is through an increase in focused attention: involvement in the arts improves children's focus—that is, their ability to pay attention—and that affects other cognitive skills.

The second pathway is through an increase in motivation:

An interest in a performing art leads to a high state of motivation that produces the sustained attention necessary to improve performance and the training of attention that leads to improvement in other domains of cognition.

I've discussed in other chapters how a child's passion (what I call their "lemonade stands") can drive learning. The scientists, however, don't discount the notion that some children may be more motivated to pursue the arts than others, and this, Gazzaniga says, relates to temperamental (or biological) differences among children:

As you practice, it's appealing to your motivational system [and] it's appealing to your temperament. All of a sudden, one hour of practice a day isn't enough—it's got to be two.

A few weeks after interviewing Mike Gazzaniga, I participated in a May 2009 summit on learning, arts, and the brain convened by Johns Hopkins University and designed to amplify the work of the consortium. At the summit, Michael Posner of the University of Oregon, a member of the consortium (and profiled in chapter 1, on focus and self control), amplified this finding that when children have training in the arts, they learn to pay attention, to stay focused, and to resist distraction, noting that these skills lead to improvements in "fluid intelligence and in IQ."

The Dana report outlined a number of specific connections between training in the arts and cognitive skills:

links between the practice of music and skills in geometry;

correlations between music training and learning to read, perhaps through an increased ability to differentiate sounds; and

connections between training in acting and improvements in memory.

In addition, the report stated that people who have dramatic training in high school score more highly in social situations than people who don't. Gazzaniga says:

In acting, you have to imagine the other person's mind. Empathy building, perspective taking—the world would be a lot better off if people could do that more often.

A study by Martin Gardiner of Brown University and his colleagues sheds light on the importance of sequenced skill development in the arts. In this study, children in eight first-grade classrooms in public schools participated. The children in four of the classrooms received an intense music and arts curriculum that emphasized sequenced skill development, while the children in the other four classrooms received the school systems' regular music and art curriculum. The children in the experimental classrooms happened to begin the program significantly behind those in the regular classrooms but ended the year catching up to them in English achievement and surpassing them in math. Gardiner explains that this program emphasizes more than the facts in that it teaches children "how to think."

When I asked Gazzaniga why the arts are so important—beyond their contributions to cognitive attainment—he replied that he feels the arts may have survival value in enabling us to reach beyond ourselves, to imagine, to understand metaphor, and perhaps to prepare for the unknown.

Because the arts have been under siege in school budget cuts, I asked Gazzaniga to reflect on the place of the arts in our educational system. He hopes that the research being conducted by the Dana Foundation will make the arts more credible as being valuable in and of themselves as well as playing a role in "achieving overall scholarly academic improvements." Perhaps if this knowledge were more widespread, the arts might not be cut back, he says.

Making usual connections and making unusual connections happen in many forms of learning, from science, math, language, and the arts.

This chapter has a deliberate trajectory. It begins with a discussion of children's inborn capacities—an object sense, a space sense, and a number sense—and discusses how these are the origins of physics, geometry, and math. It then moves into a discussion of executive functions of the brain, concluding with creativity. That's because all of these are tied together—connected—in the skill of making connections. We make connections as we build on our seemingly inborn capacities in these domains, and we can make unexpected connections as we reflect on what we know in new and creative ways.

HOW CAN YOU PROMOTE MAKING CONNECTIONS IN CHILDREN?

Babies are deeply driven and passionate about understanding the world and understanding the people around them. A baby's whole essence is about plugging into the world.

—KAREN WYNN, YALE UNIVERSITY

SUGGESTION 1: GIVE CHILDREN MANY OPPORTUNITIES TO SEE CONNECTIONS IN FUN AND PLAYFUL WAYS.

Karen Wynn finds that we promote learning on the deepest level when we tap into children's passion and enthusiasm and build on it. There are many opportunities to help children see connections that build on their interests and passions. For example, when Philip became interested in superheroes, we introduced him to superheroes of the past—knights in shining armor. That led to a few years where he was fascinated with knights in history: reading about them, playing games about them, and writing stories about them.

A PARENT'S PERSPECTIVE: THE WEATHERMAN

My older son loves weather. He's gained a whole new vocabulary by learning weather terms. He's also become quite proficient on the computer, because the first thing he wants to do in the morning is check the weather on www.weather.com. Just to check the weather, he's had to learn how to turn the computer on, spell the password and then type in the Web site name, use the mouse and find the letters on the keyboard, and then navigate different pages on the site to find hourly, daily, and weekly projections. His teacher now lets him be the weatherman at school. He clips the weather section of the newspaper and brings it in to share with the class. Each day he fills in the high temperature on a weather graph bar chart. It's been a great way for the teacher to help the class learn about graphs and weather.

SUGGESTION 2: ACKNOWLEDGE THAT MAKING MISTAKES IS NOT ONLY OKAY, IT IS A PART OF LEARNING.

Making errors is fundamental to learning. Some errors have to do with the process of learning—we often don't get it right until we get it wrong first.

Other mistakes can be developmental. As an example, Liz Spelke notes that young children can have a very difficult time seeing certain kinds of connections, such as figuring out which puzzle pieces fit into three-dimensional puzzles:

> *[Let's say] you have a box with a triangular-shaped hole in it, and you give a child two blocks and ask the child to pick the block that will go into the hole. One of the blocks is the shape of a triangle and the other is the shape of a circle. This is extremely difficult for children up to two years of age. You will see the child picking up any object and pushing—as if somehow pushing or wishing is going to make the thing go through.*

This kind of task can be difficult for adults, too. Spelke reminds us of the face-vase illustration, below. Can you find the faces in the vase?

It is impossible for us to see the faces and the vase at the same time. When your children make mistakes, remember that, in Spelke's words: "some of the errors that children are making spring from the way we understand the world, and continue to apply to us as adults." Rather than being judgmental or critical if your child makes a mistake, talk to your children the way you would like to be talked to when you make a mistake: "That is really close," or "That is hard and you are really working at it."

SUGGESTION 3: PROMOTE AN OBJECT SENSE. PROVIDE MANY EXPERIENCES WITH HOW OBJECTS FUNCTION.

As a parent, I always looked for what I thought of as open-ended toys. These were toys that had "sticking power," toys that my children could use, assemble, and reassemble in many different ways—things like balls, different kinds of blocks, and figures representing people and animals. My children could use these to make sense of the world and to create their own experiments.

The bathtub was a perfect place for experiments with objects. At three, Lara went through a phase I not so fondly referred to as the "dirty hair club." She *hated* to have her hair washed. By hanging out with other parents, I found that many of their kids belonged to the same club, and they gave me lots of ideas for ways to make sure that Lara had clean hair, every once in a while. Many of them involved experiments in the bathtub with how objects function—little boats that we could try to sink, bubbles that she could blow with soapy water. But the best solution was to put an unbreakable mirror in the tub and let her create shampoo sculptures with her hair, making all kind of funny shapes. She was learning about science—and she was getting clean!

A TEACHER'S PERSPECTIVE:
IT'S HOT ENOUGH TO FRY AN EGG

Many years ago a very curious little boy was in my child care program. One very, very hot summer when he was four and a half years old, I reminded the children that we needed to put on sunscreen before heading outside. This little boy said, "My father told me you could fry an egg outside today!" Another child laughed, and the first child looked at me and said, "Can you?"

I decided to use this as a way for us to learn about the strength of the sun. We cracked an egg into a small metal pan. Then we placed the pan outside on the front walkway. We set the kitchen timer to check every twenty minutes. After forty minutes, the white of the egg began to change. The little boy was very excited, and he shouted, "I think my dad was right!" After about three hours it was clear to everyone that the egg was cooking in the sun. Not only did this demonstrate how to scientifically test an idea, but it allowed the boy to feel very proud of his father. The mailman, on the other hand, was distressed when he saw the egg!

SUGGESTION 4: PROMOTE OBJECT, SPACE, AND NUMBER SENSE BY GIVING CHILDREN MANY OPPORTUNITIES FOR EXPLORATION AND FOR PRETEND PLAY. BUILD ON THEIR INTERESTS BY PARTICIPATING AS "GUIDE," NOT "BOSS."

Roberta Golinkoff of the University of Delaware and Kathy Hirsh-Pasek of Temple University and their colleagues conducted an experiment they call the MegaBloks Study to determine what kind of play experiences contribute to an understanding and use of language related to space.

Golinkoff explains that there were three conditions in the study. In the first, children between the ages of three and four and a half years old were presented with a prebuilt block structure and invited to play with it. In the second condition, children were given blocks and told what to build. In the third condition, children were given blocks and simply invited to play. At this point, children in the three groups were shown a card with a picture of a structure and asked to re-create it. The researchers found that those children in the third condition who were able to use the blocks simply to play—to create structures for themselves—used many more words and concepts related to space and math than the other two groups. Golinkoff says that the children in the free play situation used words like *next to, in front of, behind, littlest, biggest,* and so forth. She concludes:

When we give [children] toys that are preassembled or that ask for one right answer, we minimize the amount of spatial language. This is important because spatial language serves as the basis for understanding how we navigate in the world as well as for many mathematical concepts.

The researchers also evaluated how learning changed when the children's parents helped them address problems they were facing in building, such as how to get a block into the "middle" of the structure. According to Kathy Hirsh-Pasek:

> *When a parent joins in, we call it "guided play," and it always elevates the level of play. So parents shouldn't feel like they have to stay out and let the kids play on their own—they should join in, but they can't be the boss. They have to follow the child's lead and talk about the kinds of things that the child is interested in.*

You are being the boss if you take over and start telling children what to do, such as "Put the block here, don't put it there." You are being a guide if you ask questions such as "Where do you think this block should go? Hmm. Looks like it doesn't fit. Do you think it is too long? Can you find a shorter block?" You are also being a guide if you describe children's experiences, such as "You made that building really tall."

In a paper summarizing math education today, Herbert Ginsburg and his colleagues write that play in and of itself is not enough to help children *mathematize*—"to interpret their experiences in explicitly mathematical form and understand the relationship between the two." That's where you come in! If you listen carefully to your words when you are guiding children's play, especially with objects, you will find that one of the things you are doing is helping children bridge (or make connections among) their experiences and larger concepts of quantity and space.

AN EXERCISE: GUIDED PLAY

Think about a time when you took over your children's play and a time when you guided them. What is the difference in these two approaches? How did your child respond to the different approaches?

SUGGESTION 5: USE WORDS TO DESCRIBE SPACE.

Recently one of my colleagues brought his fourteen-month-old son to a staff holiday party. The child gravitated to a large empty carton that had contained a gift and climbed right in. Of course many of us surrounded him as he played in the box. Someone would scoot the box forward and say, "Do you want to go ahead?" Then she or he would pull the box backward and say, "Back we go!" After this child had played "train" around the office for a while, he discovered the box had a lid and pulled it over his head. That, of course, prompted a peekaboo game with many more words related to space: *inside, outside, up, down,* and so forth. Using this language and tying it to everyday fun experiences is the way we make connections between what begins as a space sense but extends to more complex concepts and descriptive language.

SUGGESTION 6: PLAY GAMES THAT INVOLVE CHILDREN FINDING THEIR WAY IN SPACES.

Hide-and-seek is the classic game for promoting space sense. It can entail people hiding or objects being hidden, and it can have many variations that add excitement, novelty, and challenge. Make the game more elaborate for older children by giving geographic clues: "It is on the left side of the room." When the children get older, play Treasure Hunt. For Philip's birthday parties, we used to have treasure hunts, writing silly (and intentionally confusing) rhymes for clues. Treasure hunts, especially when they are challenging, are fun for both kids and adults.

When you are driving somewhere, have older children help track where you are going either by using a map or, if you have one, by a GPS system. With younger children, you can narrate your navigation: "Now we'll drive down this street until we see your preschool on the left, and we'll turn left into the parking lot. That will be in one, two, three blocks."

SUGGESTION 7: TALK ABOUT QUANTITIES IN MANY WAYS.

As noted earlier, three different parts of the brain are involved with numbers—one for approximate numbers, one for verbal numbers, and one for written Arabic numerals. Susan Levine emphasizes the importance of talking about number and quantity in a variety of ways. In a study she and her colleagues are doing in classrooms serving children of different socioeconomic levels, they've learned that the teachers' "language of mathematics" makes a big difference. She reports: .

> *What we're finding is that the kids whose math knowledge increases more over the school year are [those in] the classrooms where the teachers are talking more [about math ideas]. It doesn't matter if it's a Head Start classroom, where the kids, on average, [come from] families with lower incomes, or a middle-income, tuition-based nursery school classroom. What matters is what's going on in the classroom and what the teacher is doing. Preschool teachers can have a big effect on [children's] lives just by talking about shapes, numbers, [and] quantity with kids.*

Levine says that it's not just what is said but how it's said that matters. As an example, she describes teachers who talk about three in words, but also hold up three fingers:

> *That gives the child a lot [more] information—they're saying "three" and they're showing them what a set of three things [is].*

Levine makes it clear that she is not advocating handing out worksheets to kids but using *math talk* in everyday, real-life conversations and situations, such as: "Give each child two cookies" or "Today is Wednesday. How many days have we been in school so far this week?"

Children are thus making connections between numbers and their everyday life experiences.

A PARENT'S PERSPECTIVE:
WHY SO MANY "WHY" QUESTIONS?

We count things during our walks with our three-and-a-half-year-old daughter. Recently we counted the flowers in the neighbors' yards. Sometimes we count the clouds when we sit outside or in the park. These games not only teach her to count, but they also help us keep the conversation moving from object to object and allow her to notice new things. By noticing new things, she asks numerous questions about them, and all the questions begin with "why." My wife and I learned to love and hate the "why" questions because they are so challenging!

SUGGESTION 8: GIVE CHILDREN FAMILY WORK THAT INVOLVES COUNTING.

There are numerous opportunities to use counting as a part of family life: making grocery lists, determining how many people will be home for dinner and then counting out the correct number of napkins and utensils, cooking, saving money for things children want to buy, using calendars and checking off each day, to name just a few. When they were school-aged, Philip and Lara had seasonal clothes allowances (to avoid the "gimmes," I made them responsible for budgeting and buying their clothes). Managing their allowances to decide whether they could afford a high-priced pair of sneakers and what they'd have to give up if they bought them involved no end of financial calculations, as well as self control.

A PARENT'S PERSPECTIVE:
HOW MANY SECONDS UNTIL WE GET THERE?

When my children were toddlers and young preschoolers, I would encourage them to touch things to be sure they counted each one. Later we also used counting to help them handle impatience (waiting for the toaster to pop or to get somewhere on a trip) or calm down from a fit. As they've gotten older, we've started counting in more complex ways: by twos, evens and odds, and by keeping time—counting seconds and minutes.

SUGGESTION 9: BUILD ON CHILDREN'S SENSE OF APPROXIMATE NUMBERS.

Liz Spelke believes that we can help children understand exact relationships among numbers by building on their sense of approximate numbers. She has been experimenting with incorporating children's sense of approximate numbers into concepts of addition and subtraction for kindergarten classes. Rather than give children exact numbers to work with, Spelke and her colleagues give them word problems:

We use cartoons, and we say, "Here's Mary. Mary's got twenty marbles in this bag, and now she gets fifteen more." And then we say, "Here's John. He's got fifty marbles. Who's got more, Mary or John?"

She notes that children can use their sense of approximate numbers to answer the question, and many do it very well.

Spelke then wanted to know if approximate number sense could be used to help young children begin to understand the inverse relationship between adding and subtracting—something that can be hard to grasp using exact numbers:

If you give a child a problem like the following—"Mary's got twelve marbles. She gets seven more and then her sister takes twelve away. How many marbles does she have?"—children will go, "Let's see: twelve plus seven equals twelve, thirteen, fourteen, fifteen. . . ." They'll try to do the exact calculation instead of realizing that twelve minus twelve equals zero, so there must be exactly seven that are left. So then we went on to ask, "Suppose now we present the problem using only number words, [asking], 'Does Mary have more or fewer marbles than her sister?'"

The quantities must differ by a significant amount for younger children to be able to figure out the answers using their approximate number sense, but through this and other word problems, children can gain experience with the fundamental concepts of addition and subtraction.

Rochel Gelman, too, has found that building on children's sense of approximate numbers is a very effective pathway into math. When children as young as three make numerical predictions and then count to check themselves, their counting is better than if they only count.

Bob Siegler's research has concluded that children who play more board games have a better sense of numbers than those who do not. This includes any games where children spin a spinner or throw the dice and move a playing piece forward or backward.

Most children's board games provide opportunities for making connections through matching—animals, letters of the alphabet, and colors. Dominoes is a great game for both matching and counting.

SUGGESTION 10: DEVELOP GAMES THAT ADAPT THE RESEARCHERS' TASKS FOR MAKING NEW CONNECTIONS.

Many of the tasks used by the researchers I've interviewed that draw on executive functions of the brain can be adapted as games you can play with your children. Remember, however, that executive functions are orchestrated by the prefrontal cortex of the brain, a part of the brain that doesn't really begin to mature until kids are older preschoolers. So while you can play some of these games with younger children, it's important not to push children beyond their developmental capacities—an experience that would be frustrating for you and even more frustrating for them. Games must be fun in order to be effective, so if you find that your children don't want to play, stop and wait for a better time or a better age.

With two-year-olds, you can play sorting games. When my children were young, I bought a series of big colorful plastic stacking containers to aid and abet Philip's joy in sorting. In one, we had big Legos; in another, we had plastic animals that Philip and Lara could use in their Lego constructions; in another, we had small table blocks for further building; and in another we had stuffed animals. Both children mixed and matched the contents of these containers (and the containers themselves) in any number of ways. And when it came time to clean up, that, too, became a sorting and categorizing game.

With two-year-olds and older, you can also make your own playing cards. Phil Zelazo uses pictures of everyday objects such as stars and trucks for the Dimensional Change Card Sort, but you can use any kind of picture. For example, cut and paste pictures from magazines or from copies of your children's drawings, or print out clip art from the Internet. You could also build on your child's passions: if your child loves dogs, use different images of dogs (black dogs and white dogs, dogs with spots and dogs without spots).

With two-year-olds and older, you can play the color game, where children put all the pictures of one color together, or the **shape game,** where children put the same objects together, or the **size game,** where children put all big objects or little objects together. Don't try to switch the rules (from the color to the shape game) with children under four, however. That's a skill they will obtain later.

You can make this game more complex for children between five and seven, as Zelazo does in his research, by embedding the rules in the cards. A black border around the edge of the cards means that the child is to play the color game, while no black border indicates that the child will play the shape game.

At four and older, you can play the Reverse Categorization Task, where children first sort toys in the baby bucket and the mommy bucket and then switch and put the baby toys in the mommy bucket and the mommy toys in the baby bucket.

Create a game like the Flexible Item Selection Task (FIST). Here you set out a series of three cards, each with a picture (for example, a red dog, a black dog, and a black cat). You can ask your child to pick out "two pictures that go together in one way"—without any explicit directions for how they might be matched. Your child might pick the two dogs. Then you can ask your child to pick "two pictures that go together in another way." Your child might pick the black dog and the black cat because both are black. You could also ask: "How do all the pictures go together?" (All the animals have fur . . . tails . . . noses . . . mouths . . . eyes . . . etc.) You can make lots of different cards to promote this kind of sorting.

SUGGESTION 11: PROMOTE MAKING NEW CONNECTIONS BY GIVING CHILDREN FEEDBACK ON THEIR THINKING.

Zelazo reports that some studies have found that giving children feedback on the Dimensional Change Card Sort improves their performance on the tasks. Specifically, children were helped to see the cards in different ways. They might be told: "This card shows a yellow flower, so if we are playing the color game, it would go with the yellow car, but if we are playing the shape game, it would go with the red flower." This kind of feedback helps children to reflect and see different possibilities for making connections.

SUGGESTION 12: HELP CHILDREN SEE THINGS IN DIFFERENT WAYS.

Above, we talked about the vase-face illusion. Looking at illusions provides good practice for older children in making new connections. For example:

Can you find the older woman in this drawing of a young woman?

Can you find the rabbit in this drawing of the duck?

If you enjoyed these, here is a Web site for older children that you and/or your older children might find fun to look at, too: http://kids .niehs.nih.gov/illusion/illusions.htm.

CHAPTER FIVE

SKILL FIVE:
CRITICAL THINKING

When Lara was in preschool, she came home from a friend's birthday party with a drawing she seemed particularly proud of. It was of a birthday girl—more stereotypically drawn than her usual whimsical style—but she had signed it at the bottom with her trademark loopy *L*.

We had a gallery of our children's drawings displayed along the hallway walls—from Philip's clowns to his dragons, monsters, and fantastical machines; from Lara's colorful abstractions to her "dal-may-shi-on" series (her pronunciation for the Dalmatian dog that she was pressuring us to give her). The birthday girl drawing was hung prominently in the gallery.

A few months later, we had a group of Lara's friends and their families over to our house. Spotting the birthday girl drawing on the wall, one of her close friends ran over to it and said, "That's *my* drawing. I did it. I want it back!"

We handed the drawing to its rightful owner. Lara had conveniently disappeared, but uncharitable thoughts were swarming through my mind. I pictured her as a teen, lying about where she was going, wearing provocative clothes, driving recklessly, hanging out with the wrong people, living dangerously. I suddenly remembered the time when she had taken money from my purse but insisted she hadn't taken it, though the evidence of the crime—the money—was grasped tightly in her hand. In my mind, my beloved child turned into a scheming liar, a future juvenile delinquent, in a flash.

Fortunately, because some time elapsed between the other kids leaving our house and my having the opportunity to confront Lara, I could calm down before I acted. I realized that in order to help her learn to make thoughtful decisions, I had to make thoughtful decisions about how to teach her.

We had a traditional process for problem solving in our family, so while I was making polite conversation with the other parents at our house, I was deep in thought, trying to apply this process to the situation:

1. Identify the dilemma, problem, or issue. At the time, I would have just said, "What's the problem?" but now I sometimes use the word *dilemma* because *problem* implies that there's an immediate solution, whereas so many of the situations we deal with as parents aren't clear-cut. In his book *Get There Early*, Bob Johansen of the Institute for the Future makes the point that most of the issues we address in this day and age are dilemmas rather than problems because they don't have easy answers—they're recurring, complex, messy, and puzzling. While Johansen was writing about the business world, I think it's also a perfect description of parenting.

To determine the dilemma, I had to try to fathom its causes as accurately as possible. In this case, as in her taking the money, I suspected that when Lara wanted something really, really badly, fantasy and reality became blurred. As a preschooler, occasionally her wishes had become her realities.

2. Determine the goal. If the cause of this behavior at this age was that she might have been blurring fantasy and reality when gripped by the desire for something, then my goal became to help her separate them, to help her learn that there's a difference between what you want and what's real. Ultimately, I wanted her to understand the truth and tell the truth, and not take things that didn't belong to her.

3. Come up with alternative solutions. If one of my goals was to help her distinguish between fantasy and reality, punishing her for lying didn't seem like the right solution, since I suspected that, just as in the money incident, she wasn't fully aware that she was lying. Even if she was lying, punishing her for it might only convince her that she needed to do a better job of deception next time.

The solution that made sense to me was to tell her that she had *wanted* the drawing to be hers, but there was a difference between wanting something to be true and its being true. The drawing was Leland's. I decided to tell her that if she wanted Leland's drawing next time, she could ask Leland to make one for her, as well as to tell her that we strongly valued truthfulness.

4. Consider how these alternative solutions might work. To figure that out, I first had to think about my own state of mind. Did I really want to shame her because I was bothered by the fact that my friends and hers knew that Lara had taken Leland's drawing and passed it off as her own? Or did I want to try to move beyond my embarrassment and help her behave differently in the future? And then I had to try to put myself in Lara's shoes. What would get through to her? What would make her want to act differently in the future?

5. Select a solution to try. After the other kids left, I told Lara that I felt awful that I had made such a big deal about the birthday girl drawing when it wasn't hers, and that I was sure she felt awful, too, when she had to give it back to Leland. I told her that sometimes people want something so much that they begin to think it's theirs—they feel entitled to it. If she wanted one of Leland's drawings to be hers in the future, she could ask Leland to make one for her. If the issue was that she wanted to draw the way Leland did, we wanted her to know that we loved the way she drew. I also told her that it was important in the future to tell me—as best she could—what really happened, even if it was uncomfortable for her.

A few days later, I went to our local librarian and asked her for children's books in which the characters in the story lied. It turned out there are lots of them! I began to intersperse these books into our "special time" at night. When we got to a place in the story where someone lied, I asked Lara what she thought the character should do in that situation and what the result might be. It was a mini-morality course, but talking about the issues through the characters in books made the discussions less inflammatory than talking about Lara herself.

6. Evaluate the outcome and, if the solution isn't working, try something else. I had always thought that one of the gifts I wanted to give my children was to help them be good "dilemma resolvers," and both are. It isn't that we didn't have lots of tough times. I could have written about the time Philip stuffed the mailbox of a new kid in the neighborhood with unwelcoming messages, or took a toy car from the variety store without paying for it, or even drove off in my car without asking. But because I learned to use this process in dealing with them, they *usually* (I emphasize the word *usually*—because strife is normal as kids grow up) trusted me to handle difficult situations well. And because they learned to use this process for themselves when they had tough issues to deal with, they were *usually* forthright and honest with me. In the end, we got through the school-age and teen years with a lot less conflict than is typical in most families because we used an essential skill—the skill of critical thinking. It is a skill that we continue to draw on daily.

CRITICAL THINKING DEFINED

Critical thinking is *critical* in life, in matters both large and small. Think about it: how many novels, movies, television shows, and even news features revolve around decisions that people have made and the foreseen and unforeseen consequences of those decisions? It is in ferreting out the story behind the story—by using the skill of critical thinking—that we make the best decisions.

We want the others in our lives to be good critical thinkers, too. We want our political leaders to use the best possible knowledge to guide our country into greater safety and economic stability. We want the pilots of our airplanes to know how to respond if the plane runs into turbulence, icy conditions, bird strikes, thunderstorms, or mechanical troubles. We want our employers to be resourceful problem solvers when the economy turns sour. We want to believe that our husband, wife, friends, or doctor will make the right decisions if we fall ill and can't make decisions for ourselves. And as families, we want those to whom we entrust our children—their babysitters, child care providers, and teachers—to be able to handle everyday and serious problems.

At its core, critical thinking is *the ongoing search for valid and reliable knowledge to guide our beliefs and actions.* Sometimes the task is self-imposed—I had to figure out the best way of handling the birthday-girl drawing incident. And sometimes the search for valid knowledge is externally imposed—by a teacher, a parent, a friend, or a boss.

Like the other essential skills, the skill of critical thinking follows a developmental path throughout childhood and into adulthood, but its use must also be promoted. For those schooled in the sciences, I'm sure you see the resemblance between my problem-solving process and the scientific method: determining the issue to be addressed, posing hypotheses, conducting unbiased experiments to test the hypotheses, and drawing conclusions.

Critical thinking draws on *all* the skills that I've been writing about in this book. It takes *focus* to pursue knowledge. It takes *self control* to define the issue and determine our goals (rather than responding defensively or impulsively), to consider alternative solutions (rather than going on automatic pilot and taking the easy way out), and to evaluate the evidence to determine whether our solution is working (rather than justifying our own action). We're *making connections* when we brainstorm alternative solutions. We're exercising *perspective taking* when we consider how our solutions affect others. And since others are involved in the process, the skill of *communicating* is required as well.

In addition to all these, critical thinking involves "thinking about our thinking" by reflecting, analyzing, reasoning, planning, and evaluating.

> Critical thinking is the ability to step back and look at what you're doing, to look at the dimensions of the task, and to evaluate.
>
> —FRANK KEIL, YALE UNIVERSITY

> Critical thinking is closely related to reflection: instead of accepting one's initial characterization of a situation, subjecting that characterization to a critique, stepping outside of that characterization, refusing to take it for granted that it's sufficient, and considering it

in relation to other ways of thinking about the situation. Reflection results in and makes critical thinking possible.

—PHILIP DAVID ZELAZO, UNIVERSITY OF MINNESOTA

Critical thinking is therefore a higher-order skill among executive functions of the brain.

AN EXERCISE: DAILY DILEMMAS

Think about a tough decision you had to make lately that involved critical thinking. Did you use any of the steps I outlined above? Did you make a decision that feels right, or would you do it differently if you could?

A PARENT'S PERSPECTIVE: MAKE A WISH

When my eight-year-old Cate's plans for the weekend fell through, she was upset and didn't want to do anything. "There goes my weekend, too," I thought. I knew I had to come up with a plan. I suggested we play a "make a wish" game. She had one wish to do something special over the weekend, but she had to figure it out. I told her it couldn't be an impossible wish, but something we could afford and something that was doable. She went on the computer to look up what was going on and found something. She wanted to go to the craft store and get beads to decorate her T-shirts. She got her wish, and I got mine, too—a fairly peaceful weekend.

WHAT'S VALID AND RELIABLE KNOWLEDGE?

What would happen if you showed four- to eight-year-old children a large metal machine with buttons, dials, wires, and lights and told them that it could transform objects—that it could:

Change photographs into real objects (such as change a photograph of a stuffed animal into an actual stuffed animal)?

Make real objects shrink in size (such as make a large flashlight into a small flashlight)?

Turn toy objects into real objects (such as turn a toy watch into a real watch)?

You might guess that kids this age would say, "You've got to be kidding!" That was exactly the assumption of Megan Bloom Pickard and Judy DeLoache of the University of Virginia and Gabrielle Simcock of the University of Queensland in Australia when they began a series of experiments to determine how children would react to "impossible" events that they observed with their own eyes.

In the first experiment, while parents waited nearby, the experimenter brought four- to seven-year-olds, one at a time, into a room and showed each child this "transformation machine," explaining:

This is my special machine. This machine can change things in all sorts of ways—it can make big things little, it can turn pictures into real things, and it can make toys turn real, too! Let's turn it on and see what it can do.

For each of the three transformations listed above, the experimenter took an object from a nearby shelf (let's say the large flashlight), put it in the machine, and asked the child to push a green button on the machine to make the flashlight turn little. When the button was pushed, a prerecorded noise came on and lights flashed. Through a trapdoor concealed in the back of the machine, the experimenter retrieved a little flashlight and showed it to the child, saying, "Look at that! The machine made that [flashlight turn little]."

When the child had seen nine transformations, the parent was brought into the room. Using questions that the researcher supplied, the parent interviewed the child about what had taken place (the researchers specifically chose to use the parents as interviewers because the children might be reluctant to be forthright with the experimenter). The parent asked such questions as: "What do you think happened?" "What did the machine do?" "What were the names of the things you changed?" "Did the machine really do that?" "Was it a trick?" "Was it a magic machine?"

The extent to which many of the children believed that these transformations had actually taken place surprised the researchers. Children said things like "She put in the keys and they turned into real keys!" In fact, 100 percent of the four-year-olds, 88 percent of the five-year-olds, 71 percent of the six-year-olds, and even 33 percent of the seven-year-olds completely bought into the notion that this machine had worked magic.

Wondering if children were predisposed to believing that such transformations were possible, using the same procedure as before, the researchers asked a different group of children about *impossible events:* "Do you think that this flashlight could turn little?" "Is there anything we could do to make this flashlight turn little?" "Could a machine make this flashlight turn little?"

To up the ante, they included questions about live animals, asking, for example, if a photograph of a hamster could turn into a real hamster. Children were also asked about possible events, such as, "Do you think someone could use this flashlight to see in the dark?" Overall, the children were pretty accurate in their assessments: two out of three times, they said that nothing could be done to make the changes that were claimed to have occurred in the first study.

In their third study, the researchers upped the ante again, including live animals among the objects being transformed—for example, a toy lizard seemingly turned into a live lizard in identical plastic cages. They also involved older children in the experiment—five- through eight-year-olds. Once again, the results were striking: 88 percent of the five-year-olds, 58 percent of the six-year-olds, 65 percent of the seven-year-olds, and 40 percent of the eight-year-olds believed what they saw and what the experimenter told them.

The researchers were again surprised by these findings, and I was, too. But then I thought of Lara wishing so much that the drawing of the birthday girl was hers that she seemed to believe it.

A PARENT'S PERSPECTIVE:
ALL THE TOYS ARE SLEEPING

My two-and-a-half-year-old daughter doesn't like to go to sleep at night, similar to me when I was a child. Sometimes she'll be hanging out in our bed at 10 P.M. and she'll ask to watch TV. I tell her that Dora and Diego, Max and Ruby—all the Backyardigans—and even the Little Einsteins are all sleeping. I tell her what time they went to bed and what books they read before bed. She says, "Shhh! They are sleeping," and she stops asking me to turn on the TV. We cuddle and then she goes to bed. I wonder: does she believe me, or does she know it's pretend?

Maybe it's not so surprising that children believe these transformations could happen. Think of the changes that have occurred over the past century that must have seemed impossible at the time, even to adults. Thinking this way puts children's seeming gullibility into perspective.

My mother was born in 1907. They rode in horse-drawn carriages and had blocks of ice delivered to their house to keep food cold in the summer. I remember my mother talking about many of her miraculous firsts—first ride in an automobile, first ride on a plane (scary-looking by today's standards), first television set. And then there are my firsts— first computer, first fax machine, first cell phone (heavy and clunky). I remember going to a luncheon in the early 1980s and sitting next to a scientist from MIT who talked about a watch that could be used to track us if we got lost, call people, retain encyclopedic amounts of information, and play movies and music. It seemed ridiculous to me thirty years ago, but when I got my first iPhone, there it was—as magical a machine to me as the machine was to the children in the DeLoache experiments.

Given the world our children are inheriting—a world that is a whirlwind of change, awash in information—how do we help them become critical thinkers? In the DeLoache experiments, children directly *experienced* and *heard* impossible things from an apparently reliable adult.

That can happen in the real world, too. How do we help children know when to trust their own experiences and when to dig deeper, ask more questions, and test out more possibilities? How do we help them learn to discern which people are reliable providers of information and which people aren't? When you think about all the "Should I believe this or not?" and "Is this the best solution?" decisions you make every day, you can understand why critical thinking skills will be essential to our children in school, at work, and in life.

A PRECURSOR TO CRITICAL THINKING: THEORIZING

We constantly construct, test, and revise our theories about people and things. It's a pretty invisible process much of the time, except when one of our theories collapses. You can see it on the news repeatedly. After a crime suspect is caught, think of how often the neighbors of the suspect go on TV to say, "This person didn't seem like a criminal at all. Maybe a little quiet, but not a bad person." Or after a corporate collapse, the formerly squeaky-clean executive, canonized for being a business whiz, turns out to have had a darker side that few people detected.

Creating a theory involves analyzing the evidence, drawing a conclusion, and then testing that theory against further evidence. Does one incident of tampering with Halloween candy mean that Halloween trick-or-treating isn't safe—or just that it isn't safe under some circumstances? Our theories are important because they guide our beliefs and our behavior.

Children are constantly developing theories, too. Alison Gopnik of the University of California at Berkeley says:

Children are using the same kinds of processes as scientists. They're making up theories about what's going on around them; they're checking to see if those theories fit what they see and what other people are telling them. And they're testing those theories by asking questions and making predictions. You [can] see this in their play.

Gopnik and David Sobel constructed a "magical" machine to look at how young children construct and test theories. Gopnik explains:

> What we've done is invent this little machine, the "blicket detector," that lights up when you put things on it. And sometimes it lights up and sometimes it doesn't.

The machine looks like a photographer's light box—a box with a clear top that lights up from inside when children put certain objects on top of it. Although it appears that the children's actions are making this machine go on and off, in fact, the experimenter is masterminding the lights with a switch hidden beneath the table.

In one experiment, the experimenter shows the child four identical wooden blocks and says, "Look." Then she puts the first block on the machine. The light goes on. The experimenter returns the first block to its original position and tries the second block: nothing happens. With the third block, the machine lights up again. With the fourth, the machine is dark. As Gopnik describes it:

> We can show children patterns of evidence about this new machine that they've never seen before, and we can see what kinds of conclusions they draw about what makes this detector light up.

The experimenter tells the child the first block is a *blicket* and asks the child if she or he can point to the other blicket. Even children as young as two and a half typically know that the third block is the other blicket (note that the children are not using visual cues, because the blocks are identical). The experimenter then asks children to detect patterns from sets of many different materials placed on the light box. Gopnik says:

> What we see is that children already understand a lot about how different objects can have different causal effects: one thing can make something happen and another thing cannot make it happen.

Developing theories requires that a person understand nonobvious causal relationships. That's what the children are doing. Figuring out what blickets are isn't at all obvious!

Frank Keil of Yale University has spent years studying how children acquire knowledge and create and refine theories. He points out that theories require an understanding of the "essence" of something. In a study that also used the device of making possible and impossible transformations, Keil and his colleagues looked at how children understand these transformations. For example, could you change a raccoon into a skunk? Keil describes this study. First an experimenter told the following story to the children:

> "You take a raccoon, and a doctor [would] do surgery on it and put a sack inside it of smelly stuff and train it to squirt out whenever it gets mad."
>
> We asked the kids: "When they're all done, do you have a raccoon or a skunk?" The younger kids said, "Now it's turned into a skunk." But pretty quickly they learned that no, no, what matters to being a skunk or a raccoon is some inner kind of essence [that is responsible for the surface features that differentiate one animal from another].

However, they found that even young children show a different pattern of thinking when it comes to objects made by humans—artifacts. They are aware, for example, that if you "did surgery on" a bookshelf to turn it into a desk, it would *become* a desk.

Keil notes that most of us have incomplete theories about a lot of things. For example, many of us might think that we have a pretty good idea of how a human heart works, but when we are asked to actually provide the details, we may find ourselves stumped. Keil also points out that when we—adults and kids alike—learn something new, we're like the kids figuring out what's a skunk and what's a raccoon. It takes time to perceive the essence of something, compared with what's just surface.

There are, however, some predictable patterns of learning as children develop the ability to think critically that are helpful in knowing how best to promote this skill. They involve learning from others and learning from our own experiences.

LEARNING FROM OTHERS—YOUNG CHILDREN TEND TO TRUST OTHERS WHO ARE HELPFUL

Because we get so much of our information from other people, it's important to look at how our trust in others as information providers develops. It begins with a *people sense.* Infants appear to be wired to understand people in very specific ways far earlier than they could have been taught these perceptions. Amanda Woodward of the University of Maryland has conducted studies revealing that from infancy on, children pay attention to people's intentions and goals. They don't see people's actions and speech as random or arbitrary—they focus on what the people in their lives seem to *want* to convey.

But they pay attention to more than just intentions, as can be seen in a study conducted by Kiley Hamlin, Karen Wynn, and Paul Bloom of Yale University. One at a time, ten-month-old babies were brought into a darkened room, where they sat on their parents' laps and watched a show that took place on a steep hill made of foam core on a puppet stage. Hamlin describes the scene:

A red circle with plastic googly eyes tries to climb the hill. He goes up the hill and then falls back down, twice! Two tries to get up to the top of the hill and he always fails.

Then along comes another character onto the puppet stage:

A blue square character, also with googly eyes, comes from the bottom of the hill and bumps [the red circle] up to the top of the hill so that he's actually successful at his goal, thanks to the blue square.

The red circle jumps up and down, as if to express success and happiness. But then there is another scene and a new actor:

The climber tries again—twice—to get to the top of the hill, failing each time. Then a yellow triangle character comes down from the top and bumps him to the bottom of the hill [and] so prevents him from getting his goal.

When the circle reaches the top, it jumps up and down—to signal success. When it is pushed to the bottom of the hill, it rolls over and over—to express defeat. Hamlin continues:

Babies see this a number of times, one after the other, until their looking time decreases—until they get nice and bored with it.

An experimenter then comes into the room. She or he doesn't know whether the triangle or the square is the helper or the hinderer so as not to prejudice the child. Parents, too, keep their eyes closed. The experimenter puts the square and the triangle on a tray to see which one the baby reaches for. According to Hamlin:

Impressively—almost one hundred percent of babies preferred the more positive character: the helper over the hinderer.

They achieved these results when the square was the helper but also when the triangle was the helper, so it wasn't just a matter of children preferring one shape over another. And when they tried the experiment with even younger children—six-month-olds, who are just getting adept at reaching for things—the results were the same. Hamlin says:

They were very robustly choosing the helper over the hinderer.

Thus, infants build on their people sense to begin to make value judgments about people. The authors write that this biological process may serve as the foundation of moral thought and action. This study shows that young children are more inclined to prefer people who are helpful rather than hurtful, which can affect whom they come to trust as providers of information.

Other studies by Kristina Olson and Elizabeth Spelke of Harvard University have looked at how this process of selecting what Spelke calls *social partners* unfolds in preschool-aged children. Their research suggests that there are three general principles that underlie whom children are most willing to turn to, share with, listen to, and learn from:

> *One is a principle that says, "Cooperate with kin"; a second is a principle that says, "Cooperate with other people who cooperate with you"; and a third is a principle that says, "Cooperate with other people who are cooperative in general," whether with you or with someone else.*

LEARNING FROM OTHERS—CHILDREN TEND TO KNOW WHEN THEY NEED TO TURN TO OTHERS FOR INFORMATION

You might now be thinking, "Well, we all know helpful and cooperative people (including relatives) who don't provide reliable, trustworthy information." Somewhere along the line, we learn to seek out people who are not only cooperative but are also knowledgeable about the things we need to know: we ask computer-savvy people how to retrieve a lost document, dog-savvy people about preventing our puppy's "accidents," and our wisest friend about a heartache. Critical thinking entails being able to separate fact from fiction. It begins with children knowing whom they can ask for specific help.

Frank Keil's interest was piqued by this issue because of research he'd been conducting with adults:

> *I've done a number of studies with adults showing that we underestimate just how little we understand about the world. We are incredibly dependent on knowledge in others' minds; we lean on others' minds; we outsource our understandings all the time.*

AN ENTREPRENEUR'S PERSPECTIVE:
I MISS MY BRAIN TRUST

I recently started my own solo marketing business after more than twenty years of working in a big public relations firm. The one thing I miss is my "brain trust"—the fact that there were several hundred people around, one of whom was almost guaranteed to have some firsthand experience, some idea, some bit of helpful information, some thread of useful thought, about a problem I might be wrestling with and feeling at a loss to solve. I didn't realize the huge volume of information I was absorbing this way about what was going on in my company, my profession, and even society. Now that I'm on my own, I have to build that brain trust more deliberately: call, e-mail, and meet with people, stay more current with trade publications and blogs, and find ways to feed my own brain. It takes a lot more time!

How early do we know we need a brain trust? When do children know they need help? Keil developed a study to investigate this issue:

> The idea behind the Deserted Island Study was to see if children are sensitive to what kinds of knowledge they can acquire just on their own, without having interactions with the world, and what kind of knowledge requires access to others.

Children from kindergarten through the early elementary years were asked a series of questions prefaced by "If you grew up on a deserted island, would you know" and completed in various ways: e.g., "birds can fly," "the sky is blue," "the Pledge of Allegiance," "how to build a roller coaster." It turns out that children as young as five years old are pretty accurate in differentiating between what they could have observed and what they would need to be taught:

> They're able to realize that something such as knowing that the sky is bluish-colored—even if they don't know the word blue—is

something that would be obviously immediately accessible to a child, but that something else, such as knowing the name of a popular TV show or knowing how to fix a complex artifact, would be outside their realm.

Children, as you might expect, had some very clever answers to the questions. One child I observed in this experiment said that a child on a deserted island might not know that birds fly because "the island doesn't have birds!"

LEARNING FROM OTHERS—STARTING IN PRESCHOOL, CHILDREN CAN DISCERN THOSE WHO CAN HELP THEM LEARN

Keil also found that preschool children are selective about whom they ask for help:

You'll see kids in a preschool running to different adults to ask different kinds of questions. They seem to know "one person fixes my cuts and one person fixes the trucks" and they're not necessarily the same.

To explore how children categorize knowledge, Keil and his colleagues designed a study he calls the Expert Study. Children in kindergarten, second grade, and fourth grade, as well as college students, were asked if they knew what an expert was. If they said yes, they were asked to give examples. The experimenter also provided examples to make sure this concept was understood: a doctor is an expert because a doctor "knows all about how to fix people and make them feel better, and a car mechanic is an expert because a car mechanic knows all about how to fix cars and make them work."

Then children were asked a series of questions, accompanied with illustrations. For example:

Adam knows all about why:
People sometimes fight when they are tired.

What else is he more likely to know?
Why people smile at their friends when they see them?
OR
Why salt on people's icy driveways makes the ice melt sooner?

The example above assesses knowledge of social psychology. Children might say that Adam would know more about why people smile at their friends if Adam knows about fighting because "both are about feelings."

Keil provides another example: if someone knows about why hitting a nail harder makes it go in farther, would she or he be more likely to know why a boat takes a long time to stop or why best friends sometimes fight? He says:

> When the kids are asked to explain—assuming they put together
> the boat and the hammer—they'll say, "Well, they both have to
> do with things pushing," and they know that is very different from
> interpersonal relations.

Beginning in the later preschool years, children have a rudimentary sense about how knowledge is categorized:

> Even the youngest children we looked at—as young as four and a
> half—are able to look at what's happening in the world in terms of
> different kinds of causal patterns: those of naive physics, [which is
> about] forces acting on objects; those of naive psychology, which is
> [about] how beliefs and emotions influence behavior; those of na-
> ive chemistry, which is about [how] substances influence changes in
> matter; those of naive economics, which is about what things cost
> in exchange. They know nothing about the details, but they sense
> these are different and that knowledge is going to cluster according
> to those domains.

It's fascinating that children so young already have a basic ability to distinguish among categories of knowledge, that the categories they rec-ognize have parallels in any university course catalog—from economics to chemistry to physics—and that they can even differentiate among people who are knowledgeable about the questions they might have.

LEARNING FROM OTHERS—YOUNG CHILDREN CAN DIFFERENTIATE BETWEEN PEOPLE WHO PROVIDE ACCURATE INFORMATION AND THOSE WHO DON'T

But what if the people whom children turn to don't provide accurate information? Discerning whom we can trust for information in itself requires critical thinking. Paul Harris of Harvard University and Melissa Koenig of the University of Minnesota designed a series of studies to assess this issue. In their first experiment, three- and four-year-olds were presented with two actors who appeared in a video. The experimenter, who was in the room with the child, said:

> *I've got these two friends. One has a blue shirt and one has a red shirt. They are going to show you some things and tell you what they are called. Let's watch.*

As the children watched the video, they saw a third actor ask the blue- and red-shirted actors to label a familiar object. One answered correctly—"That's a ball"—while the other incorrectly called the ball a "shoe." Then to see if the child knew the correct name of the object, the child was asked, "Can you tell me what this is called?" This overall process was repeated with two other familiar objects, with one of the actors being consistently correct and the other incorrect.

Following this experience, the children were given *test trials*, where they were asked to identify which of the people in the video was not very good at answering questions. This was followed by *prediction trials*, where the children were shown a picture of something they would know—a banana—and asked to predict what each of the actors would call the object. The question was: would the children be able to predict which actor would give the correct name of the banana?

Although three-year-olds could say which actor was more accurate in the test trials, they stumbled when it came to "predicting" which one would give the correct name of the banana. The four-year-olds, however, didn't stumble.

The same pattern held true when three- and four-year-olds saw the two actors name unfamiliar objects. The four-year-olds were more likely to trust the actor who had been accurate in naming familiar objects, while the three-year-olds again stumbled.

During the preschool years, children are beginning to learn whom to ask for information and whom to believe. Why were four-year-olds more competent in making these judgments than three-year-olds? the researchers asked. And what would happen if one of the people said she "didn't know" rather than mislabeling objects? They designed another study to find out.

In this study, with different children of the same ages, one of the actors always named the objects correctly (a ball, a cup, and a book), while the other professed ignorance, saying, "I don't know." The children were then led through a series of trials very similar to those in the first experiment. The results revealed that three- and four-year-olds could distinguish knowledgeable and "ignorant" people and could use that information to anticipate who would be knowledgeable in the future. However, in studies where the actors were sometimes correct and sometimes incorrect, there was a difference between children of these two ages. In an article reviewing this research, Harris writes:

> Three-year-olds are relatively unforgiving—an informant who has made a single error is judged as harshly as someone who has made several. Four-year-olds . . . appear to adopt a more nuanced assessment, recognizing that overall—despite the occasional error—one informant may still be more trustworthy than another.

Koenig and Harris suggest that inaccuracy and ignorance undermine the trust of the older children, but only ignorance undermines the trust of the younger ones. They write:

Children, and adults, are deeply dependent on other people for their knowledge of the world. Our results demonstrate that young children do not navigate this "sea" of testimony with unquestioning credulity, but with an interest in the validity of what they are told.

There is a developmental path on which children first recognize that some people "don't know" and then, later on, can recognize that some people make mistakes or are even deceitful.

LEARNING FROM OTHERS—CHILDREN TEND TO HAVE LESS TRUST IN THOSE WITH A VESTED INTEREST

When do children learn to distinguish among another person's "not knowing something" or being mistaken, versus someone being biased (wanting something to be true so much that the person believes it's true) versus being deceitful—that is, lying? Detecting these differences is an essential part of critical thinking.

I wanted my kids to have this skill so they could know when someone was trying to sell them something on television or on the playground by making false claims. I also wanted them to know when someone was trying to influence them to make bad decisions—like when Philip stuffed the mailbox of a new neighbor with unfriendly messages because another child in the neighborhood told him to do it. As they grew up, I wanted them to know the difference between hype and facts, between propaganda and authenticity.

AN EXERCISE: WHY DO YOU WANT YOUR CHILDREN TO BE CRITICAL THINKERS?

Can you think of a time in your own life when, if you'd asked more questions or gotten better information, you might have made a different and better decision?

A PARENT'S PERSPECTIVE: HE'LL GROW OUT OF IT

My son was late in saying words that made any sense, but his pediatrician kept insisting he would grow out of it. So I let months pass, waiting for him to grow out of it. Finally, I took him to another doctor, who realized that the ear infections he'd had as a baby were affecting his hearing. The doctor said, "No wonder! Since he can't hear well, he can't talk well." Fortunately, it was fixable.

At first I beat myself up, regretting those months I let pass when the world must have been a discordant symphony of sounds to him. Finally, I said to myself, "I can't go backward in time, so I will go forward as my son's advocate. If advice doesn't feel right to me, I will keep asking."

Frank Keil and a former graduate student, Candice Mills, developed a study, as he says, "to try to see if children are able to take what people say with a grain of salt."

One at a time, children in kindergarten, second grade, and fourth grade were told stories accompanied by simple drawings. In some cases, the ending of the story was ambiguous. For example:

We showed children [pictures of] people in a running race. We would describe the race as having an ambiguous outcome—it's not clear who won, it was too close to call. Then one of the participants in the race claimed that he [or she] won—and if you won the race, you got an enormous prize.

The children were asked to rate how much they believed the main character on a scale of 1 (do not believe at all) to 5 (completely believe). Next they were told an identical story but with a different ending. Here the main character acted against personal interest and denied winning, even though the outcome of the race was also ambiguous and the winner would receive a big prize.

The findings revealed that the older children—in the second and fourth grades—were less likely to believe the characters who acted *in* their own self interest under ambiguous circumstances than those who acted *against* their own self-interest. The opposite was true of kindergartners: "kindergartners seemed to assume that someone who wants to win a prize or achieve a goal will do so."

When do children begin to understand this issue of bias—that wanting to have something happen doesn't necessarily make it happen, and that bias can blind us to reality? To investigate this question, the researchers added children in the sixth grade to their study and developed another series of stories where the ending was crystal clear, not ambiguous at all: the race had a winner and a loser, but the loser claimed to win. The experimenter made it explicit to the children that "this character was really wrong, that he came across the finish line behind his friend and so should not win."

Then the experimenter showed the children three drawings depicting various reasons why the loser might claim to win. One explanation was that the character *lied:* "Michael knew that he crossed the finish line behind his friend, but he said he was ahead because he wanted to win. His wanting to win made him try to trick his friend." A second explanation involved *bias*—the character wanted to win so much that he thought he really did. A third explanation involved *making a mistake:* "It was just a mistake. He could have just as easily thought he was behind." The experimenter asked the children to select the drawing with the best explanation of what had happened.

This study found that in general the children were more likely to think that the loser had lied; however, kindergartners, second graders, and fourth graders rarely thought that the loser was biased (wanting is believing), but the older children did. In fact, sixth graders were just as likely to think that the loser was biased as that he was a liar. Keil told me that he finds it interesting that younger children tend to paint more of a black-and-white picture, seeing people as being deceptive or not, rather than as being "blinded" by ambition.

Being able to discern what part self interest plays in what people say is obviously essential to whether we trust their words, but that kind of information is not always obvious (even to those of us older than sixth graders), nor is it necessarily easy to obtain. I remember the days when an advertisement could make all sorts of false claims, such as that nine out of ten dentists highly recommend a certain brand of toothpaste. But who were those nine out of ten dentists? Were they dentists who had been paid by the toothpaste company? Were they the best friends of the people who created the ad? Today, making false claims in the media is harder to do—not necessarily because those with self interest have listened to their better angels, but because they're prohibited by law from false advertising. In the virtual Wild West of the Internet, however, there are fewer better angels to stand guard. Have you ever wondered if an e-mail allegedly from your credit card company is really from your credit card company or a scam? The regularity of these scams has even introduced a new word into our vocabularies—*phishing*.

LEARNING FROM OTHERS— THE "CURSE OF KNOWLEDGE"

Evaluating information from others ultimately calls on the skill of perspective taking, of trying to project yourself into someone else's mind to understand what he or she might feel, think, and believe. Remember that as children get older, they become more adept at understanding the perspectives of others.

Paul Bloom of Yale University and a former graduate student, Susan Birch, set out to design an experiment complicated enough that adults—not just children—would have trouble with it. In this experiment, undergraduate students at Yale read a story about a child named Vicki who was playing a violin and then put it away in one of four containers in the room—a blue container—to go outside and play. While she was outside, her sister moved the violin to a different container and then rearranged all four containers, moving them to different places in the room. Of course, the question was: where will Vicki look for her violin?

There are different next steps in the story. One-third of the students read that the violin was moved to "a different container"; the second third read that the violin was moved to a "red container"; and the remaining students read that the violin was moved to a "purple container."

The students were then shown a drawing of the rearranged room with the red container placed where the blue one had been. The students were asked to estimate the chances—in percentages—of where Vicki would first look for her violin. Slightly more than seven in ten students— both those who didn't know where the violin had been placed and those who were told the violin was in a purple container—guessed that Vicki would look in the blue container, where she had left the violin. But those students who were told that the violin was now in a red container—and could see that the red container had been moved to the same location where the blue container originally housing the violin once was—were much less likely to think that Vicki would look in the blue container. The researchers call this a "curse-of-knowledge bias." We filter our understanding of what we hear from others through many layers. Among these filters is prior knowledge of "the final answer." That knowledge can interfere with our ability to reason about what someone else might think. This is true both for children and for adults.

All of these experiments about learning from others make it clear that the task of learning to be a critical thinker is complex and eventually involves understanding the motives and knowledge of others.

LEARNING FROM EXPERIENCE—
THE ROLE OF CURIOSITY

Children also learn from their direct experiences. Indeed, young children often seem compelled by curiosity, driven to understand and to master information.

AN EXERCISE: BE A RESEARCHER

Watch a young child trying to learn something. What do you see? What is the child trying to understand or do? What role does curiosity play in the drive to learn? How does this child pursue his or her goal? What happens if there are setbacks?

A GRANDPARENT'S PERSPECTIVE:
LESS PULLING, LESS SWATTING

My nineteen-month-old granddaughter began following our cat around the house, calling "Cat, cat," and pointing to it. Initially the cat was tolerant until my granddaughter pulled at its fur, and then the cat swatted her. It wasn't a hard swat, but the cat had communicated: "Stop!" And it worked for a while. When my granddaughter tried the same thing later that day and the next, she received the same response. She began holding out her hand and saying "Cat" very sadly.

Our family responded by saying "Gentle," and demonstrating a gentle stroke. My granddaughter continued to experiment with approaching the cat. Although she was curious, she figured out that it was important to be cautious, so she waited until the cat would lie down and she began touching in a gentle manner. My granddaughter learned, and the cat learned, too—and there was less pulling and thus less swatting.

The picture that comes to my mind when I think of one of my children learning something new is Philip learning to walk. Ever curious, he got tired of waiting to be carried or crawling. He was determined to get where he wanted to go on his own two legs. He was like a windup toy that sometimes hits a wall but the motor keeps going and the toy keeps spinning around. His legs and arms were in constant motion, scooting him along until he found something to use as a hoist for standing up. Then off he would go, taking a few stumbling steps until he tumbled to the floor. Undaunted, he'd scoot to the next hoist and begin again. Up and down, up and down, trying to get to whatever it was that he wanted. When I think of that time in his life, the words that come to mind are *persistence, passion,* and *profound curiosity.*

Laura Schulz of MIT has been studying what propels children to learn from direct evidence and the role that curiosity plays in this learning. We typically think of children as being naturally curious—I certainly saw both of my kids this way—but Schulz has determined that curiosity is more complex:

The first thing you might think about curiosity is that we're curious about the novel; we're not curious about the familiar.

And that's true. There's a great deal of evidence indicating that children are drawn to what's new. But Schulz says:

We often seem to be curious about things that aren't particularly novel—they just puzzle us.

Her quest to understand curiosity has led to new insights:

I think there are two different things that can provoke curiosity. The simplest one is a violation of your prior beliefs. You go [into an experience] with a certain expectation that "this is the way the world is," and then you see some evidence that's inconsistent with that.

When this happens, Schulz says:

You have to do something with that evidence. You can deny it. You can try to explain it away. You could realize that your beliefs are wrong and that they have to change. But one way or another, you need more information to figure out what to do. So that's a condition under which you should explore.

My own study of parental development has shown that we—as parents—grow and change when we have an expectation of ourselves, of our children, of the world that doesn't come true, that doesn't fit with reality (such as "I am never going to yell at my kids—I am always going to be patient and kind"). Then either we stay stuck and get upset or angry or we grow—by changing our behavior to live up to our expectations or by creating more realistic expectations. So in children and adults alike, a clash between what we expect and what actually happens can be a trigger for curiosity and learning.

Children also become curious when they have two competing expectations or theories. Schulz explains:

The other time you might be curious is if you see evidence that fails to distinguish [among] competing beliefs. There are many things that might be true, and the evidence just doesn't determine which one is the case.

In scientific terms, when people are trying to understand how things work, they are typically trying to understand causal relationships—what causes something to happen. A toddler might be trying to understand what happens if she pushes her rubber duck underwater in the bathtub. Does it always rise back up to the surface? Yes, it does. That kind of evidence, in scientific terms, is *unconfounded:* there's a clear and consistent cause and effect. When Schulz talks about "competing beliefs" where "many things might be true," she's talking about *confounded* evidence: it's not clear exactly what the causes are.

Schulz and one of her graduate students, Elizabeth Baraff Bonawitz, created a study to test whether children tend to stick with a puzzling situation until they understand it. They designed a red jack-in-the-box toy that has two levers, one on each side. When both levers are pushed simultaneously, two toys—a straw puppet and a duck—pop up. This toy demonstrates a confounded experience: there's no way to determine how the toy works simply by looking at it. There are a number of possibilities: (1) both levers, working together, could control the puppet and the duck; (2) only one of the levers could control both the puppet and the duck; or (3) one lever could control the duck and the other lever could control the puppet.

In the experiment, an experimenter shows preschool-aged children this toy. The experimenter says to each child, "You push down your lever and I'll push down my lever at the same time." They count to three and each pushes one of the levers. Both the puppet and the duck pop up. Although they repeat this action several times, the child can't deduce from this process which lever controls which pop-up toy.

A second group of children is introduced to the toy in a different way. After the experimenter and the child push down the levers at the same time, they each take turns. The child can see which lever controls the duck and which lever controls the puppet. Then, Schulz explains:

We take that jack-in-the-box away. We bring it right back out along with a brand-new box that the children have never played with before.

That brand-new toy is a yellow jack-in-the-box with a single lever.

Everything we know about play and curiosity in children says [that] if four-year-olds have been playing with [the red box with two levers] for a while, they should go immediately to play with the new box—because it's something they haven't seen.

The researchers found that the children who knew how the old box worked (that is, they had unambiguous or unconfounded information) went to play with the new box. But the children who didn't know how it worked (they had ambiguous or confounded information) kept playing with it:

They recognize that information is ambiguous and they keep play-ing until they discover how it really works.

Becoming adept at disentangling cause and effect, especially when the evidence is ambiguous (or confounded), is a step toward critical thinking because children are learning how to assess whether their knowledge is accurate and valid. But, as these researchers acknowledge, life may not be as simple as this experiment. The experience may be too complex for children to figure out on their own, they may not pay enough attention to the evidence, or they may jump to hasty conclusions.

I have only to think about my own experiences, when the television remotes don't turn on the television (and in my house it is television re-motes—we have three remotes for reasons that I don't fully understand), when my cell phone doesn't work, or when everything on my computer screen suddenly freezes, to be vividly reminded how confusing it can be to detect the way things work. That's where learning from others—experts, adults, and other children—comes into the picture.

LEARNING FROM EXPERIENCES WITH OTHERS— ADVENTURES IN A SCIENCE MUSEUM

Maureen Callanan of the University of California at Santa Cruz has been examining parents' role in promoting children's scientific reasoning in everyday activities. She calls one of her early studies the Diary Study:

> We asked parents to keep track of their children's "why" questions for about two weeks. The children came up with these amazing questions, [like] "If fish are in the water, why don't they drown?"

I certainly remember how many of my kids' questions stumped me and sent me running to look for answers. I couldn't remember—if I ever knew—how lightbulbs work and what lightning is, for example. Callanan says that when we search for answers, we demonstrate a process for inquiry to our children:

> What I think is important about the way parents tend to respond is that they are usually encouraging the kids to do this kind of questioning, guiding them in thinking about how [to find] answers to questions.

Studies show that children are more likely to ask questions when there is time to reflect, like riding in the car or when they're actively doing things together. And what better place for finding out "how" and "why" than in a science museum?

Callanan has been teasing apart how parents support children's scientific and critical thinking by videotaping conversations at the Children's Discovery Museum in San Jose, California. In one study, the researchers observed children from ages four through eight at an exhibition of a zoetrope. A zoetrope is a cylinder (think of a large tin can without a label and without a top or bottom). The cylinder has vertical slits like narrow windows cut all around it. By spinning it and looking straight into the slits, you can see a horse in motion, galloping. But if you look through the top, you see that this motion is an illusion created by static drawings that freeze the movement of a horse into still frames that circle around the inside of the cylinder. A zoetrope provides children with a demonstration of how cartoon animations are created.

The researchers found that children were more engaged and spent more time at the exhibit if they explored it with their parents than if they explored it alone. They also found that parents promote their children's scientific thinking by:

> **Helping children focus on the evidence.** Parents highlight what children should pay attention to and what's important, saying, for example, "It looks like the horse is running."

> **Helping children gather new evidence.** Children might not notice that if you spin the cylinder in the other direction, the horse appears to be running backward. That is the kind of evidence that parents often point out.

> **Helping children interpret the evidence.** Parents offer brief explanations to enhance children's understanding of what they're seeing and relate this experience to broader concepts, such as telling the children, "This is how cartoons work." Callanan and her colleagues call these brief explanations *explanatoids* because they provide *just-in-time information,* or information at the moment that children need it.

TEACHING SCIENTIFIC THINKING TO CHILDREN

Our parental explanatoids may be accurate ... or not, leaving me with the question: what are some of the best ways to promote critical thinking in our children? Although the research of David Klahr of Carnegie Mellon University was designed to inform the teaching of science in schools, as a parent I find his research very insightful. He has been concerned that science education focuses on the subject matter, while the teaching of scientific thinking *processes* (such as helping children think about cause and effect, how to design a valid scientific experiment, and how to interpret findings) have been given short shrift. He explains:

Many people, like Alison Gopnik and her colleagues, have discov-
ered that even infants have a rudimentary understanding of causal
relations—they can understand that one thing is caused by an-
other—but by the time they get to second, third, or fourth grade
and you ask them to design an experiment, [they falter].

Throughout this book, I've referred to the ability of very young children to grab onto different kinds of knowledge before it could have been
taught as their having a *sense*. Klahr is referring to a *causal sense*, but
I've also shared research on young children's *language sense*, *people sense*,
number sense, and *space sense*. David Geary of the University of Missouri
at Columbia calls those inborn abilities *primary abilities*, and the related
abilities we have to learn *secondary abilities*. David Klahr elaborates:

With respect to scientific reasoning and experimental design,
[young children have] a rudimentary ability to identify causes—
that A caused B and C didn't cause B—but as soon as you make it
a little bit more complex, then it has to be taught.

That's where, according to Klahr, our educational system has fallen
short. As he reviews state standards and observes classroom teaching, he
finds far too little emphasis on promoting the learning-related skill of
scientific thinking. Helping children learn to disentangle cause and effect, especially in more complex situations where the evidence is ambiguous (or confounded), becomes essential in promoting critical thinking
with older children. It's a bit like that adage of giving someone a fish
versus teaching them to fish: which is most likely to keep that person fed
for life?

What kind of teaching and learning experiences are most effective in
promoting scientific thinking, and can children learn this skill on their
own through discovery learning experiences, or do they need it to be
directly taught? Klahr designed a series of studies that directly contrast
these two approaches.

I observed one of his studies, developed with Milena Nigam, in which
children in the third and fourth grades were asked to determine what

makes a ball roll farther on two wooden ramps positioned side by side, where they could vary: (1) the *steepness* of the ramps—setting them high or low; (2) the *surface* of the ramps—inserting a rough or smooth surface; (3) the *location of the gates* that opened to release the balls—setting them at the top or the middle of the ramp to make a long or a short runway; and (4) the *type of ball*—using rough balls (golf balls) or smooth balls (rubber balls). At the end of each ramp was a series of steps, gently inclining up, that provided an accurate measure of how far the ball had rolled.

To begin, each child was tested on his or her "initial beliefs" about what makes balls roll farther. Next the experimenter asked the child to set up an experiment to test how steepness affects the distance that the ball rolls. One child I watched made one ramp high and the other one low. But then he added other things beyond the steepness of the ramp that would affect the results—such as a smooth surface on one ramp and a rough surface on the other.

After the boy ran his experiment, an experimenter asked him, "Can you tell *for sure* from this comparison whether the steepness of the ramp makes a difference?" The boy shook his head no. The experimenter asked him to set up another experiment to test whether the steepness of the ramp makes a difference. This time, the only thing that this child varied was the steepness of the two ramps, demonstrating that at some level he understood that his first experiment had been flawed. When asked what he had found, he said, "Steepness really does affect the rolling of the ball!" When asked if he knew this *for sure,* he replied yes, because "everything that was not the [steepness of the] ramp was the same."

At this point in the study, half the children were provided with discovery learning experiences and the other half with direct teaching experiences. The boy I was observing was in the discovery group. He was asked to conduct other experiments, testing, in turn, whether the steepness, the surface, the length of the run, or the type of ball made a difference. Some of this boy's experiments were unconfounded, but then he got interested in whether different types of balls were affected by different surfaces and designed some mixed-up experiments. After each experiment, the experimenter asked him if he knew *for sure,* for example, that the surface of the ramp made the difference in the finding of his experiment, but otherwise he was given no feedback.

The other group of children was given "direct teaching" experiences. Here the experimenter set up a deliberately confounded experiment and showed each child why this kind of experiment was not a "smart choice," saying that there was a "better way." After constructing another experiment where *only* the height of the ramp varied, she said, "*This* is now a good way to find out *for sure* if steepness makes a difference—since it is the only thing different between these two ramps." After each experiment the children in the direct teaching group were given feedback about the accuracy of their experiments.

Finally, there was a post-test phase where all the children were tested on what they had learned. Klahr and Nigam found a striking difference: only 23 percent of the children in the discovery learning group became "masters"—that is, they set up at least three out of four unconfounded experiments in the post-test phase, whereas 77 percent of the children receiving direct instruction became "masters." Klahr describes the differences in the two approaches:

> In the discovery [experiences], the challenges are the same, the materials are the same, but the experimenter never says you're right or wrong and the experimenter never says why this is a good experiment or a bad experiment. So the child may come away with a misconception. On the other hand, of the kids whom we taught directly—many more do very well. We concluded from this study that direct instruction was more effective.

But would this learning skill be transferred to a new and different experience, especially one that is similar to what kids might do in science class?

To pursue this question, Klahr created a follow-up study, conducted with Mari Strand Cary, in which children evaluated science posters made by children for science fairs. The children doing the evaluations received either direct instruction or discovery experiences. At various times afterward (one week and three months), the experimenters showed the children real science fair posters.

One poster, for example, reported on an experiment conducted by a girl that asked: "Do girls have a better memory than boys?" It described an experiment in which boys and girls were shown a series of twenty-five objects, which were subsequently hidden from the children's sight, and they were tested on how many of these objects they remembered. The study found that girls remembered eighteen objects, while boys remembered only four. The poster concluded that girls have better memories than boys. Klahr laughs:

> It's a really cute poster and it gets even cuter when you see the objects. The objects that had to be memorized are lipstick, high-heel[ed] shoes, a compact, a purse. We liked that poster because it actually has a confound in it.

Obviously, the "confound" is that these objects would be less memorable to boys than to girls. Klahr's conclusion:

> We found, as usual, that a very high proportion of the kids in the direct instruction [experiences] got really good at [evaluating evidence in experiments].

Fewer children who had discovery learning experiences were able to evaluate the science posters to detect whether the experiments were confounded or not. However, if they had managed to learn how to design good experiments using ramps—even in the discovery condition—they were just as good at evaluating posters three months later as those who had learned from direct instruction:

> This means it doesn't matter how you learned it. What matters is whether you learned it or not!

From Klahr's work, it's clear that it's important for us to "guide" learning at times, being direct in pointing out to children in the later preschool and early elementary school years the difference between using unambiguous and ambiguous information to inform their conclusions. By doing so, we're promoting their critical thinking.

HOT AND COLD ISSUES

Not all issues are equal when it comes to critical thinking. Deciphering ambiguous evidence is one thing if the focus is ramps and balls, but quite another if it involves disputes among friends, a serious conflict among coworkers, or a teacher who seems to bear a grudge toward a child.

Phil Zelazo of the University of Minnesota uses the terms *hot* and *cold* for these different situations and the demands they make on the executive functions of the brain:

> Cool executive function *refers to deliberate, goal-directed problem solving as it's usually assessed by laboratory measures. For example, sorting cards by shape and color—nobody really cares that much about whether the cards go here or go there, so it's really a relatively abstract situation. In contrast, in the real world, people normally do care about the problems that they're solving—there's something at stake, there's something that stands to be gained or lost as a consequence of one's behavior.*

This is a very important point. Critical thinking sounds like a purely intellectual process, but that's not true. We may think critically about issues we don't care much about, but more often we are called upon to make judgments when we do care, and our emotions are very much a part of the process.

This hot-cold distinction is illustrated in an experiment called Less Is More conducted by Stephanie Carlson of the University of Minnesota and her colleagues. The premise is that children have to point to a smaller number of delicious treats (like candy) in order to receive a larger amount of them—and that's clearly a hot issue!

Three- and four-year-olds are brought into a classroom-type laboratory setting, one at a time. Carlson says:

We first established that children are motivated to receive these treats, so we gave them a choice of different treats to ensure that they want [them] and that they'd want the larger amount.

The experimenter introduces a monkey (a puppet) named Chris to the child, explaining that Chris is a naughty monkey who likes to get all the treats for himself—he doesn't share, and that's why he is naughty. Then the child is shown one tray with two treats and another tray with five treats:

We say, "In this game, whichever [tray] you point to, those treats will be given away to the naughty monkey who doesn't share, and you'll get the other treats."

If the child points to the larger amount of treats, they go into a clear plastic cup beside the monkey and the smaller amount goes into the child's plastic cup, so the child can observe as the treats accumulate. Like many tasks measuring executive functions of the brain, this experiment asks the child to inhibit the automatic response (pointing to the treats she or he wants), and instead do the opposite to get the bigger reward:

They can see that if they're not performing well and continually pointing to the larger amount, they're actually getting less and less than the monkey.

Three-year-olds have trouble with this game. Carlson notes that either they can't seem to help pointing to the larger amount or they respond randomly. By age four, however, the children pick up on the rule—that pointing to the smaller amount gets you more.

This study has real implications for critical thinking. It demonstrates what it takes for children to think critically about an issue that's hot—that matters—to them. Carlson thinks that children have to learn to step back from the immediate situation in order to obtain a more thoughtful, reflective perspective to guide their thinking and their actions. She says:

Psychological distancing does play a role in self control in executive function.

HOW CAN YOU PROMOTE CRITICAL THINKING IN CHILDREN?

SUGGESTION 1: WATCH YOUR CHILD FORMING THEORIES ABOUT HOW THINGS WORK.

Observe your children at play and see what they're attempting to understand. Play is the way that children often try out ideas. We do it, too—but we do it by playing with ideas in our minds rather than acting them out, as children do.

AN EXERCISE: BE A RESEARCHER

Remember the last time you had to go to a new place or meet new people. How did you prepare for it? Did you imagine what the place or the people would be like? Did you run through scenarios in your mind about what to expect or what might go wrong or right?

Now watch your children and see what they're trying to figure out in their play. Are they doing what you just did?

A PARENT'S PERSPECTIVE: A MENTAL REHEARSAL

I volunteer for the neonatal intensive care unit (NICU) where my child stayed when he was born prematurely. I recently launched a scrapbooking program called "Scrap and Chat." We bring scrapbooking supplies, and new parents can make a crib decoration or a page for their baby book. Before the first event, I pictured parents attending and I mentally rehearsed how I would briefly share my story and what kind of questions I would ask them about their children. I also imagined how I would help them with their scrapbooking. I wanted to be prepared, because I really *know* what a roller-coaster emotional ride it is to be the parent of a premature child and I wanted them to be comfortable.

A PARENT'S PERSPECTIVE: A RESEARCHER OF HINGES

My thirteen-month-old has been discovering that many things have hinges, and it's his work to find them everyplace he goes. He will crawl to a door and sit there and swing the door open and nearly closed. He also enjoys opening and closing all the kitchen and bathroom cabinets. We got him a toy that has hinges, but he lost interest in that rather quickly and headed back to the real thing—the kitchen—to continue his own research.

SUGGESTION 2: PROMOTE YOUR CHILD'S CURIOSITY.

While children are born with a drive to understand—to be curious—this drive can be weakened or strengthened by what we do. As Laura Schulz concludes, children are especially curious when something they expect doesn't come true and when they experience a situation where "the evidence fails to distinguish between competing beliefs." This is especially true when they're trying to determine what causes something to happen.

To promote children's curiosity, be careful not to jump in too quickly to fix things they're struggling with, since working with the "confounding" situation is where critical thinking is promoted. Instead, where possible, help them figure out how they can resolve it for themselves. For example, let's say your child is working on a puzzle and just can't get one of the pieces in the right place. Rather than take over, help her look for clues to where the piece might go: "It is a blue piece. Do you see any other part of the puzzle that is blue? Why don't you try to see if the piece would fit there?" Or "This piece of the puzzle is shaped like the sliver of the moon. Do you see a shape in the puzzle that has the same curved shape?"

Or let's say that your child is trying to understand why his rubber toy always rises to the top of the water in the bathtub, even when he pushes it down hard. You can help your child create some experiments for understanding floating better: "Do you think that this wet washcloth would float? What about the empty shampoo bottle? What would happen if we filled the empty bottle with water? Here is the bottle. I'll help you fill it up." You are helping your child create and test hypotheses, like a scientist.

You can also help your child refine the learning by providing what Maureen Callanan and Kevin Crowley call *just-in-time* information: "Look—if we fill the bottle with heavy marbles it doesn't float, but if we leave it empty, it does. Seems like heavy things don't float, but lighter things do. Let's see if that is always true."

SUGGESTION 3: PROMOTE YOUR CHILDREN'S "LEMONADE STANDS."

Throughout this book I've talked about the importance of what I call "lemonade stands," so called because of my daughter Lara's passion for having a lemonade stand when she was between six and seven. She moved on to other interests—especially understanding what life was like for women in different cultures, in different parts of the world, and in different periods of history. So when Lara's class studied the early days of New York City—or New Amsterdam—Lara at age seven tried to find out everything she could about women in this Dutch settlement at the tip of Manhattan in the early 1600s. And when her class studied Egypt or China or ancient Greece, Lara often gravitated to the topic of women for her papers, book reports, presentations, and plays.

We were fortunate that Lara went to a school where teachers encouraged her to pursue her interest while learning other academic subjects, year after year. Frank Keil reports that a national commission he served on concluded that this kind of teaching should be the norm, not the exception:

> I was involved in a study done by the National Research Council [of] the National Academy of Sciences asking about how recent discoveries in cognitive science might be relevant to science education. And we put out a book called Taking Science to School. We made a number of recommendations, but one of them was the idea of learning progressions. Rather than [cover] science "a mile wide and an inch deep," what you want to do is to try to pick an idea and grow it over time.

He says that the committee found some remarkable teachers who embody this approach, including a woman who taught science to children in grades one through six at Saint Ann's School in Stoughton, Wisconsin:

> Sister Gertrude Hennessey takes these kids and teaches them science years and years ahead of grade level by taking an idea—such as the nature of motion—and growing it year after year and building on that idea rather than just doing a thin survey [of science facts] each year.

Students begin with real questions about why things are the way they are. They are challenged to ask questions, conduct experiments, analyze findings, and then explain the reasoning behind their findings. They are living the scientific approach in their own pursuit of knowledge—living the learning—rather than experiencing learning as the acquisition of factual information. In a paper she wrote, Sister Gertrude Hennessey quotes an essay by an eleven-year-old student named Kathryn, describing this approach:

> I think learning in science is about wondering about the world, how it works, and then asking yourself questions that you find challenging.

This child compares learning about science to putting together the pieces of a puzzle:

You can have all 1000 pieces but if you don't take the time to fit them together you will never see the picture.

Kathryn contrasts this approach with the more typical approach found in schools:

Most school learning is like collecting the pieces of the puzzle and keeping them in a box. Teachers reward you for collecting enough pieces, the more pieces you collect the better rewards you get!

Kathryn has also learned to reflect on her own thinking (what scientists would call *metacognition,* or thinking about thinking). Upon reflection, Kathryn concludes that the analogy of a puzzle isn't perfect, because there's only one correct way to put a puzzle together, whereas "there is more than one way to fit science ideas together."

SUGGESTION 4: BE AN EXPERT—TRY TO PROVIDE ACCURATE AND VALID INFORMATION TO YOUR CHILDREN.

We can model critical thinking by encouraging our children to ask questions and by responding with accurate information, always keeping in mind what they are ready to understand.

This can include looking up information when we don't remember or don't know the answers (often true in my case—I forgot almost everything I had learned about some subjects, if I ever truly learned it). It is also true when kids ask us tough questions.

My friend Chloe has a seven-year-old son who came home from school one day, rattled off a list of swear words, and asked her what they meant. She said that this hadn't been her vision of how she was going to spend her evening with her son, but he was old enough, she felt, to be given this information. So she took a deep breath and tried to define each as simply as she could. Explaining that these words are used to insult others, she told her son not to say them.

"But you said a bad word when you hurt your finger," he shot back. "That's right, I did," she said. "It hurt so much that I said it, but I was sorry I did because I am not helping you learn not to say these words when I say them." She decided that being truthful was more important than explaining away her response.

Since children tend to model themselves after us, what about white lies—telling them ourselves or telling our kids to say, for example, that they loved a birthday present, when in fact they hated it? When that happened at our house, I would *try* to help Philip or Lara find something nice to say, but not to lie—for example, to say that it was very nice of their friend to give them a present rather than say that they loved it.

SUGGESTION 5: HELP YOUR CHILDREN FIND OTHER "EXPERTS" TO LEARN FROM.

Frank Keil's research indicates that children increasingly know to turn to others for their expertise. Think about your friends, your family, your neighbors, and your colleagues as experts who can share their experiences, their knowledge, and their passions with your kids. Friends have shared their worlds of pottery, of expeditions to find the *Titanic*, of Egyptian history, of the science of earthquakes, of Chinese healing exercises, of making crayons, and of many more fascinating interests with my kids.

SUGGESTION 6: HELP CHILDREN EVALUATE INFORMATION FROM OTHERS.

Remember that children progress in their ability to evaluate the accuracy of information from others, moving from an understanding that others might not know something to an understanding that others may be intentionally or unintentionally deceitful. If you suspect that a child has been given information that is wrong, help him or her gain the skills to tell the difference between rumor and reality. You can ask: "How can you find out if this information is true?" Especially as children get older, help them learn about fact checking, about looking up information in a valid place (in a book or on a reliable site on the Internet).

If you think that someone has lied, help your child pursue the truth. But I wouldn't stop there. I would engage your child in looking at the reasons behind why this person might have lied: "Do you think that he wants you to like him or to be impressed?" You can teach your children the importance of telling the truth at the same time that you give them an understanding about why others might lie.

SUGGESTION 7: PROMOTE CRITICAL VIEWING SKILLS.

When we watched television with our school-aged kids, we would dissect the ads. Like film critics, we'd talk about:

What is that commercial trying to sell?

Why do you think the advertising company chose that way of selling the product? Were they trying to get you to think that all cool kids wear this brand of clothes? Were they trying to use peer pressure or sex or adventure or humor to sell this product?

Does this ad work? Does it make you remember the name of the product? Do you want to buy it? Why or why not?

Is this ad accurate? Are the claims they are making true?

Do you get sick of seeing this ad or is it fun to keep watching it? Why?

David Considine, writing for the Center for Media Literacy, suggests that parents help children view television programs, thinking about:

The content of the program. Can they remember the story, how it is being told, what happens and why?

The look and feel of the program. Why is the program presented as it is? For example, if it's a suspenseful show, does having dark spaces and lots of shadows make it feel scarier?

The external forces shaping the program. How does a news channel that is liberal present a news story versus one that is more conservative?

The connection with reality. How accurate or stereotypic is the presentation of an issue or a group of people?

When Philip was in high school, he got annoyed because he thought that teenage boys were being stereotyped on TV. To prove it, he kept a notebook by the TV to tally how often boys were depicted in negative versus positive ways. Critical thinking at work! His tally showed that his impression was right. So we talked about whether he thought this portrayal would prejudice adults against teenage boys, seeing them as delinquents in the making.

He then argued that teenage boys were presented more negatively than girls, so he kept another tally, comparing how boys and girls were depicted. Again he was right. He concluded that television was correcting a societal bias against girls by swinging too far in the other direction. He also concluded that bad news, unfortunately, sells.

SUGGESTION 8: HELP CHILDREN UNDERSTAND CONFOUNDS.

Philip's self-selected research project would be a great one for a group of children because it would have emotional appeal for most kids and it could help them disentangle competing causes. For example, was it that bad news sells more than good news? What about the fact that boys— then and now—are presented on TV more often than girls, so there are more opportunities for boys to be depicted doing something wrong? Were the shows that Philip liked to watch more likely to feature boys than other shows? Given the population of girls and boys, what proportion of each group commits juvenile crimes? How does that proportion compare to television coverage of boys and girls?

There are many daily opportunities to make sure that kids don't jump to conclusions.

The idea that there might be competing causes is one that we struggle with all the time, especially in situations we feel strongly about—be it a problem at work or a world event that has political implications. It's easier, of course, to have a simple answer. But it is better by far to have an answer that connects us firmly to reality than one that may lead us astray.

SUGGESTION 9: WHEN DEALING WITH PARENTING DILEMMAS, USE A PROBLEM-SOLVING PROCESS THAT DRAWS ON CRITICAL THINKING SKILLS.

When I reread my interview with Philip Zelazo, I realized that he had described how each step in the problem-solving process I typically use (the one I wrote about at the beginning of this chapter when addressing Lara's childhood deception) draws on executive functions. In general, executive functions of the brain come into play whenever we engage in behavior that is *deliberately goal directed.* Zelazo says:

> *If you want to start to characterize more precisely what's meant by executive function, think in terms of the sequential steps that people must undertake in order to solve any problem in a goal-directed fashion.*

When you or your children use this problem-solving process, you are drawing on—and possibly strengthening—executive functions of the brain.

1. **Identify the dilemma, problem, or issue.** The first step, Zelazo says, is asking a series of questions: Where am I now? Where would I like to be? What are some of the possible moves that I might make to allow me to get from where I am now to where I ultimately want to be?

2. **Determine the goal.** Since problem solving is ultimately about being goal directed, it's important to determine what your goal is

for yourself or for your children—or, if you are helping children learn to use this process for themselves, to help them determine their goals.

3. **Come up with alternative solutions.** Zelazo notes that considering alternative solutions requires inhibiting "the tendency to do what one has done before in that situation." It also requires thinking flexibly in the pursuit of new possibilities, and that involves our imagination. Paul Harris writes that when we imagine, we draw on our past and project into the future; we conjure up new possibilities to use as the basis for making causal and moral judgments.

4. **Consider how these alternative solutions might work.** In order to do so, we must inhibit our own view of the world to view the solution from the perspective of others.

5. **Select a solution to try.** That, of course, calls on reflecting and critical thinking.

6. **Evaluate the outcome, and if the solution isn't working, try something else.** Zelazo talks about reviewing whether the plan we've made has achieved its intended results, and if not, being willing to change the plan or implement it more effectively.

He notes that executive functions might break down during any one of these sequential steps:

Somebody might fail to represent the problem adequately, for example, because they're rigidly insisting on representing it in a particular narrow fashion. Or maybe they have represented the problem adequately, but they failed to plan effectively. Or maybe they have planned effectively and they've even chosen a plan, but they get distracted and the plan goes out of their minds. Or they do keep the plan in [their] mind, but they may fail to detect their own errors—fail to monitor them, fail to benefit from feedback, fail to learn flexibly.

Change is never easy, but this problem-solving process can create a road map for change.

When Philip was a toddler and young preschooler, I felt as if I couldn't live through one more temper flare-up. I had tried everything. You name it; I had tried it. Desperation was behind my creating this problem-solving process, which I came to use in handling the toughest issues.

One day when Philip was a preschooler, I took him out to lunch. While we were having a good time, I brought up this issue, telling him that I needed to find a way to get him to stop; that he *had* to stop when I said stop; there was no choice. So I set the goal, which is the role of the parent. And he knew why—he wanted to control his temper as much as I wanted him to.

I said, "What ideas do you have that will make you stop when I say stop?" I took out a piece of paper to write down all of his ideas and mine. We discussed and evaluated each of the ideas. He finally came up with a plan—a "very secret phrase" that only he and I would know. He wanted me to say this secret phrase when I needed him to stop.

I asked him, "How do I know this will work?" We had had some false hopes before. "There has to be some consequence if it doesn't work," I said. "And the consequence has to be something you *really* care about." So we brainstormed consequences until we arrived at one that he cared about.

Did it work? Not always, but it worked much more often than not. The more he got his own behavior under control, the longer the sunny stretches in our days and the more he could use his fantastic energy, his passion, and his persistence in positive ways. Both he and I liked that a lot. And now the secret phrase, which both Philip and I remember, makes him laugh!

CHAPTER SIX

SKILL SIX:
TAKING ON CHALLENGES

AN EXERCISE: STRESS AND YOU

Think about the last time you felt really stressed. Now step back and analyze your experience as if you were analyzing someone else's:

What triggered your feelings of being stressed? Did something unexpected happen? Was there an actual danger?

How long did it take you to react to the experience that triggered your feelings of being stressed? Did you react quickly, was there a slow buildup, or was your reaction somewhere in the middle?

On a scale of 1 to 5, with 5 being "very intense," how intense were your feelings?

What were your emotional reactions to the stress? Did you feel overwhelmed, angry, anxious, like running away, or like fighting back?

How long did these feelings last?

How did you manage to downshift and move beyond these feelings? Did these feelings simply pass, or did you do something deliberate to recover? If so, what did you do?

Those of you who have watched *Mister Rogers' Neighborhood* on television probably remember Fred Rogers singing, "You Are Special," with the words "you are the only one like you." That's certainly true about how we react to stress—each of us is unique, responding in a different way.

INVESTIGATING CHILDREN AND STRESS

Having spent years studying workplace stress, I'm fascinated by how we learn to manage stress in childhood, so I was particularly interested in the work of Megan Gunnar of the University of Minnesota, who is one of the foremost authorities on stress and coping in children. When the trip to meet with her was planned, little did any of us know that just days beforehand, our country would be plunged into the severe national stress of September 11, 2001.

We decided to proceed with the visit, traveling by train rather than by plane. After thirty-six hours of sitting in an overcrowded train, with food in short supply and tensions ricocheting through the train cars, but also with the camaraderie of sharing stories about 9/11 among strangers, we felt it only fitting to arrive at Gunnar's lab to film her collecting cortisol samples from young children to measure their stress levels, and to discuss what had prompted her interest in stress and coping and what she was learning from her research:

I was a research assistant for a woman by the name of Eleanor Maccoby, who was studying sex differences in children's behavior. One of the things that they were trying to test was: were girls more fearful than boys? We had these little mechanical toys that made noise. We'd plop those down in front of children and turn them on. Then we'd see who got frightened, who ran back to Mom, and so on. I was watching these children at twelve months [and] I was thinking, "Why are they afraid of these mechanical toys?" I mean, I've heard babies make a lot more noise than these toys make.

Gunnar wanted to go deeper—to understand the biology of stress. That necessitated that she study animals, where there were more opportunities in that era to study the biological underpinnings of stress. When she returned to child development research, opportunities were still limited. For example, *cortisol,* the stress hormone, could be obtained only from blood or urine samples, so Gunnar began by studying infants in hospitals following their births, where blood samples to test cortisol levels were more readily available. Her early studies were instrumental in revealing that newborns experience pain—which, perhaps surprisingly to us now, was not fully understood thirty years ago. As soon as procedures to obtain cortisol from children's saliva became available, Gunnar began studying preschoolers.

Gunnar defines stress as physiologists and psychobiologists do:

Stress is when demands on your body or your expectations of those demands exceed your ability to handle them.

Most of the time, our bodies are functioning on automatic. When something happens to disrupt the process of normal functioning, which Gunnar calls *growth and repair* mode, our bodies need to recruit "extra resources to meet extra demands."

THE PHYSIOLOGY OF STRESS

What specifically does "recruit extra resources to meet extra demands" mean? With Megan Gunnar as a guide, I took a trip into the body to follow the process.

The first step is the emergence of a threat or challenge. While these stressors can be internal—you fall and hurt yourself—let's use an external threat as an example: you feel as if someone is following you too closely as you and your child walk down an unfamiliar street at dusk. This sensation sends messages through circuits to the thinking and reasoning parts of your brain (the *cortex*) and the emotional and memory parts of your brain (the *limbic system,* including the *hippocampus* and *amygdala*) so you can interpret the situation: is this a serious threat or not?

Let's say the threat seems serious. You catch a reflection of the person following you in a store window and see he has his hand in his pocket (a weapon?). He's getting closer and closer.

The cortex and the limbic systems send messages to your hypothalamus, which alerts your *autonomic nervous system* (ANS). Made up of nerves connected to your heart, lungs, stomach, glands, and blood vessels, the ANS operates on automatic most of the time to regulate your heart rate, circulation, breathing, and digestion.

One part of your ANS is the *sympathetic nervous system,* responsible for your *fight-or-flight response.* When a danger seems real, it stimulates the rapid release of *adrenaline* and *noradrenaline,* to prepare you for fight or flight. Secreted from the central part of your adrenal glands (located over your kidneys), these hormones send messages to your circulatory, respiratory, and digestive systems to respond to the danger—and the symptoms you associate with stress quickly appear: your pupils dilate; your breathing accelerates; your blood pressure rises; your heart rate increases to send blood and oxygen where they're needed—for example, giving you the energy to run away. Your attention becomes highly focused, and your digestive system activity is reduced, so you may experience a dry mouth, a lump in your throat or butterflies in your stomach, and lack of appetite. Even your perception of pain is dulled.

Your *hypothalamic-pituitary-adrenocortical* system (HPA) is also activated by danger. The hypothalamus and other parts of your brain send messages to your pituitary, which activates the outer part of your adrenal glands, the *adrenal cortex,* to release cortisol and other *glucocorticoids.* Known as the stress hormone, cortisol increases your blood pressure, mobilizes fats and glucose to give you energy to respond to the danger, reduces allergic reactions, and suppresses your immune system.

All systems—the HPA and the ANS—are now "go" to deal with the immediate danger. Gunnar elaborates:

> *These hormones—both adrenaline and cortisol—play a role in shifting body resources. They pull resources away from things that have to do with growth and repair—[such as] the immune system and physical growth—and shift them into things your body is doing to meet the immediate challenge—breaking down fats and sugars so they're in the bloodstream so your cells can use them for action.*

Now let's say that the person who was making you apprehensive rushes past you, and you realize that the danger isn't real or, at least, is over. The hypothalamus sends messages to your hypothalamic-pituitary-adrenocortical system (HPA) to throttle down, and your level of cortisol begins to decrease. It also sends messages to your autonomic nervous system (ANS) to deactivate your sympathetic nervous system and to activate a second system, your *parasympathetic nervous system,* which controls what Gunnar calls "growth and repair." It increases the energy you have stored and promotes healing and normal functioning. Once the danger has ended, Gunnar continues:

> *You want to turn those systems off and jump back into that nice growth mode and repair what you took away from it.*

AN EXERCISE: STRESS AND YOU, CONTINUED

Go back to the experience of feeling stressed that you thought about in the beginning of this chapter. There, I asked you about your psychological experience with stress, but think about your physical reaction.

What were your physical reactions to the stress? Did your heart pound? Did you feel shortness of breath? Was there a knot in your throat or in your stomach? What else?

Learning about how the body responds to stress helps me understand what happens to me after a near-miss accident in the car—why my legs start to shake *after* the danger has passed. Or why, when I was in an actual car crash, I didn't feel pain right away. Or why doctors ask you about your stress level if you are finding it hard to lose weight (you are storing fats in case you need them for energy).

THE IMPACT OF STRESS

As parents, we may want to shield our kids from all stress, but that's neither possible nor positive. Megan Gunnar says:

A childhood that had no stress in it would not prepare you for adulthood. If you never allow your child[ren] to exceed what they can do, how are they going to learn to manage adult life—where a lot of it is managing more than you thought you could manage?

A normal childhood has challenges in it—where children feel like "Oh, maybe I'm going to fail" or "Maybe this won't work" or whatever. [For example], no matter what a parent does, we can't make friends for our children. We can try to help them make friends, but we can't make other children like our child. There are challenges, and we need to help our children understand how to manage themselves, but not protect them completely from those challenges.

While such challenges are normal, *severe and very prolonged stress without the help of others to recover* can have a negative impact on children (and adults). It can affect their ability to remember, to pay attention, and to have self control, and it can also increase their negative emotions. Gunnar says:

When you move from the normal stresses and challenges of life to kids who are really in overwhelming circumstances, we may be talking about some fairly important effects on the way the brain develops, the way it reacts to stress later, and the way it processes information.

What makes the difference in whether stress is positive or harmful? You might be surprised by some of the findings from research.

FACTORS THAT MATTER—THE NATURE OF THE STRESS

It goes without saying that there's a difference between the impact of stress triggered by a child's trip to the doctor for a regular pediatric checkup and the stress caused by the illness or death of a loved one or a frightening accident. A review of the research on stress and children by the National Scientific Council on the Developing Child, based at Harvard University and directed by Jack P. Shonkoff, states that the stresses caused by everyday challenges like "meeting new people, dealing with frustration, entering a new child care center, getting an immunization, and overcoming a fear of animals" are positive as long as the child has the support that he or she needs to master these situations. Learning to adjust to this kind of experience, they write, is "an essential feature of healthy development."

What about the impact of more serious incidents? The council has concluded that it's not so much the nature of the severe stress that affects children, but how long it lasts, and whether there are supportive adults in the child's life "who create safe environments that help children learn to cope with and recover from major adverse experiences."

FACTORS THAT MATTER—HOW LONG THE STRESS LASTS

As the National Scientific Council on the Developing Child notes, the length of time children are under severe stress (in combination with the presence or absence of a supportive adult and other factors) makes a difference. That's understandable given the way the stress system works. The longer the child's system is bathed in stress hormones and the longer the growth and repair system is tamped down, the greater the potential impact.

If you're like me, reading this might be stressful in itself, and I don't mean to be alarmist. Recovering from some difficult experiences—like a divorce or the death of someone you love—simply takes time. The main thing to remember is that many factors matter, and the ones I describe below are things that you can do something about.

FACTORS THAT MATTER—CREATING A RELATIONSHIP OF TRUST WITH YOUR CHILD

Study after study reveals that children who have warm, caring, and trusting relationships with their mothers, fathers, and other significant people in their lives are less prone to stress. In measuring children's production of cortisol during doctor visits, Gunnar traced these patterns:

> *We found that newborns up through about two months of age have a really reactive system. Just picking the baby up will often provoke a slight increase [in cortisol].*

That shouldn't worry parents, Gunnar says. It's just the way newborns are. However, within a few weeks, things begin to change:

> *Sometime between ten and twelve weeks of life, [infants] become less reactive to handling. They're able to regulate their responses. By four to six months, we get less of a reaction to the doctor exam and inoculations.*

As children turn one to two years old, the cortisol response to a doctor exam "dampens down" even more.

What about other stressful situations—such as separations from a parent?

> *At nine months, we found that the babies who cried more were producing more of a cortisol response, but the response wasn't that great. And we tried doing it with thirteen-month-olds. Babies were upset, but they didn't show any increase in this hormone.*

So the same pattern is evident—as they grow, children's stress systems become more regulated. But this isn't because they are ready to handle stress on their own. In fact, what is happening over the first year of life is that the infant's stress biology is coming under strong social control. Those months involve a major shift in babies' development that helps to explain their growing ability to manage stress:

> *This period near the end of the first year is when babies begin to use one or a few people as sources of security. The fact that the babies*

seek security from one or a few people is the thing that seems to be helping to control the child's bodily stress reactions.

The key is trust. Children with adults whom they learn to trust to care for them can weather stormier situations. Gunnar says:

When babies get upset, they cry to the adult: "I don't like this. I'll let Mom and Dad know I don't like this."

They get distressed, they cry, and they cling:

They're acting scared. They are scared. But they have a strong expectation that "as long as I'm with you, Mom, Dad, then I know I'm safe."

Gunnar summarizes:

Remember, stress is when challenge overwhelms your capacity to manage it. With a trusting relationship with a parent who's been there for you and [who's] accessible, you're not overwhelmed.

FACTORS THAT MATTER—HOW STRESSFUL EXPERIENCES ARE CONVEYED

So *you* matter—and that includes how you convey stressful situations to your child.

In a now classic experiment, Joseph Campos of the University of California at Berkeley demonstrated how parental concerns are transmitted to children. The impetus for the study grew out of observing a transition that occurs when babies begin to move around—to crawl, walk, explore, and get into everything. Campos describes this all too familiar scene:

Parents' emotional communication with that child changes drastically; they are going to start trying to regulate the child's behavior—

encouraging the child to explore certain things but also restricting exploration of things the child might damage; for example, knocking over a vase. The communication from the mother or from the father—encouraging or discouraging—sensitizes the child to pay attention.

When you hit that stage of parenthood, I suspect that you've not only noticed the changes in your own behavior, but also the changes in your child's. Here's what typically happens. Your child approaches something new or forbidden and then looks back at you to read your reaction, as if to ask, "Is this okay?" This behavior is called *social referencing*. It occurs when young children are confronted with ambiguous situations and search for information from others to guide what they should feel and do.

A PARENT'S PERSPECTIVE: IT'S ONLY CLOTHES

My daughter often looks at me before doing something new or something she knows she shouldn't be doing. If it's something new, I think she's looking to see if I will say, "Everything is going to be okay." If it's something she shouldn't be doing, I think she's looking to see if I will really get upset.

Last week, we were at the beach but not prepared for swimming because it was a spur-of-the-moment thing. We were wearing our regular clothing and shoes. Amelia had on jellies, so they could get wet, but I didn't have a change of clothes for her, so didn't want her going into the water beyond her feet.

She had other plans, but as she inched into the water, she kept staring at me more and more intently. It was as if she was saying, "C'mon, let me in. And if I do it, please go with it . . . it's only clothes!" I found the whole thing amusing. I would have done the same thing as a child.

To investigate social referencing, Campos and his colleagues wanted to use an ambiguous situation that was somewhat frightening. They se-

lected an experimental strategy developed in the 1950s by the late Eleanor Gibson of Cornell University: the *visual cliff*.

Essentially, the visual cliff is a large table with wooden railings on all
four sides and a tabletop made of clear Plexiglas. Half the table is covered
with a checkered patterned material just beneath the surface, so children
can't see through it to the floor below. In the middle of the table, however,
there's a visual drop-off. Although the Plexiglas continues, so the table is
perfectly safe, the top becomes see-through, and the checked pattern is
now visible far below the clear surface, close to the floor. It reminds me of
walking on a sidewalk and suddenly coming upon a subway grate expos-
ing a netherworld beneath—an adult version of the visual cliff.

Infants from nine to twelve months are lifted by an experimenter
onto the part of the table where the checkered pattern is just beneath the
surface. The child's mother (mothers took part in the original experiment, but it would work with fathers, too) is at the other end of the table,
holding out an appealing toy. The mother smiles at the baby until she or
he reaches the place where the checkered pattern on the surface ends and
the child can see the visual cliff below. Campos explains:

> [W]hat we attempted to do is to understand the extent to which
> the nonverbal facial communication coming from the mother to
> the child—when the child looked up to the mother—affected that
> baby's behavior.

Just before the baby reaches the visual cliff, the mother is told to
make either a happy or a fear face. For this study, the mothers are trained
in how to express happiness and fear, based on standardized facial proto-
types of these emotions. To make a fear face, mothers raise their eyebrows,
drawing them together; their eyes are wide open, and their mouths are
also open. They truly look frightened, although they don't use any words,
sounds, or gestures.

It is amazing to watch this study in action. The babies crawl or scoot
up to the visual cliff and then hesitate, glancing at their mothers, then
back at the safe place where their journey began, then back again at their
mothers. In response to a fear face, some of the babies even shake their

heads no, while others stick a toe across the line marking the beginning of the cliff as if to "test the waters" before retreating to safety. Campos describes the findings:

> *If the mother is posing a fear face, the baby typically does not cross this visual cliff. On the other hand, if the mother poses a smile or somehow poses a nonverbal communication that is not prohibitive but encouraging, the child is much more likely to cross over to her. This particular study powerfully demonstrates the role of nonverbal communication in determining the child's behavior in an uncertain context.*

It's not just babies who react this way. I remember being on a bus that sputtered, made harsh grinding sounds, and slammed to a stop on the highway. I did what babies do—I looked at other passengers and the driver so I could figure out whether I should be alarmed or not. Campos comments:

> *By eleven to twelve months of age, the baby is already doing what all of us do when something unusual happens—we look around to figure out how other people are reacting.*

Although some experiences are inherently frightening, adults also communicate whether situations are scary or not in many subtle and not so subtle ways, giving children clues about whether a situation is stressful. This research tells us that we should be more *intentional* about what we want to convey, because children do pick up our clues and cues, whether we're aware of what we're expressing or not.

A PARENT'S PERSPECTIVE:
PLEASE DON'T DO THIS AGAIN

I was testing out a lock in my daughter Lucy's room (she's eight now). I wasn't paying attention and ended up closing the door and locking us in the room. There was no one else in the house at the time—of course my husband was miles away, on a business trip.

At first I just laughed at myself so that Lucy wouldn't get upset at the situation and told her that Mama did something stupid. She instantly corrected me for using the "s-word"! I began to look around her room to test out things that would release the lock but was unsuccessful. She started giving me suggestions, like jumping out of the second-story window.

I continued to try to laugh and joke about our situation, but Lucy began to intuit my stress despite my best efforts. Finally she said, "Mama, I'm scared that we're going to be locked in here forever." I tried to assuage her fears. Then I happened upon a bejeweled bobby pin, which I inserted into the knob. It worked. Lucy looked at me and said fearfully, "Mama, please don't lock us in my room again."

FACTORS THAT MATTER—SUPPORTING CHILDREN IN MANAGING THEIR OWN STRESS

You may think that helping children learn to master their *own* stress is possible only when children are older, but that's not true. It is possible at the very beginnings of life, even with babies born prematurely, as research by Heidelise Als of Children's Hospital Boston and the Harvard Medical School demonstrates.

Als began her career in her native Germany as a teacher of third-grade boys. She was fascinated by the differences among children. She says:

> *I very quickly learned that each of these children took my teaching in very different ways. I remember very clearly this one boy Reinhard.*

She recalls that Reinhard always came to school early, sat down in his seat close to the front of the classroom, lined up all his pencils and books on the desk, and was ready for the school day to begin. He worked unusually hard and got good grades. Since Reinhard was doing very well, Als decided to move him farther back in the room so that another child who needed extra help would have a seat in the front. She continues:

Reinhard moved promptly, yet the next day he didn't come in. He had never missed a day of school. I was very concerned. He didn't come the next day. The note [from his family] said he wasn't feeling well, but [there was] no explanation.

After a few days, she stopped by the bakery his family ran:

His mother was behind the counter and she said, "Reinhard isn't feeling well. He did have a little vomiting, but the doctor says there is nothing the matter." I said, "What do you think is happening?" And she said, "Well, he did tell me you moved his seat and he's now sitting further back. But I don't think that could do it."

Als told Reinhard's mother to tell him that he, of course, could have his seat back:

I learned from that that despite [seeing] the image of a very competent child, I should have known from his organization—from his need to have everything [lined up at the start of the school day]— that he didn't have the flexibility that other children had.

Als's sense that you have to understand the language of children's behavior to figure out how they function best and then build on their positive self-regulation strategies was reinforced after she moved to the United States to attend graduate school and had her own child, who is significantly brain damaged. She had to learn to read the language of his behavior to help him. She brought that sensitivity into her early research on premature babies, born ten to twelve weeks before their due dates. Through advances in technology in the 1970s, these babies, who couldn't yet breathe on their own, could be kept alive with medical ventilators that, in effect, breathed for them. What really interested Als was "to see what these babies were up against" and how they were handling those challenges.

As she observed them, it became clear to her that good medical care was coming at the price of supporting the baby's development. I find her description of the care of babies in that era particularly poignant because my son, Philip, was born prematurely. At almost three pounds, Philip never had medical problems and didn't need a ventilator, but I still get chills thinking about the picture Als paints of what the care of tiny babies was like:

[The premature babies] would be pinned down, held down, strapped down, and even chemically treated, if needed, so that they would not breathe against the ventilator [in order] to let the ventilator do the work that it needed to do.

A similar kind of scene took place when a nurse or doctor wanted to check on a baby and listen to his heart rate or change him:

When a baby was touched, his fingers would splay, [his face] would start to scrunch, his color would change, and his heart rate would go up.

When they turned a child over, they actually called it *flipping*—because that's the way they handled these newborns:

The baby would just splay out—all four limbs would fly out, and then the baby would try to grasp at something, but the nurse by then would already be [putting her] stethoscope on the chest, listening to the chest sounds. And then she would turn the baby over again and listen to the back, and then she would start to suction [his lungs], and then she would give a nebulizer treatment.

By then, Als reports, the baby would be beside himself:

The alarm would go off and [the nurse] would increase the oxygen. Then she would lift the ankles and change the diaper and wipe the baby clean and put the clean diaper on—ankles up and ankles down again. And then the baby would go limp typically and stop breathing.

It was clear to Heidelise Als, from her own training and from her work with the well-known Harvard pediatrician T. Berry Brazelton, that the medical care was so focused on caring for these premature babies' hearts or lungs that they were overlooking the care of the whole child:

> It seemed we were wasting a lot of the baby's energies that were very precious. We were going against the baby. We were pushing the baby to become exhausted and give in.

When a baby who was initially feisty gave in, the medical charts would record that the baby had become well adjusted. But Als saw a different reality:

> The baby had given up. The baby just let the world happen to [him or her].

Als says that a similar process happens to older children when they are overridden long enough—"they just let it happen and become depressed." Als observed the same effect in the hospital *neonatal intensive care units* (NICUs):

> We see depression in the nursery as early as thirty-two, thirty-four weeks' [gestation]. You can see a baby [over] the course [of] admission to a few weeks later having given up. [It] isn't worth it any longer for the baby. The baby doesn't put the energy out anymore to fight to live.

Als and her colleagues—nurses and doctors—set out to change care in a more developmentally supportive way and to document that it makes a difference:

> We started with a study of the babies who were called the most difficult babies in the nursery. These were babies who had developed or were on the course of developing severe lung disease.

Funded by a small grant, they began to document the babies' behavior. They thought of this as listening to the babies' behavioral "language." Als says:

If we can understand the "words" the baby is saying, maybe we can fill in the meaning of the "sentence" and understand the "message." And if we get into the body of the baby and envision what the immature nervous system is currently experiencing, perhaps we can formulate ways [of caregiving] that work for that [particular] baby.

These observations led to solutions. For example, if the baby's hands splay out, give the baby something to hold on to. If the baby is squirming under the bright lights, make the lighting softer. If the baby is getting agitated, cradle the baby with your hands until his or her breathing becomes more stable.

After documenting and recording behavior, they launched into a study where the nurses "read" and then responded to the baby's behavior in ways that built on that baby's own strategies and thus gave the baby more control. Als reports:

When we analyzed the data, the babies came off the ventilator significantly earlier [than babies typically did in their NICU], came out of [being given] oxygen significantly more quickly, and gained weight better. They had much better ability to regulate their motor systems—they didn't go pale so easily or go into rapid breathing; their lung disease was so much less bad.

It wasn't clear, however, whether the care itself had made the difference. Critics argued that these changes might have been a result of improvements in medical care during the year when the experiment was conducted, compared with medical care given to the *baseline* group the year before. So Als and her colleagues continued to improve the developmental care before launching a new study. For example, they used tiny pacifiers like fingers for the babies to suck. And because tightly swaddling the babies in blankets caused them to feel restricted and get stressed, they created soft clothes so that the babies could move while feeling comforted:

> *We wanted a kind of a cocoon. So we made a bunting with a hood and a soft roll in the bottom to tuck the feet into.*

They even created welcoming furniture, so that mothers who had had Cesarean sections could touch their babies on the warming table and not hurt themselves. Overall, these babies received care that was individualized, responsive, and respectful—care that provided:

Consistency. Each child was assigned a team of medical and nursing caregivers who continued to work with the baby and the family.

Time for rest and recovery. The medical and nursing care was timed to coincide with the babies' sleep-wake cycles.

Support for the family. Parents were welcomed. They were supported in how to read their baby's behavior and take a significant role in providing care for their newborn (versus being observers from the sidelines, as was more typical at that time).

Comfort. Parents were encouraged to hold their babies so that the babies were more comfortable during caregiving. Babies were no longer made to stay on their backs in the incubators; they would be put on their sides so that they could curl up easily, wrapped in their cozy buntings.

Skin-to-skin holding.

Pleasant, calm feeding experiences.

Quiet, soothing environments. Rather than bright lights and harsh beeps from the medical equipment, the environment was quiet and restful. Parents were encouraged to consider the space around their babies' bedsides as their own space and to decorate it.

The research team trained a group of interested nurses in these procedures and then randomly assigned premature babies to the Newborn Individualized Developmental Care and Assessment Program (NIDCAP) followed by the trained nurses or to traditional care that included excellent medical services, yet not the attention to the individual infant's language with the corresponding adaptations of the environment and care to support the infant. Again the results were impressive, and with this experiment, they could be certain that the results stemmed from the developmental care, since the decision about which babies received developmental care was made randomly. The results included decreased intraventricular (brain) hemorrhages, reduced severity of chronic lung disease, improved growth, and earlier release from the hospital. In addition, the hospitalization of these babies was significantly less costly, since the babies who received developmental care went home much earlier.

In subsequent experiments, Als and her colleagues found that developmental care enhances brain structure and brain functioning, mainly in the left frontal part of the brain, where executive functions take place as the child grows up. Thus, Als says that developmental care will affect the babies' future ability to manage stress, to be less impulsive, to better make plans, and to prioritize.

I have visited NICUs that offer the Individualized Developmental Care and Assessment Program. These environments look as if Heidelise Als and her colleagues are giving these tiny babies the kind of experiences they might have had if they had remained in the womb. But there is a much more important difference:

> In traditional care, the baby is seen much more as an object; the baby has various organs, and these organs are cared for by experts in that organ's care. In the developmental model, the baby is considered a person; the baby is actively constructing [his or her] own development.

And that's what is critical. Children, even those as young as premature infants, are less prone to the harmful effects of stress when they are supported in managing *their own* stress by being helped to use the strategies that even these tiny infants have for coping and for calming down. Als says:

> Some may think [developmental] care might lead to overindul-
> gence on the parents' part or [being] spoiled on the child's part,
> [reflecting the point of view that] "you have to toughen the child
> up from early on." On the contrary, we find that the more in tune
> the parent is with the child's competencies, the more the parent is
> equipped to support the competencies.

The take-home message for parents: If we dwell on what the child *can't* do—the child's inadequacies—those inadequacies will likely pro-liferate. If we focus on what the child *can* do—the child's strengths— these will likely be fortified. That's the true meaning of taking a strength-based and developmentally supportive approach, Als says.

What happens if a child doesn't get that care? My son, Philip, was born before Individualized Developmental Care had been created or implemented. He spent his first five weeks in a NICU, and although he didn't experience the rough handling that Als describes, and although he was a healthy premature baby who didn't require any severe medical in-terventions, he was in a glaringly lit, noisy, impersonal, and isolating en-vironment. Parents were considered "risks"—we might bring germs into the NICU. No parents were ever allowed in, although it didn't escape my notice that the maintenance staff were allowed easy access to the NICU to pick up the garbage a couple of times a day. So we found a nurse who was willing to break the rules to allow us to hold and cuddle Philip; we gave him the best possible care we could when he came home from the hos-pital; and we fought with some other parents and doctors and eventually succeeded in having the rules changed in that hospital. It was not an ideal beginning to his life, but it hasn't harmed him, either. That's why I can say with assurance that every day is a new day in parenthood: every day we can make a difference, despite what has happened in the past.

FACTORS THAT MATTER—GIVING CHILDREN SOME CONTROL IN LEARNING HOW TO MANAGE STRESS

What Heidelise Als was doing was developing care that gives these premature infants some control in managing their own stress, building on their own coping capacities. Remember Megan Gunnar's story of how she became interested in studying children's stress and coping after assisting in a study assessing children's fear levels when shown little mechanical toys? Gunnar found herself wondering why these toys were so scary, because, after all, she'd heard these babies make a lot more noise than the toys. It dawned on her that the difference might have been that the children were making the noises themselves. She tested her idea in a study:

> I set up a way for children to turn on the mechanical toys themselves, or the toy came on according to a pattern of what another child had done.

This study revealed that having control over whether the toy turned on or not was an essential factor in children's responses:

> We got a beautiful set of data that by twelve months [of age], the children's control over making arousing things happen was important in helping them decide whether they liked it or [whether] it was scary. The children who didn't have control were more fearful. And the ones who had control thought it was the greatest thing they'd done in a long time—they were laughing and giggling.

This is aligned with the research on learned helplessness:

> Having control is the principal variable in determining whether a body responds to stress when situations are potentially dangerous or not, or threatening or not.

Helping children gain control comes in many forms. We give them the tools for managing and gradually turn things over to them so that they can use these tools.

A PARENT'S PERSPECTIVE: WHOSE JAM IS IT?

June does not do well with long-term projects, like science projects. We have helped her by setting minigoals with the reward of Internet time: no goal, no Internet.

Now that she is twelve years old, we see that she also needs to experience the consequences of her own actions. If she chooses to stay up late the night before her project is due, we will *not* be available to help her out of her jam.

Another way of helping children learn to cope is helping them know whom to turn to for help.

A PARENT'S PERSPECTIVE: WE WILL BE THE FALL GUYS

Sometimes helping our children learn to cope meant letting them "use" us. We always told our children that if their friends were doing—or planning to do—something they felt was a bad or dangerous idea, they could opt out and blame it on their mean, old-fashioned parents. This took the peer pressure off them, and we were happy to be "vilified" in any way that kept our kids out of trouble.

This became an important tool for them in their teens. Once, when our son was in high school, he came to me and said, "Mom, the guys want me to go with them to a country cemetery tonight— and I think it's a bad idea. Please tell me I can't go."

Recently, following a speech I had given to parents, a mother approached me, saying that her preschool son balked at new experiences and that these instances typically deteriorated into battles. I suggested that she talk with him during a calm moment and say, "We keep having the same problem again and again when we have to go someplace new: you say no, I say yes, and then we fight. Sometimes there is no choice— we have to go. What ideas do you have that would help you manage?" Later, I heard that he decided to bring his favorite small "comfort" toy in his pocket. It wasn't the toy that helped him as much as it was taking control of the situation and coming up with his own coping plan.

A MANAGER'S PERSPECTIVE: BEATING THE WORRY HABIT

I was a worried little kid. I worried all the time, about everything. When I attended a new school, I worried whether I could remember the combination for my locker; whether I could find my way around; whether I would drop my lunch tray—and that was just until I could find other things to worry about. The only thing bigger than my worry was my ferocious interest in learning. Once I got into the new situation, I became engaged with whatever we were learning, and the rest of the stuff sort of worked itself out. I grew to become someone who displayed great competence, but my coping style of worry was always there inside.

Working in a high-pressure job, I began to see that worry was sapping my energy to solve complex problems. The problems were getting bigger and bigger, and I realized that the stress of my worry habit was going to eat me alive unless I learned to cope differently. I could see, too, that it would hold me back from progressing in my career, because the big problems that came with big responsibility would produce an overwhelming amount of worry. So I developed a mantra: "Worry doesn't work." Every time I started to worry, I'd say it. Then I'd ask myself, "Okay, so what can I do instead?" "Well, you could ask so-and-so for some advice . . . you could make one phone call today to get this started . . . you could research this or that item . . . you could assemble a team to do the parts of this you can't do . . . you could set up a schedule for getting the project done" . . . etc. Of course, as I took these baby steps, I'd get engaged: I'd learn new things, gather information, enroll other people in the process, learn more questions to ask, brainstorm ideas, and move the project or problem forward step-by-step until it was done. Mountains of work and seemingly unsolvable problems could be mastered in this way. As I look back, I see that I was swapping action for worry, and specifically the kind of action where I felt powerful and excited: learning something and working with others to do so. I guess I've also learned that it's up to me to separate the task from how it feels. The task is just the task. I can choose to complete it from a different emotional place.

FACTORS THAT MATTER—YOUR CHILD'S TEMPERAMENT

Obviously, the child who balks at or worries about new experiences is going to react to going to new places differently than one eager for adventure. That kind of uniqueness is called *temperament*. As parents, we instinctively understand temperament. We know that each of our children has been unique from the moment of birth on, that what works with one doesn't necessarily work with another, and that the way we parent each child—including twins—differs.

It's been challenging for scientists to define and measure temperament. While they agree that temperaments are inborn and are tied to biological and genetic differences, there's been an evolving understanding of what constitutes temperament. Alexander Thomas and Stella Chess were among the first to define temperament in the 1960s through the 1980s. Based on a study of one hundred children, they saw children as having nine different dimensions of temperament.

Another model, developed by Mary Rothbart and Douglas Derryberry of the University of Oregon, provides the definition I find most compelling. First, children vary in how they *react* to new experiences, specifically in:

the starting point or threshold of their responses;

how long it takes them to respond; and

how intensely they respond.

Second, children vary in how they *regulate* their responses; in other words, how long it takes them to manage the new situation, calm themselves, and return to normal.

The questions I asked you about your own responses to a stressful experience in the beginning of this chapter followed these themes.

Because of the challenges in studying temperament, I was eager to talk with Jerome Kagan of Harvard University, the man who has been called the "father of temperament" because his studies have led to so many breakthroughs in understanding what is unique in each child. Among other issues, he has pursued an ongoing quest to determine how much of behavior is inborn and how much is influenced by experience. Kagan recalls that when he became a developmental psychologist in the 1950s, the role of experience was considered primary:

> *For my generation of twenty-one-year-olds to choose [to be developmental psychologists, you were seen as] choosing God's work because you were going to learn what [caused] psychosis, achievement, depression. And then you'd tell the parents of America what to do and you could retire to a mansion in heaven. [We felt that] we were within a decade of understanding it all—what formed a child, what made a child delinquent or a genius. Honest, we believed that.*

He continues:

> *Of course, the bubble burst. We realized it's a lot more complicated. Yes, your mother's important, but there are other factors. We didn't understand the role of biology at all. We didn't understand the role of culture, of class, of historical era—none of that.*

An experience changed his worldview. During a yearlong sabbatical in Guatemala, Kagan observed a very different form of child rearing. Because the Mayan Indians living in northwest Guatemala believe that "an infant in his first year is vulnerable to the evil eye of adults and therefore you don't want adults looking at the child," these children were raised in ways that parents in the United States might consider neglectful or substandard. At the end of their first year, the infants look "sallow" and have "no vitality."

> *But at five years of age, they look like New York children. They're vivacious, they play, they [communicate]. And that's when I changed; that's when I realized that I was ignoring the role of biological maturation. And so then I began to acknowledge the role of biology, the role of larger culture, and I think my work got better.*

In 1979 Kagan began studying the role of temperament in toddlers. A few years later, he, his colleague Nancy Snidman, and another colleague launched a longitudinal study in which they screened 462 middle-class four-month-olds and found that one group of infants, about 20 percent of the total, were what they called *high reactive*. In response to new experiences, these children became physically agitated and distressed.

Another group of about 40 percent fell at the other end of the continuum: they were *low reactive*—"They're very relaxed babies, they babble a lot, they sleep well."

As all the babies grew up, the researchers continued to look at how these two groups differed biologically and how they responded to new experiences:

> *In the second year, we brought each child with its mother [to our lab] and over a two-hour period, [the child] encountered seventeen unfamiliar events—unfamiliar women, a woman with a gas mask, unfamiliar toys, unfamiliar rooms.*

They filmed the children to see which children reacted by holding on to their mothers' hands, looking tense and fearful, and which children weren't bothered.

Kagan explains how the high-reactive children responded:

> *[They] are born with a temperament that biases this child to react to anything new—new person, new food, new situation—with caution, reserve, until they assimilate it.*

The words he uses are deliberately chosen to reflect what he found. Explaining why he uses the word *bias,* he says:

Notice I'm not using the word determined. *[Children's inherited biology] doesn't determine anything. It's a push. That's temperament.*

He also uses the word *reserve.* "Notice I didn't use the word *anxiety,* but *reserve . . . vigilance."*

In contrast, the low-reactive children have a different bias: "They're biased to be the *sociable, bold* kids."

Kagan and his colleagues continued to follow these children until they were eleven years old, observing them, interviewing the children's mothers and teachers, and as the children got older, conducting biological tests including an *electroencephalogram* (EEG) to determine the electrical activity in their scalps in response to unfamiliar events. Their research question was: which children retained their inborn temperament and which children changed? Kagan summarizes the statistics about the reserved children:

I start with twenty out of one hundred of these [reserved] *infants. At adolescence, seven will be very introverted; the remaining thirteen will look average, but not one will be a highly exuberant, highly bold, highly extroverted child.*

Kagan notes that you can't push biology that far; however, children who retain the biology of a shy child can learn to behave in a relaxed way. Therefore, he concludes:

You can't judge a book by its cover. We have some children who were high-reactive infants—they cried, they were very fearful at two. At age eleven, they are not shy; they appear relaxed. The mother says, "My kid's not shy." On the other hand, we have a small number of children who were low-reactive infants, fearless at age two, who were very shy at age eleven, but they don't show any of the biology.

In other words, while the child's biology is important, it doesn't fully determine how that child will react to stress. Kagan concludes:

The behavior you see in a child is like observing the sky without a telescope. You just see a little. You've got to peer deeper.

FACTORS THAT MATTER—PARENTING STYLES

When you peer deeper into temperament, what do you see and what makes a difference? That's a question Nathan Fox has investigated at Harvard as a graduate student of Kagan's and now at the University of Maryland, where he has conducted seminal research on temperament.

Fox and his colleagues present four-month-olds with new sounds and sights and then videotape and code the infants' behavior to measure their *reactivity*—how intense their physical response is and what emotions they express. Like Kagan, they have been particularly interested in infants who responded to new people, new places, and new events with intense physical behavior and negative emotions. Of the 433 children screened, they've studied 153 children over time to find the biological and brain underpinnings of *inhibited* behavior. Fox has found that such children represent 15 percent of this age group.

These researchers and others believe that a specific brain circuit is involved. This circuit links the amygdala (an almond-shaped structure deep within the brain that processes emotions and memory) to parts of the prefrontal cortex and enables children to respond to threat and then to regulate their reaction. For those children who have trouble responding to threat, Fox thinks:

The amygdala [gets] overexcited and [these children's] ability to regulate [it] is not that effective.

As they continued to "peer deeper," the researchers made a very important discovery: they identified, for the first time, genes that may underlie children's tendency to be anxious, fearful, and stressed when faced with new experiences.

When I first read about this, I thought, "What if my child has those genes? Are genes destiny?" The answer from Fox's research is an unqualified no. He put it well in an interview with the National Scientific Council on the Developing Child:

> *Think of it as similar to having an allergy to peanuts; you only get*
> *ill if you eat peanuts.*

That is, you may be born with a certain set of genes, but those genes only give you the *disposition* to become shy. You need certain experiences over time to develop a shy personality.

The good news from his research is that he and his colleagues are identifying the aspects of the environment that make a difference. One is parenting style. If children who get upset and stressed by new experiences have parents who don't help them learn to *regulate* their emotions, they're likely to become more fearful and anxious as preschoolers and as school-age children.

Exactly what do these parents do? I asked Fox. Although in their research articles they use many different words to describe the parenting styles that are not helpful, Fox says it comes down to two characteristics:

Parents who are *alarmist.* These parents see danger everywhere. Fox uses the example of a child building a block tower. The parent might say things like "The tower is going to fall" or "You are going to hurt yourself."

Parents who are *intrusive.* Fox says that you could call this overprotective—these parents interfere with what their children are doing. They don't let their children explore:

> *If a nine-month-old is crawling off the blanket toward a toy, the*
> *parent picks up the toy and moves it toward the child so that the*
> *child doesn't have to move. [With] an older child, the parent man-*

ages the child's interactions with other children. They redirect the conversation: "Take this toy and give it to the other child." They move the situation along.

I asked Fox how his coders would differentiate between parents who are *guiding* their children's behavior and parents who are *interfering*. He says that it's a matter of degree—taking over rather than building on the child's own strategies for managing. That echoes back to Heidelise Als's research, where parents and health professionals built on premature babies' *own* coping strategies.

Fox says that the difference between guiding and interfering is also a matter of emotion. The parents who are being alarmist or intrusive have negative emotions written all over their faces and reverberating in their voices. That links to Joe Campos's research on social referencing and how attuned young children are to seeing their parents' "fear face" and thus deciding not to cross the visual cliff.

FACTORS THAT MATTER—OTHER ADULTS, CHILD CARE, AND OTHER CHILDREN

There was a surprising finding in the longitudinal study that Fox and his colleagues have been conducting. Among those four-month-olds who had behavioral markers for becoming inhibited later in life (negative emotions and intense physical behavior when confronted with new experiences), those children who attended child care in their first two years were more likely to change; in other words, they were less likely to be fearful and anxious at four years of age. The researchers postulate several possible explanations for this finding. Perhaps the children in child care learn to be more comfortable with new experiences and new people. Perhaps they're expected to be more independent. The more conclusive explanations haven't yet been found, and Fox and his colleagues continue to investigate them.

FACTORS THAT MATTER—PARENTS WHO THEMSELVES HAVE SUPPORTIVE RELATIONSHIPS

In one of his latest studies, Fox has found that when we as parents have people to turn to—people on whom we can rely when we feel stressed—that affects our children's social development. Even if our children have a genetic predisposition to becoming fearful and anxious, they're far less likely to manifest that disposition if we can manage our own stress and if we have friends who can help us.

A MINDSET THAT MATTERS

Remember the story of Heidelise Als's young student Reinhard, who stopped coming to school when he was moved from the front of the class, because he needed the security of being close to the teacher and thrived better in that situation? A fear of losing her seat in the front of the class was a formative experience in shaping the career of Carol Dweck of Stanford University, who studies how children take on challenges. As she tells it:

> I think I've always been interested in the question[s] of intelligence, dealing with challenges, and being resilient. If I had to trace this back, I'd trace it back to my sixth-grade class. Our teacher, Mrs. Wilson, seated us around the room in IQ order. Mind you, this was already the top-IQ sixth grade in an upwardly mobile, academic-type neighborhood. Yet she thought that your IQ score summarized you—not just your intelligence, but your character as well. She would not let a lower-IQ student carry a note to the principal, erase the blackboard, or carry the flag in the assembly.
>
> Even though I knew there was something wrong with this, it was so powerful that part of me got sucked in and part of me looked on as an observer. It made me really think about it, [questioning]: Is [intelligence] fixed? I know these kids, and I know they can all learn. I had both of these views at war within me.

I was so aware of how I had loved to learn before, but in that class, it was "look smart at all costs." I did not want to lose my seat to someone else.

After that, even though I did well in school, the possibility of doing poorly—not getting an A—loomed so large for me that I really wondered about the origin of that. I was fascinated with people who could take on something difficult, roll with the punches, get up again, start again. I was fascinated by resilience, so I just wanted to figure it out.

Dweck carried that question "of how children cope with challenges and setbacks" into graduate school, where she had another formative experience:

In my very first study, I gave kids impossible problems to solve. Some were thrilled by it. They said things like "Wow, I love a challenge" or "Yes, I was hoping this would be informative." I looked at them and thought: "Where are they from?" I have dedicated my career to unlocking their secrets—and maybe bottling them—so that all children could feel this way about learning.

To unearth their secrets, Dweck did another study where she gave fifth-grade children tasks (like those found on intelligence tests) that became increasingly difficult. When children began to stumble and make mistakes, she asked them to share their thinking processes aloud:

We found that children who were vulnerable and upset thought that that difficulty meant that they weren't smart or they weren't good at the task—a very discouraging conclusion, whereas students motivated by the setback thought, "Well, that just means I need to try harder or try a different strategy." It was the students who wanted to learn who explained the setback or difficulty in terms of their effort or strategies.

This was a seminal moment that ultimately led to Carol Dweck's theory of *mindset*. She found that these two groups had fundamentally different beliefs about their capabilities. The children who "wilted" in the face of stress or a challenge saw their abilities—their intelligence—as an unchangeable trait; they had a *fixed mindset*. Whereas the students who continued to pursue the challenge saw their abilities as something that they could develop: they had a *growth mindset*.

To test the hypothesis that different mindsets predicted how children cope with challenge, Dweck created a questionnaire to assess children's theories about their intelligence:

> *We asked them questions like this: "Your intelligence is something very basic about you that you can't really change—agree or disagree." We call that a fixed view of intelligence. Another question [that] measures the growth mindset is: "No matter who you are, you can always become a great deal smarter."*

Then, to test whether the children's mindset or view of their capacities affected their response to setbacks, Dweck and her colleagues gave them increasingly difficult problems to solve, such as puzzles from a nonverbal IQ test, anagrams, and other tasks that were new to them. She says:

> *We give them a few trials where they do pretty well; then we give them more difficult problems. We see what happens to their strategies, what happens to their enjoyment of the task, what happens to their persistence.*
>
> *We found that [when] the students who endorsed the fixed view of their intelligence hit difficulty, [they] started blaming their ability for failure; they started not liking the task anymore, and their performance plummeted. The students who thought their intelligence was something they could increase or develop saw the challenge as exciting. They thought, "I just [need] more effort or different strategies"; they maintained their enjoyment; they maintained their performance.*

Dweck and her colleagues wondered about the implications of their findings for everyday life. For example, would children with a growth mindset do better in school? To test this idea, they followed children through their transition to seventh grade—often a tough period in children's lives:

> We measured the students' theories [of intelligence] at the beginning of seventh grade and followed them over two years. [W]e found that those initial theories predicted their goals in school—whether they wanted to learn or just look smart—predicted how they confronted setbacks, and predicted their grades. Even though the two groups [children with a fixed mindset and children with a growth mindset] entered seventh grade with identical math achievement, they showed diverging grades over the next two years, so that by the end of eighth grade, they had significantly different grades in math.

Of course, the question arises: how do children develop a fixed versus a growth mindset, and can their mindsets be changed? For clues, Dweck turned to the way people talked with children:

> This was in the late nineties—it was the height of the self-esteem movement. The self-esteem gurus were telling parents [and] teachers, "You must praise your child at every opportunity. Tell them how talented and brilliant they are. This is going to give them confidence and motivation."
>
> We took a poll of parents: 85 percent agreed, "You must praise your child's ability to give them confidence and motivation." But we had been studying mindsets and saw that children who were overly focused on intelligence were the vulnerable ones—not the motivated and confident ones—and we wondered whether praising children's intelligence would put them in a fixed mindset, make them fragile rather than hardy.
>
> Well, the great thing about research is that you can take these questions and put them to the test. So we gave [fifth graders] problems from a nonverbal IQ test. After they finished ten problems and did pretty well, we gave them one of three forms of praise. A third of

the children were told, "Wow, that's a really good score. You really must be smart at this." [In other words, we gave them] intelligence praise. A third of them got effort praise: "Wow, that's a really good score. You must have worked really hard." We had a third group where they were just told, "Wow, that was a really good score." [It was] like "Good job."

We then asked them what kind of problems [they'd] like to work on now: "I have some problems here that are like things you're good at—you'll look really smart," or "I have some very challenging problems—you'll make mistakes, you might not feel smart, but you'll learn something important."

Right away, we found that the students praised for intelligence mainly wanted the task that would make them look smart. They did not want to risk their "gifted" label. Whereas the students praised for effort overwhelmingly wanted the hard task they could learn from. They were like my original kids who said, "I love a challenge."

The story doesn't end there. The researchers told the children in all three groups that they wanted them to tell children in another school about this experience. They gave children a sheet of paper to write about their experiences and left a place for them to write down the score they'd received on the hard problems. The results were revealing and actually sad:

Almost forty percent of the children praised for intelligence lied— they reported a score higher than the one they actually earned. Very few children [who were praised for effort] thought that they had to puff themselves up in this way. So not only did the intelligence praise harm [children's] confidence, harm their motivation, [and] harm their performance, but they were so humiliated by it that they could not report their score truthfully—even to someone they would never meet.

These are important findings because they reveal that although mindsets emerge early, they're not set in stone (much like our capacities). Children respond to the situations they're in. If they're praised for their effort and for the strategies they're using, they're more likely to want to learn and to try harder. If they're praised for their intelligence, they're more likely to pull back. As I said earlier, every day is a new day in being a parent—it is never too late to try new ways with our children, and our changes do matter.

A PARENT'S PERSPECTIVE: SHE'S AN ORIGINAL

Our daughter is very creative and original. She loves art and loves to dress inventively. When she was a young girl, her hairstyle changed almost daily. I wasn't quite sure what to say about this, as I didn't want her to focus too much on her looks. Finally, I said what I truly felt. I told her how much I enjoyed anticipating and seeing how she looked each day. It's now years later, and she still mentions how much that comment meant to her.

GETTING BACK ON THE HORSE

When I first began contemplating this skill, I saw it as managing stress. As I thought about it more deeply, I saw it as the skill of resilience. But now it's clear to me that the real essential skill is taking on challenges—being proactive rather than reactive when difficulties arise. My mother always called it "getting back on the horse after falling off." As with so many of her momisms, she was right.

A friend, Toni, recently said to me that it is not how we handle the good times in our lives that shapes us in the most profound ways; it is how we handle the bad times. I am convinced Toni is right.

A PARENT'S PERSPECTIVE: I CAN'T FIX EVERYTHING

When I was twenty-two weeks along in my pregnancy with twins, I began preterm labor and was hospitalized for one week. I then went on strict bed rest, took medication, and had to primarily lie on my left side. I was incredibly scared and felt very guilty for having the preterm labor: maybe I'd done too much . . . maybe I'd worked too hard. But as I realized the seriousness of the situation and what was at stake, I began to let go of the blame because it served no purpose, and I instantly forgot about my work to-do list (even though I was a major workaholic).

Instead, I instantly became a mom (before my children were born), because I realized that in some ways it was no longer about me. I had to protect my babies but also take care of myself. Rather than focus on the negative, I tried to imagine positives.

When they were born three months premature, there were a slew of medical issues to deal with. The parenting lessons I learned were many, but this is my favorite: I can't fix everything for my children. Things will happen, and we all have to try to stay strong.

HOW CAN YOU PROMOTE TAKING ON CHALLENGES IN CHILDREN?

SUGGESTION 1: MANAGE YOUR OWN STRESS.

Nathan Fox has found that our stress spills over onto our children. That's no surprise to me. In my *Ask the Children* study, when I surveyed a nationally representative group of children in the third through the twelfth grades, asking them what they'd say if given one wish to change the way their mother's or father's work affected their lives, the largest proportion wished that their mothers and fathers would be less stressed, less tired.

Intrigued, I asked children in in-person interviews how they knew if their parents were stressed or had had a bad day. The kids' answers revealed that they almost had a sixth sense about detecting parental stress. It's as if they were detectives, expert at figuring out what was going on. Some called their parents at the end of the workday to gauge their parents' moods from their tone of voice—information they used to decide whether or not to clean things up before their parents got home. Others noticed the way their parents arrived home from work—the way the front door was opened, how the footsteps sounded, how work stuff was put down. Others listened to their parents' telephone conversations, sitting around the corner unseen while Mom, for example, talked to a friend on the telephone. Still others listened at the top of the stairs at night to their parents' conversations below. In one enterprising family, the older kids sent the youngest into the room when their parents argued. The parents thought that this young child was too young to understand the meaning of their words (and that was partially true), but the child was not too young to parrot back some of the words she had heard to her older brothers and sisters.

What's the point of this espionage? According to the children in my study, it was to know if there was a serious problem. More important, it was to find out if *they* were the cause of their parents' troubles. Had they done something wrong?

The lesson I learned from asking the children was not that parents should try to erase stress. Just as it's impossible to give children a stress-free childhood, so it's impossible for us to have stress-free adult lives. I've always loved the findings from a longitudinal study conducted by George Vaillant. The original researchers selected Harvard undergraduates in the late 1930s who seemed destined for success because of their physical and psychological fitness. These men signed up to be followed for the rest of their lives. Vaillant found that in general they encountered significant stresses at one time or another in their lives but that it was those who could respond to stress positively who fared best.

What does it mean for parents to respond to stress positively? It means, first, to admit that you're feeling stressed. You can tell your children directly that you had a bad day. Most know it anyway from reading the nonverbal language of your behavior. Make sure you tell them that it isn't their fault, if it isn't, because blaming themselves is a natural conclusion for many children. Then share with them how you are going to cope. Mention and use coping strategies, such as:

"I need a time-out, just like you need a time-out when you are upset and can't manage."

"I always feel better if I exercise, so I am going to . . . [do whatever exercise you do to make yourself feel better]."

"A friend said something to me that upset me. I'm thinking about how to respond."

Remember to tell your children "the rest of the story." Just as they are watching you like detectives to understand the source of your stress, they are also watching you to learn how to handle tough times. One child told me that he always heard what had gone wrong in his father's workplace, but never how his father dealt with it. He was looking to learn from how his father handled problems.

Creating a ritual for managing the transition from work to home can help. One commuting mother picked a spot on the road where she switched off the work chatter in her mind and turned on her "child-centered mode." I especially like my son's solution to my bad days. When he was a teenager, he made a tape for the car of upbeat music and gave it to me with the label *Prozac for Driving*. And it is! No matter how stressful my day, how bad my mood, it is hard to stay stressed when I listen to *Prozac for Driving*.

A PARENT'S PERSPECTIVE:
LEARNING NOT TO HYPER OUT

When my son was about nine, he ran away from home. He was entirely justified, because I'd been screaming at him for something or other and was pretty much out of control. He went into his room and shut the door. When he didn't come out for a long time, I knocked and, hearing no answer, opened the door a crack. He wasn't there.

He'd climbed out his window, which was at ground level. But he was kind enough to leave us a note. It said, "Dear Mom, you were really mean and I am running away. I won't cross the street and I will be home at 7." When he did, indeed, return around seven, I apologized, hugged him, and promised to *try* not to "hyper out"—my children's phrase for me when something made me crazy—in the future.

SUGGESTION 2: TURN TO OTHERS WHO CAN HELP YOU MANAGE YOUR OWN STRESSES.

There are times when our own coping strategies aren't enough. Nathan Fox and his colleagues found that parents who have friends to turn to are less likely to transmit stress to their children. Sometimes friends aren't enough, either. So if you need to find some professional help to get over a rough patch, do so.

SUGGESTION 3: TAKE TIME FOR YOURSELF.

Families and Work Institute's studies consistently find that people who take time for themselves experience less stress in their lives. We also find that time for oneself has decreased for both fathers and mothers. Taking time for ourselves when we have children can feel selfish—yet this time can be a key destressor. Remember that part of being a good parent is having positive energy, so think about something you love to do, something that reenergizes you, and plan to do it as regularly as you can.

SUGGESTION 4: DON'T SHIELD YOUR CHILD FROM EVERYDAY STRESSES.

Remember Megan Gunnar's words about children and stress—that learning to deal with stress is a necessary part of life. And then think about Nathan Fox's studies—that parents who are overprotective of their shy children can actually do more harm than good. That doesn't mean throwing your children in the lake when they don't know how to swim, but it does mean helping them figure out how to cope—or to use my mother's analogy, how to get back on that horse after they fall off.

SUGGESTION 5: KNOW THAT A WARM, CARING, AND TRUSTING RELATIONSHIP WITH YOUR CHILD MAKES YOU A STRESS-BUSTER.

Megan Gunnar finds that having a warm and caring relationship with parents helps children feel more safe and secure. That's true for adults, too. Think of being in a stressful situation, such as encountering turbulence on a plane. If you're with someone who helps you feel safe rather than scared, you can manage the situation much better. It's even better if that person is an off-duty pilot! Luckily for them, young children think their parents can do and know everything. So when they really trust that we are there for them, they can learn from everyday setbacks and challenges, while their body and brain stay in the "growth and repair" mode and out of the stress mode.

SUGGESTION 6: TRY TO KEEP YOUR OWN "ALARM BUTTON" ON LOW.

It's important to help your children want to venture out, to take a reasonable amount of risk. Philip was the kind of preschooler who was fearless, so it was a constant struggle not to overreact to the shock of some of his adventures. He stuck his fingers into electric sockets; he plunged down our steep steps inside a wastebasket; he took the screens off the windows on the second floor and dangled outside; he grabbed a handful of deadly nightshade from the side of the road and stuffed it into his mouth; and he locked himself into the bathroom of a motel. At least while he was locked in the bathroom, Norman and I felt reasonably assured that he wasn't going to hurt himself, so we had a brief respite until the management arrived to take the door off its hinges and rescue him.

Our strategy was to tell him that his sense of adventure was a great quality, but he needed to manage it so that "he was taking good care of himself." That worked (some of the time) until he was older and more adept at understanding the consequences of his actions.

SUGGESTION 7: UNDERSTAND YOUR CHILD'S TEMPERAMENT—OBSERVE WHAT YOUR CHILD DOES TO CALM DOWN, AND BUILD ON HIS OR HER STRENGTHS.

Remember that children's temperaments have two components:

how they *react* to a new experience—specifically what triggers their response, how long it takes them to respond, and how intensely they respond; and

how they *regulate* their response—how much time it takes them to manage the new situation, calm down, and return to normal.

Just as our children play detective to figure out our stresses, we need to play detective for theirs—to read the "language of their behavior" and figure out how they cope best with challenging circumstances. When they're very young, watch their behavior when they get upset. Do their hands splay out, like the premature babies in Heidelise Als's studies? If so, give them something to hold on to. For young children, distraction is also effective. When my children would get into a crying jag, they would stop when I turned the lights off and on and then let them flip the light switch themselves. Power!

For preschoolers and older children, engage them in a conversation about what helps them when they're upset. Is it putting their head down on the table until they calm down? Is it taking deep breaths? Lara came up with an idea for coping with bad dreams that worked for her: she'd imagine the dream as if it were inside a soap bubble, and then she'd pop the bubble. Philip made a sword out of cardboard and aluminum foil to keep by his bedside to chase away bad dreams.

When children get older, they can come up with solutions for dealing with other stresses, such as what will help them if they get upset before a test or when going to a new place. If they're asked in a calm moment, and if they know you'll take their ideas seriously, most children have creative solutions for managing their own challenges.

A GROWN-UP'S PERSPECTIVE:
MEMORIES AS A SAFETY BLANKET

Coping strategies aren't just for little kids. As a college freshman, I was excited by the academic challenges, but also stressed by them—and periodically homesick, too. When I wanted to calm down before sleep, sometimes I'd visualize summer evenings at home when my parents and I would wander next door and hang out with the neighbors on their screened porch, all of us just sitting there in the dark, listening to the night sounds, smelling the new-cut grass, talking about this and that. I was always calmed by being able to conjure this mental picture of the continuity and safety of home. Even today, I feel comforted when I recall those summer evenings.

SUGGESTION 8: PROMOTE "GOODNESS OF EXPECTATIONS."

In their writings about temperament, Alexander Thomas and Stella Chess described the concept *goodness of fit*. By that they mean that an individual (including his or her temperament and motivation) is adequate to meet the demands, expectations, and opportunities offered by others. Our children's behavior is strongly affected by the views of others. If a child is slow to warm up to a new situation, that may be just fine in one family but a disaster in another. Thomas and Chess saw goodness of fit as the foundation of children's positive self image.

Parents' expectations are pivotal in this process, as Jerry Kagan explains:

Parents have ideals for their children. In my generation, [parents] were more inflexible. I'm thinking of a case where one of these shy, inhibited boys [had a] father who was the football coach at this small-town high school. He wanted his son to be a fullback. This boy was temperamentally not cut out [to be a fullback]. And the father, in either explicit or implicit ways, let his son know he was disappointed. This boy, as an adult, was so anxious, so tense.

That's less common today. Parents are more sophisticated. But yes, there's a fit [that's important]: does the child's personality match the parents' ideal for that child? If there's a poor fit, that's the worst possible situation.

In my study of parental development, I found that expectations are the drivers of good or bad times in parenthood, too. Whenever a parent was upset, angry, or disappointed, I found an unfulfilled expectation lying—even lurking—beneath the negative feelings: "I want my child to be . . ." (fill in the blank) or "I want myself to be . . ." (also fill in the blank).

The positive news is that I found that either adjusting those expectations to fit reality or changing reality to fit the expectation—or both—is the driver of adult growth. Using Kagan's example of the football coach, if the father could have accepted that his son was not going to be a fullback but had other wonderful qualities, the father could have grown and his son might have had a better life. We can choose to stay stuck, or not. So if you are feeling upset about your child, ask yourself what you are expecting—of yourself as well as of your child—and whether or not your expectation is realistic. If it is realistic, try to live up to it. If it is not realistic, try to find the expectation that is real.

SUGGESTION 9: GIVE YOUR CHILD APPROPRIATE LEVELS OF CONTROL IN MANAGING STRESS.

COROLLARY 1: YOU SET THE PARAMETERS, BUT WITHIN THOSE, HELP CHILDREN FIND WAYS TO MANAGE THEIR OWN STRESS. Involving children in addressing the problems they face can be misunderstood as permissiveness—letting kids do whatever they want—but it isn't the same. I've always found it useful to think of parental guidance as the guardrails on a high bridge. They help the child feel safe. Within those boundaries, children, especially as they get older, should be increasingly involved in coming up with solutions for facing challenges. With this approach, you're helping children learn to manage challenge rather than fixing things for them.

We started this approach when our kids were preschoolers. Philip, as you can imagine, had a hard time sitting still if we went out for dinner. So we would talk about it beforehand: "What ideas do you have for managing?" He often thought of bringing toys to amuse himself.

COROLLARY 2: HELP CHILDREN SET CONSEQUENCES FOR NOT FOLLOWING THROUGH ON THEIR PLANS AND BE ACCOUNTABLE. It's not enough to have your kids make plans for managing stress; have them also come up with plans in case their solutions don't work. For example, we had Philip make a plan for what was going to happen if he couldn't manage at the restaurant. This usually involved leaving the table and walking around with a parent until he could calm down.

One of my favorite examples of how to teach children to take responsibility for dealing with challenges comes from Lara's preschool teacher, Suzanne Carothers. Now a professor at New York University, Carothers says that her work with three-year-olds "has informed every single thing [she has done] professionally since that time." She recalls the story of a very high-energy child in one of her classrooms of three-year-olds.

A TEACHER'S PERSPECTIVE:
"YOU'RE NOT THE BOSS OF MY LEGS"

Harry was the tallest three-year-old in my classroom. He learned about his world by being engaged with it. He could dress himself; he had command of language.

One day our class was going to the park. As I stood with the children on the school steps, I asked them, "What's a safe way for us to get to the park?" We had this discussion every day before we went to the park. And, of course, the children said, "We should walk, because if you run, drivers of cars cannot see little children."

As soon as we got off the steps of the school, Harry charged down the hill, running as fast as his long legs could carry him, doing everything that we had just talked about *not* doing. So I turned to the group, and I said the obvious: "Harry is running down the hill, so I'm going to need to go very quickly to make sure Harry is safe while you stay with the student teacher." If I had just started running down the hill, all twenty three-year-olds would have been running down the hill.

So I'm taking these giant steps to get to Harry, who stops right by the curb. I get down very low and look him right in the eyes, and I say, "Harry, you ran down the hill." And he looked right back at me and said, "You're not the boss of my legs. You can't tell them which way to go!"

I looked right back at him and I said, "You're absolutely right. So you now tell your legs to turn around and walk back up the hill so that you and your legs can have a conversation about how to move down the hill safely on the next school day."

So we turned around and together we walked right back up the hill because he had instructed his legs. When we passed the group, I said to the rest of the class, "Harry is going to go to another teacher's class and he is going to talk with his legs about ways to get down the hill safely." And that was the end of the discussion.

When Harry told me I wasn't "the boss" of his legs, it was hilarious but it was so true. I was not the boss of his legs. Sometimes teachers really feel like they're the boss of children, but they're not. But I can engage children in a conversation about what they've done in a way for them to have some power over the situation. Harry was probably about to turn four then and, you know, "fours" need some power in their lives!

Notice, in this story, that the teacher does not give the control to this young child. It is her job as a teacher, just as it is our job as parents, to set the rules or guidelines ("You can't run into the street"). The control or power we provide is figuring out how to help the child comply with the rules or guidelines, and setting consequences for when the child doesn't comply. This is an essential point in helping children learn how to take on challenges.

SUGGESTION 10: IF YOUR CHILD IS SHY, LET HIM OR HER WATCH NEW SITUATIONS FIRST, AND THEN INTRODUCE CHANGE SLOWLY.

Studies by Nathan Fox and his colleagues have shown that shy children tend either to watch a new situation or to occupy themselves but not get involved with the other children right away. When I asked Jerry Kagan for advice for the parents of shy children, he said:

For the shy child, the advice is very simple. It's something your grandmother would give. Don't overprotect. Gradually expose the child to the events he or she is afraid of. Invite other children into the house, one at a time, and talk to your child.

Expectations are important in children's lives, just as in adults' lives. Help your child rehearse what will happen when another child visits or when your child goes to a new place. This can help desensitize your child to this experience. Kagan notes that many children know what they need to overcome—he cites one six-year-old who said: "I've got to practice being not shy."

SUGGESTION 11: PROMOTE YOUR CHILD'S "LEMONADE STANDS."

In his ongoing study of children who were highly reactive as babies (the babies who became physically agitated and distressed in response to new experiences) but didn't turn out to be shy or inhibited as older children, Kagan observes that a number of these children had a special interest and talent. As I've said, I call this a "lemonade stand," after my daughter Lara's passion for her lemonade stand as a school-aged child. My choice of the word *passion* is deliberate, too: this should be something your child really cares about.

I can understand how passion counteracts fear in my own life. There are a number of things that I find scary, such as climbing on steep rocks.

But when I have my camera in hand and am in pursuit of a particular photograph, I can be unbelievably brave, doing things that might have frightened me under any other circumstance.

A PARENT'S PERSPECTIVE: CAR CRAZY

My son is scared of amusement rides. At the same time, he is vehicle obsessed . . . cars, planes, trains, buses, etc. We went to an amusement park and, as I expected, he was very timid and didn't want to try anything. Then he saw a ride called the "crazy bus," which went way up in the air and swung down with great speed.

I felt sick just looking at it, and I was enormously surprised when Asa pointed to it and said, "Go." So I took a very deep breath, and he went on the ride with my mother-in-law. He enjoyed it so much that he had to go a second time. This, from the same three-year-old who was afraid of the carousel and the Pony Express rides for one-year-olds!

SUGGESTION 12: CULTIVATE A GROWTH MINDSET IN YOUR CHILDREN.

After conducting a number of studies on children's mindsets, Carol Dweck and her colleagues wondered whether and how a growth mindset could be taught. They began by creating a workshop for seventh graders. Since children's grades frequently decline at this time, it was an apt window for an intervention. Dweck says:

We divided [the students] into two groups: the control group got eight sessions of fabulous study skills; the experimental group got six sessions of great study skills but two sessions [on] growth mindset.

Dweck describes what the children learned in the growth mindset sessions:

They learned that the brain is like a muscle—it gets stronger with use. They learned that every time they work hard, their brain forms new connections, and they also learned how to apply this to their schoolwork.

Applying this theory to their schoolwork meant paying more attention in class, but it also meant realizing that if they don't understand something, they can continue to persevere. Dweck points out that the children found these messages reassuring. She tells the story of one child:

One boy was kind of the bane of our existence. He wouldn't sit still; he was always cutting up with his friends; but when we started on this message, he sat in his seat, he looked at us, and said, "You mean I don't have to be dumb?"

Their results indicated that teaching good study skills to children is not sufficient. Dweck elaborates:

We found that the group that just got great study skills continued to show declining grades. They didn't have the motivation to put those skills into practice. But the group that got the study skills and the growth mindset message showed a significant rebound in their grades.

We asked the teachers, "Did you notice any changes in your students?" The teachers didn't know what workshops the students were in—they didn't even know there were two different [types of workshops]. [Yet] they singled out three times as many students from the growth mindset workshop, [reporting] that they had noted remarkable changes in [these children's] study habits, in their turning in their homework on time, [and] in their asking for feedback from the teacher.

In a subsequent project, Dweck and her colleagues created computer-based workshops where children learn more about the brain as well as how to promote their brain's health, such as by eating better and getting enough sleep. Dweck reports that these workshops changed children's views not only of themselves as learners, but of school—from a place that tests and judges them to a place that provides them with resources for learning.

What are the implications for us as parents? We can help change our children's views of their capacities from being something they're born with to something that they can cultivate and improve.

SUGGESTION 13: PRAISE YOUR CHILD'S EFFORT AND STRATEGIES, NOT HIS OR HER PERSONALITY.

One of the main ways that we can change children's views about themselves and their world is by how we comment on their accomplishments or failures. Rather than praising their personalities or intelligence ("You are so smart" or "artistic" or "athletic"), criticizing them ("You are so stupid" or "uncoordinated"), or attributing their accomplishments to luck, we can praise their efforts or strategies. I watched this process at work in the Bing Nursery School at Stanford University. Children were given a very difficult puzzle to work on, and most agonized over it. The teacher's comments continued to reinforce their problem-solving strategies: "Look, you turned that piece around and around to see where it would fit" or "You looked for a place that was the same color as the piece you are holding." The children struggled, but they didn't walk away; they didn't give up. They were taking on challenges!

Does this mean that we should *never* comment on our children's attributes? I plan to continue to tell my children that they look great or are talented—but only every once in a while!

CHAPTER SEVEN

SKILL SEVEN: SELF-DIRECTED, ENGAGED LEARNING

The drive to master our environment is a basic human characteristic from the beginning—from birth.

—JACK P. SHONKOFF, HARVARD UNIVERSITY

I began the quest that led to this book to reconcile two contrasting images. One is an image of infants who are unstoppable learners—eager to see, touch, understand, and master everything. Anyone who has ever watched a baby or child engaged in pursuing a goal can see that children are born to learn. Stanislas Dehaene of the Collège de France in Paris calls it a *learning instinct*—a survival skill, but also a source of deep pleasure and joy. The eyes of young children are burning brightly as they explore their world.

The other image is of children from across the country, in the sixth through the twelfth grades, whom I interviewed about learning for a study I was conducting. I asked about their experiences of learning—at home, in their neighborhoods, in school, in church, anywhere. Despite coming from very different backgrounds and communities, they told me very similar stories.

Far too many—from all kinds of families, schools, communities, and parts of the country—seem deadened by the notion of learning. There was little, if any, fire in their eyes when they talked about learning. What happens to extinguish that passion? What happens to dull their eyes?

So I have spent the past eight years delving deeply into the science of children's learning, asking:

How do children *learn best*?

What makes them stay *motivated and engaged* in learning, to see themselves as learners, and to be ongoing, lifelong learners?

What can be done to *rekindle that motivation* if it has been dulled?

What are the essential learning skills that will help them along this path?

Although I've been actively pursuing answers to these questions for the past eight years, my quest actually began much earlier. Understanding learning has been important to me for as long as I can remember. In fact, in my first year as a teacher of preschool children, I knew what I and the other teachers *thought* we were teaching, but I was unsure of what children were actually learning, so I devised some simple experiments to try to find out. And as a parent, I've continued to wonder which of the life lessons I am trying to impart are sticking, which aren't, and why.

BEYOND EITHER/OR—IT'S NATURE *AND* NURTURE

Some of the debates about learning that have concerned philosophers, scientists, educators, and families for centuries have been largely resolved in scientific circles (though perhaps not by the general public). One such debate is the nature versus nurture debate. Is the mind a blank slate, to be written on by experience, or are our minds primarily programmed by genetics? In the late 1990s, the National Academy of Sciences convened a committee of scientists from a number of academic child development perspectives to try to resolve this and some of the other issues (and confusions) about brain development that have been swirling around in the media and in all of us. One of the conclusions of this Committee on Integrating the Science of Early Childhood Development was:

It is time to reconceptualize nature and nurture in a way that emphasizes their inseparability . . . [and] not their distinctiveness: it is not nature versus nurture, it is nature through nurture.

The expression of genes, the committee continues, is truly unimaginable apart from the environment. It is this ongoing communion between our heredity and our experiences that shapes us. That mystery, Jack P. Shonkoff, the committee chair, reflects, "is what is magical about human development."

And that's where learning comes in. Dehaene writes:

We are born into a complex world that cannot be completely predicted in advance and thus our brain cannot be fully prewired.

It is through learning that we realize our potential. It is through learning that our minds become attuned, ready to meet whatever life brings. As the world changes, so can we, for as long as we live—as long as we learn.

So how do we promote self-directed, engaged learning in our children throughout their lives? I've concluded that there are seven principles. To look at how to foster learning, let's first look at what stands in its way.

AN EXERCISE: ROADBLOCKS IN LEARNING

Think about a time when either you or someone else wanted you to learn something, but it didn't happen. Why not? What stood in the way of your learning?

Chances are there's a person in your story—someone who didn't make you feel good about yourself, who didn't connect with you or with what you felt you needed to know, who was confusing, or who didn't seem to care. Those were the kinds of roadblocks I heard from young people all over the country when I asked them to recount their experiences of being turned off by learning.

Now let's look at the principles that unleash children's passionate desire to learn.

PRINCIPLE 1: ESTABLISH A TRUSTWORTHY RELATIONSHIP WITH YOUR CHILD

There is no development without relationships.
—JACK P. SHONKOFF, HARVARD UNIVERSITY

A central conclusion of the Committee on Integrating the Science of Early Childhood Development is that human relationships "are the building blocks of healthy development." The committee goes on to say that all of young children's achievements occur "in the context of close relationships with others."

THE POWER OF THE "STILL-FACE"

It may seem obvious that trusting relationships enhance children's learning, but it wasn't obvious not so long ago, when Edward Tronick of the University of Massachusetts Boston became interested in the subject.

In the early 1970s, Tronick collaborated with the pediatrician T. Berry Brazelton at the time when Brazelton was creating the Neonatal Behavioral Assessment Scale, a tool designed to interpret what newborns are communicating through their behavior (which I described in chapter 1, on focus and self control):

> *On Saturday mornings, Berry [Brazelton] and Jerry Bruner [the psychologist, now at New York University] and I would go to the newborn nurseries and examine babies together. We did this for seven, eight months in a row. Berry would show us things about babies that we had no idea babies could possibly do, and then we would talk about it afterward. It was just the most exciting sort of thing! The social development in infants had never really been studied. Pretty much at that point in time I said, "This is what I'm going to do."*

Tronick's goal has been to pursue how relationships affect children's development:

I [wanted] to understand what's going on in the exchange [between a parent and child] that allows a relationship to be "good" or "smooth." What do these words mean? Can we describe them, and can we come to an understanding of that process?

Tronick began his studies with infants, using a new scientific procedure he developed called the *Still-Face*. In Tronick's lab, the baby is placed in an infant seat on a table across from his or her seated parent so that they're literally face-to-face. The experimenter instructs the parent to play with the baby. One mother I observed played "This little piggy went to market" with her six-month-old daughter's toes. The baby squealed with delight when her mother ran her fingers up to the baby's nose as the "little piggy cried 'Wee! Wee! Wee!' all the way home."

The experimenter then instructed the mother to turn away and then to return to the face-to-face position, but *not* to react in any way—to keep a still (or frozen) face.

AN EXERCISE: AN EXPERIMENT WITH THE STILL-FACE

Before I share the experiment's results, try it yourself with two people. Give each instruction in private, so that neither knows what the other is supposed to do. You can write the instructions on index cards or tell them.

Tell the first person:
"You are the speaker.
Please tell the other person about one of the following: something happy that happened to you recently; or something that caused you great anger or sadness."

Tell the second person:
"You are the listener.
While the other person is speaking, assume a 'still-face'—maintain eye contact, but do not show any expression on your face, use any gestures, or say anything."

After two to three minutes (if they last that long), ask them:
"How did it feel to be the speaker?
How did it feel to be the listener?"

I am sure you will get highly emotional responses as we do when we use this exercise in the Learning Modules for Teachers that we have developed. This experience reveals just how essential the normal give-and-take interaction with others is to us.

Tronick describes what usually happens in this experiment with babies. Even children as young as three months pick up on the fact that their mothers aren't responding:

They greet the mother. You know how three-month-olds have a really big greeting and that wonderful smile. They give that big smile, and [then] many of them just sort of stop. They're waiting for the mother to respond, and she's not responding. They might look at her, then turn away, and then they'll [turn] back typically and try to [get her to respond]. Then some of the babies kind of collapse. They lose postural control. They may look at the mother out of the corner of their eyes, but they don't turn to her—[they have a] sad, helpless look.

Tronick remembers when he first presented this experiment on film to his professional colleagues at a Society for Research in Child Development meeting:

When the film ended, there was a silence in the hall. And I'm up there thinking, "This is terrible. They don't like it." My heart literally stopped. I thought, "Okay, I'll find another career." And then people burst into applause because it really is so stunning.

What's stunning is how early the child comes to expect a response from his or her parent. And how powerful it is when the parent wears a "still-face," devoid of feeling. Tronick says:

It speaks to the incredible emotional capacities [of] the infant—to pick up on the fact that the mother's not reacting emotionally the way she normally does, that her social behavior is completely changed.

The baby has not only this ability to process what's [happening] and make meaning out of it, but [also] the capacity to respond in a really appropriate way—that is, they try to get the mother's attention, and then when they fail, they give up, with a sense of their own helplessness. They may be angry and then they become sad.

Of course, the experimenter tells the parent to resume reacting normally and the child quickly recovers. Tronick has conducted this experiment with two-year-olds, and you just tried it with adults. The results are always the same—when the connection between us and another person is broken, we wonder if there's something wrong with us, we try to engage the other person, and then, if there is no response, we pull back—if not physically like the infant, at least emotionally.

I have shown the video of this experiment to many parents and teachers, and it usually makes them wonder, "Does this mean we have to be constantly 'in sync' with children, responding to their every move?"

Tronick had the same question. When he and his colleagues began conducting the Still-Face experiment, they believed that the more the parent and child were in sync, the better. But they've since learned that this isn't the case:

Only maybe twenty, thirty percent of the time is the interaction "perfectly" in sync. The rest of the time, you're in sync, you're out of sync, you're getting back into sync.

In fact, Tronick has found that moving in and out of sync with others—repairing a mismatch with a match—is not only normal, it can be a positive learning experience for both parent and child:

This not being in sync frees up parents from that constant burden of being perfect—because you can't be perfect. No matter how hard you try, you can't be.

When mismatches are repaired, he says, children's "emotions can go from really negative to really positive":

The experience of repair gives children a sense of reparation, a sense of trust, a sense of mastery—"I can do this. I learned different ways of [reconnecting] with my mother and with my father."

A PASSENGER'S PERSPECTIVE: OUT OF SYNC, IN SYNC

A toddler and his father were sitting in front of me on the bus. As we pulled up to a stop, the toddler looked out the window and saw a poster of Pinocchio. "Pinoko!" said the toddler, tugging on his father's sleeve. From his seat, the father couldn't see the poster. "Hmm?" he said. "Pinoko!" the toddler repeated, looking from the window to his father. "Bus stop?" the father said, trying to get it right. "What do you see? The people?"

By now this child was getting frustrated. He pressed his forehead against the window (without letting go of his father's sleeve) and whimpered loudly, *"Pinookoo!"* As the bus pulled away from the stop, the poster came into the father's field of vision. "Oh—Pinocchio! Yes, I see it—Pinocchio, buddy!" Immediately the boy relaxed. His frown turned to a smile, and he settled back against his father, whispering, with a contented sigh: "Pinoko."

Tronick points out the benefits of this learning:

When you reconnect, one of the things that can happen—not always, but some of the time—is that you create something new. You figure out a new way to do something together that you have never done before. If you create something new, you grow. And babies are about growing.

THE POWER OF IMITATION

There's a feedback loop in this kind of learning: the infant does something, the parent responds, the infant responds in turn—back and forth. This process is normally invisible—we're far too busy living our everyday lives to pay attention—but when the action is artificially stopped, as happened in the Still-Face experiment, we can see how this process unfolds and how the baby works to reengage the parent's attention. Even more startling, Tronick says, we can see that the infant, even by the third month of life, has developed an expectation of how people usually respond and has the capacity "to pick up on the fact that the mother's not reacting emotionally the way she normally does, that her social behavior is completely changed." The infant has developed expectations, and this experience violates them.

In addition to feedback from our responses to their behavior, children obviously learn by what we actively seek to teach them. In chapter 3, on communicating, I described how children learn by what we say (*parent-speak*), what we look at (*parent-look*), and what we point to (*parent-gesture*). Given children's attunement to us, we can do a great deal to promote essential skills intentionally.

Children also learn by imitating us. This form of learning has captivated Andrew Meltzoff of the University of Washington:

> *The reason that I am so interested in imitation is that parents always say that the child somehow is changing [his or her] behavior, but it isn't just reinforcement learning where we praise or punish the child. And it isn't just maturational development, where if you leave the child alone, the child automatically develops these skills— like a caterpillar turning into a butterfly.*
>
> *Nonetheless, it is obvious that the child is radically changing his or her behavior. There needs to be a third channel for development and change—and the third channel is observational learning or imitation. Children are learning from us, but they're learning on their own. They're absorbing the information, transforming what they see into their own actions.*

In an article titled "Foundations for a New Science of Learning," Meltzoff and his colleagues write that imitation "accelerates learning and multiplies learning opportunities. It is faster than individual discovery and safer than trial-and-error learning."

Imitation also provides a measure of children's emerging ability to remember. To investigate how imitative learning works, Meltzoff brought babies one at a time into his lab and showed them a series of "novel things to do with toys"—a *new* action with a *new* toy—and then handed the toy to the child, who typically mimicked the action. When I saw him conduct this experiment with eighteen-month-olds, the novel actions included pulling apart a toy dumbbell, flattening a collapsible toy with the palm of his hand, and touching his head to a light box, which turned the light on. Meltzoff says:

> *Even when I did this novel behavior of leaning forward and touching the light panel with my head, the baby leaned forward with her head. There's remarkable imitation at eighteen months of age.*

These aren't actions babies would do spontaneously with these toys:

> *We have control groups of babies that we give those objects to play with on their own. They don't perform these particular odd and unusual actions when left to their own devices. We could prove that the children were learning these actions from us, and this helps to show the power of imitative learning.*

Meltzoff wondered how long babies would remember these "novel actions," especially since at the time people didn't think babies had very long memories:

> *People used to say that young babies had memories of one minute; thirty seconds; ten seconds—[or] perhaps a few hours.*

His experiments have demonstrated that this view is wrong:

> *We showed the babies a series of actions on one day and didn't let them play with or touch the toy. We sent them home from our laboratory; then they would come in the next day and we would hand*

them the toys. We were able to demonstrate that the children—at fourteen months and even as young as nine months—would re-member what they had seen the day before. They would do just what they had seen the adult do with the toys.

How long would they remember and imitate? Meltzoff and a colleague tested this with twelve-month-olds:

We started off using a twenty-four-hour delay, and we were able to show that babies would imitate after the twenty-four-hour delay. We moved rapidly from there to a one-week delay. Lo and behold, babies could imitate after one week, even if we changed the context and they needed to recall the information in a different room from where they had learned it.

In the final study, we did a memory delay of four months with children of fourteen to sixteen months. I was personally quite sur-prised that after having watched me do a gesture for just twenty seconds, babies could imitate from memory four months later. It is a dramatic demonstration that they learn from us and remember what we do.

We may not realize just how much young children watch what we're doing. Meltzoff marvels:

Children are sitting wide-eyed in their high chair across the din-ner table and we don't know it, but they are watching us and they are committing our actions to memory. We wonder why chil-dren begin acting like Dad, or acting like Mom, and sometimes people think it's genetics and inborn dispositions, but it's partly the power of imitative learning. We are role models for our chil-dren starting from early infancy. They want to be like us. This has important implications for parenting, emotional development, and early education.

A PARENT'S PERSPECTIVE: DON'T STOP THE ACTION!

At twenty-three months, it's daily imitation now. Niko dips his fingers in my contact lens case and puts this finger to his eye as I am putting on my contacts. When I put on lip balm, he needs some, too. When I apply face cream, it's the same. The funniest is when he gets interrupted midaction: he has to go back to the very beginning of the routine and start all over again.

BABIES AS EAVESDROPPERS?

Nameera Akhtar of the University of California at Santa Cruz traces her fascination with what children can learn "when no one is teaching them—when they're *eavesdropping* or overhearing other people's conversations"—in part to growing up surrounded by multiple languages. She says:

> I actually [learned] one language primarily through overhearing. My parents spoke one language to me and my siblings, but a different language between themselves. We were very motivated to understand what they were saying to each other.

In one of her studies, young children from two to two and a half years of age are shown an exciting toy to play with. The hope is to capture their attention and "distract" them, in order to determine how motivated they will be to pay attention to an overheard situation. In the experiment I observed, the distracter toy was a row of dinosaur eggs—each egg could be popped open to reveal a baby dinosaur. On the other side of the room, two adults (the experimenters) sat on the floor on either side of a row of buckets, each of which held a "novel" toy:

> We use objects that children would not be familiar with—they haven't seen them before, but they're interesting and fun objects for them to play with.

One of the experimenters lifted a toy out of each container, but named only *one* of them, using a made-up name: a *modi*. It was amazing to watch the children observe the action across the room. Some played with the distracter toy for some time before looking over; others peered over their shoulders right away; still others descended from their chairs to stare at the two experimenters directly. Akhtar says:

> One of the surprising findings for us was that [children] tended to look up when they heard this new word. That was very interesting because it wasn't something we were necessarily looking for. They were more likely to disengage from the distracter toy when they heard this new word.

After the experimenters had repeated this routine three times, they put all the toys on the floor for the child to play with and then put them on a tray. The experimenter asked the child, "Can you show me the modi? Which one is the modi?" Without fail, most pointed to the correct object. Akhtar concludes:

> I think these experiments show how motivated children are to pay attention to adults' conversations—even though they are not in-volved or being directly addressed—and how motivated they are to learn new information.

It is important to note that very young children—under one year of age—have trouble differentiating two voices, even saying familiar words, including their own names, unless the distracter voice is less intense than the voice they are supposed to be listening to. Rochelle Newman of the University of Maryland calls this *the cocktail party effect*. She says:

> Infants are in noisy environments a lot. If you have an infant and you take them out into the grocery store with you, there's noise in the background; if your child is in a day care setting, there's noise; if you have more than one child in the household, there's noise; if you have a TV on or the radio on, there's noise. In order to be able to

learn language from those settings, they've got to be able to separate the sound of the person talking to them from that background noise.

WHY A TRUSTWORTHY RELATIONSHIP IS SO IMPORTANT TO LEARNING

Trustworthy relationships that foster learning are caring and reliable relationships where adults can be depended on to:

Keep children *safe*. Megan Gunnar's studies, which I discussed in chapter 6, on taking on challenges, reveal that if children are fearful and stressed—if they're in a *fight-or-flight* mode for long periods of time—they're less able to pay attention, to remember, and to have self control. Children need to feel safe in order to learn.

Make them feel *secure*. The day-in, day-out security of children's relationships with the important people in their lives makes it possible for them to try new things, to learn new things. This is dramatically visible when children go somewhere new. Typically, they'll turn to you to see if it's okay to venture out, as researcher Joseph Campos found in his experiment with young children checking out their mother's facial expressions before daring to cross a *visual cliff*—a tabletop covered with clear Plexiglas revealing a "floor" beneath (which I also described in the chapter on taking on challenges). If the mother posed a smiling face, the children tended to cross the visual cliff; if she posed a fear face, they tended to retreat.

Robert Pianta of the University of Virginia, an expert on early childhood education and teacher quality, describes the same process between children and teachers:

A lot of people talk about the relationship between kids and a teacher as [providing] a secure base for exploring the world. A good teacher-child relationship is going to offer the child the opportunity to stretch and risk a little bit socially, emotionally, or in learning something hard and new. It's going to provide just the kind of support that the child needs to be able to master what's being offered.

Give them *structure*. Part of being reliable is providing structure, a routine and pattern to their lives that children can count on. Children need an understandable and regular structure in their lives in order to learn.

PRINCIPLE 2: HELP CHILDREN SET AND WORK TOWARD THEIR OWN GOALS

Executive function is a behavioral construct that, broadly speaking, refers to the deliberate, goal-directed control of behavior.
—PHILIP DAVID ZELAZO, UNIVERSITY OF MINNESOTA

That's why helping children set and work toward goals is critical to helping them be self-directed and engaged learners. But, you could argue, how can goal setting be done with very young children, since the brain's executive capacities don't seem to emerge until children are preschoolers? Adele Diamond explains:

> *People used to think that young children couldn't exercise executive functions. For example, preschools and kindergartens were often organized so that the teacher would exercise executive functions for the children or would try to organize situations so the children wouldn't need to exercise executive function.*

Yet we know that infants and toddlers are driven to understand and master their own experiences. Much of children's early behavior—twisting until they can turn over on their own, scooting across the floor until they can crawl, grabbing onto everything in sight to pull themselves upright until they can stand on their own two legs, babbling until they can say words that others can understand—is fueled by the drive to master their environment. I see this drive for mastery as nature's precursor to goal setting—a drive that we can promote through nurture.

ENCOURAGE CHILDREN'S DESIRE TO EXPLORE

Craig Ramey of Georgetown University has spent his career asking whether and to what degree human development can be altered and optimized:

> *Can we put our hands on the levers that we think are going to be positive influences [on children's] development? [Can we] use those levers to help children get a better start in life and then follow them and find out whether they had an influence on how their life unfolded?*

The Abecedarian Project, which I'll describe shortly, was the first of many rigorous experiments that Ramey and his colleagues conducted to pursue these questions.

Craig and his wife, researcher Sharon Ramey, reviewed approximately eight hundred studies to identify what parents and caregivers do that best promotes the development of intelligence, social competence, and academic achievement, which they've written about in their book, *Right from Birth*. The first principle they write about is encouraging exploration. Craig Ramey says:

> *When we encourage [children] to explore, we let them know that the world is a very interesting place and that they are going to have a great time as they sort of meander through it—if they keep their eyes and ears opened and their sense of touch going. They're going to discover things about the world that will be of enormous benefit to them.*

Ramey encourages parents to make a big deal out of children's explorations, whether they're discovering that water changes shape when you pour it from one kind of container to another or discovering a bug inching along the sidewalk. He says:

> *We think of explorers as the people who get into spaceships and go into outer space or the people who generations ago got into boats*

*and went across the ocean. Well, every child is an explorer, be-
cause children always have first experiences with the most elemen-
tal things in the world. [These] may be old hat to us but [they're]
brand-new to them. The parents who can keep that enthusiasm for
discovery [alive], who say, "Go ahead and try something a little bit
more—take the risk," [have children who] later in life are likely
to come up with novel insights, new ways to do things and solve
problems.*

HELP THEM LEARN TO PLAN

Helping children learn to plan helps them build ways to satisfy their
drive for discovery and mastery. Surprisingly, children are able to plan
earlier than we may have thought. In a study of twenty-one- and twenty-
seven-month-olds by Patricia Bauer of Emory University and her colleagues, an experimenter showed individual children two nesting cups
and a small wooden block and let the children play with them to see if
they spontaneously assembled these objects to form a rattle. Next the objects were removed from the child's sight so that the experimenter could
assemble a rattle by putting the block inside one of the nesting cups and
snapping the other cup on top of it (like a lid). The experimenter then
showed the newly assembled toy to the child, saying, "You can use this
stuff to make a rattle." She took it apart (again, out of the child's sight)
and gave the cups and block to the child to see if she or he could plan the
steps necessary to make the rattle.

If the child did not make the rattle, the experimenter removed the
cups and ball, showed the child the sequence of actions, and again encouraged the child to make a rattle, with such prompts as "Now it's your
turn; you make a rattle."

You can see how this process is similar to the imitation procedures I
discussed earlier—but rather than giving the child *one* action to mimic,
there are *three sequential steps* for the child to remember and repeat. It
turns out that two in five toddlers could plan the sequence of steps necessary to make the rattle, and virtually all of them were able to repeat the

sequence once it was demonstrated for them, indicating that the ability to plan to reach a goal emerges early—an important finding.

In writing about their experiment, Bauer and her colleagues ask us to imagine what it would be like if someone showed us a lemon meringue pie and then handed us all the individual ingredients and told us to make a pie. Yes, there are more ingredients and more steps in making a pie than in making a rattle, but following directions to create something is not necessarily an easy task for children or adults! Seeing this experiment reminds me of the agony of reading directions for a new product I have bought and then struggling to assemble it.

We can help children build on their emerging ability to plan to reach goals by articulating their goals when they're small, such as saying, "You are trying so hard to stand up." When they're preschool age and older, we can help them form and achieve goals by asking them to make plans, stick to them, and then evaluate how the plans have worked—an activity that you've probably seen in good educational programs.

PUTTING IT ALL TOGETHER: GOLD-STANDARD EXPERIMENTS IN EARLY EDUCATION

In 2006 the Committee for Economic Development (CED) offered me a unique opportunity. The leaders of CED (a nonprofit, nonpartisan organization of top corporate executives and university presidents "dedicated to policy research on the major economic and social issues of our time") invited me to revisit three "gold-standard programs" of high-quality early education to determine what made them so effective. (I say "revisit" because I visited two of them in their early years.) These three early childhood programs—the HighScope Perry Preschool Project, the Abecedarian Project, and the Chicago Child-Parent Centers—were launched respectively in the 1960s, 1970s, and 1980s and have been extensively researched ever since. There are a number of reasons that these programs are considered "gold standard":

They enrolled children deemed at highest risk for subsequent problems in school: children from families who were low-income and struggling with all the issues that poverty in America entails. By illuminating what it takes to keep children engaged in learning under difficult circumstances, we can see what it takes to promote learning in *all* children.

They used rigorous research designs, such as comparing the children who were randomly selected to participate in their programs with children who were not selected to participate.

They were longitudinal, following the children from the time they enrolled in the program until the present day.

Finally, they used several different measures of children's success.

The children in these programs now range from their twenties to their forties. Financial calculations have revealed that the benefits of participating in these programs far outweighed their costs, including less special education, better grade retention, higher high school graduation rates, higher college attendance rates, higher employment rates, and higher monthly earnings.

I was eager to revisit the programs by interviewing the researchers who evaluated them, because these three programs have been used to justify *any* and *all* early childhood programs, and because revisiting gave me the chance to ask the original researchers what *they* think made the critical difference in their program's success. For example, many analyses have shown that factors like the number of adults per children (or adult-to-child ratio) and the size of the group were important, but I know from my own research that you can have those things and not have a good program. From the HighScope Perry Preschool Project, I interviewed Larry Schweinhart of the HighScope Educational Research Foundation; from the Abecedarian Project, I interviewed Craig Ramey and Sharon Ramey of Georgetown University; and from the Chicago Child-Parent Centers, I interviewed Arthur Reynolds of the University of Minnesota.

Here are some of my findings:

The children were seen as active learners.

The creators of these programs did not subscribe to the "empty vessel" model of learning, where knowledge is poured into the child. They assumed that children have a drive to learn and explore, and the program creators built on this drive.

As such, children were expected to take increasing responsibility for their own learning—to become more goal directed. As an example, Larry Schweinhart described a classroom for three- and four-year-olds at the HighScope Perry Preschool Project in the 1960s:

The classroom was divided into activity areas, like mini-rooms— clearly delineated areas with certain kinds of materials in [them].

These areas would have included a science area, a reading area, and a block area:

When the children came in, they would all assemble. They might be reading storybooks or anything during that time. When the formal part of the program began, the children were called upon to make plans, carry out the plans, and review the plans.

In other words, the children set and carried out goals. The program's intent was to give children increasing responsibility for their own learning. Schweinhart says:

The reason we want children to be involved as initiators is because it works better for their education and, in fact, it makes them better citizens in the long run. The basic cornerstone of that daily routine is children making plans, then carrying out the plans, and then getting back together and reviewing the plans, under the guidance of the teacher.

The program creators saw setting goals as critical to helping children develop lifetime habits of engaged learning.

THE LESSONS LEARNED: AN EXPERIMENT IN EDUCATION AND SOCIAL CHANGE

A new, equally seminal experiment in education and social change that's under way and being evaluated now is the Harlem Children's Zone (HCZ). The CEO and president—a true visionary—Geoffrey Canada, recounts his history with HCZ:

> I've been at the same job for more than twenty-five years. Originally, we had this idea that if we could get kids early (and that was by the first grade), and if we can get these kids on track, that by middle school, they would be fine. We went about doing that and we thought we were doing a great job.
>
> By 1990, people were saying, "Wow, you guys are really doing great work." I thought we were doing great work. I looked around— we were being written up in the newspaper, people were saying these wonderful things about our organization.
>
> And then I really began to look at the data of what was happening to children in Harlem, and I had to admit that things were actually worse for these kids than when I first began in the field. Harlem has been at the bottom of positive outcomes for children in New York State.
>
> So I went to my board and I said, "Look, some places—and Harlem is one of those places—there's not one thing that's going bad for kids, it's everything . . . and if we can get kids past one of those hurdles, they get tripped up by another one." So I said we had to think about a new way of working with these young people, not by running individual discrete programs but [by] trying to rebuild a community around these kids— one where the adults were playing a much more active role, and all of us who were there, either paid or unpaid, had to step up our game.
>
> We chose one hundred blocks and we said that the kids in that area were going to be "ours" and we were going to do everything— we said everything, we meant everything—to help these children.

Encompassing almost one hundred blocks in Harlem and serving over eight thousand children, HCZ has steadily grown over the last decade, adding the following programs: in 2000, a parenting program called The Baby College for families who are expecting or who have young children; in 2001, the Harlem Gems preschool programs; in 2004, Promise Academies charter public schools, which are planned to extend into the high school years. These programs include extended days and Saturday programs. There are also initiatives to improve children's health, and all the programs provide healthy food.

In its brochure, Canada describes the ultimate goal of HCZ: "getting our kids into and through college." In the HighScope Perry Preschool Program, the children were asked to set daily goals; in the HCZ, there is a larger goal that the families, the community, and the Zone have set for all the children: that *every single child* in the program will enroll in and graduate from college. It is a goal that Canada acknowledges critics have deemed difficult, but this opposition fuels Canada and his team even more.

HCZ makes sure that this goal is visible and reinforced daily. For example, in the Promise Academy elementary program I observed, the children line up in the hallway every morning and state this goal as their creed. Canada says:

> *If kids are saying their creed, "I will go to college; I will succeed,"*
> *if their parents are thinking that, if the teachers are thinking that,*
> *then you've got thirty percent of the work done.*

Because the children who participate in HCZ are chosen by lottery, it is possible to compare their success with those who weren't selected. An evaluation conducted by Will Dobbie and Roland Fryer of Harvard University has found that the HCZ program has been "enormously effective" in reducing the racial and economic achievement gap between these children and other children in New York City. Its middle school program has eliminated the gap in mathematics and reduced it in English language arts, and its elementary school program has closed the gap in both subjects.

As these programs show, in ways small and large, it is important to ensure that we help our children articulate goals, make plans for how to achieve them, work toward them, and evaluate their progress. This can include everything from helping them make a plan for how to spend a rainy Sunday to establishing larger goals for their lives.

A PARENT'S PERSPECTIVE:
"A LITTLE EVERY DAY"

When Madison started school, she couldn't read. Lots of other kids in her class were reading. The teachers told me not to be concerned because all children progress at different rates. Honestly, I wasn't concerned about her reading abilities, but I was concerned about her self esteem. She felt bad about not being able to read and compared herself to others. Her teachers told me that she should try to read a little every day, but whenever we sat down to read, she would get frustrated and walk away.

I told Madison that she was really good at working toward a goal, and it didn't matter how long it took her to get to a goal—it mattered whether or not she tried. So I made a monthlong calendar on a big piece of paper, and each day of the week was boxed and depicted in a different color. I then asked Madison to set a goal for each day in the month by telling me how long she wanted to read. We wrote her time goal in each day's box. (She set times like five or ten or fifteen minutes.) I thought of a lot of things we could do together to help get her into the world of reading, such as having her tell me stories of books without words or picking out a word in a book she knew by heart (such as *Hop on Pop* by Dr. Seuss). We hung the calendar in the kitchen. Each day, she was determined to put a huge X through the box, indicating that she had done her work! The calendar became a game—she was so focused on wanting to meet her goal and cross out the box that she was very happy spending the time reading.

So, as Canada says, with clear and agreed-upon goals, "you've got thirty percent of the work done" toward promoting self-directed, engaged learning. But it's only thirty percent. There's still—by Canada's calculations—seventy percent of the way to go. That's where these other principles come in.

PRINCIPLE 3: INVOLVE CHILDREN SOCIALLY, EMOTIONALLY, AND INTELLECTUALLY

While we adults tend to differentiate among different types of learning to ensure that we're focusing on all of them with children, it's important to bear in mind that in the lives of children—indeed, in our own lives— these aren't necessarily distinct, especially when children are truly engaged in learning. Larry Schweinhart of the HighScope Perry Preschool Project says:

> *We don't have cognitive learning now, but no social learning and no emotional learning, and then have emotional learning later for a set period of time—they are all together.*

BEYOND EITHER/OR: SOCIAL, EMOTIONAL, AND COGNITIVE LEARNING ARE, AT THEIR BEST, CONNECTED

Think back to the Still-Face experiment I described at the beginning of this chapter. It's clear that the baby was learning, but what part of that learning was social, what part was emotional, and what part was cognitive?

AN EXERCISE: THINK ABOUT A TIME WHEN YOU WERE LEARNING

Recall a time when you learned something, whether recently or long ago. Describe the experience to yourself. Then ask yourself:

What part of that learning was social (i.e., you learned from others)?

What part was emotional (i.e., you cared about what you were learning)?

What part was intellectual (i.e., you learned new information or a new concept)?

While academia has divided human development into different disciplines (for example, social psychology and cognitive psychology), while teachers tend to talk about social-emotional development and intellectual development as if they are distinct, and while many people think of learning as predominantly cognitive, this exercise makes it clear that those boundaries are far more fluid than one might think. Studies of the brain in action likewise reveal that different networks within the brain typically work together when the child is learning. Kurt Fischer of Harvard University says:

> *One of the most beneficial things that brain research has done is it's made it very hard for us to split cognition from emotion. For example, the areas of the brain most involved in memory—the quintessential cognitive function—are strongly tied to the emotion areas.*

Carol Dweck of Stanford University reiterates this point: neuroscience shows that

> *we can't carve people up—there isn't the cognitive person, the emotional person, the motivational person, the social person. All of these co-occur in the brain.*

Although there are times when learning is more cognitive than social or more emotional than cognitive, when children are *truly engaged* in learning, they are engaged on all three levels. Karen Wynn of Yale University says:

> *You can never put the child in a cognitive bubble where there's only a cognitive context and no emotional or social context or vice versa.*

Similarly, the National Scientific Council on the Developing Child (a multidisciplinary collaboration of scientists and scholars from universities across the United States and Canada designed to bring the science of early learning to bear on public policy decision-making) concluded:

Cognitive, emotional and social capacities are inextricably intertwined throughout the life course.

A PARENT'S PERSPECTIVE:
A LIFETIME INTEREST (SO FAR)

My daughter Emma was obsessed with monkeys. We lived near a zoo for the first four years of her life, and she visited the monkey house several times a week. She loved *Curious George*.

At seven, she insisted she wanted a pet monkey. It would have been *so* easy to say, "No, a pet monkey is not a good idea. Sorry." But instead (in one of my better parenting moments), I suggested she do some research on monkeys as pets. I asked her to present everything she learned about monkeys to me, and we would consider getting one as a pet. She was thrilled, energized, and eager to begin her first research project.

Emma called the zoo and spoke to a monkey house attendant who told her about natural versus domesticated environments. She went on the Jane Goodall Web site and learned about monkey behavior. She learned that monkeys were wonderful pets—until they turned two. Then they tend to eat furniture, ruin houses, and fight with other household pets, especially dogs. We had a three-year-old Labrador retriever.

Emma made the decision, with the saddest look on her face, that a pet monkey was not a good idea. But her love of monkeys didn't fade. Throughout elementary school and middle school, she referenced and used her learning research project as something she was really proud of—something she knew about that others didn't. In high school, she was selected to participate in a three-year science research project, and she conducted a comparison of the cognitive abilities of monkeys with those of two-, three-, and four-year-old children in terms of sorting and numeracy.

My lesson from this experience is that when children are *fully* engaged and "own" their learning process, there's no end to the possibilities that can result.

═══════════════════════════════════

OPTIMIZING LEARNING AND REMEMBERING

When we talk about learning, we have to talk about memory, because we can't benefit from what we've learned if we can't remember it, either consciously (as in a remembered fact) or unconsciously (as in a habit we've acquired). Researcher Patricia Bauer affirms the pivotal role of the "phenomenon of memory":

[V]irtually every other kind of higher cognitive function depends on memory. You can't talk about something unless you have something to talk about; you can't think about how two different things are related unless you can think about—[that is,] remember—the properties of each of those objects. When we try to solve a problem, when we read, when we communicate with others, when we try to make a persuasive argument—all of those abilities depend on memory, either very directly or at least indirectly. Therefore, it's extremely important that we understand how [memory] develops.

Why do we remember some things and forget others? That's one fascinating question Bauer investigates. She and her colleagues have found that memories are better preserved and recalled under some circumstances than others. Her findings have profound implications for how we promote children's learning and remembering. Children are more likely to recall their experiences when:

They have direct experiences rather than act as bystanders. Bauer notes:

One of the things that we've found that helps babies to remember is being allowed to be engaged in the activity. This is true for adults as well. If we're passive observers of something, we don't have as strong a memory for it later on.

To test this, Bauer and her colleagues have used procedures such as the nesting cups and the blocks that form a rattle:

Some babies only get to watch—they sit across the table and watch us make the rattle, but they don't ever get to do it themselves. Other babies get to see us make the rattle, and then get an opportunity to imitate right away. When we bring the babies back and test their memory, we see that the babies who've been allowed to imitate us right away have [a] better memory for that experience, relative to the babies who only had an opportunity to watch.

They have multiple experiences. Children are more likely to remember experiences that happen more frequently than those that happen less frequently, as Bauer explains:

We've found that children have better memory for something they've seen more than one time. This is probably something any parent of a young child can tell you—that [children] want the same book read to them over and over and over, and if you try to skip a page because you're tired, your child will bring you right back to that page and make you start over. They like that repetition. That repetition allows [children] to have better memory for an experience.

There are verbal cues and visual prompts. We can all attest to the fact that we remember things better if there are reminders or clues. Building on the experiment of making a rattle, Bauer has found that both hearing words and seeing the objects again help children remember:

What we have done is ask the child to remember the rattle either by just giving them the objects as their cue, or giving them the objects and also saying to them, "We used that stuff to make a rattle. Show me

*how you do that." [With children] even as young as thirteen months,
we find that providing the verbal label for that experience [and the
materials] facilitates their memory, allows them to show better memory performance than if we don't provide them with that.*

AN EXERCISE: WHAT HELPS YOU REMEMBER?

*When you're trying to remember something, what helps you
retrieve it? If you are trying to remember something (like
the name of a person you just met), what do you do to help
yourself?*

The experiences are meaningful and purposeful. When children
see sequences of actions that are random rather than meaningful
and purposeful, they forget them more easily. I think Bauer's studies
show that even tasks that seem primarily cognitive—such as creating
a rattle from cups and a block—are more likely to be remembered
when emotional and social engagement are integrated with the cognitive work: when children find meaning in the process, when they're
involved hands-on, and when there's conversation about what they're
doing. In fact, Bauer reports that children are "highly motivated" to
imitate these experiences.

A PARENT'S PERSPECTIVE:
"I HOPE SHE NEVER STOPS"

When my girl falls for something, she falls hard—obsessive, en-
gulfing, constant worship. Lately we're into bugs. She sleeps with
jars of spiders in her bed. After dinner, she and I head to the library and check out every book on arachnids. She has an imaginary
friend—Ickson, a blue spider that "lives" on the ceiling in her room.
She asks for Spider Juice or Spider Nuggets for dinner. I had a friend
make a shirt for her with a spider on it, blue of course, for Ickson.
She wore it for eighteen days straight. She agreed to go to preschool only because I told her spiders live there, and she can keep
a jarred spider in her coat cubby. We went to dinner as a family, and

somehow this child found a spider in the corner and spent the entire meal eating under the table, talking to her new friend.

I love her voracious appetite for learning. Sometimes she'll get shorter, less intense obsessions—dinosaurs, scorpions, and volcanoes were recent hits. She is three and a half years old and can tell you more about hot magma than I can. We even have a fish named Hot Magma.

I enjoy all of this because I can feel like a kid again, learning about this giant, amazing world as if for the first time. I hope she always stays this curious, this questioning. I hope she has teachers who act graciously toward her and her thirst for learning. Above all, I hope she never stops seeing this world as an incredible place.

THE IMPORTANCE OF PHYSICAL LEARNING

Bauer's research makes it clear that learning is physical: babies do better at remembering how to make the rattle when they have a chance to try it immediately after watching someone do it. Furthermore, children also learn best when they're well taken care of physically—when they're feeling healthy, well fed, well rested, and have time during the day for physical activity and play. That's why programs like the Harlem Children's Zone begin the day with breakfast, but also have their own cooks to ensure that the food children eat is healthy—the Harlem Children's Zone is a no-junk-food zone.

But even healthy foods may not always be healthy for your child. You need to monitor your children's reactions to foods. We found, for example, that Philip used to get very tired in kindergarten. It turned out that he had an adverse response to the eggs he was craving. We experimented and ultimately removed eggs from his diet, and he had a lot more energy.

THE IMPORTANCE OF MULTIPLE KINDS OF LEARNING

Because of the effectiveness of social, emotional, and cognitive learning, the three gold-standard early childhood programs and programs like the Harlem Children's Zone emphasize all kinds of learning, not just so-called cognitive learning. Geoffrey Canada says it is vital to recognize that children learn in different ways and are good at different things, and these need to be promoted:

> We want great music, great art, great sports. We want young people to excel in multiple things, not just in academics.

The day I visited HCZ, I saw a grade school class focusing on the meaning of Gustav Klimt's painting *The Tree of Life* and drawing their own versions of it. (For more information on the connection between the arts and learning, see chapter 4, on making connections, and my interview with Michael Gazzaniga.)

PRINCIPLE 4: ELABORATE AND EXTEND CHILDREN'S LEARNING

Memory researchers have investigated what children remember about their lives and have again found differences in what they remember and why.

AN EXERCISE: WHAT ARE YOUR EARLIEST MEMORIES?

Think about how your own memory has developed. What are your earliest memories? Why do you think you remember those experiences?

My own earliest memory is of my first day of school at Mrs. Helene Dick's nursery school and kindergarten. I was three and a half, and according to my mother, I was wearing a new dress that had butterflies and roses on it (which she said that I pronounced as "budderfwies" and "wooozes"). My dress has become part of our family's lore, and I only remember this because I have been told about it so often. Central to my own memory are the steps down to the school—dauntingly long, steep steps down a vertical West Virginia hillside. That memory was not courtesy of my mother, who learned of my trepidation at first sight of Mrs.

Dick's steps only years later, when I was an adult. Clearly my emotions played a role in the enduring vividness of this memory decades later, outweighing even my probable excitement about wearing my brand-new "budderfwies and wooozes" dress.

We have our own personal memories, and then there are memories we share as a generation. How many of us who are old enough remember President Kennedy's funeral?

AN ADULT'S PERSPECTIVE: NOVEMBER 1963

I am four years old, and I am watching TV coverage of President Kennedy's funeral. I remember the prancing, gleaming horse with the boots backward in the stirrups, and the flag-draped coffin being borne along the street, and how the camera panned over the faces of the military men and the crowd. It feels to me as if I watched for hours and days, and perhaps I did. I remember looking very hard at the faces of the crowd, especially those tall-standing uniformed soldiers, and being afraid at how somber everyone looked. I watched and watched to find one tiny flicker of a smile or crinkle in the eyes. Nothing. I knew that this must be a sad time beyond understanding. My mother has told me that in preschool during that time, I played "funeral," putting a doll in the baby carriage, draping a blanket over it, and wheeling it around. She said that for a while after that I would ask her, "Mommy, when will you die?" She would try to say reassuring things like "Oh, not for a long, long time, when you are all grown up, and you will be old, and I will be very old, and that will be a very long time from now." And I would seem to accept that for a while, but then pretty soon I'd circle back and say, "But, Mommy, when will you die?"

Bauer notes that we are not atypical in having our earliest memories originate in the early preschool years and revolve around an emotional experience. She says:

If I ask you to think about your earliest memories, the average age for earliest or [verbal] memory is about three to three and a half years of age. And that phenomenon—infantile or childhood amnesia—has been documented for over a century now.

Since the 1980s, Robyn Fivush, a colleague of Patricia Bauer's at Emory University, has been studying children's memories of their experiences. She and her colleagues taped conversations between mothers and their preschool-aged children talking about past experiences. In this and subsequent studies, the researchers found that mothers had diverse styles of recalling the past with their children, which they term *high elaborative* and *low elaborative* styles of reminiscing. In a high elaborative style:

The mother discusses the past experience in rich detail.

She asks lots of open-ended questions, which the researchers call "wh" questions: *why, what, where,* or *who* questions. For example, after a trip to the zoo, a highly elaborative parent might ask: "Who did you go to the zoo with? What animals did you see there?" This kind of question differs from yes/no "just the facts" questions, such as "Did you like the zoo?" By being asked questions, the child is invited to participate in the conversation, or *co-construct* it.

The mother often repeats what the child says ("You saw a lion!"), thus encouraging the child to say more.

As they go back and forth, the mother provides feedback to the child as well as more information: "The lion was growling. Was that a scary noise?"

The mother shows a genuine interest in what the child is saying.

Does the mother's style of discussion matter in the development of her child? Yes, it does. This and other studies have found that the children of more elaborative mothers are more likely to have more robust memories, better language and literacy skills, and a better understanding of the perspectives of others. "Children of more highly elaborative mothers come to tell more detailed, more elaborated, and more coherent narratives of their personal past than do children of less elaborative mothers."

In other words, children are learning that life is not simply a series of events that take place, but that it is linked to how they and others think and feel. They are creating a story about themselves—in a real sense beginning to "write" their own autobiographies, developing a richly detailed understanding of themselves and the world. This ever-deepening understanding is what they bring to their learning, to their everyday lives, to their future friends and partners, and to their work.

Daniel J. Siegel of the UCLA School of Medicine further explains the processes by which children begin to write their own autobiographies:

> *Around the second birthday, children begin to develop this ability to talk about the past [and] the present, and to discuss the anticipated future. As they do this, parents have the opportunity to engage with their children in creating these stories together about events they shared.*

Siegel reports that the parents who create stories with their children have children with a deeper understanding of themselves and others. He also reports that when children feel secure in their relationship with their parents, they are more likely to create stories about who they are that are "rich and full of detail." And what better place to share these stories than around the dinner table!

FROM ELABORATING TO EXTENDING

Although Fivush and others have found socioeconomic and cultural differences in elaborating, I think that elaborating is an important way for all of us to promote our children's learning—whatever our differences. So many of the studies I've shared in this book reveal that elaborating *and extending* children's experiences are essential to promoting learning. Think, for example, of Catherine Snow's studies, profiled in chapter 3, on communicating. She and her colleagues have found that mothers, fathers, and teachers who have *extended discourse* with children—conversations that go beyond the here and now, that include "wh" questions, that ask children to think about the past, the present, and the future—have children with better literacy skills in their school-age years.

I was struck by how each of the three gold-standard early childhood programs worked to extend children's learning: each based their curriculum on closely observing the children and then providing activities that moved the children from where they were to the next step in learning.

For example, the curriculum of the Abecedarian Project was designed, in Craig Ramey's words, to "get away from the one-size-fits-all" notion of curriculum. He describes what we might have seen on a classroom visit:

> Let's just say we were talking about a child who is eighteen months to two years of age, the time when children are just beginning to do two-word combinations, typically a noun and a verb—the classic of "Look ball." If the child says "Ball," then the teacher might say, "That's great. [You have] the red ball." And we would measure whether the child over a two-week period came to label that as a "red ball."

If you had walked into that program, it might have seemed as if the children were just being spontaneous and having fun—and they were. But they were also learning a great deal from a curriculum that the teachers had carefully created based on observing the children, seeing what they were attempting to master, and then planning an activity to extend that learning. Carollee Howes, a UCLA researcher who has looked at what makes educational programs work, says that extending children's learning is not just changing the topic of the conversation; it is giving children "a more complex way of doing something."

GIVE EACH CHILD HIS OR HER OWN
"LEMONADE STAND"

Throughout the book, I've talked about the importance of each child having what I call a "lemonade stand": an interest, a passion, something they genuinely want to learn. This can become the fertile ground for your elaborating and extending their learning.

Lemonade stands can come in handy when you're stuck with a cranky child. I remember a trip we took when Lara was eight. We wanted to see museums, but every time we stepped inside one, Lara was ready to leave—"Are we done yet? When can we leave—how many minutes, how many *seconds*?" Not fun. But (probably with inspiration born of desperation), I remembered her interest in women of different times in history from her school social studies classes. I could also see she was drawn to a painting of the Madonna in one room because it was golden and glowing. So I asked her to find paintings of the Madonna in that and other rooms—to see what was different about them. And she began to notice that sometimes the Madonna had blond hair but sometimes dark hair. Sometimes the Madonna was very round and full and sometimes very thin. As we elaborated on what she was noticing, we began to notice other things about the paintings. When were they painted? What country was the artist from? Did other paintings from that era or that country have people in them that looked similar? What did that tell us about the backgrounds of the paintings? We also could talk about the religious significance of the paintings. Pretty soon she had stopped hammering at us to leave and was actually taking us around the museum to share her discoveries!

Schools can be designed with this express purpose—to engage children and then extend their learning. A good example is the Normal Park Museum Magnet School in Chattanooga, Tennessee, which serves children from prekindergarten through eighth grade. In 2001 this school was listed as a low-performing school. Since then, it has been transformed, now scoring at 100 percent of proficiency in reading and language arts.

The architect of the turnaround is school principal Jill Levine, who created the school and connected it with seven local museums. Each unit of study involves the children in a nine-week inquiry in which they ask questions, pursue the answers through direct experience, and then share what they've learned by creating museum-quality exhibits.

As an example, the third grade was studying the ecology of their state. One project involved going to the aquarium to study the habits and habitats of local fish. Each child had a fish to follow, marking its path every five seconds with colored dots on cellophane that covered the side of the tank. They brought the cellophane back to the classroom and mapped the journeys of their fish. "What is important," says Levine, "is to get children to ask question after question."

At the end of each unit, the children create a museum-quality display of what they have learned. These exhibits are not just posters attached to the wall. These third-grade children built caves, forests, lakes, and streams. At the opening of their exhibit, the children served as docents, explaining to their families what they had learned. Levine told me:

> I always wanted to do something that promotes curiosity and celebrates learning and I have!

Extending children's learning also involves challenging them. In business, these are called "stretch assignments," where we're pushed a little further than we think we can go. We know, however, from our research on adults that too great a stretch can lead to unproductive stress—that it's important to challenge people, but by successive degrees outside their comfort zone. The same applies to children. We need to calibrate how far to challenge children, and if it is too far, rein in.

A PARENT'S PERSPECTIVE: FROM MONEY TO MEANING

My son (age seven) has been interested in money. He wants to earn a lot of money. When he began saying that, I thought "What! A Bernie Madoff in the making." So I told him that earning money just to have money shouldn't be his goal. He should want to earn money so he could do something he feels passionate about or so that he could do something good for the world.

His class had been studying children in different parts of the world, and he was very upset when he found out that some children go hungry. He said, "Why don't they just go to the grocery store?" It upset him that some kids don't even have the essentials. So he decided that he wanted to make money so no child would ever be hungry.

He started to ask for money for everything he did. He would come to me and say, "I cleaned my room. Can I have money?" "I listened to you. Can I have money?" "I got dressed. Can I have money?" I told him that these are things that you just do—not things you get paid for doing.

He has been thinking about what he could do when he grows up to earn lots of money. His latest idea is that he would own an aquarium. He would make the tickets and sell them, his grandfather would keep it clean, his father would play music, and his grandmother would cook the food.

And me. He wants me to be his personal assistant. That's the perfect definition of a mother if I ever heard one!

A PARENT'S PERSPECTIVE:
FROM LEMONADE STANDS TO KIDS' CAFÉS

My daughter, Grace, is eight years old and passionate about many things, including animals. She studied the rain forest in third grade this year and became concerned about endangered animals, and she wanted to do something to help. So she and several of her school friends set their own goal: set up a kids' café to raise money for Amazon Watch.

There was no stopping these children. They decided on the date ahead of time, planned a menu, figured out who would make the red velvet cake and who would make the tiered vanilla cake, who would bring the lemonade and who would bring the iced tea, all with just a little help from their parents. They created illustrated menus, price lists, and posters and announcements to send to our neighbors and to their classmates at school. They were so passionate about what they had learned and what they might do to help that they turned themselves into social entrepreneurs, advocates, bakers, accountants, and event planners—unified by a single-minded goal. The day came for the kids' café, cold and dreary, as luck would have it, but they set up their tables as planned, and the customers showed up. They made $86.30 to help save the animals!

PRINCIPLE 5: HELP CHILDREN PRACTICE, SYNTHESIZE, AND GENERALIZE

Extending their learning is something that children in time begin to do for themselves, if given the right cues. In their book, *Right from Birth*, Craig and Sharon Ramey point to the importance of helping children "rehearse and extend" the skills they're learning. Craig Ramey explains:

> *If you've never played tennis before, [or] never played golf before, you are unlikely on your very first outing to shoot a par under two, or play a great set of tennis. Life just doesn't work that way. [When they're learning something new], kids need the opportunity to try and try again, in a good atmosphere where there's a chance to refine the skill.*

LEARNING AT THE BRAIN LEVEL

Consolidating what one has learned is part of the fundamental pattern of how we learn. Learning and growth, according to Kurt Fischer of Harvard University, happen in spurts—spurts we have all observed as parents:

> *We're now at the point where we can pin down when there are abrupt changes in development—dramatic spurts in understanding, for example—and when there are continuous changes. One of them is at about two years of age, when kids are mastering language: vocabulary takes off, pretend play takes off, children show a new capacity to represent things [understand that one thing can stand for another], all within a common age period. At about age four, there's another cluster of spurts.*

What's fascinating is that these spurts in behavior happen at the brain level, too. Fischer points out that there were clues to these brain changes as early as the 1940s, when scientists conducting a longitudinal study, the

Berkeley and Yellow Springs Longitudinal Studies, observed that the actual size of children's heads changed at four years old—a time when their cognitive capacities were also changing. Now scientists can see even more:

> It looks like for each of the jumps in behavior [where] we see new capacities emerging [during] certain age periods, there's a reorganization going on in the brain that at its crudest may be reflected in brain size, but more deeply it's reflected in changes in brain process. In particular, there is a jump in the energy in brain activity, in the connections between cortical areas; [that is,] in the way that parts of the brain are connected to each other.

Interestingly enough, another pattern parents observe is also reflected in brain processes—where children take two steps forward in their growth and then take one step backward; they seem to regress:

> When you [see] a huge jump in performance, then shortly after you see a big drop. Generally the increase is bigger than the drop. You see a sudden jump, then a drop, then another sudden jump, then a drop. That's one of the basic mechanisms in development.

Importantly, these surges in children' capacity involve consolidating their knowledge or capacities:

> When we look at how people build knowledge in the short term, one of the most basic processes we see is that people need to build knowledge over and over and over and over in order to get more general stable knowledge.

You can see this in children and in adults, Fischer says, recounting his own experiences with computers:

> I can remember when I was first learning to use computers, I would get a new computer and I would say after five minutes, "This computer is broken"—and then miraculously over the next hour it

would fix itself. The computer wasn't broken; it was just that I was figuring out how to use the computer in a general way.

He was consolidating his knowledge of how to use a computer. "Practice makes perfect," "If at first you don't succeed, try, try, again," and other axioms speak to the importance of practice in remembering, consolidating, and generalizing new knowledge. But we also know that "drill and practice" can become "drill and kill," where our engagement in learning is dulled, put to sleep.

WHAT MAKES THE DIFFERENCE? PROMOTING CHILDREN'S CURIOSITY

In chapter 5, on critical thinking, I described the research of Laura Schulz of MIT. She and others have found that children are curious about anything new, so extending children's learning with new information as they build knowledge and skills helps maintain their motivation to practice.

Schulz has also found that children are curious when something happens that contradicts their prior understanding that "this is the way the world is." I've talked about *confounding expectations* research in other chapters—how even very young babies literally look longer or sometimes even look astonished when something happens that isn't what they expect. In effect, when the "story" children are learning about the world changes, children become alert and engaged, and there's a golden opportunity for learning. Schulz says:

You have to do something with that evidence. You can deny it. You can try to explain it away. But one way or another, you need more information to figure out what to do.

The second reason that children become curious is that they have two competing or conflicting understandings:

There are many things that might be true, and the evidence just doesn't determine which one is the case.

So introducing new and perhaps puzzling information continues to keep children motivated to practice.

WHAT MAKES THE DIFFERENCE? HAVING CHILDREN EXPLAIN WHAT THEY'RE LEARNING

Robyn Fivush's research reveals how much children learn from their everyday conversations with their parents, but what if parents only *listen* and don't talk?

Bethany Rittle-Johnson of Vanderbilt University has been investigating the *transfer of knowledge*—applying something learned in one instance to a new situation. Specifically, she has been interested in whether *explaining* to someone what you've learned can improve the transfer of this knowledge to a new problem or situation.

She and her colleagues tested this idea by giving children pattern problems (because these are crucial in math learning). Four- and five-year-olds were shown a game board with seven squares on it. The experimenter put objects in a pattern on the game board: for example, a green grasshopper, a green grasshopper, a blue spider, a green grasshopper, a green grasshopper, and a blue spider. The child would be asked what comes next in the pattern (on the seventh square) and shown nine different objects from which to choose. The answer is—a green grasshopper. A harder problem would involve using three objects to create patterns—a red spider, a red bee, and a blue bee.

First children were pretested by being given problems to solve so that the experimenter could determine whether the child should be given the easier or harder problems. The children were also asked to explain how they made their decision in selecting the seventh object. Then they were randomly assigned to three different *conditions* for the experiment:

1. They were *not* asked to explain their reasoning in solving the pattern problems.

2. They were asked to explain their reasoning *to themselves.*

3. They were asked to explain their reasoning *to their mothers,* who were instructed to listen but not respond.

The children were then given six pattern problems to solve at the appropriate level of difficulty. The experimenter always gave the children feedback on whether they made the correct selection or not.

For the post-test part of the experiment, the children were given four new problems. Two followed the structure they were accustomed to—the seventh square was left empty. Two, however, were designed to see if the children could transfer their learning to a new situation. For example, the fifth, not the seventh, square might be left empty.

The researchers found that having a listener—even one who doesn't respond—matters. Children did better when they had to explain their problem-solving process to their mothers. And the children who explained their thinking to themselves did better than those who did not explain their thinking at all. The authors speculate that having an audience might:

help children make their implicit understanding more explicit;

lead children to focus on the principles behind what they're learning and not just the facts, making them more able to apply the principles to new situations; and

make children feel more motivated and focused.

The authors conclude:

The general lesson might be that if you are having difficulty in understanding something, you should try explaining it to your mom.

I certainly know, as others do, that having children who are struggling in school mentor other children improves their motivation and knowledge. "Each one teach one" should be more often a maxim in families and in schools. It is certainly a way to practice without drill and kill.

A PARENT'S PERSPECTIVE: IN THE GROOVE

Christopher has always been the kind of child who is cautious—watching, observing every detail, taking it all in. He works slowly and methodically and doesn't want to get it wrong. We tell him that mistakes are how you learn, and to be really good at something requires lots of practice. How many hours did Vladimir Horowitz spend at the piano? Hundreds? Thousands? Tens of thousands?

We so wish at times that Christopher could relax more and just enjoy experiences rather than focusing on whether he's doing it right—or well—but his temperament seems to drive him to do otherwise: to fret and to focus on his opinion of how he's performing.

But when we go to our house near the ocean and go down to our rocky cove, Christopher is transformed. He has been walking and running over these rocks, building dams and catching crabs, all his life.

We had some friends visiting, and all the kids were down in the cove, preparing for their fishing adventure. It's nature's perfect cycle—you catch crabs under the rocks, use them as bait for the fish, and then use the fish heads and backs as bait to lure the crabs from under the rocks. Christopher explains how all this works to his friends.

To watch him in action here is a joy—this shy, reserved child is transformed into the truly seasoned fisherman that he has become. He skims along the rocks—sharp in places and ultraslippery where the seaweed is attached—barefoot, without missing a beat. He checks the crab baits and expertly grabs the crabs just so to avoid getting pinched. He dumps them in the bucket, and we all watch as the yield grows.

Several of our friends comment on how skilled Christopher is at this whole process. He could easily be the adult in charge here. In this cove, there is no complaining, no doubting, no worrying—just the wild abandon of Christopher being in his element and showing others how things work.

WHAT MAKES THE DIFFERENCE? EXPECTING CHILDREN TO STRIVE FOR THEIR "PERSONAL BEST"

Marty Lipp, communications director at the Harlem Children's Zone, says:

> We certainly love the kids and want the best for them, but [that] doesn't mean letting them get off easy. It means challenging the kids; having expectations and beliefs that they can do well and don't have to be coddled. The kids are taught respect and are given challenging work and are constantly challenged, constantly pushed.

Lipp says that this atmosphere pervades the organization. He describes CEO Geoffrey Canada as a "no-excuses boss," and those expectations cascade from the teachers to the children. The superintendent of the HCZ, Daryl Rock, elaborates on the importance of a solid work ethic:

> We believe strongly that kids have to spend more time on tasks—that makes a difference—and develop a work ethic (you're never going to be a good student if you don't), and understand that it's not always fun. To be a good student, you have to spend some [time] doing things that you don't like to do.

Craig Ramey makes the point that practicing is most effective when it encourages one "to work *toward* perfection—to challenge oneself to come to a new level of performance. I love the concept of 'personal best.' We can all have our personal best in everything we want to do."

Ramey's point also applies to motivation. Often motivation is defined as besting others rather than besting ourselves. If we're driven by the desire to do our personal best, practice becomes part of that motivation. Daryl Rock notes:

> The best way to learn something is to try and teach it, and that works very well in the classroom. It also develops a sense of commu-

nity that "we're in this together"—that I'm not trying to become smarter [to keep] you down, [but] that we're all going to pull each other up.

BEYOND EITHER/OR: DIRECT INSTRUCTION AND DISCOVERY

For years, the debate has flourished—is it better to let children discover knowledge or to teach them directly? This is the wrong debate. The studies by David Klahr and his colleagues at Carnegie Mellon, described in chapter 5, on critical thinking, indicate that there are many times when we need to provide children with information (such as how to create a scientific experiment that will allow us to clearly identify the cause of an outcome). But direct teaching needs to engage and motivate children to discovery—not just cram knowledge into them. Likewise, discovery without explanation can leave children floundering or drawing incorrect conclusions.

It is time to realize that *how* we encourage children to discover and *how* we provide information are key. Both should, in Robert Pianta's words, make children feel as if they are being offered a meal at a good restaurant—they want to "dig in" to what is being offered.

PRINCIPLE 6: HELP CHILDREN BECOME INCREASINGLY ACCOUNTABLE

The need to measure achievement is undoubtedly as old as learning itself. As parents, we use praise—to spur children on and to acknowledge their accomplishments. We also use punishment. Grades and test scores merge both praise and punishment—they are intended to let children know where they stand and motivate them to forge forward.

In a world that often feels praise-crazy and test-crazy to me, I think it's important to return to the fundamental purpose of these strategies and thus use them in constructive ways.

MAKE EXPECTATIONS FOR SUCCESS CLEAR

Often praise and grades feel subjective to children and only have a weak connection to what's expected. At the Harlem Children's Zone, I observed a good example of making expectations clear. The children were deriving how to write from looking at writing techniques in the children's books they were reading. Their writing specialist, Hilda Reyes, created a rating matrix that spelled out how these techniques applied to their own writing, on a scale of 1 to 4. For example, they learned that the author often begins with a "small moment story" to engage the reader. Importantly—and more about this later—the 1, or lowest level, is called an "oops" rather than a bad or failing grade.

CATCH CHILDREN DOING SOMETHING POSITIVE

This phrase came from Dennis McKesey, principal of the Promise Academy, which I visited in the Harlem Children's Zone. In the morning hall assembly, the teachers shout out the good things that children have done. They mention not only children's academic achievements but also actions such as being helpful to others. McKesey says:

It's very important to me that we acknowledge [children] being caught doing something positive, [such as helping] someone else out, whether it be an adult or another child. It gives everyone an opportunity to feel special and to feel as if there is a goal that's attainable. All three hundred and sixty-six students in the school feel, "I have a chance today of being acknowledged."

A clear lesson from the research I've discussed throughout this book is the importance of parenting from children's strengths, not their weaknesses. That means acknowledging what children are good at and building on those things.

On the other hand, all children have weaknesses, so how do we deal with those? I think it's important for children to know that making mistakes is an essential part of learning. That's why I like the rating system used at HCZ—not A, B, C, D, and F but 1 to 4, where 1 is an "oops." Daryl Rock describes HCZ's philosophy:

We give [children] the freedom to make mistakes. We teach our kids that failure is not a way of labeling who you are—it's just a way of identifying what you don't know and what you need to put more effort into. When kids understand that, they're not hesitant about trying something, because if they fail, it's not a reflection on them. That just tells them: "This is an area we need to work on."

PRAISE EFFORT, NOT INTELLIGENCE

As Carol Dweck's studies (which I shared in chapter 6, on taking on challenges) have shown, the children most willing to take risks, to feel comfortable making mistakes, and to take on learning that is hard for them are those who are praised for their effort, not for their intelligence.

As I've said, we live in a praise-crazy, test-crazy world. And nowhere is this more apparent than as children head into standardized test season. In New York State, these are called Regent Exams. My grandson Antonio and his ninth-grade classmates received this letter from their science teacher, Dan Brownstein, after the exams. However one feels about this kind of testing, this is a good example of how to give praise. It proves that even when the pressure to pass standardized tests is high, we can find ways to focus on the things that motivate our children, even if that's learning how to work under pressure.

A TEACHER'S PERSPECTIVE: "YOUR HARD WORK AND COMMITMENT ARE YOUR SUCCESS"

Dear Students:

Great news! Phenomenal results on the Regents!!! 72% of you scored over 85%! Even more impressive, 56% were above 90 and a whopping 25% of you had a 95 or higher!!! There were also MANY students who struggled ALL YEAR on exams and PASSED the Regents. I am just as excited by those achievements—especially since it would have been so much easier to just "give up." Wow!!!!

I cannot begin to tell you how pleased and proud I am of your effort(s). I know that the past several weeks have felt like boot camp for many of you. However, I do want to point out that I have ALWAYS said that I knew that you (as a group) had enormous potential, but it didn't seem that many of you knew how to reach it. Throughout the year, I felt that many of your grades did not reflect your ability or your knowledge of the subject. I also felt that there was a general lack of understanding of what it meant to "work hard" towards a goal. I do hope that the last several weeks prove to you that your efforts were NOT wasted. I saw you guys come together and almost thrive under the intense pressure that many of you felt leading into the Regents. You did not fall apart . . . you rose to the occasion. The quality of your homework improved, your critical thinking improved, your commitment to the subject improved (we had record attendance at most of our reviews—especially the "mega" one on Tuesday), and your overall desire to succeed was greater. While the mega review was exhausting (at least for me), and you wouldn't stop chatting, I was definitely impressed by how many of you came AND how many of you stayed for the full four hours. I think you would have stayed longer if I hadn't ended it!

This is a remarkable achievement and really demonstrates your ability and your potential. It also means that you ALL are capable of working well under pressure and can achieve well beyond what you might have previously thought. I do hope that you take this lesson with you into your courses next year. And please don't use just the grade as a measure of success.

Your hard work and commitment, in my mind, ARE your success. I consider a 65 by a student who struggled to pass an exam all year, but never gave up, just as much of a success as a 98 by another student. There was improvement across the board, in nearly every category. I am proud of ALL of you. Great Job!!! Thanks so much for your hard work. It is so nice to end the year like this.

PRINCIPLE 7: CREATE A COMMUNITY OF LEARNERS

WE TEACH BEST WHEN WE ARE LEARNING

In study after study that my organization has conducted on parenting or on early education, we arrive at similar findings: adults who continue to learn about children—about parenting them and teaching them—make the best parents and the best teachers.

That conclusion also rang loud and clear in my interviews with the creators and evaluators of the three gold-standard early childhood programs: these programs worked because their creators were learning, the teachers were learning, the parents were learning—and thus the children were learning. Larry Schweinhart describes the HighScope Perry Preschool Project as a "learning community":

> *The teachers were studying Piaget . . . and reading other authors to develop their own curriculum.*

In the Abecedarian Project, the teachers' processes changed in response to their engaging in an ongoing cycle of observing the children, planning activities that challenged the children, and then evaluating and planning the next activities. Similarly, in the Chicago Child-Parent Centers, staff meetings were a time to share observations and assess what was working and what wasn't in order to plan next steps.

When I asked Ron Lally, an expert on early childhood development from WestEd, what he believed made these programs work, he told me he thought that all of the commentaries on the programs had missed one of their key ingredients:

> *[If] we're looking at really taking the science seriously, [we're] saying that the teacher needs to act as a researcher—to view the child and then to step back and [ask]: what is my hypothesis for what I should be doing next and [then] making the distinction between what works and what doesn't work.*

WE TEACH BEST WHEN WE ARE PRACTICING WHAT WE ARE PREACHING

In thinking about the repercussions of brain science for education, Kurt Fischer goes back to the basics of how we—adults and children—learn:

> There's a basic mechanism for learning: [when] we find something interesting to us, we try to control it, we try to make it happen again, we try to change it, or we try to manipulate it. You see very early in babies—that they're trying to reproduce interesting things; take control of interesting things.
>
> In a lot of our schools, the teacher tells us what we have to know, and then we repeat it. That's not very interesting. It's much more interesting if you can take some of what the teacher told you and start playing with it, start working with it, start arguing with somebody about it, start trying to use it. That meshes in general with what we know from cognitive science and neuroscience—learning is much more effective when you use what you need to know actively; when you try to manipulate it and control it.
>
> Teachers need to change their interaction patterns in the classroom so that they're engaging in learning with the students. A common question I get [is]: "How do I teach my students to become critical thinkers?" The answer is very straightforward: "Do critical thinking in class—talk about complicated problems and come at [these problems] from different perspectives. Work on that with students and they learn how to do critical thinking. You can't tell them what to do for critical thinking—they actually have to do it to learn it."

In other words, as parents and as teachers, we keep trying to do our best. Marty Lipp of HCZ sees the analogy between good teaching and good parenting:

> A good parent does "whatever it takes." There're no barriers for a parent. A parent doesn't say, "Oh, my job stops here." If the child

needs it, a good parent tries to supply it. And that's what we do. We're constantly assessing what we do and looking at how we can do it better.

GIVES AND GETS

If you think all this sounds child-indulgent, it isn't. Doing whatever it takes involves saying no as well as saying yes. And it means children giving as well as getting. One of the aspects of Harlem Children's Zone that impressed me the most is that all the children are expected to give back to others. In the first grade, a leadership group of children is selected to be ambassadors of the school—to greet visitors and to tell them about their school. In all the classes, children are expected to help one another ("each one teach one"). And all are expected to and are given tasks to improve their community. Canada says:

We really want kids to understand and believe in service. Young people all have to know they have something to offer the world— something to offer their families, their communities, their friends, and the larger society. We want our kids to grow up learning "you have gifts that are valuable and important to the world"—and to give back.

A PARENT'S PERSPECTIVE: A LEARNING RELATIONSHIP IS A LIFETIME IN THE MAKING

My father-in-law is an anesthesiologist and an amateur landscaper/ botanical enthusiast. Long before I met him, he bought a flat piece of property and began creating a verdant vision. He carved out a pond and stocked it with fish, sculpted hills and rock gardens, and planted trees, bushes, and flowers of all colors, shapes, and sizes by the dozen. He would plant a tree and find, maybe several years later, that it really should be five feet to the left. This was somewhat annoying and mildly torturous for my now husband, who spent weekends during his teenage years as his father's assistant, digging and filling holes.

Last weekend as we were visiting—myself, my husband, and our young son—I looked around and what I saw—a labor of love more than twenty years in the making—took my breath away. It was as though that very day everything came together, every blade of grass, every tree and bush that had taken root and grown, every flower in bloom.

My son is sixteen months old. He is learning so much so rapidly. When I think back to the little peanut I gave birth to, I am amazed by who he is today—a busy, curious, mostly happy, sometimes cranky little boy. He has also, completely unbeknownst to him, become my greatest teacher. I have so much to learn! Together we stumble through, sometimes with a plan, sometimes playing it by ear. Step forward, step back, stall. There are perfect moments, and others that are not.

Last weekend, I was so struck by those trees and landscape. Seeing them and knowing how they came to be, I felt to be true what I already knew to be so—that this mother-and-son learning relationship is a lifetime in the making.

CONCLUDING THOUGHTS

Mind in the Making: The Seven Essential Life Skills Every Child Needs. That is the premise of this book, but . . . when you heard that children need these skills, did you initially have an image of a bunch of "experts" sitting in judgment on parents? Did you think that you were to learn about studies that would show you that you had done something wrong as a parent and it would be too late to fix it?

If you had those thoughts, I'm glad that you suspended them and took this journey with me through the eight years I have spent on *Mind in the Making,* because I think you will have seen how inspiring, insightful, and transformational the research is. And I hope you will have enjoyed meeting the researchers I introduced you to on the pages of this book:

> Like good parents (and most of them are parents), they are driven by questions, by the desire to better understand children and their development.
>
> Like good parents, they've made wrong turns—some big, some small, but they've kept going.
>
> Like good parents, they've tried something different and pursued new directions until they've gotten closer to a genuine understanding.
>
> And like good parents, they are learners.

I have always been strongly influenced by the views of Edward Zigler of Yale University, an eminent researcher and a hero to me. He believes that the ultimate purpose of developmental research is to improve all of our lives.

Throughout the book, I have emphasized that these essential skills are *not for children only*—they are as important to us as they are to our children. Think of the father who was just about to leave a to-do list for his procrastinating teenage son beside his breakfast cereal when he realized that he would hate finding such a list from his boss on his desk at work. Taking the perspective of his son helped him come up with a more effective way of handling his son's procrastination.

These essential skills don't call for expensive programs, fancy materials, or elaborate equipment. They simply call for doing the everyday things you do with children in new ways. When I once asked children what they would remember most about their childhoods, they told me about small moments, everyday traditions they had in their families. If you think back to your own childhoods, you probably remember similar things—it is the small moments that make the biggest difference.

And finally, it should be very clear that it is never, ever too late. My mother was "parenting" me into her late nineties, and I am parenting my grown children now—meaning that I am continuing to learn from them as they are continuing to learn from me. As a parent whose story I share in the book said—her learning relationship with her child is "a lifetime in the making."

I hope that this book has given you an understanding of what you can do to keep the fire of learning burning brightly in your children's eyes and the skills to help them be all that they can be. If so, then I will have achieved my most enduring dream.

NOTES

INTRODUCTION

2   *"sea of sounds"* Jenny R. Saffran, "Words in a Sea of Sounds: The Output of Infant Statistical Learning," *Cognition* 81, no. 2 (2001): 149–69; Bruna Pelucchi, Jessica F. Hay, and Jenny R. Saffran, "Statistical Learning in a Natural Language by 8-Month-Old Infants," *Child Development* 80, no. 3 (2009): 674–85; Jenny R. Saffran, Richard N. Aslin, and Elissa L. Newport, "Statistical Learning by 8-Month-Old Infants," *Science* 274, no. 5294 (1996): 1926–28.

3   *number sense* Fei Xu and Elizabeth S. Spelke, "Large Number Discrimination in 6-Month-Old Infants," *Cognition* 74, no. 1 (2000): B1–B11.

    people sense Amanda L. Woodward, "Infants Selectively Encode the Goal Object of an Actor's Reach," *Cognition* 69, no. 1 (1998): 1–34.

    who's helpful and who's not J. Kiley Hamlin, Karen Wynn, and Paul Bloom, "Social Evaluation by Preverbal Infants," *Nature* 450, no. 7169 (2007): 557–59.

4   *"We found impressively"* Kiley Hamlin, interview with the author, August 14, 2008.

    driven by goals Philip David Zelazo, interview with the author, December 8, 2008.

    using our working memory Adele Diamond, interview with the author, October 4, 2008.

    reflect, analyze, plan, and evaluate Zelazo, interview.

5   *"neuronal workspace"* Stanislas Dehaene, *Reading in the Brain: The Science and Evolution of a Human Invention* (New York: Penguin/Viking, 2009), 318.

    predict children's achievements Diamond, interview.

    Marshmallow Test Jonah Lehrer, "Don't!: The Secret of Self-Control," *New Yorker,* May 18, 2009; Yuichi Shoda, Walter Mischel, and Philip K. Peake, "Predicting Adolescent Cognitive and Self-Regulatory Competencies from Preschool Delay of Gratification: Identifying Diagnostic Conditions," *Developmental Psychology* 26, no. 6 (1990): 978–86; Walter Mischel, interview with Hank O'Karma, June 8, 2006.

    many executive functions Michael Posner, interview with the author, June 26, 2008; M. Rosario Rueda et al., "Training, Maturation, and Genetic Influences on the Development of Executive Attention," *Proceedings of the National Academy of Sciences* 102, no. 41 (2005): 14931–36.

6   *"outside-in perspective"* Elizabeth Haas Edersheim, *The Definitive Drucker* (New York: McGraw-Hill, 2007), 45.

    Ross Thompson Ross Thompson, interview with the author, September 28, 2001.

    Alison Gopnik Alison Gopnik, interview with the author, November 29, 2001; Laura Capage and Anne C. Watson, "Individual Differences in Theory of Mind, Aggressive Behavior, and Social Skills in Young Children," *Early Education and Development* 12, no. 4 (2001): 613–28; Anne C. Watson et al., "Social Interaction Skills and Theory of Mind in Young Children," *Developmental Psychology* 35, no. 2 (1999): 386–91. Gopnik was referring to the research of Janet Wilde Astington of the University of Toronto. See, for example: Janet Wilde Astington and Janette Pelletier, "Theory of Mind, Language, and Learning in the Early Years: Developmental Origins of School Readiness," in *The Development of Social Cognition and Communication,* ed. Bruce D. Homer and Catherine S. Tamis-LeMonda, 205–30 (Mahwah, NJ: Lawrence Erlbaum, 2005).

    Larry Aber Larry Aber, interview with the author, August 2, 2006; J. Lawrence Aber et al., "Resolving Conflict Creatively: Evaluating the Developmental Effects of a School-Based Violence Prevention Program in Neighborhood and Classroom Context," *Development and Psychopathology* 10, no. 2 (1998): 187–213; Stephanie M. Jones, Joshua L. Brown, and J. Lawrence Aber, "Classroom Settings as Targets of Intervention and Research," in *Toward Positive Youth Development: Transforming Schools and Community Programs,* ed. Marybeth Shinn and Hirokazu Yoshikawa, 58–77 (New York: Oxford University Press, 2008); J. Lawrence Aber et al., "Changing Children's Trajectories of Development: Two-Year Evidence for the Effectiveness of a School-Based Approach to Violence Prevention" (New York: Columbia University, National Center for Children in Poverty, 2003).

7   *Kathy Hirsh-Pasek* Kathy Hirsh-Pasek, interview with Amy McCampbell, February 22, 2005; Kathy Hirsh-Pasek, e-mail to the author, August 6, 2009.

    spoken and written communication skills Families and Work Institute, "National Study of Employers" (unpublished data, Families and Work Institute, New York, 2005).

    Anne Fernald Anne Fernald, interview with the author, April 19, 2008; Anne Fernald and Thomas Simon, "Expanded Intonation Contours in Mothers' Speech to Newborns," *Developmental Psychology* 20, no. 1 (1984): 104–13; Anne Fernald, e-mail to the author, August 31, 2009.

7   *more child-directed speech* Nereyda Hurtado, Virginia A. Marchman, and Anne Fernald, "Does Input Influence Uptake? Links Between Maternal Talk, Processing Speed, and Vocabulary Size in Spanish-Learning Children," *Developmental Science* 11, no. 6 (2008): F31–F39; Fernald, e-mail.
    parent-gesture and parent-look Amanda Woodward, interview with Hank O'Karma, January 17, 2003; Susan Goldin-Meadow, interview with Amy McCampbell, October 16, 2006; Amanda L. Woodward, "Infants' Use of Action Knowledge to Get a Grasp on Words," in *Weaving a Lexicon*, ed. D. Geoffrey Hall and Sandra R. Waxman, 149–72 (Cambridge, MA: MIT Press, 2004); Susan Goldin-Meadow, "Pointing Sets the Stage for Learning Language—and Creating Language," *Child Development* 78, no. 3 (2007): 741–45.
    taping parents interacting Catherine Snow, interview with the author, September 17, 2001; Patton O. Tabors, Kevin A. Roach, and Catherine E. Snow, "Home Language and Literacy Environment: Final Results," in *Beginning Literacy with Language: Young Children Learning at Home and School*, ed. David K. Dickinson and Patton O. Tabors, 111–38 (Baltimore: Paul H. Brookes, 2001); Barbara Alexander Pan, Rivka Y. Perlmann, and Catherine E. Snow, "Food for Thought: Dinner Table as a Context for Observing Parent-Child Discourse," in *Methods for Studying Language Production*, ed. Lise Menn and Nan Bernstein Ratner, 205–24 (Mahwah, NJ: Lawrence Erlbaum, 2000); Catherine Snow, e-mail to the author, August 17, 2009.
8   *playing board games* Robert Siegler, interview with the author, July 23, 2008; Geetha Ramani, interview with the author, July 23, 2008; Geetha B. Ramani and Robert S. Siegler, "Promoting Broad and Stable Improvements in Low-Income Children's Numerical Knowledge Through Playing Number Board Games," *Child Development* 79, no. 2 (2008): 375–94.
9   *Researcher Philip David Zelazo* Zelazo, interview; Sophie Jacques and Philip David Zelazo, "The Flexible Item Selection Task (FIST): A Measure of Executive Function in Preschoolers," *Developmental Neuropsychology* 20, no. 3 (2001): 573–91.
    "The essence of creativity" Adele Diamond, e-mail to the author, August 16, 2009.
    "In a Google generation" Hirsh-Pasek, interview with Amy McCampbell.
10 *National Scientific Council* "Excessive Stress Disrupts the Architecture of the Developing Brain" (working paper no. 3, National Scientific Council on the Developing Child, Harvard University, Cambridge, MA, 2005).
    "fixed mindset" and "growth mindset" Carol Dweck, interview with the author, April 17, 2008; Carol S. Dweck, *Mindset: The New Psychology of Success* (New York: Ballantine Books, 2006); Carol I. Diener and Carol S. Dweck, "An Analysis of Learned Helplessness: Continuous Changes in Performance, Strategy, and Achievement Cognitions Following Failure," *Journal of Personality and Social Psychology* 36, no. 5 (1978): 451–62.
    gold-standard early childhood programs Ellen Galinsky, *The Benefits of High-Quality Early Childhood Education Programs: What Makes the Difference?* (Washington, DC: Committee for Economic Development, 2006), www.ced.org; Larry Schweinhart, interview with the author, August 2, 2006; Craig and Sharon Ramey, interview with the author, October 25, 2005; Craig Ramey, interview with the author, June 30, 2006; Arthur Reynolds, interview with the author, October 24, 2005.
11 *Nobel Prize winner James Heckman* James Heckman, "Investing in Disadvantaged Young Children Is Good Economics and Good Public Policy" (speech, annual conference of the National Association for the Education of Young Children, Chicago, November 8, 2007); James J. Heckman, "Skill Formation and the Economics of Investing in Disadvantaged Children," *Science* 312, no. 5782 (2006): 1900–1902; James J. Heckman, "Policies to Foster Human Capital," *Research in Economics* 54, no. 1 (2000): 3–56.

CHAPTER I

13 *Many kids, too, feel rushed* Ellen Galinsky and Kimberlee Salmond, *Youth and Violence: Children Speak Out for a More Civil Society* (New York: Families and Work Institute, 2002), 45.
    Jeanne Brooks-Gunn Greg J. Duncan et al., "School Readiness and Later Achievement," *Developmental Psychology* 43, no. 6 (2007): 1428–46.
14 *"Attention [skills]"* Jeanne Brooks-Gunn, interview with the author, April 8, 2008.
    "Executive functions" Adele Diamond, interview with the author, October 4, 2008.
15 *"If you ask"* Philip David Zelazo, interview with the author, December 8, 2008.
    global neuronal workspace Stanislas Dehaene, *Reading in the Brain: The Science and Evolution of a Human Invention* (New York: Penguin/Viking, 2009), 318.
    "It's a theoretical construct" Stanislas Dehaene, interview with the author, June 1, 2009.
    The prefrontal cortex is responsible Dehaene, *Reading in the Brain*, 318.
18 *Adele Diamond defines cognitive flexibility* Diamond, interview.
20 *Adele Diamond defines working memory* Ibid.; Adele Diamond, e-mail to the author, August 16, 2009.
23 *effortful control* Mary K. Rothbart et al., "Developing Mechanisms of Temperamental Effortful Control," *Journal of Personality* 71, no. 6 (2003): 1113–43.
    "the ability to resist" Diamond, interview; Diamond, e-mail.
    "[There's] inhibition at the level of attention" Ibid.
24 *Diamond goes on to say* Diamond, e-mail.
    "There's also inhibition at the level of behavior" Diamond, interview.
    We also need inhibition Diamond, e-mail.
    "Let's say there's a friend" Diamond, interview.
26 *"Executive functions are very fragile"* Ibid.

29 *"We still didn't think babies"* T. Berry Brazelton, interview with the author, January 24, 2002.
    Neonatal Behavioral Assessment Scale T. Berry Brazelton and J. Kevin Nugent, *Neonatal Behavioral Assessment Scale*, 3rd ed. (London: Mac Keith Press, 1995).
    "The thing that came to me" Brazelton, interview with the author.
    Brazelton had observed T. Berry Brazelton, interview with Hank O'Karma, January 8, 2003.
    stimulating the newborn Brazelton and Nugent, *Neonatal Behavioral Assessment Scale*.

30 *"Michael Posner is one"* Mary K. Rothbart and M. Rosario Rueda, "The Development of Effortful Control," in *Developing Individuality in the Human Brain: A Tribute to Michael I. Posner*, ed. Ulrich Mayr, Edward Awh, and Steven W. Keele, 167 (Washington, DC: American Psychological Association, 2005).
    "We all know" Michael Posner, interview with the author, June 26, 2008.

31 *Signals are sent* Ibid.; Michael Posner, e-mail to the author, August 11, 2009.

34 *"When I found out"* Clancy Blair, interview with the author, September 29, 2008.

35 *Blair measures children's cortisol levels* Clancy Blair, Douglas Granger, and Rachel Peters Razza, "Cortisol Reactivity Is Positively Related to Executive Function in Preschool Children Attending Head Start," *Child Development* 76, no. 3 (2005): 554–67.
    "We ask children to think" Blair, interview.

37 *"There are three kinds of ADHD"* Diamond, interview; Diamond, e-mail.
    F. Xavier Castellanos F. Xavier Castellanos, "Neuroscience of Attention-Deficit/Hyperactivity Disorder: A Summary," NYU Child Study Center, http://www.aboutourkids.org/articles/neuroscience_attentiondeficit-hyperactivity_disorder_summary.

38 *"We believe that by measuring"* Ibid.

39 *"How can you"* Diamond, interview.

40 *Michael Posner and his colleagues* M. Rosario Rueda et al., "Training, Maturation, and Genetic Influences on the Development of Executive Attention," *Proceedings of the National Academy of Sciences* 102, no. 41 (2005): 14931–36.
    Tools of the Mind Elena Bodrova and Deborah J. Leong, *Tools of the Mind: A Case Study of Implementing the Vygotskian Approach in American Early Childhood and Primary Classrooms* (Geneva, Switzerland: International Bureau of Education, 2001).
    the researchers found Adele Diamond et al., "Preschool Program Improves Cognitive Control," *Science* 318, no. 5855 (2007): 1387–88.

41 *"As you let go"* Heidelise Als, interview with the author, February 19, 2002.

42 *"Every time babies"* Brazelton, interview with the author.
    "I think that we should be focusing" Diamond, interview.

45 *"The game is that you're all to walk"* Ibid.

46 *Goodnight to the stars* Margaret Wise Brown, *Goodnight Moon* (New York: HarperCollins, 1947).

47 *"The typical scenario"* Diamond, interview.
    The first game involves a cartoon M. Rosario Rueda et al., "Training, Maturation, and Genetic Influences."

48 *"[The children] have to really control"* Posner, interview.
    To develop the skills of Ibid.; Posner, e-mail.

49 *"I had given a lecture"* Daniel Anderson, interview with the author, July 11, 2008.
    In an early study Daniel R. Anderson and Stephen R. Levin, "Young Children's Attention to 'Sesame Street,'" *Child Development* 47, no. 3 (1976): 806–11; Stephen R. Levin and Daniel R. Anderson, "The Development of Attention," *Journal of Communication* 26, no. 2 (1976): 126–35.
    To investigate this question Daniel R. Anderson et al., "The Effects of TV Program Comprehensibility on Preschool Children's Visual Attention to Television," *Child Development* 52 (1981): 151–57.

50 *age-appropriate, meaningful, and educational* Samuel Ball and Gerry A. Bogatz, "Summative Research of 'Sesame Street': Implications for the Study of Preschool Children," in *Minnesota Symposia on Child Psychology*, ed. Ann D. Pick, vol. 6, 3–17 (St. Paul: North Central Publishing, 1972).
    "If you design programming" Anderson, interview.
    "Watching aggression begets" Ibid. See also Marie Evans Schmidt and Daniel R. Anderson, "The Impact of Television on Cognitive Development and Educational Achievement," in *Children and Television: Fifty Years of Research*, ed. Norma Pecora, John P. Murray, and Ellen Ann Wartella, 65–84 (Mahwah, NJ: Lawrence Erlbaum, 2007).

51 *"The study came about"* Anderson, interview; Daniel Anderson, e-mail to the author, August 11, 2009. See also Marie Evans Schmidt et al., "The Effects of Background Television on the Toy Play Behavior of Very Young Children," *Child Development* 79, no. 4 (2008): 1137–51.

53 *Dimensional Change Card Sort* Philip David Zelazo, "The Dimensional Change Card Sort (DCCS): A Method of Assessing Executive Function in Children," *Nature Protocols* 1, no. 1 (2006): 297–301.
    "Three-year-olds have no trouble" Diamond, interview.

57 *Peg-Tapping Game* Blair, Granger, and Razza, "Cortisol Reactivity."
    Day-Night Task Cherie L. Gerstadt, Yoon Joo Hong, and Adele Diamond, "The Relationship Between Cognition and Action: Performance of Children 3½–7 Years Old on a Stroop-like Day-Night Test," *Cognition* 53, no. 2 (1994): 129–53.
    Adele Diamond has found Diamond, interview.

57   *Stroop-like exercises* John Ridley Stroop, "Studies of Interference in Serial Verbal Reactions," *Journal of Experimental Psychology* 18 (1935): 643–62.

58   *Say "ten" fifteen times* Richard Weissbourd, e-mail to the author, November 22, 2008.
     Say "pots" ten times Andrea Cameron, personal communication with the author, August 21, 2008.

59   *Hearts and Flowers* "EF Tasks," Developmental Cognitive Neuroscience, University of British Columbia, www.devcogneuro.com/eftasks.html.
     Diamond adds a complication Diamond, interview.
     Flanker tasks Ibid.; "EF Tasks."

60   *if you include the reverse flanker* Diamond, e-mail.
     Anthony Pellegrini Anthony D. Pellegrini, *Recess: Its Role in Education and Development* (Mahwah, NJ: Lawrence Erlbaum, 2005).

62   *Gil Gordon* Gil Gordon, *Turn It Off: How to Unplug from the Anytime-Anywhere Office Without Disconnecting Your Office* (New York: Three Rivers Press, 2001).
     Maggie Jackson writes Maggie Jackson, *Distracted: The Erosion of Attention and the Coming Dark Age* (Amherst, NY: Prometheus Books, 2008).

63   *Marshmallow Test* Walter Mischel, interview with Hank O'Karma, June 8, 2006; Walter Mischel and Ebbe B. Ebbesen, "Attention in Delay of Gratification," *Journal of Personality and Social Psychology* 16, no. 2 (1970): 329–37.
     "We were trying" Mischel, interview.

64   *This experiment began* Jonah Lehrer, "Don't!: The Secret of Self-Control," *New Yorker*, May 18, 2009; Yuichi Shoda, Walter Mischel, and Philip K. Peake, "Predicting Adolescent Cognitive and Self-Regulatory Competencies from Preschool Delay of Gratification: Identifying Diagnostic Conditions," *Developmental Psychology* 26, no. 6 (1990): 978–86.
     "The longer the young children" Mischel, interview.

66   *"The correlations are"* Ibid.
     "inhibition has a downside" Alison Gopnik, *The Philosophical Baby: What Children's Minds Tell Us About Truth, Love, and the Meaning of Life* (New York: Farrar, Straus, and Giroux, 2009), 13.

CHAPTER 2

71   *functional magnetic resonance imaging* Rebecca Saxe and Nancy Kanwisher, "People Thinking About Thinking People: The Role of the Tempo-Parietal Junction in 'Theory of Mind,' *Neuroimage* 19, no. 4 (August 2003): 1835–42; Rebecca Saxe, "Uniquely Human Social Cognition," *Current Opinion in Neurobiology* 16, no. 2 (2006): 235–39; Rebecca Saxe, Susan Carey, and Nancy Kanwisher, "Understanding Other Minds: Linking Developmental Psychology and Functional Neuroimaging," *Annual Review of Psychology* 55 (2004): 87–124.

72   *Siblings* Judy Dunn and Carol Kendrick, *Siblings: Love, Envy, and Understanding* (Cambridge, MA: Harvard University Press, 1982).

73   *"well before age 3"* Ibid., 121.
     "understanding the other" Ibid., 100.
     "In families where the mothers" Ibid., 220.

75   *Ross Thompson* Ross Thompson, interview with the author, September 28, 2001.
     Studies have found Janet Wilde Astington and Janette Pelletier, "Theory of Mind, Language, and Learning in the Early Years: Developmental Origins of School Readiness," in *The Development of Social Cognition and Communication*, ed. Bruce D. Homer and Catherine S. Tamis-LeMonda, 205–30 (Mahwah, NJ: Lawrence Erlbaum, 2005).
     Daniel Stern Daniel Stern, interview with the author, October 12, 2001.
     "The real reason" Ibid.

77   *"I went there every day"* Ibid.

78   *number sense* Stanislas Dehaene, *The Number Sense: How the Mind Creates Mathematics* (New York: Oxford University Press, 1997); Jim Holt, "Numbers Guy: Are Our Brains Wired for Math?" *New Yorker*, March 3, 2008, 42–47.
     people sense Amanda L. Woodward, "Infants Selectively Encode the Goal Object of an Actor's Reach," *Cognition* 69, no. 1 (1998): 1–34.

79   *familiarization procedure* Robert L. Fantz, "Visual Experience in Infants: Decreased Attention to Familiar Patterns Relative to Novel Ones," *Science* 146 (1964): 668–70.
     In this experiment Woodward, "Infants Selectively Encode," 1–34.
     "In one new event" Amanda Woodward, interview with Hank O'Karma, January 17, 2003.
     replacing the person's arm Woodward, "Infants Selectively Encode," 1–34.

80   *"This suggests that by"* Woodward, interview with Hank O'Karma.
     "For literally thousands of years" Alison Gopnik, interview with the author, November 29, 2001.

81   *Gopnik and her colleague* Betty M. Repacholi and Alison Gopnik, "Early Reasoning About Desires: Evidence from 14- and 18-Month-Olds," *Developmental Psychology* 33, no. 1 (1997): 12–21; Alison Gopnik, e-mail to the author, August 11, 2009.
     "I would have some" Gopnik, interview.

82   *crayon box with paper clips* The original study, based on previous researchers' designs, was: Alison Gopnik and Janet W. Astington, "Children's Understanding of Representational Change and Its Relation to the Un-

derstanding of False Belief and the Appearance-Reality Distinction," *Child Development* 59, no. 1 (1988): 26–37. In the original study pencils were placed inside a candy box, rather than paper clips inside a crayon box. There are several variations and expansions of this experiment, including: Alison Gopnik and Virginia Slaughter, "Young Children's Understanding of Changes in Their Mental States," *Child Development* 62, no. 1 (1991): 98–110, a study that used birthday candles inside a crayon box.

82 *"The four-year-olds"* Gopnik, interview.
Renée Baillargeon Kristine H. Onishi and Renée Baillargeon, "Do 15-Month-Old Infants Understand False Beliefs?" *Science* 308, no. 5719 (2005): 255–58; Renée Baillargeon, e-mail to the author, August 4, 2009.

83 *"In order to predict"* Rebecca Saxe, interview with the author, July 9, 2008.

84 *"A puppet has a snack"* Thompson, interview; Ross Thompson, e-mail to the author, August 28, 2009.

85 *"just the facts"* Ibid.; see also Deborah J. Laible and Ross A. Thompson, "Mother-Child Discourse, Attachment Security, Shared Positive Affect, and Early Conscience Development," *Child Development* 7, no. 5 (2000): 1424–40.
parents have different styles Lenna L. Ontai and Ross A. Thompson, "Patterns of Attachment and Maternal Discourse Effects on Children's Emotional Understanding from 3 to 5 Years of Age," *Social Development* 11, no. 4 (2002): 433–50.
"We began to wonder" Thompson, interview.

86 *"Children who get in fights"* J. Lawrence Aber, interview with the author, August 2, 2006.

87 *Kennneth Dodge* Kenneth A. Dodge, "A Social Information Processing Model of Social Competence in Children," in *Minnesota Symposium in Child Psychology*, ed. Marion Perlmutter, 47–125 (Hillsdale, NJ: Lawrence Erlbaum, 1986).
Aber and his colleagues Aber, interview; Larry Aber, e-mail to the author, September 3, 2009.
hostile attribution bias J. Lawrence Aber et al., "Resolving Conflict Creatively: Evaluating the Developmental Effects of a School-Based Violence Prevention Program in Neighborhood and Classroom Context," *Development and Psychopathology* 10, no. 2 (1998): 187–213; see also J. Lawrence Aber, Joshua L. Brown, and Stephanie M. Jones, "Developmental Trajectories Toward Violence in Middle Childhood: Course, Demographic Differences, and Response to School-Based Intervention," *Developmental Psychology* 39, no. 2 (2003): 324–48.
attributional retraining Aber, interview.
children become less aggressive Aber, Brown, and Jones, "Developmental Trajectories Toward Violence."

89 *Authority Stage* Ellen Galinsky, *The Six Stages of Parenthood* (Reading, MA: Perseus, 1987).

91 *Ross Thompson found* Ontai and Thompson, "Patterns of Attachment," 433–50; Laible and Thompson, "Mother-Child Discourse," 1424–40.

92 *"human needs underlying"* Thompson, interview; Thompson, e-mail.
"[Parents should] try" Ellen Galinsky, *Ask the Children* (New York: Quill, 2000), 354–55.

93 *good communication is like* Urie Bronfenbrenner, personal communication with the author, 2001.

96 *"were failing"* Gopnik, interview.
When, for example, a child Alison Gopnik, Virginia Slaughter, and Andrew N. Meltzoff, "Changing Your Views: How Understanding and Visual Perception Can Lead to a New Theory of the Mind," in *Children's Early Understanding of Mind: Origins and Development*, ed. Charlie Lewis and Peter Mitchell, 157–81 (Hillsdale, NJ: Lawrence Erlbaum, 1994); Alison Gopnik, Andrew N. Meltzoff, and Patricia K. Kuhl, *The Scientist in the Crib: What Early Learning Tells Us About the Mind* (New York: HarperCollins, 2001).

97 *"end of that training"* Gopnik et al., "Changing Your Views."
"We told [children]" Gopnik, interview.

98 *"What's it like"* Ibid.
other-oriented discipline Martin L. Hoffman, "Parent Discipline and the Child's Consideration for Others," *Child Development* 34, no. 3 (1963): 573–88.

99 *In their first studies* Aber et al., "Resolving Conflict Creatively"; Aber, Brown, and Jones, "Developmental Trajectories Toward Violence."
4 Rs Program Stephanie M. Jones, Joshua L. Brown, and J. Lawrence Aber, "Classroom Settings as Targets of Intervention and Research," in *Toward Positive Youth Development: Transforming Schools and Community Programs*, ed. Marybeth Shinn and Hirokazu Yoshikawa, 58–77 (New York: Oxford University Press, 2008); Aber, e-mail.

100 *"It's learning that helps"* Thompson, interview.
Studies have found Astington and Pelletier, "Theory of Mind, Language, and Learning."

101 *"One of the things"* Gopnik, interview.
Without this ability Stern, interview.

CHAPTER 3

102 *MIT neuroscientist Rebecca Saxe* Rebecca Saxe, interview with the author, July 9, 2008.
"I wanted to understand" Roberta Golinkoff, interview with Amy McCampbell, February 22, 2005.
journey into the mind Kathy Hirsh-Pasek, interview with Amy McCampbell, February 22, 2005; Kathy Hirsh-Pasek, e-mail to the author, August 6, 2009.

104 *"There is a debate"* Families and Work Institute, "National Study of Employers" (unpublished data, Families and Work Institute, New York, 2005).

105 *brain-imaging technique* Raye-Ann deRegnier et al., "Neurophysiologic Evaluation of Auditory Recognition Memory in Healthy Newborn Infants and Infants of Diabetic Mothers," *Journal of Pediatrics* 137, no. 6 (2000): 777–84.
"The only way [this baby]" Charles Nelson, interview with the author, September 26, 2001; Charles Nelson, e-mail to the author, August 6, 2009.

106 *"What can they hear in the womb?"* Patricia Kuhl, interview with the author, October 30, 2001; Patricia Kuhl, e-mail to the author, August 5, 2009.
"If she spoke French" Kuhl, interview; Kuhl, e-mail. See also Patricia Kuhl, "Speech, Language, and Developmental Change," in *Emerging Cognitive Abilities in Early Infancy,* ed. Francisco Lacerda, Claes von Hofsten, and Mikael Heimann, 111–34 (Mahwah, NJ: Lawrence Erlbaum, 2001).
Janet Werker Krista Byers-Heinlein, Tracey C. Burns, and Janet F. Werker, "The Roots of Bilingualism in Newborns," *Psychological Science* (in press); Janet Werker, e-mail to the author, August 15, 2009.

107 *Janet Werker and Athena Vouloumanos* Athena Vouloumanos and Janet F. Werker, "Listening to Language at Birth: Evidence for a Bias for Speech in Neonates," *Developmental Science* 10, no. 2 (2007): 159–64.
"We give [newborns]" Janet Werker, interview with the author, October 5, 2008. See also Athena Vouloumanos and Janet F. Werker, "Tuned to the Signal: The Privileged Status of Speech for Young Infants," *Developmental Science* 7, no. 3 (2004): 270–76.
"We went for one year" Anne Fernald, interview with the author, April 19, 2008; Anne Fernald, e-mail to the author, August 31, 2009.

109 *Fernald recorded German mothers* Anne Fernald and Thomas Simon, "Expanded Intonation Contours in Mothers' Speech to Newborns," *Developmental Psychology* 20, no. 1 (1984): 104–13.
"When we brought men and women" Kuhl, interview.

110 *auditory preference methods* Anne Fernald, "Four-Month-Old Infants Prefer to Listen to Motherese," *Infant Behavior and Development* 8 (1985): 181–95.
"I had the moms speak to me" Fernald, interview; Fernald, e-mail.
was it the music Anne Fernald and Patricia Kuhl, "Acoustic Determinants of Infant Preference for Motherese Speech," *Infant Behavior and Development* 2, no. 3 (1987): 279–93.
"[In] the next experiment" Fernald, interview.

111 *adults from two very different cultures* Janet F. Werker and J. E. Pegg, "Motherese in Both the Voice and Face: Empirical Evidence from Chinese and English Speaking Mothers" (invited address, The Early Relationship: A Conference with Dr. Daniel Stern, Vancouver, Canada, February 22, 1997).
They found three typical faces Werker, interview; Werker, e-mail.

112 *"not universal listeners"* Werker, interview; Werker, e-mail; see also Chandan R. Narayan, Janet F. Werker, and Patrice Speeter Beddor, "The Interaction Between Acoustic Salience and Language Experience in Developmental Speech Perception: Evidence from Nasal Place Discrimination," *Developmental Science* (in press).

113 *"Babies begin to learn"* Fernald, interview.

114 *Curious to know if tone* Anne Fernald, "Approval and Disapproval: Infant Responsiveness to Vocal Affect in Familiar and Unfamiliar Languages," *Child Development* 64, no. 3 (1993): 657–74.
"These little American babies" Fernald, interview.

115 *"pretty baby"* Jenny R. Saffran, "Words in a Sea of Sounds: The Output of Infant Statistical Learning," *Cognition* 81, no. 2 (2001): 149–69.

116 *Saffran and her colleagues* Jenny R. Saffran, Richard N. Aslin, and Elissa L. Newport, "Statistical Learning by 8-Month-Old Infants," *Science* 274, no. 5294 (1996): 1928.
a similar technique to present Italian words Bruna Pelucchi, Jessica F. Hay, and Jenny R. Saffran, "Statistical Learning in a Natural Language by 8-Month-Old Infants," *Child Development* 80, no. 3 (2009): 674–85.
. "sea of sounds" Saffran, "Words in a Sea."

117 *children were even more facile* Erik D. Thiessen, Emily A. Hill, and Jenny R. Saffran, "Infant-Directed Speech Facilitates Word Segmentation," *Infancy* 7, no. 1 (2005): 53–71.
"Imagine you're standing" Amanda Woodward, interview with Hank O'Karma, January 17, 2003.

118 *"It turns out that babies"* Woodward, interview with Hank O'Karma.
"golden nuggets of sound" Kuhl, interview.
Woodward has explored Amanda L. Woodward, "Infants' Use of Action Knowledge to Get a Grasp on Words," in *Weaving a Lexicon,* ed. D. Geoffrey Hall and Sandra R. Waxman (Cambridge, MA: MIT Press, 2004), 149–72.
"it's the gombie" Ibid.

119 *Susan Goldin-Meadow* Susan Goldin-Meadow, "Pointing Sets the Stage for Learning Language—and Creating Language," *Child Development* 78, no. 3 (2007): 741–45.
"the royal point" Hirsh-Pasek, interview with Amy McCampbell.
"I like to say that" Susan Goldin-Meadow, interview with Amy McCampbell, October 16, 2006; Susan Goldin-Meadow, e-mail to the author, August 10, 2009. See also Susan Goldin-Meadow et al., "Young Children Use Their Hands to Tell Their Mothers What to Say," *Developmental Science* 10, no. 6 (2007): 778–85.

120 *children use gestures before their first words* Jana M. Iverson and Susan Goldin-Meadow, "Gesture Paves the Way for Language Development," *Psychological Science* 16, no. 5 (2005): 367–71.
In studying fifty-three children over time Meredith L. Rowe, Seyda Ozcaliskan, and Susan Goldin-Meadow, "Learning Words by Hand: Gesture's Role in Predicting Vocabulary Development," *First Language* 28, no. 2 (2008): 182–99.

120 *In a subsequent study* Meredith L. Rowe and Susan Goldin-Meadow, "Differences in Early Gesture Explain SES Disparities in Child Vocabulary Size at School Entry," *Science* 323, no. 5916 (2009): 951–53.
"*Mothers, [fathers, and other caregivers]*" Goldin-Meadow, interview with Amy McCampbell.
121 "*anchors*" Golinkoff, interview with Amy McCampbell; Roberta Golinkoff, e-mail to the author, August 6, 2009.
"*We [have] learned that babies pay attention*" Hirsh-Pasek, interview with Amy McCampbell.
How Babies Talk Roberta Michnick Golinkoff and Kathy Hirsh-Pasek, *How Babies Talk: The Magic and Mystery of Language in the First Three Years of Life* (New York: Penguin Putnam, 2000), 70.
123 "*The way [we conduct naming experiments]*" Anne Fernald and Neredya Hurtado, "Names in Frames: Infants Interpret Words in Sentence Frames Faster than Words in Isolation," *Developmental Science* 9, no. 3 (2006): F33–F40; Fernald, interview.
children's vocabularies seem to take off Kathy Hirsh-Pasek, Roberta Michnick Golinkoff, with Diane Eyer, *Einstein Never Used Flash Cards: How Our Children Really Learn—And Why They Need to Play More and Memorize Less* (Emmaus, PA: Rodale Books, 2003); Hirsh-Pasek, e-mail.
[Babies at] Fernald, interview.
124 *how efficiently children process new words* Virginia A. Marchman and Anne Fernald, "Speed of Word Recognition and Vocabulary Knowledge in Infancy Predict Cognitive and Language Outcomes in Later Childhood," *Developmental Science* 11, no. 3 (2008): F9–F16.
"*The baby is sitting on Mom's lap*" Fernald, interview. See also Anne Fernald et al., "Looking While Listening: Using Eye Movements to Monitor Spoken Language by Infants and Young Children," in *Developmental Psycholinguistics: On-line Methods in Children's Language Processing*, ed. Irina A. Sekerina, Eva M. Fernandez, and Harald Clahsen, 97–135 (Philadelphia: John Benjamins, 2008).
"*Where's the baby?*" Marchman and Fernald, "Speed of Word Recognition"; Fernald, e-mail.
125 "*At eighteen months*" Fernald, interview.
Children who processed language Anne Fernald, Amy Perfors, and Virginia A. Marchman, "Picking Up Speed in Understanding: Speech Processing Efficiency and Vocabulary Growth Across the 2nd Year," *Developmental Psychology* 42, no. 1 (2006): 98–116.
"*little differences can add up*" Anne Fernald, interview with Amy McCampbell, April 23, 2009. See also Nereyda Hurtado, Virginia A. Marchman, and Anne Fernald, "Does Input Influence Uptake? Links Between Maternal Talk, Processing Speed, and Vocabulary Size in Spanish-Learning Children," *Developmental Science* 11, no. 6 (2008): F31–F39.
"*For the young child*" Fernald, interview with Amy McCampbell.
126 "*I could review the literature*" Catherine Snow, interview with the author, September 17, 2001.
The Home-School Study Patton O. Tabors, Kevin A. Roach, and Catherine E. Snow, "Home Language and Literacy Environment: Final Results," in *Beginning Literacy with Language: Young Children Learning at Home and School,* ed. David K. Dickinson and Patton O. Tabors, 111–38 (Baltimore: Paul H. Brookes, 2001).
127 "*We started with a group of eighty*" Snow, interview.
taping family dinnertime conversations Tabors, Roach, and Snow, "Home Language and Literacy Environment"; Catherine Snow, e-mail to author, August 17, 2009.
"*extended discourse*" Barbara Alexander Pan, Rivka Y. Perlmann, and Catherine E. Snow, "Food for Thought: Dinner Table as a Context for Observing Parent-Child Discourse," in *Methods for Studying Language Production*, ed. Lise Menn and Nan Bernstein Ratner, 205–24 (Mahwah, NJ: Lawrence Erlbaum, 2000).
128 "*Extended discourse means*" Snow, interview.
130 *The Home-School Study of Language* David K. Dickinson and Allyssa McCabe, "Bringing It All Together: The Multiple Origins, Skills and Environmental Supports of Early Literacy," *Learning Disabilities: The Research and Practice* 16, no. 4 (2001): 186–202.
"*Teachers use 'cognitively engaging talk'*" Snow, interview.
131 *Megan McClelland* Megan M. McClelland, Alan C. Acock, and Frederick J. Morrison, "The Impact of Kindergarten Learning-Related Skills on Academic Trajectories at the End of Elementary School," *Early Childhood Research Quarterly* 21, no. 4 (2006): 471–90.
The results are striking Ibid. See also Megan M. McClelland et al., "Links Between Behavioral Regulation and Preschoolers' Literacy, Vocabulary and Math Skills," *Developmental Psychology* 43, no. 4 (2007): 947–59.
The researchers also followed Claire C. Ponitz et al., "A Structured Observation of Behavioral Self-Regulation and Its Contribution to Kindergarten Outcomes," *Developmental Psychology* 45, no. 3 (2009): 605–19; Megan McClelland, e-mail to the author, August 9, 2009.
132 *Catherine Snow says* Catherine E. Snow and Connie Juel, "Teaching Children to Read: What Do We Know About How to Do It?" in *The Science of Reading: A Handbook,* ed. Margaret J. Snowling and Charles Hulme, 501–20 (Malden, MA: Blackwell, 2005).
understand what is communicated Ibid.
Hirsh-Pasek, Golinkoff, and others Kathy Hirsh-Pasek et al., *A Mandate for Playful Learning in Preschool: Presenting the Evidence* (New York: Oxford University Press, 2008).
Judy DeLoache Robert S. Siegler, Judy S. DeLoache, and Nancy Eisenberg, *How Children Develop* (New York: Worth Publishers, 2002).
133 *concept of print* Dorothy Strickland, interview with Emily Prince, June 8, 2006; Snow and Juel, "Teaching Children to Read."
meaningful experiences with books Snow and Juel, "Teaching Children to Read"; Strickland, interview.

133 *share their ideas* Snow and Juel, "Teaching Children to Read."
phonemic awareness Developing Early Literacy: Report of the National Early Literacy Panel (Washington, DC: National Institute for Literacy, 2008), www.nifl.gov/publications/pdf/NELPReport09.pdf.
different forms for self-expression Snow and Juel, "Teaching Children to Read."
brains are not prewired to read Stanislas Dehaene, *Reading in the Brain: The Science and Evolution of a Human Invention* (New York: Penguin/Viking, 2009).
134 *"Reading is a completely novel"* Stanislas Dehaene, interview with the author, June 1, 2009.
"Mark Changizi" Ibid.; see also Mark A. Changizi and Shinsuke Shimojo, "Character Complexity and Redundancy in Writing Systems over Human History," *Proceedings of the Royal Society B* 272 no.1560 (2005): 267–75.
138 *"The possibility exists"* Snow, interview.
common wisdom Ibid.
139 *Linda Espinosa* Linda M. Espinosa, "Challenging Common Myths About Young English Language Learners," *FCD Policy Brief Advancing PK–3*, no. 8 (January 2008).
Using the "preferential looking" Werker, interview; Whitney M. Weikum et al., "Visual Language Discrimination in Infancy," *Science* 316, no. 5828 (2007): 1159.
occasional code switching Werker, interview; Werker, e-mail.
141 *"Language is a tool"* Janellen Huttenlocher, interview with Amy McCampbell, October 16, 2006.
"There are so many ways" Hirsh-Pasek, interview with Amy McCampbell.
142 *"Think of yourself"* Kuhl, interview.
"Rather than buy" Ibid.
"Children learn language" Snow, interview.
144 *"simple, concrete, repetitive"* Ibid.
"Think about how many meanings" Golinkoff, interview with Amy McCampbell.
145 *Meaningful Differences* Betty Hart and Todd R. Risley, *Meaningful Differences in the Everyday Experience of Young American Children* (Baltimore: Paul H. Brookes, 1995).
146 *"At twelve months of age"* Golinkoff, interview with Amy McCampbell; Golinkoff, e-mail.
147 *"extremely intense interests"* Judy S. DeLoache, Gabrielle Simcock, and Suzanne Macari, "Planes, Trains, Automobiles—and Tea Sets: Extremely Intense Interests in Very Young Children," *Developmental Psychology* 43, no. 6 (2007): 1579–86; Judy DeLoache, e-mail to the author, August 21, 2009.
I recorded the following Ellen Galinsky, *Beginnings: A Young Mother's Personal Account of Two Premature Births* (Boston: Houghton-Mifflin, 1976), 3.
148 *"kids who are taken places"* Strickland, interview with Emily Prince.
149 *"Books do something"* Snow, interview.
150 *children don't comprehend* Patricia A. Ganea, Megan Bloom Pickard, and Judy S. DeLoache, "Transfer Between Picture Books and the Real World by Very Young Children," *Journal of Cognition and Development* 9, no.1 (2008): 46–66.
151 *reading using electronic books* Molly F. Collins and Julia Parish-Morris, "Electronic Books: Boon or Bust for Interactive Reading?" (poster presented at the Boston University Conference on Language Development, November 3, 2006); Hirsh-Pasek, interview with Amy McCampbell.
152 *"Books can take us"* Hirsh-Pasek, interview with Amy McCampbell.
153 *Dorothy Strickland suggests* Strickland, interview with Emily Prince.
154 *Catherine Snow feels that invented spelling* Catherine E. Snow, M. Susan Burns, and Peg Griffin, *Preventing Reading Difficulties in Young Children* (Washington, DC: National Academy Press, 1998).
cognitively engaging talk Snow, Tabors, and Roach, "Home Language and Literacy Environment."
Janellen Huttenlocher Janellen Huttenlocher et al., "Language Input and Child Syntax," *Cognitive Psychology* 45, no. 3 (2002): 337–74.
156 *"It's very important"* Huttenlocher, interview with Amy McCampbell.
"As I've watched my own child" Kuhl, interview.
"Language development is" Kathy Hirsh-Pasek, interview with Victor Zimet, September 27, 2006.

CHAPTER 4
157 *predictable patterns of growth and development* Ellen Galinsky, *The Six Stages of Parenthood* (Reading, MA: Perseus Books, 1987).
"ask the children" Galinsky, *Ask the Children* (New York: Quill, 2000).
159 *"One important thing"* Alison Gopnik, interview with the author, November 29, 2001.
160 *core cognitive capacities* Elizabeth Spelke, interview with the author, September 23, 2008. See also Elizabeth S. Spelke and Katherine D. Kinzler, "Core Knowledge," *Developmental Science* 10, no. 1 (2007): 89–96.
number sense Stanislas Dehaene, *The Number Sense: How the Mind Creates Mathematics* (New York: Oxford University Press, 1997); Jim Holt, "Numbers Guy: Are Our Brains Wired for Math?" *New Yorker,* March 3, 2008.
161 *now a classic experiment* Philip J. Kellman and Elizabeth S. Spelke, "Perception of Partly Occluded Objects in Infancy," *Cognitive Psychology* 15, no. 4 (1983): 483–524.
"If you show a baby a rod" Spelke, interview.
163 *Subsequent experiments* Philip J. Kellman, Henry Gleitman, and Elizabeth S. Spelke, "Object and Observer Motion in the Perception of Objects by Infants," *Journal of Experimental Psychology: Human Perception and Performance* 13, no. 4 (1987): 586–93.

163 *space sense* Barbara Landau, Henry Gleitman, and Elizabeth Spelke, "Spatial Knowledge and Geometric Representation in a Child Blind from Birth," *Science,* new series, 213, no. 4513 (1981): 1275–78.

165 *geometry of the environment* Linda Hermer and Elizabeth S. Spelke, "Modularity and Development: The Case of Spatial Reorientation," *Cognition* 61, no. 3 (1996): 195–232.
cognitive maps Barbara Landau, "Early Experience and Cognitive Organization," in *Encyclopedia of Cognitive Science,* ed. Lynn Nadel (London: Nature Publishing Group–Macmillan, 2002).
Amazonian tribe Stanislas Dehaene et al., "Core Knowledge of Geometry in an Amazonian Indigene Group," *Science* 311, no. 5759 (2006): 381–84.
"stand for" relationships Landau, "Early Experience and Cognitive Organization."
Judy DeLoache Judy S. DeLoache, "Young Children's Understanding of the Correspondence Between a Scale Model and a Larger Space," *Cognitive Development* 4, no. 2 (1989): 121–39.

166 *"To my astonishment"* Judy S. DeLoache, interview with Amy McCampbell, August 3, 2006; Judy DeLoache, e-mail to the author, August 21, 2009.
Children's capacity to make connections Judy S. DeLoache, "Symbolic Functioning in Very Young Children: Understanding of Pictures and Models," *Child Development* 62, no. 4 (1991): 736–52.
"There's nothing that sets" DeLoache, interview with Amy McCampbell.

167 *Herbert Ginsburg of Teachers College* Herbert P. Ginsburg, Joon Sun Lee, and Judi Stevenson Boyd, "Mathematics Education for Young Children: What It Is and How to Promote It," *Social Policy Report* 22, no. 1 (2008): 1–24; Herbert P. Ginsburg, e-mail to the author, August 20, 2009.
Ginsburg comments Herbert P. Ginsburg, interview with Amy McCampbell, October 6, 2006; Ginsburg, e-mail.
"People don't go" Susan Levine, interview with Amy McCampbell, October 16, 2006.

168 *"What we're finding in our studies"* Susan Levine, e-mail to the author, August 25, 2009.
"the foundations of human science" Spelke, interview.
Fei Xu Fei Xu and Elizabeth S. Spelke, "Large Number Discrimination in 6-Month-Old Infants," *Cognition* 74, no. 1 (2000): B1–B11.

169 *"[Half the babies] first see"* Spelke, interview.
Subsequent studies have further refined Fei Xu, Elizabeth S. Spelke, and Sydney Goddard, "Number Sense in Human Infants," *Developmental Science* 8, no. 1 (2005): 88–101.

170 *"We found that babies"* Spelke, interview.
the honks of a car Jennifer S. Lipton and Elizabeth S. Spelke, "Origins of Number Sense: Large-Number Discrimination in Human Infants," *Psychological Science* 14, no. 5 (2003): 396–401.
"hard for me to see" Spelke, interview.
Rochel Gelman Rochel Gelman, interview with Amy McCampbell and Emily Prince, May 11, 2006; Rochel Gelman, e-mail to the author, August 10, 2009.

171 *In a now classic experiment* C. R. Gallistel and Rochel Gelman, "Mathematical Cognition," in *The Cambridge Handbook of Thinking and Reasoning,* ed. Keith J. Holyoak and Robert G. Morrison, 559–88 (New York: Cambridge University Press, 2005).
"The game involved" Gelman, interview with Amy McCampbell and Emily Prince; Gelman, e-mail.

172 *Gelman and her husband* Gallistel and Gelman, "Mathematical Cognition."
Karen Wynn Karen Wynn, interview with the author, August 14, 2008.
testing five-month-olds' looking time Karen Wynn, "Addition and Subtraction by Human Infants," *Nature* 358, no. 6389 (1992): 749–50.
"They would see one little Mickey Mouse" Wynn, interview.

173 *experiments with subtraction* Susan Carey, "Evidence for Numerical Abilities in Young Infants: A Fatal Flaw?" *Developmental Science* 5, no. 2 (2002): 202–5.
three parts of the brain Stanislas Dehaene, "Précis of 'The Number Sense,'" *Mind and Language* 16, no. 1 (2001): 16–36.
"What we're looking at" Wynn, interview.

174 *"Number sense is a term"* Robert Siegler, interview with the author, July 23, 2008; Robert Siegler, e-mail to the author, August 6, 2009.
children's ability to estimate Julie L. Booth, "Development of Numerical Estimation in Young Children," *Child Development* 75, no. 2 (2004): 428–44.
"Young children, at first" Siegler, interview.

175 *"We've found that"* Ibid.; Siegler, e-mail.

177 *"We started asking"* Siegler, interview.
Siegler and Geetha Ramani Geetha B. Ramani and Robert S. Siegler, "Promoting Broad and Stable Improvements in Low-Income Children's Numerical Knowledge Through Playing Number Board Games," *Child Development* 79, no. 2 (2008): 375–94.

178 *Ramani notes that* Geetha Ramani, interview with the author, July 23, 2008.

179 *"Traditionally, parents in the U.S."* Siegler, interview.
"In the initial phase" Philip David Zelazo, interview with the author, December 8, 2008. See also Stephanie M. Carlson, Dorothy J. Mandell, and Luke Williams, "Executive Function and Theory of Mind: Stability and Prediction from Ages 2 to 3," *Developmental Psychology* 40, no. 6 (2004): 1105–22.

180 *Dimensional Change Card Sort* Philip David Zelazo, "The Dimensional Change Card Sort (DCCS): A Method of Assessing Executive Function in Children," *Nature Protocols* 1, no. 1 (2006): 297–301. The card sort described in this article uses different pictures (rabbits, flowers, and sailboats in addition to the trucks I mention) than those described in the book from my visit to Zelazo's lab, but the procedure remains the same.
"Children are told explicitly" Zelazo, interview.

181 *FIST* Sophie Jacques and Philip David Zelazo, "The Flexible Item Selection Task (FIST): A Measure of Executive Function in Preschoolers," *Developmental Neuropsychology* 20, no. 3 (2001): 573–91.
Being able to make connections Stuart Marcovitch et al., "Self-Reflection and the Cognitive Control of Behavior: Implications for Learning," *Mind, Brain, and Education* 2, no. 3 (2008): 136–41; Zelazo, interview.

182 *Zelazo writes that* Philip David Zelazo, "Executive Function Part Two: The Development of Executive Function in Infancy and Early Childhood," *AboutKidsHealth*, May 13, 2005, www.aboutkidshealth.ca/News/Executive-Function-Part-Two-The-development-of-executive-function-in-infancy-and-early-childhood.aspx?articleID=8036&categoryID=news-type.
These are the capacities, Zelazo says Zelazo, interview. See also Clancy Blair, Philip David Zelazo, and Mark T. Greenberg, "The Measurement of Executive Function in Early Childhood," *Developmental Neuropsychology* 28, no. 2 (2005): 561–71.
"The essence of creativity" Adele Diamond, interview with the author, October 4, 2008; Adele Diamond, e-mail to the author, August 16, 2009.
facts are "at your fingertips" Kathy Hirsh-Pasek, interview with Amy McCampbell, February 22, 2005.
"For a number of years" Mitchell Resnick, interview with Amy McCampbell, August 30, 2006; Mitchell Resnick, e-mail to the author, August 6, 2009.

184 *Michael Gazzaniga* Michael Gazzaniga, interview with the author, April 21, 2009.
learning, arts, and the brain Michael Gazzaniga, organizer, *Learning, Arts, and the Brain: The Dana Consortium Report on Arts and Cognition*, ed. Carolyn Asbury and Barbara Rich (Washington, DC: Dana Press, 2008).
"There is growing evidence" Gazzaniga, interview.
"An interest in a performing art" Michael S. Gazzaniga, "Arts and Cognition: Finding Hints at Relationships," in *Learning, Arts, and the Brain*, v.

185 *"As you practice"* Gazzaniga, interview.
"fluid intelligence" Michael Posner, "How Arts Training May Influence Cognition" (presented at Learning, Arts, and the Brain—An Educational Summit, Johns Hopkins University, Baltimore, May 6, 2009). See also Mariale Hardiman et al., *Neuroeducation: Learning, Arts, and the Brain* (Washington, DC: Dana Press, 2009).
The Dana report outlined Gazzaniga, "Arts and Cognition," vi.
"In acting" Gazzaniga, interview.
A study by Martin Gardiner Martin F. Gardiner et al., "Learning Improved by Arts Training," *Nature* 381 (1996): 284; Martin Gardiner, e-mail to Sharon Huang, October 20, 2009.

186 *"how to think"* Martin Gardiner, interview with the author, June 4, 2008.
survival value Gazzaniga, interview.

187 *"Babies are deeply driven"* Wynn, interview.
Karen Wynn finds Ibid.

188 *"[Let's say] you have a box"* Spelke, interview.
face-vase Edgar Rubin, *Synsoplevede figurer* (Copenhagen: Gyldendalske Boghandel, 1915).

190 *MegaBloks Study* Roberta Golinkoff, interview with Victor Zimet, September 27, 2006; Wendy L. Shallcross et al., "Building Talk: Parental Utterances During Construction Play" (poster presented at the 16th International Conference on Infant Studies, Vancouver, Canada, March 2008).
Golinkoff explains Golinkoff, interview with Victor Zimet.

191 *"guided play"* Kathy Hirsh-Pasek, interview with Victor Zimet, September 27, 2006.
mathematize Ginsburg et al., "Mathematics Education for Young Children."

193 *Susan Levine emphasizes* Raquel S. Klibanoff et al., "Preschool Children's Mathematical Knowledge: The Effect of Teacher 'Math Talk,'" *Developmental Psychology* 42, no. 1 (2006): 59–69.
"What we're finding is" Levine, interview with Amy McCampbell.

195 *"We use cartoons"* Spelke, interview.

196 *Rochel Gelman* Rochel Gelman, "Young Natural-Number Arithmeticians," *Current Directions in Psychological Science* 15, no. 4 (2006): 193–97.
Bob Siegler's research Ramani and Siegler, "Promoting Broad and Stable Improvements."

197 *Phil Zelazo uses* Zelazo, interview.

199 *older woman in this drawing* W. E. Hill, "My Wife and My Mother-in-Law," *Puck* 16, no. 11 (1915).
rabbit in this drawing Joseph Jastrow, "The Mind's Eye," *Popular Science Monthly* 54 (1899): 299–312.

CHAPTER 5

201 *Get There Early* Bob Johansen, *Get There Early* (San Francisco: Berrett-Koehler, 2007).

204 *"Critical thinking is the ability"* Frank Keil, interview with the author, October 26, 2008.
"Critical thinking is closely related" Philip David Zelazo, interview with the author, December 8, 2008.

206 *"This is my special machine"* Megan Bloom Pickard, Gabrielle Simcock, and Judy S. DeLoache, "Children's Reactions to 'Real' Impossible Events" (manuscript in preparation), 11.

206 *"Look at that!"* Ibid., 12.
207 *impossible events* Ibid., 16; Judy DeLoache, e-mail to the author, August 21, 2009.
209 *Alison Gopnik* Alison Gopnik, interview with the author, November 29, 2001; see also Alison Gopnik and Laura E. Schulz, "Mechanisms of Theory Formation in Young Children," *Trends in Cognitive Science* 8, no. 8 (2004): 371–77.
210 *"What we've done"* Gopnik, interview. See also Alison Gopnik and David M. Sobel, "Detecting Blickets: How Young Children Use Information About Novel Causal Powers in Categorization and Induction," *Child Development* 71, no. 5 (2000): 1205–22.
211 *nonobvious causal relationships* Gopnik and Sobel, "Detecting Blickets," 1206.
       theories require an understanding Keil, interview; Frank C. Keil, *Concepts, Kinds, and Cognitive Development* (Cambridge, MA: MIT Press, 1989), 184.
       "You take a raccoon" Keil, interview.
       Keil notes that most of us Frank C. Keil, e-mail to the author, September 2, 2009; Leonid R. Rozenblit and Frank C. Keil, "The Misunderstood Limits of Folk Science: An Illusion of Explanatory Depth," *Cognitive Science* 26, no. 5 (2002): 521–62.
       learn something new George E. Newman and Frank C. Keil, "Where Is the Essence? Developmental Shifts in Children's Beliefs about Internal Features," *Child Development* 79, no. 5 (2008): 1344–56.
212 *people's intentions and goals* Amanda L. Woodward, "Infants Selectively Encode the Goal Object of an Actor's Reach," *Cognition* 69, no. 1 (1998): 1–34.
       Kiley Hamlin, Karen Wynn, and Paul Bloom J. Kiley Hamlin, Karen Wynn, and Paul Bloom, "Social Evaluation by Preverbal Infants," *Nature* 450, no. 7169 (2007): 557–59.
       "A red circle with plastic" Kiley Hamlin, interview with the author, August 14, 2008.
213 *foundation of moral thought* Hamlin, Wynn, and Bloom, "Social Evaluation by Preverbal Infants."
       Kristina Olson and Elizabeth Spelke Kristina R. Olson and Elizabeth S. Spelke, "Foundations of Cooperation in Young Children," *Cognition* 108, no. 1 (2008): 222–31.
214 *"One is a principle"* Elizabeth Spelke, interview with the author, September 23, 2008.
215 *"I've done a number of studies"* Keil, interview.
       "The idea behind" Ibid. See also Frank C. Keil, "The Feasibility of Folk Science." Under review.
216 *the Expert Study* Frank C. Keil et al., "Discerning the Division of Cognitive Labor: An Emerging Understanding of How Knowledge Is Clustered in Other Minds," *Cognitive Science* 32, no. 2 (2008): 259–300.
       "doctor is an expert" Ibid., 269–70.
       "Adam knows all about" Ibid., 271.
217 *Keil provides another example* Keil, interview.
218 *Paul Harris of Harvard* Melissa A. Koenig and Paul L. Harris, "Preschoolers Mistrust Ignorant and Inaccurate Speakers," *Child Development* 76, no. 6 (2005): 1261–77.
       "I've got these two friends" Ibid., 1264.
219 *During the preschool years* Paul Harris, e-mail to the author, August 7, 2009.
       "Three-year-olds are relatively unforgiving" Paul L. Harris, "Trust," *Developmental Science* 10, no. 1 (2007): 136.
220 *"Children, and adults"* Koenig and Harris, "Preschoolers Mistrust," 1276. See also Harris, "Trust," 135–38.
221 *Frank Keil and a former graduate student* Keil, interview.
222 *"kindergartners seemed to assume"* Candice M. Mills and Frank C. Keil, "The Development of Cynicism," *Psychological Science* 16, no. 5 (2005): 385–90; Keil, interview.
223 *Paul Bloom* Susan A. J. Birch and Paul Bloom, "The Curse of Knowledge in Reasoning About False Beliefs," *Psychological Science* 18, no. 5 (2007): 382–86.
226 *"The first thing"* Laura Schulz, interview with the author, July 9, 2008.
       My own study Ellen Galinsky, *The Six Stages of Parenthood* (Reading, MA: Perseus Books, 1987).
227 *"The other time"* Schulz, interview.
       Schulz and one of her graduate students Laura E. Schulz and Elizabeth Baraff Bonawitz, "Serious Fun: Preschoolers Engage in More Exploratory Play When Evidence Is Confounded," *Developmental Psychology* 43, no. 4 (2007): 1045–50.
228 *"We take that jack-in-the-box"* Schulz, interview.
229 *Diary Study* Maureen A. Callanan and Lisa M. Oakes, "Preschoolers' Questions and Parents' Explanations: Causal Thinking in Everyday Activity," *Cognitive Development* 7, no. 2 (1992): 213–33.
       "We asked parents" Maureen Callanan, interview with the author, April 19, 2008.
       Studies show that children Susan A. Gelman et al., "Beyond Labeling: The Role of Maternal Input in the Acquisition of Richly Structured Categories," *Monographs of the Society for Research in Child Development* 63, no. 1 (1998): 1–157; Maureen A. Callanan and Jennifer J. Jipson, "Explanatory Conversations and Young Children's Developing Scientific Literacy," in *Designing for Science: Implications from Everyday, Classroom, and Professional Settings*, ed. Kevin Crowley, Christian D. Schunn, and Takeshi Okada, 21–49 (Mahwah, NJ: Lawrence Erlbaum, 2001); Maureen Callanan, e-mail to the author, August 29, 2009.
       exhibition of a zoetrope Kevin Crowley et al., "Shared Scientific Thinking in Everyday Parent-Child Activity," *Science Education* 85, no. 6 (2001): 712–32.
230 *"It looks like the horse"* Ibid., 725.
       explanatoids Ibid., 730.
231 *"Many people"* David Klahr, interview with the author, July 22, 2008.

231 *David Geary* David C. Geary, "Reflections of Evolution and Culture in Children's Cognition: Implications for Mathematical Development and Instruction," *American Psychologist* 50, no. 1 (1995): 24–37; David C. Geary, *Children's Mathematical Development: Research and Practical Applications* (Washington, DC: American Psychological Association, 1994).
 "With respect to scientific reasoning" Klahr, interview.
 Klahr designed a series of studies The first experiment was: Zhe Chen and David Klahr, "All Other Things Being Equal: Acquisition and Transfer of the Control of Variables Strategy," *Child Development* 70, no. 5 (1999): 1098–1120. A second experiment was: David Klahr and Milena Nigam, "The Equivalence of Learning Paths in Early Science Instruction: Effects of Direct Instruction and Discovery Learning," *Psychological Science* 15, no. 10 (2004): 661–67. And a third study, exploring, among other things, the effects of instruction after a three-year interval, was: Mari Strand Cary and David Klahr, "Developing Elementary Science Skills: Instructional Effectiveness and Path Independence," *Cognitive Development* 23, no. 4 (2008): 488–511.
232 *"initial beliefs"* Mari Strand Cary and David Klahr, "Script for Experimenter, Control of Variables Strategy (CVS) Explicit Instruction vs. Exploration, Session 1" (Department of Psychology, Carnegie Mellon University).
233 *Finally, there was a post-test* Klahr and Nigam, "Equivalence of Learning Paths," 665.
 "In the discovery [experiences]" Klahr, interview; David Klahr, e-mail to the author, August 6, 2009.
 Klahr created a follow-up study Strand Cary and Klahr, "Developing Elementary Science Skills."
234 *"It's a cute poster"* Klahr, interview; Klahr, e-mail.
235 *"Cool executive function"* Zelazo, interview.
 Less Is More Stephanie M. Carlson, Angela C. Davis, and Jamie G. Leach, "Less Is More: Executive Function and Symbolic Representation in Preschool Children," *Psychological Science* 16, no. 8 (2005): 609–16.
236 *"We first established"* Stephanie Carlson, interview with the author, December 8, 2008.
238 *"the evidence fails to distinguish"* Schulz, interview.
240 *"I was involved"* Keil, interview.
 "Taking Science to School" Committee on Science Learning, Kindergarten through Eighth Grade, National Research Council, *Taking Science to School: Learning and Teaching Science in Grades K–8*, ed. Richard A. Duschl, Heidi A. Schweingruber, and Andrew W. Shouse (Washington, DC: National Academies Press, 2007).
 "a mile wide and an inch deep" Keil, interview.
 "I think learning" M. Gertrude Hennessey, "A Case Study of a Student's Reflective Thoughts: A Vision for Practice" (essay presented for the Role of Metacognition in Teaching Geoscience workshop, Carleton College, Northfield, MN, November 19–21, 2008).
243 *David Considine* David Considine, "Critical Viewing and Critical Thinking Skills," Center for Media Literacy, http://www.medialit.org/reading_room/article202.html.
245 *"If you want to start"* Zelazo, interview.
246 *Paul Harris writes* Paul L. Harris, *The Work of the Imagination* (Oxford: Wiley Blackwell, 2000).
 "Somebody might fail to represent" Zelazo, interview.

CHAPTER 6

248 *"You Are Special"* Mister Rogers' Neighborhood, PBS Kids, http://pbskids.org/rogers/songlyricsyouarespecial.html.
249 *"I was a research assistant"* Megan Gunnar, interview with the author, September 26, 2001. See also Eleanor E. Maccoby and Carol N. Jacklin, *The Psychology of Sex Differences* (Stanford, CA: Stanford University Press, 1974).
250 *cortisol from children's saliva* Eve B. Schwartz et al., "Assessing Salivary Cortisol in Studies of Child Development," *Child Development* 69, no. 6 (1998): 1503–13.
 "Stress is when" Gunnar, interview; Megan Gunnar, e-mail to the author, August 6, 2009.
 The first step Megan R. Gunnar et al., "Neonatal Stress Reactivity: Predictions to Later Emotional Temperament," *Child Development* 66, no. 1 (1995): 1–13; Mary C. Larson et al., "Dampening of the Cortisol Response to Handling at 3 Months in Human Infants and Its Relation to Sleep, Circadian Cortisol Activity, and Behavioral Distress," *Developmental Psychobiology* 33, no. 4 (1998): 327–37; Erikson Institute, *Early Development and the Brain: Teaching Resources for Educators*, ed. Linda Gilkerson and Rebecca Klein (Washington, DC: Zero to Three Press, 2008).
251 *"These hormones"* Gunnar, interview; Gunnar e-mail.
253 *severe and very prolonged* Elizabeth O. Johnson et al., "Mechanisms of Stress: A Dynamic Overview of Hormonal and Behavioral Homeostasis," *Neuroscience and Biobehavioral Reviews* 16, no. 2 (1992): 115–30.
 "normal stresses and challenges" Gunnar, interview.
254 *"meeting new people"* National Scientific Council on the Developing Child, "Excessive Stress Disrupts the Architecture of the Developing Brain" (Working Paper no. 3, National Scientific Council on the Developing Child, Harvard University, Cambridge, MA, 2005), www.developingchild.net/pubs/wp.html.
 "who create safe environments" Ibid., 1.
255 *"We found that newborns"* Gunnar, interview; Gunnar, e-mail. See also Megan R. Gunnar et al., "Dampening of Adrenocortical Responses During Infancy: Normative Changes and Individual Differences," *Child Development* 67, no. 3 (1996): 887–89.
256 *The key is trust* Melissa Nachmias et al., "Behavioral Inhibition and Stress Reactivity: The Moderating Role of Attachment Security," *Child Development* 67, no. 2 (1996): 508–22.
 "When babies get upset" Gunnar, interview.

256 *Joseph Campos* Mary D. Klinnert et al., "Emotions as Behavior Regulators in Infancy: Social Referencing in Infancy," in *Emotion: Theory, Research, and Experience,* ed. Robert Plutchik and Henry Kellerman, 57–86 (New York: Academic Press, 1983); James F. Sorce et al., "Maternal Emotional Signaling: Its Effect on the Visual Cliff Behavior of 1-Year-Olds," *Developmental Psychology* 21, no. 1 (1985): 195–200.
"Parents' emotional communication" Joseph Campos, interview with Hank O'Karma, August 28, 2003.

257 *social referencing* Sorce et al., "Maternal Emotional Signaling," 196.

258 *visual cliff* See Eleanor J. Gibson and Richard D. Walk, "The Visual Cliff," *Scientific American* 202 (1960): 67–71.
"nonverbal facial communication" Campos, interview.

260 *"I very quickly learned"* Heidelise Als, interview with the author, February 19, 2002.

261 *Als's sense* Billy Baker, "Reading the Body Language of Infants," *Boston Globe,* July 28, 2008.
Through advances in technology Als, interview; Heidelise Als, e-mail to the author, September 3, 2009.

262 *"[The premature babies]"* Als, interview.

263 *"depression in the nursery"* Als, e-mail; Als, interview.

264 *launched into a study* Heidelise Als et al., "Individualized Behavioral and Environmental Care for the Very Low-Birth-Weight Preterm Infant at High Risk for Bronchopulmonary Dysplasia: Neonatal Intensive Care Unit and Developmental Outcome," *Pediatrics* 78, no. 6 (1986): 1123–32.
"When we analyzed the data" Als, interview.

266 *babies who received developmental care* Heidelise Als and Linda Gilkerson, "Developmentally Supportive Care in the Neonatal Intensive Care Unit," *Zero to Three* 15, no. 6 (1995): 1–10; Als, e-mail.
Individualized Developmental Care Heidelise Als et al., "Individualized Developmental Care for the Very Low-Birth-Weight Preterm Infant: Medical and Neurofunctional Effects," *Journal of the American Medical Association* 272, no. 11 (1994): 853–58; Als, e-mail.
In subsequent experiments Heidelise Als et al., "Early Experience Alters Brain Function and Structure," *Pediatrics* 113, no. 4 (2004): 846–57.
"In traditional care" Als, interview.

267 *My son, Philip, was born* Ellen Galinsky, *Beginnings: A Young Mother's Personal Account of Two Premature Births* (Boston: Houghton Mifflin, 1976).

268 *"I set up a way"* Gunnar, interview. See also Megan Gunnar–von Gnechten, "Changing a Frightening Toy into a Pleasant Toy by Allowing the Infant to Control Its Actions," *Developmental Psychology* 14, no. 2 (1978):157–62.

271 *define and measure temperament* Nathan A. Fox, "Temperament and Regulation of Emotion in the First Years of Life," *Pediatrics* 102, no. 5 (1998): 1230–35.
Alexander Thomas and Stella Chess Alexander Thomas and Stella Chess, *Temperament and Development* (New York: Brunner/Mazel, 1977); Alexander Thomas et al., *Behavioral Individuality in Early Childhood* (New York: New York University Press, 1963).
Mary Rothbart and Douglas Derryberry Mary Klevjord Rothbart and Douglas Derryberry, "Development of Individual Differences in Temperament," in *Advances in Developmental Psychology,* vol. 1, ed. Michael E. Lamb and Ann L. Brown, 37–86 (Hillsdale, NJ: Lawrence Erlbaum, 1981); Mary Klevjord Rothbart, "Measurement of Temperament in Infancy," *Child Development* 52, no. 2 (1981): 569–78.

272 *"father of temperament"* "Jerome Kagan: The Father of Temperament," interview by Natasha Mitchell, *All in the Mind,* ABC Radio National, August 26, 2006, www.abc.net.au/rn/allinthemind/stories/2006/1722388.htm.
"For my generation" Jerome Kagan, interview with the author, February 20, 2002; Jerome Kagan, e-mail to the author, August 5, 2009.

273 *temperament in toddlers* Cynthia Garcia-Coll, Jerome Kagan, and J. Steven Reznick, "Behavioral Inhibition in Young Children," *Child Development* 55, no. 3 (1984): 1005–19.
high reactive Jerome Kagan, "Temperament and the Reactions to Unfamiliarity," *Child Development* 68, no. 1 (1997): 139–43.
low reactive Kagan, interview.
As all the babies grew up Jerome Kagan, Nancy Snidman, and Doreen Arcus, "Childhood Derivatives of High and Low Reactivity in Infancy," *Child Development* 69, no. 6 (1998): 1483–93; Jerome Kagan and Nancy Snidman, *The Long Shadow of Temperament* (Cambridge, MA: Harvard University Press, 2009). Kagan and his colleagues continue to research these children. A more recent article studied participants' temperaments in adolescence: Nathan A. Fox et al., "The Preservation of Two Infant Temperaments into Adolescence," *Monographs of the Society for Research in Child Development* 72, no. 2 (2007): 1–75.
"In the second year" Kagan, interview.

275 *specific brain circuit* Susan D. Calkins, Nathan A. Fox, and Timothy R. Marshall, "Behavioral and Physiological Antecedents of Inhibited and Uninhibited Behavior," *Child Development* 67, no. 2 (1996): 523–40; Nathan Fox, e-mail to the author, August 5, 2009.
"The amygdala" Nathan Fox, interview with the author, April 10, 2009. See also Koraly Pérez-Edgar et al., "Attention Alters Neural Responses to Evocative Faces in Behaviorally Inhibited Adolescents," *NeuroImage* 35, no. 4 (2007): 1538–46.
researchers made a very important discovery Nathan A. Fox et al., "Evidence for a Gene Environment Interaction in Predicting Behavioral Inhibition in Middle Childhood," *Psychological Science* 16, no. 12 (2005): 921–26; Fox, e-mail.

276 *"Think of it as similar"* National Scientific Council on the Developing Child, "An Interview with Nathan Fox: Member of the National Scientific Council on the Developing Child"; Fox, e-mail.
parenting styles that are not helpful Calkins, Fox, and Marshall, "Behavioral and Physiological Antecedents"; Kathryn Amey Degnan et al., "Predicting Social Wariness in Middle Childhood: The Moderating Roles of Childcare History, Maternal Personality, and Maternal Behavior," *Social Development* 17, no. 3 (2008): 471–87.
two characteristics Fox, interview. See also Kenneth H. Rubin, Kim B. Burgess, and Paul D. Hastings, "Stability and Social-Behavioral Consequences of Toddlers' Inhibited Temperament and Parenting Behaviors," *Child Development* 73, no. 2 (2002): 483–95; Heather A. Henderson et al., "Psychophysiological and Behavioral Evidence for Varying Forms and Functions of Nonsocial Behavior in Preschoolers," *Child Development* 75, no. 1 (2004): 251–63.
277 *longitudinal study* Nathan A. Fox et al., "Continuity and Discontinuity of Behavioral Inhibition and Exuberance: Psychophysiological and Behavioral Influences Across the First Four Years of Life," *Child Development* 72, no. 1 (2001): 1–21.
278 *parents have people to turn to* National Scientific Council on the Developing Child, "Interview with Nathan Fox."
fear of losing her seat Carol S. Dweck, *Mindset: The New Psychology of Success* (New York: Ballantine Books, 2008).
"I think I've always" Carol Dweck, interview with the author, April 17, 2008.
279 *"of how children cope"* Carol S. Dweck, *Self-Theories: Their Role in Motivation, Personality, and Development* (Philadelphia: Psychology Press, 1999).
"In my very first study" Dweck, interview.
Dweck did another study Carol I. Diener and Carol S. Dweck, "An Analysis of Learned Helplessness: Continuous Changes in Performance, Strategy, and Achievement Cognitions Following Failure," *Journal of Personality and Social Psychology* 36, no. 5 (1978): 451–62.
"children who were vulnerable" Dweck, interview.
280 *To test the hypothesis* Dweck, *Self-Theories.*
"We asked them questions" Dweck, interview.
Dweck and her colleagues wondered Lisa S. Blackwell, Kali H. Trzesniewski, and Carol Sorich Dweck, "Implicit Theories of Intelligence Predict Achievement Across an Adolescent Transition: A Longitudinal Study and an Intervention," *Child Development* 78, no. 1 (2007): 246–63.
281 *"We measured the students' theories"* Dweck, interview; Carol Dweck, e-mail to the author, August 7, 2009.
"height of the self-esteem movement" Dweck, interview. See also Claudia M. Mueller and Carol S. Dweck, "Praise for Intelligence Can Undermine Children's Motivation and Performance," *Journal of Personality and Social Psychology* 75, no. 1 (1998): 33–52.
282 *although mindsets emerge early* Patricia A. Smiley and Carol S. Dweck, "Individual Differences in Achievement Goals Among Young Children," *Child Development* 65, no. 6 (1994): 1723–43.
284 *Ask the Children* Ellen Galinsky, *Ask the Children* (New York: Quill, 2000), 93–95.
285 *George Vaillant* George E. Vaillant, *Adaptation to Life* (Cambridge, MA: Harvard University Press, 1998).
287 *Families and Work Institute's studies* For example: Ellen Galinsky, Kerstin Aumann, and James T. Bond, "Times Are Changing: Gender and Generation at Work and Home," *2008 National Study of the Changing Workforce* (New York: Families and Work Institute, 2008).
288 *warm and caring relationship* Gunnar, interview; Gunnar, e-mail.
290 *goodness of fit* Thomas and Chess, *Temperament and Development.*
"Parents have ideals" Kagan, interview.
291 *In my study of parental development* Ellen Galinsky, *The Six Stages of Parenthood* (Reading, MA: Perseus Books, 1987).
292 *work with three-year-olds* Suzanne Carothers, e-mail to the author, September 8, 2009.
"Harry was the tallest" Suzanne Carothers, interview with the author, April 2, 2002.
294 *Studies by Nathan Fox* Henderson et al., "Psychophysiological and Behavioral Evidence."
"For the shy child" Kagan, interview.
children who were highly reactive Ibid.
295 *workshop for seventh graders* Blackwell, Trzesniewski, and Dweck, "Implicit Theories of Intelligence."
"We divided [the students]" Dweck, interview; Dweck, e-mail.

CHAPTER 7
298 *"The drive"* Jack Shonkoff, interview with the author, September 17, 2001.
learning instinct Stanislas Dehaene, *Reading in the Brain: The Science and Evolution of a Human Invention* (New York: Penguin/Viking, 2009), 142.
I interviewed about learning Ellen Galinsky, *Youth and Learning* (unpublished data, Families and Work Institute, New York, 2001–2002).
300 *"It is time to reconceptualize"* National Research Council and Institute of Medicine, *From Neurons to Neighborhoods: The Science of Early Childhood Development,* ed. Jack P. Shonkoff and Deborah A. Phillips, 41 (Washington, DC: National Academy Press, 2000).
"is what is magical" Shonkoff, interview.
"We are born" Dehaene, *Reading in the Brain,* 142.

301 *"no development"* Shonkoff, interview.
"are the building blocks" National Research Council and Institute of Medicine, *From Neurons to Neighborhoods*, 4.
"in the context of close" Ibid., 225.
Neonatal Behavioral Assessment Scale T. Berry Brazelton, interview with the author, January 24, 2002; The Brazelton Institute, "Understanding the Baby's Language," www.brazelton-institute.com/intro.html.
"On Saturday mornings" Edward Tronick, interview with the author, February 20, 2002.

302 *Still-Face* Ed Tronick, *The Neurobehavioral and Social-Emotional Development of the Infant* (New York: W. W. Norton & Company, 2007).

303 *"They greet the mother"* Tronick, interview.

304 *"Only maybe twenty"* Ibid.; Edward Tronick, e-mail to the author, August 26, 2009.

306 *"The reason that I"* Andrew Meltzoff, interview with the author, October 30, 2001; Andrew Meltzoff, e-mail to the author, August 26, 2009.
"accelerates learning" Andrew N. Meltzoff et al., "Foundations for a New Science of Learning," *Science* 325, no. 5938 (2009): 285.

307 *Imitation also provides* Patricia Bauer, interview with the author, September 26, 2001.
how imitative learning works Andrew N. Meltzoff, "Elements of a Developmental Theory of Imitation," in *The Imitative Mind: Development, Evolution, and Brain Bases*, ed. Andrew N. Meltzoff and Wolfgang Prinz, 19–41 (New York: Cambridge University Press, 2002); Andrew N. Meltzoff, "The 'Like Me' Framework for Recognizing and Becoming an Intentional Agent," *Acta Psychologica* 124, no. 1 (2007): 26–43; Meltzoff, interview; Meltzoff, e-mail.
"novel behavior" Meltzoff, interview; Meltzoff, e-mail.
how long babies would remember Mikael Heimann and Andrew N. Meltzoff, "Deferred Imitation in 9- and 14-Month-Old Infants: A Longitudinal Study of a Swedish Sample," *British Journal of Developmental Psychology* 14 (1996): 55–64; Andrew N. Meltzoff, "Infant Imitation and Memory: Nine-Month-Olds in Immediate and Deferred Tests," *Child Development* 59, no. 1 (1988): 217–25; Andrew N. Meltzoff, "Infant Imitation After a 1-Week Delay: Long-Term Memory for Novel Acts and Multiple Stimuli," *Developmental Psychology* 24, no. 4 (1988): 470–76; Meltzoff, interview.

308 *Meltzoff and a colleague tested* Pamela J. Klein and Andrew N. Meltzoff, "Long-Term Memory, Forgetting, and Deferred Imitation in 12-Month-Old Infants," *Developmental Science* 2, no. 1 (1999): 102–13.
"We started off" Meltzoff, interview; Meltzoff, e-mail. See also Andrew N. Meltzoff, "What Infant Memory Tells Us About Infantile Amnesia: Long-Term Recall and Deferred Imitation," *Journal of Experimental Child Psychology* 59, no. 3 (1995): 497–515; Meltzoff, "Like Me."
"Children are sitting wide-eyed" Meltzoff, interview; Meltzoff, e-mail; Meltzoff, "Like Me"; Andrew N. Meltzoff et al., "Foundations for a New Science of Learning," *Science* 325, no. 5946 (2009): 284–88; Betty M. Repacholi, Andrew N. Meltzoff, and Berit Olsen, "Infants' Understanding of the Link Between Visual Perception and Emotion: 'If She Can't See Me Doing It, She Won't Get Angry,'" *Developmental Psychology* 44, no. 2 (2008): 561–74.

309 *"when they're eavesdropping"* Nameera Akhtar, interview with the author, April 19, 2008.
pay attention to an overheard situation Nameera Akhtar, "The Robustness of Learning Through Overhearing," *Developmental Science* 8, no. 2 (2005): 199–209; Akhtar, interview.

310 *the cocktail party effect* Rochelle S. Newman, "The Cocktail Party Effect in Infants Revisited: Listening to One's Name in Noise," *Developmental Psychology* 41, no. 2 (2005): 352–62.
"noisy environments" Rochelle Newman, interview with the author, July 17, 2008.

311 *"A lot of people talk"* Robert Pianta, interview with Amy McCampbell, August 3, 2006.

312 *"Executive function"* Philip David Zelazo, interview with the author, December 8, 2008.
"People used to think" Adele Diamond, interview with the author, October 4, 2008.

313 *"Can we put our hands"* Craig Ramey, interview with the author, June 30, 2006.
Right from Birth Craig T. Ramey and Sharon L. Ramey, *Right from Birth: Building Your Child's Foundation for Life—Birth to 18 Months* (New York: Goddard Press, 1999).
"When we encourage" Craig Ramey, interview.

314 *Patricia Bauer* Patricia J. Bauer et al., "Planning Ahead: Goal-Directed Problem Solving by 2-Year-Olds," *Developmental Psychology* 35, no. 5 (1999): 1321–37; Patricia Bauer, e-mail to the author, August 12, 2009.

315 *CED* CED, http://www.ced.org/about/about-ced.
"gold-standard programs" Ellen Galinsky, *The Benefits of High-Quality Early Childhood Education Programs: What Makes the Difference?* (Washington, DC: Committee for Economic Development, 2006), www.ced.org.
I say "revisit" I visited classrooms at the HighScope Perry Preschool Project in the 1960s and at the Abecedarian Project in the 1970s.

316 *benefits of participating* Lynn A. Karoly, M. Rebecca Kilburn, and Jill S. Cannon, *Early Childhood Interventions: Proven Results, Future Promise* (Santa Monica: RAND Corporation, 2005).
the original researchers Larry Schweinhart, interviews with the author, October 13, 2005, and August 2, 2006; Craig Ramey, interviews with the author, October 25, 2005, and June 30, 2006; Sharon Ramey, interview with the author, October 25, 2005; Arthur Reynolds, interview with the author, October 24, 2005.

317 *"The classroom"* Schweinhart, interview with the author, October 13, 2005.

318 *"I've been at the same job"* Geoffrey Canada, interview with the author, June 9, 2009. See also Paul Tough, *Whatever It Takes: Geoffrey Canada's Quest to Change Harlem and America* (New York: Houghton Mifflin, 2008).

319 *"getting our kids"* "Letter from the President and CEO," in *Harlem Children's Zone: Keeping the Promise* (program guide, 2009), 1.
"If kids are saying their creed" Canada, interview.
"enormously effective" Will Dobbie and Roland G. Fryer Jr., *Are High-Quality Schools Enough to Close the Achievement Gap? Evidence from a Bold Social Experiment in Harlem* (Cambridge, MA: Harvard University, 2009).

321 *"cognitive learning now"* Schweinhart, interview with the author, August 2, 2006.

322 *"brain research"* Kurt Fischer, interview with the author, August 31, 2006.
"we can't carve people up" Carol Dweck, interview with the author, April 17, 2008.
"You can never" Karen Wynn, interview with the author, August 14, 2008.

323 *"Cognitive, emotional and social"* National Scientific Council, *The Science of Early Childhood Development: Closing the Gap Between What We Know and What We Do* (Cambridge, MA: Harvard University Center on the Developing Child, 2007), 8.

324 *"phenomenon of memory"* Bauer, interview.
Bauer investigates Bauer Memory Development Lab, www.psychology.emery.edu/cognition/bauer/lab/.
"One of the things" Bauer, interview. See also Patricia J. Bauer, "Early Memory Development," in *Blackwell Handbook of Childhood Cognitive Development,* ed. Usha Goswami (Malden, MA: Blackwell Publishing, 2002), 127–46.

325 *hearing words and seeing the objects* Patricia J. Bauer et al., "Props, Not Pictures, Are Worth a Thousand Words: Verbal Accessibility of Early Memories Under Different Conditions of Contextual Support," *Applied Cognitive Psychology* 18, no. 4 (2004): 373; Bauer, interview.

326 *creating a rattle from cups* Bauer, "Early Memory Development"; Bauer, e-mail.

328 *"great music, great art"* Canada, interview.

329 *earliest memories originate* Patricia J. Bauer, "What Do Infants Recall of Their Lives? Memory for Specific Events by One- to Two-Year-Olds," *American Psychologist* 51, no. 1 (1996): 29–41; Bauer, interview.

330 *Robyn Fivush* Robyn Fivush and Fayne A. Fromhoff, "Style and Structure in Mother-Child Conversations About the Past," *Discourse Processes* 11, no. 3 (1988): 337–55.
mothers had diverse styles Robyn Fivush, Catherine A. Haden, and Elaine Reese, "Elaborating on Elaborations: Role of Maternal Reminiscing Style in Cognitive and Socioemotional Development," *Child Development* 77 no. 6 (2006): 1571.
mother's style of discussion Ibid., 1568–88.
"Children of more highly elaborative mothers" Ibid., 1580.

331 *"second birthday"* Daniel J. Siegel, interview with the author, November 28, 2001. See also Daniel J. Siegel, *The Developing Mind* (New York: Guilford Press, 1999).
socioeconomic and cultural differences Fivush, Haden, and Reese, "Elaborating on Elaborations," 1572–73.
extended discourse Barbara Alexander Pan, Rivka Y. Perlmann, and Catherine E. Snow, "Food for Thought: Dinner Table as a Context for Observing Parent-Child Discourse," in *Methods for Studying Language Production,* ed. Lise Menn and Nan Bernstein Ratner, 205–24 (Mahwah, NJ: Lawrence Erlbaum, 2000); David K. Dickinson and Allyssa McCabe, "Bringing It All Together: The Multiple Origins, Skills and Environmental Supports of Early Literacy," *Learning Disabilities: Research and Practice* 16, no. 4 (2001): 186–202.

332 *Abecederian Project* Craig Ramey, interview with the author, October 25, 2005; Galinsky, *Early Childhood Education.*
Carollee Howes Carollee Howes, interview with the author, November 27, 2001.

334 *"What is important"* Jill Levine, interview with the author, June 29, 2009.
unproductive stress Kerstin Aumann and Ellen Galinsky, *The State of Health in the American Workforce: Does Having an Effective Workplace Matter?* (New York: Families and Work Institute, 2009).

336 *"rehearse and extend"* Ramey and Ramey, *Right from Birth*; Craig Ramey, interview with the author, June 30, 2006.
"We're now at the point" Fischer, interview. See also Geraldine Dawson and Kurt W. Fischer, eds., *The Developing Brain* (New York: Guilford Press, 1994).

337 *Berkeley and Yellow Springs* Alex F. Roche, *Growth, Maturation, and Body Composition: The Fels Longitudinal Study 1921–1991* (New York: Cambridge University Press, 1992).
"jumps in behavior" Fischer, interview.

338 *children are curious* Laura Schulz, interview with the author, July 9, 2008.

339 *pattern problems* Bethany Rittle-Johnson, Megan Saylor, and Kathryn E. Swygert, "Learning from Explaining: Does It Matter If Mom Is Listening?" *Journal of Experimental Child Psychology* 100, no. 3 (2007): 215–24.

340 *The general lesson* Ibid., 223.

342 *"We certainly love the kids"* Marty Lipp, interview with the author, June 9, 2009.
"We believe strongly" Daryl Rock, interview with the author, June 9, 2009.
"to work toward perfection" Craig Ramey, interview, June 30, 2006.

342 *"The best way to learn"* Rock, interview.
343 *studies by David Klahr* David Klahr and Milena Nigam, "The Equivalence of Learning Paths in Early Science Instruction: Effects of Direct Instruction and Discovery Learning," *Psychological Science* 15, no. 10 (2004): 661–67.
"dig in" Pianta, interview.
344 *"It's very important"* Dennis McKesey, interview with the author, June 9, 2009.
345 *"We give [children] the freedom"* Rock, interview.
Dan Brownstein Dan Brownstein, e-mail to his students, June 19, 2009.
347 *study after study* Ellen Galinsky, *Ask the Children* (New York: Quill, 2000); Ellen Galinsky et al., *The Study of Children in Family Child Care and Relative Care* (New York: Families and Work Institute, 1994).
"learning community" Galinsky, *Early Childhood Education,* 9.
"[If] we're looking at really" Ibid., 25.
348 *"mechanism for learning"* Fischer, interview.
"A good parent" Lipp, interview.
349 *"believe in service"* Canada, interview.

CONCLUDING THOUGHTS
351 *Edward Zigler* Edward Zigler and Sally J. Styfco, "Epilogue," in *The Crisis in Youth Mental Health, Critical Issues and Effective Programs,* vol. 4: *Early Intervention Programs and Policies,* ed. Norman F. Watt et al., 347–71 (Westport, CT: Praeger, 2006); Edward Zigler, "Metatheoretical Issues in Developmental Psychology," in *Theories in Contemporary Psychology,* ed. M. Marx, 341–68 (New York: Macmillan, 1963).

INDEX